A People's History of Latin America

Drawing by Felipe Guamán Poma de Ayala (Peru, 17th century)

A People's History of Latin America

Hernán Horna

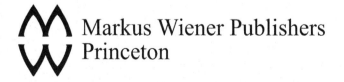

Markus Wiener Publishers
Princeton

For information, write to: Markus Wiener Publishers
231 Nassau Street, Princeton, NJ 08542
www.markuswiener.com

Library of Congress Cataloging-in-Publication Data

Horna, Hernán.
  [History of Latin America]
  A people's history of Latin America / Hernán Horna.
    pages cm
  Original title: A history of Latin America.
  Includes bibliographical references and index.
  ISBN 978-1-55876-577-1 (hardcover : alk. paper)
  ISBN 978-1-55876-578-8 (pbk. : alk. paper)
  1. Latin America—History. I. Title.
  F1410.H67 2013
  980—dc23
                        2013012715

Contents

Foreword

Who writes history? Whose narrative and interpretation of the past has the strongest impact? Which perspective and research angle give us the deepest understanding of a specific region in the world? These fundamental issues run across as an undercurrent in Hernán Horna's book about Latin American history. His synthesis is, of course, not the final chord from the historian's studio—none could be—but it is one with several merits.

The quality of a synthesis depends on the quality of the studies, investigations and research that it must rely on. The author, indeed, laments the many lacunae in Latin American historiography and the dearth of studies of gender relations, the weak standard on scholarship about ethnic groups, etc. He even deplores the professional standard among historians in Latin America itself and this underdevelopment is explained within the context of developmental conditions in that part of the world. Latin America has not been able to free itself from the dependency on those who in successive stages came to dominate so much of its economy and institutions. Historiography itself is the victim of colonialism; it has suffered from an unfinished decolonization and is the prey of neocolonialism, all this despite the vitality in almost all spheres of intellectual life.

The history of this continent needs constant revision, not least because the power relations between Latin America and the surrounding world have shifted constantly. As a consequence, the interpretation of the past has shifted as well. It reflects the asymmetry of power that goes back even to pre-Columbian times. Since history, normally, is written by the victors, the imbalance in the description of group relations also affects the period before the encounter, or rather confrontation, between indigenous cultures and European "discoverers." The first conquest concerned territories: the power over land, natural resources, and manpower. A second conquest, perhaps equally important, concerns the conquest of the minds. It was important to get the upper hand in telling what had actually happened. For a long time, the history of the so-called European discoveries and the penetration of foreign continents were written by the conquerors themselves, and the Europeans forced their exegesis on the Amerindians. The Portuguese and the Spaniards swayed their swords over and gained control of non-European territories but eventually they lost ground even in Europe itself and lost momentum in the propaganda war that shed light and spread disinformation on what happened between colonizers and colonized overseas. When the French and the Englishmen got the upper hand on the global scene, it had repercussions all over the Western Hemisphere. From the beginning, the Latin American "dependency scholars" described the situation as a chain of "centers and peripheries." Horna's historical analysis has as main variable, the interdependence between external centers of power on the one hand and on the other, the Latin American nations, states and regions. Since the early 1800s, the United States has cast its shadow over the continent and much of the analysis is devoted to U.S.—Latin American relations.

Not until our own times have pre-colonial societies been described and analyzed from within and on the basis of their own internal conditions and perceptions. It took a long time before "counter-histories" were written. In Mexico the anthropologist and historian Miguel Leon-Portilla (born 1926) was a pioneer in understanding and reevaluating Nahuatl literature. Horna has made parallel studies of other Indian cultures. He has published an enduring contribution to an authentic ethno-history of Amerindians in *La Indianidad* (Spanish 1999, English 2001, French 2010) which relies not only of traditional historical sources but also on the works of archaeologists, anthropologists, and the usual Portuguese and Spanish sources.

The author of this book is well qualified for his task. He has a background both in South and North America. He was born in Peru (Cajamarca) in 1942, where he got his upbringing and education. He went to college in several American universities and obtained his Ph. D. in history at Vanderbilt University (1970). His doctoral dissertation analyzed the Colombian transport modernization and entrepreneurship during the nineteenth century. Horna became Associate Professor of History at Western Illinois University where he was the co-founder of the Latin American Cultural Awareness Center. Since the late 1970s, Hernán Horna has had his intellectual base in Sweden, a European country with only a marginal role as colonial power in the Third World. Horna's achievements as historian of Latin America, connects well with Swedish research traditions. For example, Swedish historian Sverker Aronldsson published penetrating investigations of *La Leyenda Negra* (The Black Legend), i.e., the attempts from European powers to denigrate Spain's and Portugal's deeds as colonial powers, not least their treatment of the Indian populations. Magnus Mörner, Sweden's foremost Latin Americanist, is a leading figure in the writing of Latin American colonial history, and historian Åke Wedin contributed to a deeper understanding of Inca chronology. Uppsala University, where Horna has served as researcher and teacher for over three decades and reached the rank of Professor founded the interdisciplinary Latin American Seminar. His academic activities are not isolated events from the Swedish interest for Latin America. One is impressed by Uppsala University's versatile contacts with South America, not least in the field of botany. Several recent dissertations from Uppsala explore Amerindian cultures and their survival alternatives under adverse conditions. It is in this context that Hernán Horna has produced a Latin American history within a global perspective. In his own research he has covered a variety of topics about the Western Hemisphere's history, including ancient contacts between Asia and the Americas, and Latin American migration to contemporary Europe. The author balances skilfully national, regional, and global perspectives. All serious readers are recommended to reflect on the results of his research.

Harald Runblom
Professor Emeritus, Uppsala University

Introduction

Until very recently there has existed an absence of professional historians in Latin America because even today it is almost impossible to make a living as a historian. The writers of history were usually people from the upper classes who had enough money to sustain themselves and plenty of time to ponder what their history was about. Members of the clergy have also figured as prominent historians. Despite the very distinguished exceptions, native historical perceptions became either concoctions of the authors' elitist limitations or religious prejudices. It is the record of the local elites from the newly created national states that has constituted the traditional Latin American historiography. The pre-European past still remains in near oblivion. Most Latin American historians concentrated on writing about local history of very uneven quality. Relatively speaking, there has been a conspicuous absence of general historical surveys for the entire region. The task of writing general historical surveys has been undertaken by authors from Europe and the United States. The latter in particular have bombarded Latin America with their research activities and perceptions. Ironically, today most Latin American history is being written in the United States and in English.

The history of the Latin American lower classes, ethnic minorities, Afro-Latin Americans, gender relations and ecology remain to be written. Likewise, the region's multi-ethnic character makes it imperative that Latin American social history critically confronts that crucial problem. This is a reality that can not be rectified overnight and it can not be accomplished by historians alone; it requires an interdisciplinary approach. The uneven historical research and the region's cultural diversity have the consequence that generalizations made about Latin America as a whole naturally contain a high level of abstraction. There is still a lack of monographic research, which prevents the formulation of needed comparative conclusions. However, in several Latin American nations there is a rising group of young and talented historians, few of them educated in the United States and Europe, who are trying to write their own history despite the limited infrastructure and financial resources. They deserve at the least moral support for their pioneering struggle.

One of the Latin American geographic conditions is its proximity to the United States. Both the United States and Latin America were former European colonies, but their post-independence periods would continue to diverge in the emerging global system. The asymmetric power relations between the United States and Latin America have regional and inter-state considerations. From the mid-nineteenth century, all the nations and territories south of the United States began to be considered as part of Latin America by the media and the cognoscenti. The eighteen oldest and biggest Latin American countries achieved their independence during the first quarter of the nineteenth century, while Cuba and Panama joined the neophyte community of national states in 1898 and 1903 respectively. The emergence of Cuba and Panama as national states was intimately related to the rise of the United States as the major world power. Likewise, the "backyard" grounds developed in tandem with the growth of American entrepreneurial, political and military activities.

The Latin American identity and even the identities of the various national states are still in the making. The unity of Latin America remains a distant project despite efforts by the region's leaders, ideologists and patriots. Latin America is an area of contrasts but the geographic nearness, cultural similarities, and shared historical experience constitute the region's greatest bonds. Miscegenation found its first frontier of the world in Latin America. Latin America is in essence Amerindian, African, and European, and the boundaries of the contemporary national states do not necessarily coincide with their ethnic or racial boundaries. Their territorial borders are the result of their colonial history.

Moreover, there is a pressing need for further inter-cultural dialogues for the region to become the genuine home for all the peoples of the so-called Latin America. Latin America is not yet an economic or political unit. By the end of the twentieth century only 13% of all trade in Latin America was among its community members. But horizontal trade is in the making. The growing Asian demands for raw materials are disrupting the traditional *North-South* trade. During the first decade of the third millennium, China became Latin America's second-largest trading partner after the United States. We live in new times and defining readjustments in which middle-range economies like the G-20 are emerging. Latin America is part of such a process and it demands a greater voice in global affairs. Moreover, the United States is losing its capacity to dictate and subordinate in some of its traditional Latin American *clients*.

Latin America is the region of the Third World that has the oldest postcolonial period, and yet it still remains underdeveloped and not completely independent. Until recently, it was noted that Latin America was the most economically advanced area of the Third World. But the South East Asian transition from an underdeveloped to a "newly industrialized" region has further minimized the economic image and significance of Latin America.[1] East Asia is emerging as a paradigm of alternative modernizations and modernities. With the exception of Haiti, Bolivia and Nicaragua, Latin America was classified by hopeful economists as consisting of "middle income countries." Alas, Haiti and Bolivia have not been insignificant in the history of capital accumulation in the metropolitan centers. Moreover, the three largest and most industrialized nations, Argentina, Brazil and Mexico, account for approximately two thirds of the region's total production. Brazil alone has at least the eighth largest GNP in the world. But it has been noted that after 1973, Latin America underperformed in the Third World. The Latin American underperformance ensued in tandem with the implantation of neo-liberal economic policies in the region.

Latin America displays the classic ills of Third World underdevelopment; that is, extreme poverty of the masses and the utmost affluence of socio-economic elites. Exquisite sophistication and archaic realities are the heritages that still co-exist. The middle classes have had a lethargic development. Along with the imaginative novelists and Nobel laureates survive about 50 million illiterates. The literacy, literary and intellectual contrasts are intimately related to the socio-economic differences of Latin America. Latin America is lagging in infrastructure as well as *Research and Development* (R&D). Despite recent outstanding accomplishments in some scientific fields, Latin American universities still are behind the elite centers of world science. In the underdeveloped world of Latin America, the socio-economic gaps are staggering. In several countries 5% of the population owns over 50% of the national income while there are at least 20 million children without homes throughout Latin America. Needless to say, those that do not have homes can hardly afford a good education.

Even though Latin America was the first in the Third World to create a native school of development economics (*Dependency*), the region remains underdeveloped. For a while "Dependency" theories became an essential part of Latin American economic thought in relation to the global system. The message of Dependency and its core thesis, the *"unequal exchange,"* have not completely disappeared from Latin American economic analysis. Although neo-liberal economic science became the official orthodoxy in the West, Latin American economists and social scientists continue to debate on how state control, privatizations and market mechanisms should face neo-liberal globalization. Moreover, the Colombian economist Mario Pérez Rincón broadens the Dependency analysis and argues that there is an "ecological unequal exchange" between the Center and Periphery. The nations of the *North* avoid payment for the environmental damages in their economic relations with the *South*. According to Pérez Rincón, the metabolism of the rich industrial countries depends on strategic raw materials and primary products from underdeveloped economies. The supply of those commodities also causes inordinate ecological damages to the Periphery.[2] Furthermore, the underdeveloped world is becoming the dumping grounds for the industrial wastes from the metropolitan centers.

Prior to the Dependency analysis, Western social scientists used "modernization theory" to explain the relative lack of industrialization in Latin America. However, history has demonstrated that the stages of development in the West were not necessarily those of the Third World. Modernization theory claimed that economic growth in poor countries led to political democracy. It follows that citizens with higher incomes will demand more democratic rights. Moreover, the United States government supported its *client* and favorite dictatorships with the rationalization of modernization theory during the 1960s and 1970s. Regardless of the merits, or lack thereof, within economics and the social sciences, the Dependency analysis has an important contribution to the writing of Latin American history. Perceptively, the American historian Erick D. Langer has noted: "The most influential contribution of Latin American scholars to the project of world history was the development of the dependency theory."[3] In this work, I attempt to incorporate some aspects of the Dependency school and the *"unequal exchange"* in the writing of Latin American history. Certainly, no single theory can explain the empirical reality of Latin America. But the Dependency school still has a contribution to make in the explaining and understanding of "Latin America."

There are two separate histories of the Americas: that of Amerindian America and that of the Americas under the influence of Western civilization. Native America was a very ancient world that became the "New World" in the eyes of the *conquerors*. Despite syncretisms and cultural exchanges, the Europeans and neo-Europeans created the vision of the New World and gradually imposed it on the natives and non-Europeans under colonial rule. Latin American independence was led by *Criollo* or white elites and they would also become the real inheritors of Iberian power. Although the political term "Liberal" was first used in Spain during the struggle against Napoleon I, liberalism achieved its greatest accomplishments outside the Iberian world. The idea of democracy among the most progressive Latin American elites of the post-independence period was concerned only with the slogans of European liberalism, which led to the rise of charismatic leaders and populists from the Left and the Right. Such limitations led to the abandonment of Amerindian and dark-skinned peoples' rights. The ineffectiveness of political institutions and overwhelming challenges led many Latin Americans to support individual leaders (*caudillos*). In the transition from neo-liberalism to post neo-liberalism, the Latin American democratic process is still engendering its own institutions and new leaders.

In principle history should attempt to be neutral but that is a virtue which only few historians can claim for themselves. I begin the effort of writing this book by reflecting on the Latin American past through historiographic and interdisciplinary assessments. I daresay that I write as an almost self-exiled émigré who tries to tell a history of Latin America. It is with the awareness of the above noted limitations as well as the conviction that history must be constantly rewritten that this author has the audacity to write a Latin American history. My writing has benefited from discussions with students and colleagues as well as the many interdisciplinary debates at the Latin American Seminar of Uppsala University. Despite my own limitations and temperament, I bear full responsibility for the text and views here expressed. Furthermore, I wish to thank Carlos Arroyo, Lars M. Andersson, Hugo Cancino, Gunnel Cederlöf, Gustav Cederlöf, Ariana Horna, Lida Horna, Mary Horna, Melquiades Horna, Rubén Darío Horna, Esther Quiroz, José del Carmen Marín, Harald Runblom, Jane M. Rausch, Stanley J. Stein, Rolf Torstendahl, and Anita Wahlgren for their very helpful comments on the earlier drafts of this book.

CHAPTER I

THE AMERINDIAN ANTIQUITY

T hroughout the contemporary world, native and aboriginal peoples face disputes regarding their human rights and political participation as well as claims to their ancestral resources and existential symbols. Their excluded situation is a consequence of the historical globalization, which began in the long-sixteenth century. Natives and aboriginals were subjected to the worst side of the globalization process. Generally speaking, the indigenous peoples of the world are among the poorest of the poor. The heritages of colonial legalities are still deterrents to the contemporary ownership rights of natives.[1] At the dawn of the third millennium, ethnicity and ethnic conflicts are still blooming. The history of the vanquished has to recognize them, first of all, as the oppressed victims of colonialism. None of the European nations fought and colonized the Amerindians for humanitarian reasons. Despite civilizing and missionary policies, the present struggle of the Amerindians is, at the same time, that of those who are discriminated and excluded by the modernized world.

Amerindians migrated from Asia to the Americas before the Neolithic revolution.[2] As humans made the transition from food-gatherers to cultivators, they simultaneously learned to domesticate animals. Dogs, horses, cows, donkeys, goats, sheep and pigs became more permanent human companions as well as nutrition

1

sources in the Old World, while in the New World the Amerindians developed a similar relationship with llamas, alpacas, vicuñas, guinea-pigs, turkeys, iguanas and small hairless dogs. Unfortunately, Amerindians did not have access to draught-animals like horses or donkeys. Llamas, the strongest of the domesticated animals, cannot be loaded with much more than 25 pounds. Despite all the affirmations about the Amerindian incapacity to conceive the wheel, they did indeed know the operative principles of the mechanic wheel. Toys of four wheels that present the vehicular conceptualization were excavated after World War II. But it can be said that the wheel of Pre-Columbian America still did not have the functionality that it had in the Old World. The vehicular wheel for the Amerindians played a role something like gunpowder did for the ancient Chinese.

In the Americas, maize (Indian corn) and quinoa were the only cereals, but Indians cultivated many other farming products: beans, squash, peanuts, papaya, guava, avocado, pineapple, tomato, chili pepper, pumpkin, potato, sweet potato, yucca, cacao, tobacco and the best cotton in the world.[3] The cultivation of tubers and poisonous plants became an Amerindian specialty. The inhabitants of tropical America were the first to make good use of the manioc; from its roots they extracted their food, alcoholic beverages, and poison for hunting.

By approximately the year 1500 B.C., we observe in many parts of the Americas the development of simple farming, combined with food gathering, fishing, hunting and bee-keeping. The use of stone tools and weaving are evident. Archeological research is revealing that while farming developed even earlier in several places of the Americas, with the exception of the ancient Peruvians who had llamas, the combination of agriculture and cattle-breeding was basically a phenomenon of the Old World. With the growth of agriculture, the creed of *Pachamama* (sacred mother earth)[4] became one of the most deeply revered religious tenets among neophyte Amerindian farmers. The main nuclear centers of cultural diffusion were the central Andes and Mesoamerica where such advanced cultural and technological developments place the Indians at nearly the same level of development as the other centers of world civilization. Ironically, the indigenous populations of both regions have become the poorest in the modern Western Hemisphere.

The Amerindian population when Christopher Columbus "discovered" America was about 80 million according to the Spanish historian Guillermo Céspedes.[5] The great majority of the Amerindian population belonged to the so-called high cultures. The Amerindians included a wide range of personalities, from astronomers, philosophers, poets and engineers to liturgical cannibals. Their descendants, who survived, originate from "primitives" as well as kings, queens, nobles, merchants, artisans, peasants, philosophers and slaves. At the time of the conquest, the Maya Indians had the most developed merchant class in the Americas. Moreover, the long–distance trade in Pre-Columbian America was intimately intertwined with shamanism and luxury goods.

The similarity of cultural elements among the Amerindians as well as the discovery of archeological remains and other products away form their original places,[6] suggests that the history of the advanced and less advanced Amerindians can not be written separately and without interrelation. It must be conceded that our knowledge about the "less developed" cultures is very precarious. One of the most difficult problems in the study of those cultures has been the absence of archeological remains and ethnographic sources. It can be said that the great majority of those cultures practiced several kinds of rustic agriculture in which women played an important and often dominating role. The majority of the human groups in that developmental stage maintained a sedentary life with complex cultural and social characteristics, but they did not develop urban centers in the real meaning of the word. However, recent research has revealed, for example, that the Mississippi culture traded through river networks with one third of the North American continent; its capital *Sun City* (Cahokia, Illinois) had more than 40,000 inhabitants in the thirteenth century.[7]

More than 1,200 different dialects stemming from 140 different linguistic stocks were spoken in the Pre-Columbian American hemisphere. There were 22 cultural areas. Many physical and cul-

3

tural differences distinguished the Indian tribes, especially those of North and South America, but the pre-Hispanic inhabitants were more closely linked by their many-sided similarities than they were separated by their differences. Certainly, Pre-Columbian Amerindians represented the human crystallization of peoples that had intermingled with each other and had shared the New World for thousands of years. Although there is a growing interdisciplinary data about sporadic contacts between Asia and the Americas, the most remarkable quality about Pre-European America was its isolated development.[8]

The so-called "low" like the "high" cultures lived in a moral world in which they tried to adapt their lives to their perception of nature's laws. Their observations of nature affected their religious beliefs, and moral laws, and also taught them botanical and ecological concepts. It should surprise no one that their medical knowledge has survived up to the beginning of the third millennium, and that many pharmaceutical companies still learn and profit from their "primitive" knowledge of plants. Despite the fact that the less developed cultures had contacts with the high civilizations, they themselves did not vary from their nearly absolute disuse of metallic instruments and other artifacts enjoyed by the more "civilized" Indians.

The reasons for the different levels of development among the Amerindians have constituted a conundrum that borders on mysticism. The experts have proposed geographic, climatogical, ecological, cultural and socio-economic factors, but like the contemporary debate about industrialized and developing or underdeveloped nations, they have not reached a consensus. Apparently, the answer to this transcendental problem of yesterday and today has pluralist conceptualizations, and it is in that perspective that the research must be projected. The history of mankind has demonstrated that economic development is not a homogeneous process. Indeed, the most significant aspect of the lives of the Pre-Columbian Amerindians was their relationship to mother earth and nature, and it was that relationship that determined the use of their physical and mental capacities.

Unfortunately, one of the most neglected areas of archeological research has been the interrelations among the different Amerindian cultures. It is germane to remember that the mountains and distances never were absolute barriers. There is not any region in the American continent where signs of isolated development can be found. We know that where there were Indians with gold, the Spaniards found them. But the Spaniards "discovered" them because the Indians themselves guided them. It has been easier for scholars to accept that the Amerindians migrated from Asia and colonized the whole continent, thousands of years ago in an almost humanoid condition than for them to admit the existence of contacts among Indians at the time when the Spaniards arrived. Such an attitude reflects, at the very least, intellectual short-sightedness. But, indeed, there were contacts by land and sea.

In view of the fact that it is not impossible for humans to swim or float[9] from Europe to Africa, as well as to walk to Asia, it must be conceded that the most remarkable aspect of the ancient American civilizations was their isolated development. However, researchers continue to discover evidence of outside influences, such as Negroid people in Mesoamerica,[10] Polynesian –style artifacts, sculptures, and other cultural links in Peru and northern Chile; and pottery of ancient Japanese style (Jomon) in Ecuador. Likewise, the similarities in the iconography of Central Asia and North America are very noticeable.[11]

The astonishing similarities in art styles of Amerindian and Oriental civilizations suggest transpacific contact at the time of the high cultures.[12] Western scholars have noted artistic and architectural similarities between China of the Shang dynasty (1200 B.C.) and the Chavin (Peru) and Olmec (Mexico) cultures. Similar links have been found among the pre-Inca Indians of the Peruvian coast. The pentaphonic nature of Chinese music and that of many Indian tribes needs attention. The anthropological, cultural and linguistic similarities between the Indians of Western South America and Polynesia and Melanesia can not be ignored.

The American archeologist Betty J. Meggers noted the Asian-Amerindian contacts and the increasing probability that trans-Pacific introductions played an important part in shaping the civilizations, which existed at the time of the European discovery.[13] Viracocha, Quetzalcoal and Kukul-Chan were citizen gods who came and left by the seas. All of them were symbolically represented by dragons and fantastic serpents with arms and legs. It is the Eurocentric historiography, which asserted that they navigated through the Atlantic and conveniently attributed to them the quality of being white. Chinese historians now maintain not only that the Chinese discovered America, but that China had sporadic contacts until shortly before Columbus' arrival. The great controversy in Chinese historiography is not about whether the Chinese discovered America, but rather about which parts of America they discovered.[14]

Modern science has at least two problems to confront: Either the first Asian immigrants to the New World were not as savage as has been presumed, or there were transpacific contacts with Asia when the ancient Amerindians had already ceased to be primitives. One suspects that the evolution of Amerindian civilizations could include ingredients of both scenarios. It is imperative that scholars go beyond the debate between isolationist and diffusionist development. Such a debate undermines the Amerindian ability for cultural dialogue. Amerindians do have an ancient history that began long before it came to the attention of the Europeans.

The Mayas

The origin and collapse of the Maya civilization still remains clouded by an aura of mystery, and presently there is an ongoing lively scholarly debate on these issues.[15] The confusion remains despite the fact the Mayas left the most advanced writing system among the ancient Amerindians. The Maya language is characterized by its pictographic, ideographic and phonetic nature. Unfortunately, most of the Mayan writings and books were destroyed or burned by the fanaticism of the conquering Christians. Despite the efforts by the American epigrapher Linda Schele, the four remaining manuscripts have not been completely deciphered. A "Rosetta

Stone" has not yet been found by Western scholars and it appears unlikely that it will occur in the near future. Sophisticated computer programs have been of great help in deciphering the hieroglyphs, even though the spirit of a language can not be completely understood that way.

Researchers who study Amerindian languages and writings have found striking similarities with Asian languages and writings. The Mayan language, as well as the more advanced Mesoamerican writings, is written like Chinese: from top to bottom.[16] The Mayan hieroglyphs have constituted one of the greatest enigmas for Americanist Western scholars, but thanks to the pioneering efforts of the Russian scientist and linguist Yuri V. Knórozov, it has been possible to advance in deciphering these ancient texts. Knórozov maintained from the beginning that the Maya writing like Chinese combined pictographic, ideographic and phonetic elements at the same time.[17] Likewise, the Mayan and Chinese languages are basically monosyllabic and logographic. In addition all Maya dialects have linguistic structures significantly similar to Japanese.[18] According to the French scholar Paul Arnold, the Mayan signs are very similar to those that existed in China from two thousand to one thousand years before the Christian era. Furthermore, Mayan manuscripts, like the religious Chinese and Japanese texts, were written with long hair brushes; the comparison to old Chinese texts enabled Arnold to translate partially the Mayan manuscripts found in the libraries of Dresden, Madrid and Paris.[19] So far, the Mayan hieroglyphs up to now translated, concern dynastic, political, military and religious matters of the ruling elites, while the history of peasants, artisans and small merchants remains in deep obscurity.[20]

Many Mayanists trace the Mayan origins to the mysterious Olmecs (also the indirect ancestors of the Toltecs and Aztecs), who inhabited the Gulf Coast of Mexico in the neighborhood of Tabasco and Veracruz at about 1200 B.C.[21] The Olmecs linked almost all Central America in a trade network. They were the first users of hieroglyphs, of the vigesimal system and the Mesoamerican calendar. The Olmecs produced the oldest and most sophisticated Mesoamerican art, which was to influence the styles of the Mayas,

Toltecs and Aztecs. Olmec art includes sculptures of dragons, birds, midgets, hunchbacks, jaguars, anthropomorphic figures, and figures with anatomic organs. In addition to building great pyramids, the Olmecs sculptured gigantic stone faces of up to 18 tons. In the Olmec sculptures can be seen Asian, Negroid or Australoid faces. Olmec culture expanded to Guatemala, Honduras, British Honduras, El Salvador and Costa Rica, but the Olmecs mysteriously disappeared by the third century B.C.

The Mayas emerged as a distinctive culture in the fertile lowlands of Petén (Guatemala) at about the ninth century B.C.[22] It was the region with the most abundant and purest salt in ancient Mesoamerica. Mayan civilization reached its highest splendor between 250 and 950 A.D., an era often labeled as the Classic Period of Mayan and Mesoamerican history. During the height of this epoch, something resembling the ancient Greek City-States developed in an approximate area of 125,000 square miles comprising what is today south and southeastern Mexico, Guatemala, Honduras and British Honduras. The most widely accepted population estimate is still that of the British scholar Eric Thompson, who asserted that there were three million inhabitants in 800 A.D. By then, Tikal (in Petén), one of the biggest Mayan cities, had more than 10,000 inhabitants. The majority of the Mayas were peasants, but their cities were centers for worship, administration and commercial transactions. During the golden age of Mayan civilization, the major urban centers such as Tikal, Copán, Chichén Itzá and Palenque were connected by masonry causeways and gravel or stone roads.

The Mayas derived their living from agriculture, but there was an entrepreneurial elite of shamans who profited from trade and agriculture. These merchants used red shells and corals from the Pacific coast as money.[23] Among themselves the Mayas traded salt, calcium, cacao, obsidian, feathers, hides, textiles, ceramics, woods, medicinal herbs, natural crystals and rubber. They were seafarers and traded with the Caribbean islands, Panama, Colombia, Ecuador and Peru. From South America, the Mayas obtained mostly gold, silver, and metallic alloys.[24]

Before the Christian era, the Mayas invented a yearly calendar which eventually became more accurate than that used in Europe until the late sixteenth century; it was in fact, accurate to within seventeen seconds over a period of 365 days. Moreover, the modern calendar rests upon a year of 365.245 days with a margin of one day and a half every 5,000 years, but the Mayan astronomical year of 365.2420 days was accurate within a day during the same millennia. At least from the beginning of the Christian era, the Mayas had a number system that included the concept of the zero. Mayan mathematical knowledge was developed because the high priests and intellectuals considered it necessary for divinations and astronomical observations. Mayan scientists conceptualized the earth as round.[25] Besides informing their disciples and believers about the lucky and unlucky days, they could also predict eclipses, rains, and other natural phenomena. In the mystical Maya calculations, the world reached a cosmological and historical cycle on Sunday, December 21, 2012.

On the more practical level for the pain folk, the Mayan understanding of nature and the terrain allowed them to remove the fragile limestone shelves which exposed the subterranean water tables, thus allowing the rains to percolate through the porous limestone. Mayan water reservoirs, cisterns, and irrigation systems remain as clear testimony of how well they coordinated their way of life with nature. Until recently, there has been much perplexity among Mayanists about the Mayan ability to cultivate high yields of food for its dense population. But thanks to space and aerial photography, it has been possible to conclude that the peasants dug an intricate network of parallel canals in the swamps. They placed the excavated soil onto the areas between the canals, thus creating a series of elevated gardens. Such practices supplied the plants only the amount of water that they needed and thus prevented the rotting of roots from an excess of moisture. The Mayas of the lowland tropical zones laboriously gathered and stored water in *cenotes* (wells) while those of the highlands built distributing hydraulic canals. It was labor intensive agriculture.[26]

It is difficult to know, in historical terms, how labor was regulated by Mayan society. Some early Spanish accounts, and archeological and anthropological data indicate that it was a hierarchical society, which provided abundantly for the theocratic elite and well for the majority of its agricultural population. It was a non-egalitarian society which co-existed with slavery. The slaves were war captives or people who had committed infractions against certain social norms. They were bought and sold, could own property and had free time for their own benefit. The slaves were of two types: household slaves and those used in mass production such as in the cultivation of cacao.[27]

By about 900 A.D., the lowland Maya cities were abandoned. The tropical jungle gradually covered them, preserving them for posterity. We do witness what has been termed as a post classic renaissance in Chichén Itzá and Yucatán, but what the Europeans found there was no longer strictly Maya. The downfall of Mayan civilization has to be seen within the context of contemporaneous ecological changes throughout Mesoamerica. The droughts of those years, rendered useless the canals and aqueducts which served for transport and irrigation. In addition to dryness and ecological changes,[28] there were times of invasions by northern tribes and defensive wars against those nomads. Those disturbances further deteriorated the Maya trading system, causing scarcity and the basis for internal problems, which promoted even more external attacks.[29] The excessive tributary requests by the ruling elites caused peasant revolts. Such revolts became the most decisive factors in the collapse of the Classic Mayas. It was a social explosion. Further studies have confirmed that it was a collapse and virtual extermination of the theocratic elite rather than the majority of the population.

Although there is growing evidence that the Maya sophistication continued to develop in present-day Belize (British Honduras), the foreign attacks by northern tribes further disrupted the working masses from their elaborate chores which the steamy jungles demanded for agricultural production. Thus, the wild forest little by little transformed the ecology. It can be asserted that by about 800 A.D., the Maya civilization was one of the most developed cultural centers within a world context. The Mayas like the great non-European civilizations, which prospered during the first millennium of the Christian era, had superior material qualities to those that developed in Western Europe during that period.

The average Mayan had a social, moral, spiritual and ceremonial perception of work. There was a spirit of obedience, which allowed the elite to direct by *corvée* the construction of pyramids, temples, urban centers, and irrigation systems. The land was owned communally by clans, which produced for themselves and rendered tribute to the theocratic elite. Moreover, social discipline was deeply affected by Mesoamerican ecology. Recent research has made us aware that ecological transformations are important in global history. The impact of ecological changes in economic development by the end of the first millennium A.D., in Central Asia and the Americas still has not been analyzed scientifically from a global and comparative perspective.[30]

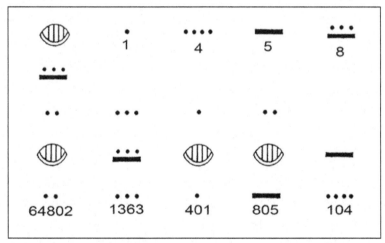

Maya Mathematics: The Mayan numerical system uses as a base the number 20. The numbers are formed through the combination of points, lines, and the figure of a sea shell. A point is the equivalent of a unit. A line is the same as five units, and the shellrepresents the numeral O. The basic column contains quantities that can reach up to 20. The following horizontal column contains numbers between 20 and 399. The subsequent column contains the numbers 400 through 7,999. Every new column increases 20 times every one of the numbers in the previous column.

The Aztecs

It is likely that the ancient Mexicans were hunters who came from the north during the paleolithic period not long after the first Asian migrations to the Western Hemisphere. It was in the eastern part of modern Mexico (Tamaulipas and Tehuacán) that the ancestors of the Aztecs became farmers sometime between 5,200 and 3,400 B.C. By approximately 1,200 B.C., we begin to see signs of organized religion when ceremonial mounds appeared at La Venta on the Gulf Coast, the Oaxaca Valley and Lake Texcoco. Likewise, during this period at La Venta, the Olmec culture emerged with far superior accomplishments than those of the other Mesoamerican tribes. At the outset of the millennium before Christ and when Western Europe was still illiterate, the Olmec elite had designed a hieroglyphic script. Apparently, the Olmec became the "mother culture" for all the higher cultures of the Mesoamerican Classic Period.

During the Classic Period (approximately 300-750 A.D.) urban centers developed throughout the present Mexican republic; among them, Monte Albán, El Tajín, Xochicalco and Teotihuacán (the place of the gods). The latter city was the most important religious Mecca for the Mexican highlands during most of the Classic Period. During its grandeur, Teotihuacán reached 250,000 inhabitants (500 A.D.). It was one of the greatest cities of the world. By the eighth century, in a process reminiscent to the fall of Rome, Teotihuacán was invaded by nomads from the north who likewise eventually deserted the city. Some of the Teotihuacán residents fled to the shores of Lake Texcoco where they continued their culture and traditions. The downfall of Teotihuacán was typical of what was to occur by the close of the Classic Period. It was a period of turmoil, invasions, migrations, bloodshed and ecological changes that engulfed most of Mesoamerica. From the ashes of such turbulence, rose many new states controlled by the Toltecs, the Mixtecs and the Aztecs. The Aztecs called these relentless invaders, *Chichimecs* (people of the dog), a Nahua-speaking ethnic group. Eventually, these war-like people with different dialects settled down and adopted the culture of the conquered peoples. The Toltecs themselves were a Chichimec group.

According to legends, in the last third of the tenth century, a Toltec "Citizen-God" and prophet took the name of the ancient deity, Quetzalcoatl (Feathered Serpent), and ruled in his name. Quetzalcoatl distinguished himself for his piety and the teaching of better agricultural techniques. He wanted to end human sacrifices, and advocated that only snakes, flowers, incense and tortillas should be offerings to the gods. Mainly due to such heresies, he was forced to abandon the Toltec capital (Tula) by a rival faction. A myth was spread by the remaining followers of Quetzalcoatl that their hero had escaped by the seas promising to return and rule over his people once again. This myth was to be used advantageously by the conquering Spaniards, who also found it convenient to add the physical characteristic of whiteness to their vision of Quetzalcoatl.

The Aztecs claiming to be the descendants of the Toltecs came from the north, wandering for many years before they finally founded the city of Tenochtitlán in 1325.[31] The city was located on an island in Lake Texcoco where the waters protected them from foreign attack. However, the official Aztec historiography noted that the "Chosen" Aztec people originated from the mythic land of Aztlán since 50 A.D.[32] The distinguished American historian Charles Gibson noted that the Aztecs "built dams, causeways, aqueducts, canals, irrigation works, terracing systems, and cities situated partly in the water and partly on land. Fish and water birds helped to provide them with one of the most balanced diets in all America, and chinampa [floating gardens] agriculture rivaled Asiatic rice-paddy cultivation in its intensity."[33]

The Spanish conquerors perceived the commercial activity of the Aztec capital to be greater than that of Rome, Constantinople and Salamanca. Hernán Cortés describes the Aztec commercial activity in the following terms: "Every trade and every kind of merchandise from all parts are found...jewelry of gold and silver, of bones, shells, corals and feathers; they sell stones, both rough and finished, adobes, bricks...There is a place for animals where all kinds of birds are sold...they sell rabbits, hares, deer...There is also a wonderful variety of herbs, roots, leaves, and seeds which are sold for medicinal purposes...There are barber shops where they wash and cut hair...There are places where food and drinks are served for a price. There are porters like in Castile who carry loads for a price...There are all kinds of vegetables...fruits...They sell bee honey and from maize...they make wine which they sell. They sell all types of cotton of all colors...They sell deerskins, raw or tanned...and of different colors. They sell much pottery of different clays and glazes and painted. They sell maize in grains and in bread...They also make lacquer ware; they set and carve emeralds, turquoises, other precious stones and pearls...They sell with much order and things are sold by units and weight...certain men go around the market place as inspectors. There is one house where a dozen old men hear complaints and where all might see them."[34]

In the Aztec, like other Mesoamerican societies, there existed a small intermediary class which included artists, artisans and merchants. The merchants constituted a group which was growing in opulence and privileges. Cortés wrote that in his expedition from Mexico to Honduras, he and his entourage were quartered in great hostelries that belonged to merchants. These merchants had all kinds of employees, maids, slaves and even excellent mapmakers.[35] However, the merchants had to wear modest clothes when meeting the emperor; they were not allowed to look at him directly on the eyes.

In Aztec times, the land was worked collectively by communal clans, each of which was composed by the same ethnic group (*calpulli*). The local community paid tribute to the political and religious bureaucrats with products and obligatory work (*cuatequil*) during certain times of the year. The majority of the calpulli's members belonged to the *macegual*class. But internally, the calpulli did not have an egalitarian nature; it was stratified, and at the bottom existed a *submacegual* or *mayeque* class that was analogous to European slavery which existed during the same time period.[36] Recent estimates assert that up to 30% of the total population belonged to the *submacegual* class.

In ancient Mexico, the slaves were not only provided by prisoners taken in war, but there already existed a market and slave trade. The slaves were from inside and outside the Aztec Empire. Although they could gain their freedom, the masters could even kill them if they deemed it to be necessary. The so-called "flower wars" that the Aztecs inflicted on their enemies were not total wars; they were opportunities to capture slaves. On certain occasions and within the context of the "flower wars," ball games were agreed upon, in which the players could win the war, lose their lives, or be enslaved. The imperial Aztec mystic ideology was intimately related to the cosmological balance of positive and negative forces. From childhood, the Aztecs were educated to admire flowers and take care of the elderly, "and on the other hand, practice war, human sacrifices…and the death cult."[37]

The state apparatus had an authoritarian bureaucracy with active political, military and shamanistic roles. Every major population center had an imperial headmaster (*tlatoque*), and his official bureaucrats, who were maintained by communal tributes. Generally the position of *tlatoque* was hereditary. Many were relatives by blood or marriage with the imperial family. The high nobility owned private land, and some of them belonged to the Military Orders like the "Eagles" and the "Jaguars." They received tributes in products and services from the *macegual* communities.[38]

The Aztec Emperor was treated almost as a divine being and his position was basically hereditary. There was always more than one candidate among the heirs of the previous monarch. The Council of Nobles together with the religious elite had certain influence in the choosing of the new emperor. Moreover, the Aztec Empire was the result of an alliance among three kingdoms. The Aztec monarch lived in luxurious palaces, reminiscent to those of oriental despots. The royal table-service was of gold, silver and fine ceramics. For every dinner the chefs prepared more than 30 different courses; the banquets were shared by more than a thousand employees, guards, guests, and dignitaries. The diners were entertained by singers, musicians, dancers, artists, buffoons and acrobats. Tobacco, refreshments and *pulque* (cactus wine) were consumed. The emperor wore his clothes only once, and never put the same clothes on twice. Besides his legitimate wife, he had numerous concubines of royal blood.[39] The Emperor bathed thoroughly everyday. He was a person of exquisite tastes and super-civilized refinements.

The Incas

No other Amerindian civilization had reached the socio-economic and political cohesiveness that the Inca Empire or Tawantinsuyo had achieved at the arrival of the Spaniards. It comprised approximately 30 million inhabitants.[40] The Tawantinsuyo was the largest American empire, and it was bigger than the Roman Empire at its maximum extension. Despite its authoritarianism, the Inca state provided for the care of the sick, lame, elderly, orphans and widowers. According to the Peruvian historian Alberto Flores Galindo the Inca Empire attempted to practice justice. This is not to say that the Inca Empire was a socialist society. However, within the context of classical Marxism, Rosa Luxemburg maintained that the Inca Empire represented the most advanced form of primitive communism, resulting from military conquests over other primitive communists. In addition, she asserted that Inca society represented the key for the understanding of primitive communism in the history of humanity and all societies.[41]

The Inca Empire produced in abundance and accumulated reserves. The Inca agricultural development was greater than that of the contemporary Andean region. The American historian E. Bradford Burns asserts on this issue: "We are challenged to understand why Incan technology, efficiency, and productivity surpassed Western technology, efficiency, and productivity or why the Inca empire of the fifteenth century was more developed than Peru, or Ecuador or Bolivia of the twentieth century."[42] From Cuzco (the belly of the world) at 3,467 meters of altitude the Incas intended to civilize their vassals. The capital city of the expansionist empire had over 100,000 inhabitants when the Spaniards arrived.

Before the rise of the Inca Empire, there were two basic periods of Andean history. The Chavín appears at about 1200 B.C. in the central Andes (Ancash). The Tiahuanaco emerged in the Bolivian highlands at almost the same time of the Mesoamerican Classic Period, and suddenly declined by the end of the first millennium of the Christian era. Both "mother cultures" were the nuclear centers of diffusion in the Andean region and western South America. The Chavín are contemporaneous with the Olmecs of Mexico and both have striking similarities. The Chavín and the Tiahuanaco expanded in the Andes and towards the Pacific. But both civilizations reached their highest level of development in the mountains. With the decline of the Tiahuanaco, several new kingdoms emerged like the Huari (Ayacucho) in the Andes as well as the Chincha and the Mochica-Chimu in the Pacific coast.

The Inca society was established between the twelfth and thirteenth centuries of the Christian era by the mythological Manco Capac and his wife, Mama Ocllo. They claimed to be the living children of the Sun. The Inca Emperor had absolute hereditary power. However, male primogeniture was not an automatic quality for succession. The heir had to be anointed by the ruling monarch as well. After the time of Emperor Tupac Yupanqui (1447-1493), the marriage between the emperor and one of his sisters was instituted in order to legitimize the succession.[43] The "sisters" of the *Inca* were all the women of his generation within his ethnic clan. The co-government with the *Coya* (empress) was created in order to avoid civil war and facilitate the peaceful transition to the heir chosen by the Emperor. The *Coya* was the personal advisor to the emperor, and she had important political-religious powers within the administrative hierarchy. The emperor was considered a divine person and disobedience to him was sacrilegious. He was accepted as lord father and protector of his people, and after his death, his mummy was placed in the *Coricancha* (the temple of the sun), where he was worshiped together with the other deities of the Inca religion.

The Inca Emperor presided over the political-religious administration. He shared his tasks with the *Uilla Umu* (high priest), who was usually his brother or an immediate relative, and the *Tucuiricuc* (imperial council). The Incas were benevolent rulers, but only the elite enjoyed a luxurious lifestyle with palaces, servants, polygamous life, and the right to chew the best coca-leaves. Inca society was flexible enough to permit individuals who distinguished themselves in the service of the emperor, especially soldiers, talented technicians, or artists, to rise in the social ladder. But it was a situation where the emperor could give everything and take all as well. One of the greatest talents of the Inca rulers was their ability to mobilize numerous workers for specific tasks. In the main, collective work had a social goal. Indeed, work was a venerated cult at every social level. Labor and upward loyalty were regulated under three major commandments: *Ama Sua* (do not steal), *Ama Quella* (do not be lazy) and *Ama Llulla* (do not lie). Infractions among the lower classes brought the death penalty for the culprit and his family.

Although the subjugated tribes of the Aztec Empire were subjected to forced contributions of different kinds, they were allowed considerable freedom in their religious and socio-economic organization.[44] The Aztec hierarchical system was less structured than that of Inca society. In the Aztec Empire, war and the threat of war kept vassals obedient. The death cult of the Mexican people was used by the State in order to control the conquest and growth of the Aztec Empire.[45] On the other hand, the Inca bureaucracy was more centralized, and exercised great diplomatic skills in the conquest and global administration of conquered vassals. The Incas routinely used threats, power demonstrations and presents as an alternative to war, and they were distributors of goods; the Incas were "takers" as well as "givers." Those policies constituted the fundamental essence of the Incas' self-appointed civilizing mission.

The administrative apparatus was organized in a decimal system. The decimal system was implanted in order to bureaucratize the different socio-political structures of the conquered ethnic groups. At the bottom of the organizational scale was the *Chunka Camayoc*, who was the chief of ten families and the communal lands worked by them. There existed a bureaucracy whose highest levels were monopolized by the imperial family and the nobility of the conquered kingdoms. As soon as a new tribe or kingdom was incorporated, the cult to the Sun god was forced on the neophyte vassals, but they were allowed to keep their local deities on a secondary level. The heirs of the local chiefdoms were taken as hostages to Cuzco, where they were inculcated with Inca traditions. Likewise, a resettlement program was initiated by which sizable numbers of the newly conquered vassals (*yanaconas*) were interspersed with loyal citizens (*mitimaes*). The *mitimaes* were not only good spies, but would teach the new vassals Quechua and the Inca ways of doing things.

In the Tawantinsuyo the State demanded tribute in metals, precious stones, wild animals and unusual objects. But that form of tribute could be done mostly by the nobility and local chiefs (*curacas*). No *curaca* could take office without being previously trained in Cuzco and accepted by the Inca elite. The Inca State received most of its tribute in labor. This emphasis on labor constitutes the great difference between the tributary systems of the Inca Empire and Mesoamerica. *Chicha* (corn-beer) and music were fundamental aspects of state labor in the Tawantinsuyo. The bureaucratic administration of production and enthusiastic labor in great scale permitted the Inca Empire to distribute food to all its inhabitants.

Despite the fact that the bureaucratizing process was in an expanding trend, the productive unit was still the family clan or ethnic group (*Ayllu*).[46] The value of production from the *Ayllu* was divided in such a way as to leave enough for the needs of the local community while the surplus went to the State and Church. Thus, the land was formally divided into three sections: for the community, the State and religion. The cultivation rested upon the shoulders of the average Inca citizen (*runa*). The *runa* was also subjected to the *mita* and *minka* which constituted obligatory work by turn for the benefit of the community and the State during some periods of the year. The agricultural production in the highlands was not only for local consumption, but to subsidize the coastal region, where due to the aridity of the desert, there were populations which could produce only one third of their needs. The rest was obtained from fishing and barter.

The lands of the State were also subdivided in three sections: common lands, those of the royal clans (*panacas*), and the private lands of the emperor. Production from the common lands covered the expenses of the administration of the imperial apparatus. When the emperor died, his lands passed to his royal clan. By the end of the Incan Empire there were twelve *panacas*. With the development of the *panacas* and the private property of the ruling elite, emerged a class of semi-slaves or *yanaconas*. It is likely that the *yanaconas* composed the main working group in the private sector.[47]

The Inca Empire was a multi-ethnic, tributary and hierarchical society. About 100 ethnic groups comprised the Inca Empire; 58 of them still survive in our days. The Inca society was a conglomerate of ethnic, inter-ethnic and supra-ethnic relations. But the Inca more than any other Amerindian state was based on the politics of reciprocity. Despite the Inca assimilation policies, each individual had to dress in the manner of his region and ethnic group. The local nobilities were allowed to keep their privileges, and marriage to the Inca nobility was permitted. Roads were built to connect the new frontiers to the royal highways leading to Cuzco. But above all, a social restructuring was effected in which the Inca tributary system of labor was implanted.

The technological knowledge developed by the Incas was unequalled by the other ancient Amerindians. And yet, most Western observers have asserted that the Incas did not have a writing system. The Incas had the *quipus*, which were woolen ropes with various knot forms. The *quipus* are considered mnemonic devises to store mainly statistic and mathematical data. The numerical *quipus* included the conception of the zero.[48] However, the word "writing" (*quilca*) existed in Pre-Hispanic Quechua in all the grammatical functions.[49] Moreover, in the Inca bureaucracy there were different officials in charge of the *quipus* and the *quilcas* (*Quipu Camayoc* and *Quilca Camayoc*). According to the Peruvian epigrapher Victoria De La Jara and the German cryptologist Thomas Barthel, the Inca writing was logographic like Chinese. A phonetic as well as numerical alphabet has already been resecued and elaborated.[50] Furthermore, the American ethnograper Gail Silverman claims that the *quipus* and *quilcas* have a binary and ternary logic like modern computers.[51] Apparently, the *quipus* and the *quilcas* were intertwined modalities of symbolic communications by the Inca elites. The sciences and history of the Incas will continue to be enigmatic as long as the *quipus* and *quilcas* are not fully deciphered. Unfortunately, the Incas like all the other Amerindians were vanquished and plundered. Their future and their past are still at the mercy of Western values and perceptions of reality.

CHAPTER II

FROM COLONIZATION TO DECOLONIZATION

C olumbus arrived at Samaná Island or San Salvador after 33 days on the high seas. The Caribbean natives lived from fishing, hunting, trading and farming. In this last activity, women had a very active role, if not the dominant one. The Caribbeans lived in towns of one to two thousand inhabitants, which were ruled by hereditary chiefs or *caciques* with varying levels of power. Some of them exercised political hegemony in several islands. Within 24 hours of Columbus' arrival, the natives informed him that there existed a mainland to the west, and that a great ruler governed those territories. Naturally, Columbus assumed that it was the Asian continent and that the ruler was the Great Khan.[1] It was, instead, a new continent, and the great ruler was the Aztec Emperor. The Indians informed Columbus that the gold and the precious stones came from the Caribbean southwest, and from the island of Haiti.[2] Columbus explored Haiti, and renamed the island as Hispaniola. The island had very fertile soils, and the richest gold-bearing lands of the Caribbean.[3] Haiti was controlled by the family of the great *cacique* Caonabó. Columbus chose to befriend the *cacique* Guacanagarí, leader of the Taino people, who were enemies and tributary vassals of Caonabó and the *Canibas* or *Caribas* (Cannibals).

By the time Columbus arrived at the Caribbean, the Tainos were the majority.[4] However, the Canibas and their allies were the dominant group. The Canibas were great merchants and controlled the contacts between the Caribbean islands and the northern South American mainland. The Tainos became the allies of Columbus. The Canibas had several outstanding technologies. In war, the Canibas used metal weapons and copper chest-protectors. Because of their use of curare as poison in their arrows and darts, they were superior in many military conflicts.[5] The Canibas were the most difficult to defeat by the white man. Indeed, they were the heroes of the Caribbean resistance. The Canibas of the Windward Islands resisted until 1797, when the British finally defeated them, and their survivors were removed to Central America. The need of Christian Spain to justify the colonization in moral terms was present from the very beginning. The Canibas have been the least known and most slandered Amerindians. When in 1503, the Crown decreed that only anthropophagous people could be enslaved, it condemned the Aztecs to the fantasy of being cannibals before they were "discovered."

Bartolomé de Las Casas categorically denies that the Canibas were anthropophagous. When comparing the letters, reports and documents related to Columbus' first voyage and those of the successive ones, we observe basic differences concerning his description of the Indians. Contrary to the documents and reports of the successive voyages, those of the first describe the Indians as kind, honest, hard-working, and a vigorous "race." The Indians were willing to cooperate with the whites and also learn the virtues of Christianity. But the necessity to justify the colonization of the New World produced a new type of documentation. It was during Columbus' second visit that his letters and reports indicated the Indians were devil worshipers, deceitful, lazy, homosexuals, prostitutes, and eat human flesh. During the first trip, Columbus specifically and explicitly addressed the question of whether the natives were anthropophagous or not. This was a question, which contemporary Europeans considered very seriously about the world outside Europe. Columbus was always looking out for anthropophagous, tailed-people, one-eyed people, dog-faced people, giants, and mermaids.[6]

The remaining sources and literature are unclear about the issue of canibalism and human sacrifices in Pre-European America. The historian Inga Clendinnen considers the allegations of human sacrifices in the water wells (cenotes) to be a historiographical fiction constructed by the friars on the inventions of tortured Indians. Clendinnen asserts: "There are at least, the same arguments to conclude the contrary."[7] In regard to the Amerindian anthropophagy, the American anthropologist William Arens concludes that the accusation is false.[8] Both Christians and Indians, despite the presence of numerous Saints and Virgins in Europe and the almost animistic indigenous worship of nature, were essentially monotheistic. Both could distinguish very clearly what was good and bad. Whites as well as Indians had profound concepts of good and evil in their mythologies, symbols and metaphors. From the plains of North America and the Amazon forests to the high civilizations of Mesoamerica and the Andes, the Amerindians engaged in mystical monologues that questioned their spiritual existence and asked for guidance from the *Great Spirit* (Huaka Tanka).[9] In the *Popol Vuh*, the sacred book of the Mayas, it is written that while many gods are worshiped, there is likewise the one "great creator and protector god."

Unfortunately, several Indian tribes and especially the Aztecs were unable to confine the ancient religious human sacrifice to a symbolic level.[10] As in the old Christian communion, the Amerindian religious sacrifices contained a cult and ideology for blood shedding. But since most of the victims were war prisoners sacrificed in the name of *Huitzilopochtli* (Master of the Sun and God of War), such a bloody practice was intimately related to the ancient causes of war, and consequently it must be explained and understood in that context. As R. C. Padden has carefully explained, that cult was intimately linked to the maintenance of Aztec imperialism.[11] There were also victims selected by the clergy, slaves acquired for the occasion, and common criminals. As to the number of executions by this method, it is likewise a matter of dispute, and much of it depends on the European sympathy or antipathy for the Indians. The first Bishop of Mexico, Juan de Zumárraga, stated that in the Aztec capital 20,000 individuals were sacrificed annually, while Hernán Cortés' secretary, who never visited America, noted more than 50,000 per year. On the other hand, Bartolomé de Las Casas set the figure at around 100 annually.[12]

Much ink and paper have been used by Western writers to explain the speed of the Spanish conquest in terms of the Indian belief that whites were gods riding on ferocious beasts and shooting thunder. In great part, this misconception is the result of Western ignorance about the existence of social classes among the Indians. Was it really true that the white gods brought darkness in broad daylight? But being white did not automatically confer treatment as a lord or God. The Peruvian historian Pablo Macera writes that when the Inca Emperor Atahualpa was under Spanish custody and in the twilight of his power, "he behaved as a prince and had social contempt for the Spaniards who were not of noble birth."[13]

One of the most puzzling aspects of the Spanish conquest is the fact that very small numbers of whites were able to subdue large Indian masses. Although the whites possessed superior military technology, this is only one of several important factors. The history of the conquest is essentially the history of kidnappings. For example, when the Spaniards first arrived at Tenochtitlán their Aztec hosts took the visitors on tours as well as "dinned" and "wined" them during a week. On the seventh day, Cortés and five elite soldiers kidnapped the Aztec monarch at sword-point in the midst of a friendly conversation.[14] When the Spaniards kidnapped Montezuma, he was about 40 years old, married, and had several concubines as well as sons and daughters. Montezuma was of delicate physique and had the manners of a prince. He was melancholic, somewhat effeminate and often cried. His nephew Cacamatzin considered the Emperor as brave as a chicken.[15] The chronicler Díaz Del Castillo, who admired Montezuma, exonerates him from having any "unnatural vices."[16] Despite rumors, the historian Ross Hassig concludes that Montezuma was not a coward when confronting the Spaniards but he was afraid to lose his political power in the Aztec society.[17] The Aztec emperor's capture was a prototype of the kidnappings of native leaders during the *conquest*. Perfidy runs across the colonization process. It took time for Amerindians to realize that whites talked with "forked tongues."

The conquest of the Americas was also a war of microbes in which the Europeans were favored. European epidemics, malnutrition and forced labor caused the Amerindian demographic catastrophe in the times of the Iberian conquest. Although initially the Aztecs militarily defeated Cortés (June 30, 1520), his soldiers left smallpox among the victorious natives. In the following year almost 40% of the population in the Mexican Central Valley died from European plagues. Likewise, before the Spaniards invaded Peru, European pests had already killed the highest Inca cadres. European epidemics gradually would anticipate the Spanish kidnappings and fire-arms. When Francisco Pizarro landed for the last time at the Inca Empire (Tawantinsuyo) during early 1532, he encountered it in the midst of a violent civil war. After the death of Emperor Huayna Capac (1493-1527), in a smallpox and measles epidemic five years earlier, the empire had been shaken by the dispute between rival candidates. Historians agree that if the Tawantinsuyo had been ruled by Huayna Capac at the time of the Spanish invasion, it would have been impossible for Pizarro to conquer the Inca Empire.

Another crucial aspect of the Spanish conquest consisted of the alliances made between *conquistadores* and the local ethnic enemies. When the besieged Aztecs finally surrendered their capital city on August 13, 1521, the armies of Cortés included more than 150,000 Indians (most of them from Tlaxcala) and only 900 Spaniards.[18] During the rule of Huayna Capac, the Portuguese adventurer Aleixo Garcia allied with Guaraní Indians already had unsuccessfully attempted to penetrate the eastern border of the Inca Empire (1524-1525).[19] The Spanish invasion of Peru could have begun only after the death of Huayna Capac. The civil war among the Incas permitted the landing of Pizarro and his troops on the northern Peruvian coast almost without Indian interference. In analyzing the Spanish conquest, the role of white-Indian alliances in the battles against other Indian ethnic groups should by no means be underrated. Indian collaboration in the defeat and domination of the Indians themselves runs through the very heart of Post-Columbian Amerindian history. The Indian assistance to white supremacy survived as a subordinate partnership in the exploitation of other Indians. Moreover until the late eighteenth century, European powers searched for alliances with "Indian Nations" in order to advance their imperial objectives.

The horses were feared not because they were ferocious magical demons, but because, in military terms, they had the advantage of being strong and fast. The horses have been perceptively called the "tanks of the conquest." It is important to keep in mind that the Indians were quick to adopt horses as fighting elements. Manco Inca, half-brother of Atahualpa and the Spaniards' puppet Emperor, made his final revolt against the Spaniards on horseback and with European weapons together with a platoon of native cavalry. His army even produced gunpowder in their resistance against the invaders.[20] Moreover, the Indians of Patagonia and those of the United States' southwest became skillful horsemen before they ever met the white man. Unfortunately for the Amerindians, horses by then had lost much of their strategic value for the white man had added other factors to the invasion and domination of the Americas.

The practice of kidnapping was not limited to military or political operations. The Catholic clergy used it to bring about the conversion of natives. The usual procedure involved kidnapping the children of the native elites in order to indoctrinate them and keep them as interns in schools operated by the Church. After these children were considered thoroughly indoctrinated, they were released to convert their compatriots of humbler birth.[21] Wherever Amerindian deities and spiritual symbols existed, the Catholic church approved and confirmed the appearance of saints and virgins. Such a prototype of colonial expediency and religious syncretism is clearly illustrated by the appearance of the *Virgin of*

28

Guadalupe (1531) in the same place where the Mexican Indians worshiped the mother goddess, *Tonantzin*. Believers and Catholic bureaucrats still verify her miracles. But *Tonantzin,* like other Amerindian goddesses, were generally connected to the "mother earth" and fertility cults. The *Virgen of Guadalupe* is transcendental to the syncretic reality that prevails in the Latin American existensialism. She is one of the virgens and saints with dark-complexion that inspires many to act with humility and search for justice in Latin America.

It has been noted that the cross and the sword acted together in the colonial enterprise. The Church defended the divinity of the Iberian monarchs, the colonial state and the ecumenical authority of Catholicism. Religious salvation and submission to the colonial system was the fundamental task of Catholic activism among Amerindians. Indians faced the dilemma of sin and rebelliousness or salvation and submission. From the outset, betrayal to the State became the equivalent of heresy. The Pope granted to the Iberian crowns the Royal Patronage (*patronato, padroado*) which theoretically allowed the State to supervise the whole ecclesiastical apparatus.

In the beginning, the Church depended for its maintenance mostly on royal subsidies, the tithes and private donations. But gradually it became involved in banking, entrepreneurial administration, mining, urban real estate and agricultural production. The Church administered and financed religious and public charity such as schools and hospitals. It produced sugar, wines, textiles and numerous consumer products. By the end of the eighteenth century, the Church controlled about 50% of the Spanish American agricultural lands. Although, these lands had belonged to the Indians, they were acquired indirectly. The lands of the Church were mainly donated by Catholic sinners who wanted to insure salvation in heaven, and many of those lands could not be sold or divided. The *mayorazgo* (entailed estate) was the effort of the upper classes to perpetuate their wealth and social hierarchy with the collaboration of the Church.

Through the Royal Patronage, the Vatican had granted the Iberian crowns the task of converting the recently discovered pagans. Thus, the first *encomenderos* (owners of *encomiendas*) were allowed by the Spanish crown to obtain tribute in products and labor from the Indians in exchange for their Christianization. In the beginning, the *encomienda* was often called *repartimiento*. It was an exploitation directly controlled by the *encomenderos* that later on would pass to the supervision of the Crown's *corregidores* (royal representatives). Ironically, the Dominicans were the first in protesting against the abuses of the *encomienda* and labor assignments. The first conflicts between the Church and the *encomenderos* culminated in the Laws of Burgos (1512-1513). Although those laws prohibited the mistreatment of the Indians, the existence of the *encomienda* was confirmed. The Spanish crown also wanted to clarify its jurisdiction in the conflicts between the *encomenderos* and the Church. The *encomenderos* and the Church had gradually become rivals in the struggle for the physical and spiritual control of the Indians. Furthermore, between the *encomenderos* and the religious fathers, the Indians preferred the latter.

Only the representatives of the king could exercise final authority. In practice, the system was clientelist at all its levels, and Iberians as well as *Criollos* participated for mutual benefit. The Viceroy, in the name of the King had as main function executive powers. A Viceroy governed for about five years. He was controlled by the *Audiencia* or judicial court, which at the end of his administration would make an evaluation (*residencia*) of his administration. During his term of office, the Viceroy could be visited by a high royal official, without previous announcement, to investigate his good or bad government (*visita*). In addition, the ecclesiastical authorities and the *Consulado* watched with great attention the policies of the Viceroy. Until the Bourbon Reforms of the eighteenth century, the *Audiencias* functioned as the favorite fiefs of *Criollo* interests.[22]

In the seventeenth century, the socio-political power of the colonies reached a great apogee. In the so-called "long century" (1670-1770) of Portuguese and Spanish imperial decadence, the private entrepreneurs greatly surpassed the State in profits.[23] For example, in the 1620s, eight or ten wealthy Peruvian *Indiano* families, who were established in Seville, controlled the European trade with Spanish South America.[24] The Indianos were mixed clans (Spaniards and *Criollos*) who after having accumulated wealth in the colonies returned to the metropolis. Their entrepreneurial networks were involved in the long-distance trade. They owned enterprises on both sides of the Atlantic and everywhere else. The wealthiest Peruvian *Indianos* were millionaires, and they conducted international transactions in millions of pesos. On Lima's *Merchant Street*, there were at least 60 merchants with more than 100,000 pesos in capital. Likewise, by the dawn of the seventeenth century, Brazilian entrepreneurs converted Brazil into the greatest sugar producer of the world. Indeed, it was the Brazilian elite that made it possible for Portugal to maintain jurisdiction over the contemporary Brazil.

From the dawn of Iberian colonialism, the export of commodities became the leading link between Latin America and the outside world. The Caribbean emerged as one of the most important international commercial depots. It was one of the earliest centers for the long-distance triangular trade. In the colonial world, the socioeconomic power of the *Criollos* became hegemonic during the seventeenth century. The landowners, miners, merchants and the Church became the main financial sources of the colonial system. The *cabildos* and *senadosdacâmera* (municipal councils), despite their limited jurisdictions, remained in the hands of the Iberian American elites (vecinos principales) during the whole colonial period; they were mini-oligarchies.

The Spaniards and their Catholic missions concentrated themselves in the areas where large and diverse Amerindian populations would do the productive work. Such a situation enabled them to make greater contacts with Amerindians than any other European power in the New World. The *encomienda* and the *repartimiento* in the frontier regions or the colonial periphery did not have the same importance as in the Andean or Mesoamerican regions. However, in the territorial peripheries of European colonialism in the

31

Americas, the relations between whites and Indians were strikingly similar. In the regions and centers that were already colonized by Spaniards, the *repartimiento* was the most important labor institution after the middle of the sixteenth century. It was first practiced in the Caribbean and became intimately connected with the *encomienda*.

During the colonial period, labor assignments took place under different regional names like the *mita* (Peru) and *cuatequil* (Mexico). The great difference between the *cuatequil* and the *mita* is that in the first case, the workers lived near their working places while the *mitayos*traveled long distances and worked for longer periods. In those days, the way for a miner or white entrepreneur to obtain *mitayos* was through a request to the colonial authorities that a number of workers be assigned for some tasks to perform during certain periods. The *mitayos* were assigned to the applicants according to the number of inhabitants in the ethnic communities. The applicant promised to pay the *mitayo* the salary determined by the assigning authorities. In many cases the right to apply for *mitayos* had a hereditary character.[25] The white applicants could also sublease their *mitayos*.[26] The *mitayos* were paid an insufficient salary for survival. In order to survive, they brought their own food and supplies from their regions. Likewise, some ethnic communities were able to develop a supply system for their recruited *mitayos*. The links between the ethnic community and the serving *mitayos* were never completely broken. If at the end of this semi-slavery, the *mitayos* had survived, they were allowed to return to their own ethnic communities. In the Andean mining centers, even the wage-earning Indians maintained *reciprocity* contacts and obligations with their ethnic communities.[27]

The Spanish crown considered the *repartimiento* as a temporal institution, which eventually had to be abolished. Therefore, by the end of the sixteenth century, the Crown began to impose restrictions on the *repartimiento* outside the mining industry, and it encouraged the importation of African slaves. For example, the *repartimientos* in the sugar mills were prohibited. However, the condition of forced labor went on despite the laws and good intentions. The *conquistadores* were the law and power at the outset, but gradually the Crown took control of the colonial administration. Such a process culminated in 1570, when the colonial bureaucracy took direct authority over the colonies. The change was the result of an interrelation of state and private interests designed to exploit the colonies for the benefit of the colonial state.

The first generation of *encomenderos* and *caciques* allowed the Crown only an indirect role, but the swift growth of mineral production in the American colonies activated the Crown's efforts to wrestle a more direct control of its colonies. In theory, the colonies were directly subordinated to the absolute power of the Spanish king. Historians of colonial Latin America assert that the labor drafts (*repartimientos*) of Amerindians enabled them to make money to pay their taxes.

During the third and fourth decades of the sixteenth century, a rivalry between the *encomendero* class and the colonial state emerged. In this conflict, the Church sided with the colonial state. The abolition of the *encomienda* by the New Laws (1542), was articulated on humanitarian terms, but likewise, the monarchical authority was at stake. The *encomenderos* attempted to control the amounts and forms of the Indian tribute as well as to maintain civil and criminal jurisdiction in their regions. The Crown feared the development of a feudal system like in Europe. After the subsequent civil wars in Peru, the Crown eliminated the radicalism of the New Laws. When the Crown prohibited the *encomenderos* from procuring free labor from the Indians, the *econcomienda* and the *repartimiento* became legally different. In the future, the Indians would have to pay their tribute to the State in money or products.

The colonial state would emerge as the legal moderator in the exploitation of Indians while promoting the market economy among them. By the end of the sixteenth century, the colonial state had established a centralized apparatus for exploiting labor from the ethnic communities. The government bureaucracy began to monopolize the tribute collection and the assigning of Indian workers for private enterprises. However, some restrictions against the *encomienda* continued. The colonial state increased its authority by taking the exclusive right to receive the Indian tribute. The tribute was the equivalent of the "pecho" duty paid by the Spanish lower classes in Spain. In Spanish America, whites and those who could pass as whites did not pay the tribute. The Indian tribute was maintained during the entire colonial period. Ironically, wherever the Indians were most numerous, the tribute prevailed in the independent Latin American republics until the mid nineteenth century.

By the end of the sixteenth century, the *encomienda* was a dying institution. However, the disappearance of the *encomienda* was primarily a consequence of the Indian demographic catastrophe. It is in this manner that the lands inhabited by Indians became vacant (*baldías*), and on them haciendas were built. During the seventeenth century, the hacienda demand for lands began to be greater than the supply, and hacienda owners began the systematic takeover (legally or illegally) of the lands held by the surviving Indians. The Indians were requested to present property titles, and the lack of papers meant expulsion from their lands. Thus, the struggle for land tenure became "the Indian problem" that subsisted until modern times.

From the outset of the colonial period, land ownership was intimately related to the power of the Church. The Jesuit missions were unique cases, characterized by their efficiency and prosperity. Despite the Jesuit vow of poverty, the Jesuits acquired enormous collective wealth. The legendary Paraguayan Jesuit missions were built because the Brazilian *bandeirantes* still were hunting Guaraní Indians, who had retreated to the Uruguay and Paraná valleys. On the other hand, the Spanish settlers of Paraguay pressured the Indians from the west. In order to solve the "Indian problem," the Spanish-Portuguese crown granted the Jesuits jurisdiction over the Indians of "Ecclesiastic Paraguay" in 1607. Ecclesiastic Paraguay extended from southern Bolivia to the Uruguayan northwest, including modern Paraguay, northern Argentina, parts of Mato Grosso, Paraná, Santa Catarina, and Rio Grande do Sul. As in other parts of the Western Hemisphere, the Jesuits created "reductions" in order to "protect" Indians which included their training and equipping with European weapons.

The Jesuits and "their Indians" defeated the *bandeirantes* on the shores of the Mbororé River in 1641. Afterwards, the *bandeirantes* diminished their attacks on the Jesuit missions. The Indian-Jesuit defensive capacity and the Brazilian importation of African slaves became the main reasons for peaceful coexistence. In the eighteenth century, the enemies of the Jesuits, both religious and civilians, argued that the Jesuits were trying to create an independent state within the colonial system.[28] When the Jesuits were expelled from the Iberian world, and finally dissolved by the Pope in 1773, the other Catholic Orders undertook the task of pacifying the Indian nomads, but they were not very successful.

At the time of the Spanish conquest, it was fateful that the Amerindians had gold and silver. After the silver mountain Potosí was discovered (1545) and until 1601, almost fifty percent of the world's silver came from its veins. The majority of Amerindian recruits died within six months of hard labor. In 1638, the Spanish monk Antonio De La Calancha claimed that "every peso from Potosí had cost the lives of ten Indians." Thirty-two years later, Count De Lemos (the Peruvian Viceroy) further added: "The stones and minerals of Potosí are bathed in Indian blood and if one is to squeeze the extracted money, more blood than silver will gush out."[29] Historiography has noted the exploitation of Amerindians in the gold and silver mines. But more tragic was the relatively unnoticed Amerindian servitude in the mercury mines. Indian illness and suffering followed them after they left the mines. Moreover, their lands and ecological environment were left with greater contamination levels.

When the Amerindians refused to be enslaved and fled to the hinterlands, the whites imported large numbers of African slaves. Miscegenation characterized the evolution of Latin America, but a pigmentocratic society has endured until our days. The more Caucasoid one's appearance was the better. Indeed, the pigmentocratic societies became the essence of Latin American racism. The pigmentocratic societies still hinder the evolution of genuine national states and a Latin American identity.

Spain, which had more Amerindians than all the European powers, imported about a million African slaves during the colonial period. More Blacks than whites would migrate to Brazil and Spanish America during the colonial period. The Spanish, French and English Caribbean possessions started out as white farming communities but were transformed into Black communities when sugar for export developed. With the decline of silver output after the mid seventeenth century, production shifted from the mines and haciendas of the interior to the plantations of the coastlands. The Latin American economic development of the post-independence period further reinforced the socio-economic power of the landed estate whose production was directed to foreign markets.

After the Portuguese discovery of Brazil, only small enclaves emerged where European trinkets were bartered for dyewood. The Pre-Columbian Brazilian population has been calculated between one and two and a half million.[30] But a century later only about 100,000 Brazilian Amerindians remained. The first encounters between Europeans and the native Tupi-speakers were friendly. The Portuguese married important Indian women in local ceremonies; their children, the Mestizos or *Mamelucos*, would help to defeat the Indians who struggled to expel the whites from Brazil. When Portuguese gangs, together with *Mamelucos* and their Indian families were almost defeated by the Tupinamba Indians and their French allies, the Portuguese crown took direct control of the colonization process. However, the intensification of the colonization also brought the enslavement of the natives.

The Portuguese brutality against the defeated Indians was as intense as that of the Spanish conquerors, and it was in the Brazilian Amazon where Indian slavery lasted the longest in the Americas. In North America as in the Amazonia, the Indian societies were rarely fully conquered. They resisted furiously or "they withdrew collectively from contact" with whites.[31] The *Mamelucos* would figure as the most infamous hunters of "enemy Indians" or *negros da terra* (local Blacks). The conquest of Brazil was intimately related to the *Mamelucos*. The first *Mamelucos* gave origin to the *bandeiras* and *bandeirantes*, which constituted the vanguard of the Brazilian colonization and the "Indian hunting."[32] However, in the

36

enclave and plantation economy, African slaves became the dominant labor force from 1580 to the end of the colonial period.

Although Indians and Africans continued revolting and escaping to the tropical jungle during the entire colonial period, the African survivors were the most notable and numerous. In the distant uncolonized regions emerged *quilombos* where fugitive slaves found sanctuary. The *quilombos,* like the Spanish American *palenques,* became the most famous refugee centers for run-away slaves. Perhaps the most famous *quilombo* was the so-called Palmares Republic (Alagôas), in which ten Afro-Brazilian towns resisted Portuguese and Dutch control for almost the whole seventeenth century. Recent research confirms Indian collaboration and especially feminine assistance in the Palmares resistance.[33] The runaway slaves were not defeated by the Portuguese crown and the *bandeirantes* until 1694. A year later, Ganga Zimba, the leader of the Palmares resistance was murdered and beheaded. However, Indians continued attacking white settlements even after Brazil became independent. Until the middle of the nineteenth century there were parts of the Brazilian coast which were totally uninhabitable for whites due to Indian attacks.

The Jesuits supported the Portuguese crown religiously and even militarily, in the subjugation of the Brazilian Indians. After the Indians were defeated, the Jesuits became the most important custodians of their freedom and labor. The Indians were congregated in *aldeias*, adjacent to Portuguese cities, and later on in distant missions. The *aldeias* were sources of labor and income for the Crown and the Church in exchange for Indian Christianization. In some ways, the *aldeias* functioned like the Indian "reductions" and "congregations" in Spanish America. Aldeias, "reductions" and "congregations" were pools of cheap Indian labor. The landowners and entrepreneurs could request paid Indian workers from the *aldeias*. However, only a small percentage of Indians lived in the *aldeias*, since the majority was hunted in "just wars." The *aldeias* were managed by Catholic orders, and especially by the Jesuits until 1757. Afterwards, the *aldeias* went under civilian and military jurisdiction. In Brazil, the Catholic Church did not achieve the opulence of its Spanish American counterpart, but until the Jesuit expulsion (1759), this order was the largest landowner. It was also the most powerful religious order. The Jesuits were the most tenacious users of African slaves and Indian servants in Iberian America.

The Latin American colonies developed a mixed labor system with the coexistence and inter-relation of wage earners and several forms of slavery and semi-slavery. However, the most characteristic type of work was coercive. Even the wage-earning workers were not entirely free. Moreover, internal forms of domination originating in pre-colonial times continued and even gained strength under colonial rule. The former slaves and semi-slaves became only semi-proletarians because they did not receive regular salaries and were kept attached to the farms through debt peonage and other means. Their unauthorized departure could make them "runaways." Debt peonage had emerged in the late sixteenth century, but rapidly expanded during the following two centuries, and it persisted even after Latin American independence. This indebtedness consisted of small loans made by the landowners to mainly Indians, so that they could pay the tithes, tributes and other obligations in exchange for their labor. Labor indebtedness could be inherited by the children and relatives of the victims from generation to generation.

By the end of the sixteenth century, Spanish mercantilism had developed mining centers in Mexico and Peru as well as agricultural and cattle-raising zones which supplied the mining and urban centers. The main purpose of mining and colonial entrepreneurship was to supply the Spanish metropolis with precious metals. It is mostly through the Indian tribute and labor that the colonizers had built a mercantilist, extractive and mining economy. The colonial enterprises were dynamic and were deeply affected by international supply and demand. The internal relations of production were not static; for example, in the mining industry, workers ranged from the best international mineralogists to slaves and semi-slaves of all races. Among the wage earners there were whites, Mestizos and Indians, but the majority of workers were neither white nor free.

The colonial economy and especially the mining industry promoted an internal market for textiles and artisan goods produced in *obrajes* (sweat shops), where Indians worked almost with the same tragic fate as in the mines. Indeed, the Pre-Columbian ethical reciprocities of labor had been replaced by the European considerations of profits, prices and costs. The *obrajes* became the first industrial organizations of the Americas.

Just like some ethnic groups enjoyed some privileges under Spanish colonialism, the less privileged classes of Pre-Columbian societies had, in some cases, the opportunity to escape from the worst oppression and exploitation. For example, the semi-slave *mayeque* class of the Aztec society continued being subordinated to the Indian upper classes, and until the end of the sixteenth century it avoided the *cuatequil* or *repartimiento*. Likewise, the Inca semi-slaves or *yanaconas* avoided the *mita* or *repartimiento* until the eighteenth century. In Mexico as in Peru, "free" Indians pretended to pass as Pre-Columbian semi-slaves in order to avoid the *repartimiento*. The *repartimiento* and the *yanacona* system were the dominant mode of production in the central Andes, even though, in some mining centers of Lower Peru the wage earners predominated.[34] The *yanaconas* and their families rapidly followed the Spaniards as their personal servants. By the end of the colonial period, there were Indians, Mestizos, castes and even *Criollos* among the *yanaconas* of the Peruvian coast.[35]

The *encomienda* in Spanish America and the first *captaincies* granted to 12 Portuguese *donatarios*, constituted concessions of authority to colonizers and private entrepreneurs in exchange for specific contributions to the imperial projects of the Crown. The Spanish and Portuguese monarchs like those of other European countries were not prepared to start and finance with their own funds the colonialist development outside Europe. In different forms, it was private enterprise, which pioneered the development of colonial regimes. Subsequently, all the European governments would make great efforts to recover the authority delegated to their entrepreneurs and private agents. Along with the European colonial expansion emerged centralized States under the sponsorship of monarchical authorities. In Spain and Portugal, the *letrados* or college graduates led the bureaucratization process. They would become more of a professional elite than a social class.[36] A kind of hereditary meritocracy soon expanded in the bureaucracy of the Iberian world.

The Spanish kings like the Portuguese monarchs had their elitist councils (*consejos*, *conselhos*) and favorites who helped them rule, legislate, collect taxes, and "make justice" in their empires. As in other types of imperialism, the State combined legality with violence in order to prevail. At the outset, the administration of Brazil constituted only a very small part of Portuguese colonialism. After the decline of Portugal, Brazil assumed a more important role in the Portuguese colonial system. With the advent of the Enlightened Despotism during the eighteenth century, the Council of Indies (Spain) and the Overseas Council (Portugal) were reorganized and formalized into ministries. It was a quest for Enlightened Despotism as well as the professionalization and the centralization of the state apparatus in the colonies. *Enlightened Despotism* also tried to increase state revenues in the colonies. In some ways, the intention was to take away privileges from the Church, the local elites and the *caciques* as well as make tributary subjects out the mixed races (castes). Those were "capitalistic" policies promoted by the State.

During the seventeenth century, the *Criollo* elites acquired hegemony within the colonial state. The Crown's authority weakened while the *Criollos* utilized the bureaucracy to increase their fortunes. Indeed, the century of Spanish decadence became times of plenty and baroque refinements for the colonies. The European economic expansion and the intensification of colonization in the American continent caused new demographic pressures and dislocations during the eighteenth century. Tensions intensified, not only between whites and Indians, but also between Spaniards and *Criollos*. The Indian rebellions of the eighteenth century were intimately interrelated with their old political and legal resistance against Spanish colonialism. Local protests and routine mobilizations were transformed into struggles that tried to eliminate the European domination, and in some cases, racial wars emerged.

Despite the Crown's efforts to promote racial separation instead of integration, castes or mixed-bloods emerged, and eventually became the most expanding group. However, the colonial fears that Mestizos, Mulattos and castes would lead Indian or Afro-Amerindian revolts motivated the Crown to sanction the legal separation of "colored people" from the sixteenth century onwards. In 1554, the Viceroy of New Spain Luis de Velasco asserted that the Mestizos "are growing in great numbers and all of them are so badly inclined and so audacious for all the wickedness that one has to fear them and the Blacks...and the Indians get from them so many bad manners."[37]

With the passing of time, even the *Criollos*, children of Europeans born in the New World, were considered inferior by the Spaniards. The fact that some of the *Criollos* had a small percentage of Indian blood in their veins evoked contempt from the Spaniards. However, for more than three centuries Spaniards and *Criollos* lived together and constituted an allied elite that enabled the longevity of the colonial system. The Mestizos and castes became subordinate allies and intermediaries in the oppression and exploitation of Indians. But when the castes came to the top, they had to behave like whites and defend the bias and interests of the system. This is the prototype of social mobility that has survived until our days.

In the areas of the so-called high Amerindian cultures, the *conquistadores* married the daughters of the Indian nobility (indios principales). Many of them and their children returned to Spain and were granted appointments and fraternized with the Spanish nobility. Some built castles and entered in the Spanish Military Orders. As a general rule, the *caciques* collaborated in the white exploitation and oppression of the ethnic communities. The Indian nobility was exempted from the tribute, the *repartimiento*, and other servile obligations. At the outset of the colonial period, their children were educated at special schools for nobles. The ethnic communities that had collaborated in the Spanish conquest were organized as *cacicazgos* (cacique fiefdoms) by their leaders. For the *caciques*, hispanization was a system of authority and a way to maintain authority. In some cases the *cacicazgos* were inherited from generation to generation according to the Spanish primogeniture system. However, the *caciques* as a social class had lost importance by the eighteenth century. By then, the success of the *caciques* basically depended on their entrepreneurial capacities like the white landowners. Indeed, they had already been assimilated to the "republic" of Spaniards.

Many Latin American *Criollos* still recall their pedigree by tracing their genealogy to Indian princesses and *conquistadores*. The gender relations of the conquest remain to be written. But native women suffered and benefited from the conquest. Native men and women survived the first encounter with Western civilization differently. The Caribbean queen Anakaona, the Inkan queen Cura Ocllo as well as the Mexican Malitzin (Malinche) experienced decisive roles during the *conquest*. Their histories have very much to teach us about the first encounters and the gender relations that emerged in the patriarchal and multi-ethnic Latin American society. As wives, mistresses and servants, Amerindian women were intimantely involved in the daily lives of the conquerors. However, as more white men and women arrived, Amerindian women and Mestizos were pushed aside from the power structure, and "many Spaniards preferred to marry a white prostitute rather than an Indian woman."[38]

The *caciques* who collaborated with the Spanish conquest were considered as "Natural Lords" which were the same titles undertaken by the Spanish monarchs. In Peru as well as Mexico, many *caciques* and the Indian nobles supported the "republic" of Spaniards, but the Andean Messianism and utopias constituted a greater ideological challenge to the Hispanic-Peruvian proto-nationalism. By the end of the Latin American colonial period, the Amerindians still constituted the most numerous inhabitants. From a total of 17 million people, only three million were whites. The Amerindians made up almost eight million, and the rest were castes and Blacks. In Brazil, of a population of three million people, only about 500,000 were whites; less than 10% would remain as pure

Amerindians. Only at the third millennium's outset, the Amerindians would exist in numbers and calculations similar to those at the time of Columbus, but from being the majority of the American population, they were converted to a minority.

Because of the European expansionism of the eighteenth century, Amerindian prophets, rebels and proto-Amerindian nationalists emerged from the Andes to the Algonkins of Canada. In 1781, the biggest Amerindian independence movement led by Tupac Amaru II was defeated in the Peruvian Andes. During five months,[39] Tupac Amaru´s armies had complete control of Southern and Alto Peru (Bolivia). He acted as an Inca monarch appointing local authorities and bureaucrats.[40] The suppression of this Andean rebellion required the mobilization of the entire Spanish colonial apparatus as well as the use of mostly Black soldiers.[41] Influenced by Andean traditions and the Enlightenment, the Amerindian nobleman Tupac Amaru II attempted to create a neo-Inca state. Although, it has been noted that the Tupac Amaru movement had internal ethnic problems, those were not the major reasons for its failure. Tupac Amaru II relied on a plan for multi-ethnic and class collaboration that was defeated. There were conflicts between local ethnic groups and newly resettled Indians (*forasteros*), but the defeat of this Andean utopia was more the result of the fragmentation in rural interests.[42] The Tupac Amaru movement was defeated with vengeance by the colonial state and its native allies.[43] Even though in defeat and under torture, Tupac Amaru II declared loyalty to the Spanish king, he had created the institutions and structures for a new social and political order. Afterwards, the colonial state systematically repressed all Indian revolutionary projects. Even the name "Tupac" was prohibited by the colonial state in the Andes.

In the Peruvian viceroyalty there were fewer whites and Mestizos than in Mexico by the end of the colonial period. In Peru the "republics" of Spaniards and Indians were more clearly visible. Moreover, a cultural Inca renaissance had emerged that attracted even some Mestizos and *Criollos* during the eighteenth century. The Andean Messianism predicted the return of a native savior called *Inkarri* that would bring a new cycle of happiness. *The*

Royal Commentaries, written by the Mestizo Garcilaso Inca de la Vega (1539-1616), which discusses the good government, justice, and material abundance during Inca rule, became a subversive document and generator of utopias. The Indian militancy intensified. It has been recorded that between 1720 and 1790, more than one hundred revolts took place against the colonial authorities in Peru and Upper Peru. Unlike the Mexican Indian revolts where *Criollos* and castes rose as leaders, the Andean Indians themselves led their mobilizations. As it has been well documented by the late Peruvian historian Alberto Flores Galindo, the understanding and dialogue between the "republics" of Indians and Spaniards was interrupted by the social conflicts and repression which erupted between 1780 and 1824.[44]

The eighteenth century is a period of economic expansion as well as an arms race among the European powers. Likewise, the Bourbons decided that the majority of fiscal revenues from Spain and the colonies should be used for military modernization. The interests of the military complex were mobilized at all the levels of the colonial apparatus.[45] Above all, it was a state effort to modernize itself along the lines of England and Western Europe. The "republic" of *Criollos* led the independence project. After the Indian rebellions of the eighteenth century and the Bourbon Reforms, the Indian elites lost most of their privileges. Even the Indian nobles who collaborated with the Crown were abandoned when they were no longer needed to administer the low levels of the bureaucracy.

One of the main reasons for the rebellion of Tupac Amaru II was the increase and reorganization of the Indian tribute by the Bourbons.[46] Spaniards and *Criollos* with all their clients resisted the bureaucratic reforms. The Indians themselves who had been indoctrinated and disciplined by almost three centuries of patriarchal rule were baffled. The Indians, who in the majority of cases were not accustomed to the use of money or its function in the "free market," were abused by the "reparto comercial" as well as the new power-brokers. The reparto comercial allowed licensed merchants to sell forcefully European products to the Indians even if the Indians were not interested in buying. Likewise, the landowners struggled to retain their control of the Indian labor force and sabotaged the Bourbon reforms.

By the outset of the eighteenth century, Portugal depended economically on England, and its military security was virtually guaranteed by the British navy. Between 1690 and 1770, there was an export boom in Brazilian gold and diamonds. The cultivation of sugarcane and cotton by African slaves constituted major items of Brazilian production, but since the seventeen century, they had lost competitiveness in international markets. Moreover, Brazilian exports were never restricted to only one or two products. Brazil exported vegetal oils, wax, spices, leather, woods, corn, tobacco, nuts, parrots and monkeys. However, sugar continued to be the biggest source of foreign income. The Brazilian historian Caio Prado asserts that the colonial economy of his country was fundamentally organized and administered in relation to international demand.[47] Brazil had emerged as the most profitable and important colony of the Portuguese Empire.

In 1720, Brazil was promoted from Governorship-General to viceroyalty.[48] The Marquis of Pombal as the Minister of the Portuguese crown (1755-1777) like the Spanish Bourbons tried to reform and modernize Portugal without too much success. Pombal led an economic proto-nationalism with an enlightened despotism that intended to promote Portuguese modernization, industrialization and to improve the administration of Brazil. Moreover, the Bourbon and Portuguese reforms did little or nothing to improve the subhuman living conditions of the unprivileged masses and the Amerindians. But in the fantasies of the Enlightened Despotism, Pombal argued that modernization would reach the Indians if they learned Portuguese and their women had children by white men.

The Bourbons introduced in Spain and its colonies the French *intendant* system in order to improve the tax collections and government policies. However until the ascent of Charles III (1759-1788), the Bourbon projects were not very successful in Spain or the colonies. The increasingly aggressive English smuggling as well as their capture of Havana (1762-1763), and its use as *entrepot* to smuggle merchandise to the Spanish American colonies, forced the Spanish crown to take more drastic measures for the modernization of the empire. After 1765, several Spanish ports were authorized to trade directly with the main Caribbean ports. Merchant companies from Barcelona, Bilbao and Zaragoza were assigned part of the colonial markets. Mostly due to the Bourbon modernizing policies, there was an increase in Spanish trade with the colonies and also in fiscal revenues. There was a swift growth in the colonial production of silver, gold, sugar, cacao, coffee, cotton, dyes, leather and tobacco. However with the advent of the French Revolution, the Spanish and Portuguese crowns looked with fear at the modernizing projects and began to delay reforms.

The French regicide and anarchy led Spain to suspend relations with France from 1793 to 1796. In the interlude, Spain sought an alliance with England in order to modernize and defend itself, but the British were not interested in modernizing the Spanish navy or the economy. Moreover, the British took over Trinidad (1797), and on two occasions attempted to capture Buenos Aires (1806-1807). The British interest was to smuggle and penetrate the Iberian American market as well as obtain raw materials and specifically precious metals. At a time when trade increased between the *Criollos* and the British, the Spanish crown required more revenues and "loans" from the colonies. Despite the *Criollos'* resentments against the Spaniards, they looked at the Crown as a guarantee against the demands of the underprivileged masses: Indians, Blacks and castes. It is the postcolonial historiography, which described the *Criollos* as patriotic heroes and notable protagonists.

Haiti was the first Amerindian kingdom to be colonized by the Europeans. European exploitation and diseases obliterated the natives. At first, Haiti and the Caribbean developed as white settlements. With the disappearance of the native population and the rise of agricultural crops for export with African slave labor, Haiti emerged as the foremost sugar exporter. Before the French Revolution, Haiti was extremely profitable to its French owners, and it constituted the greatest source of fiscal revenue for France. The ideals of the French Revolution had a direct impact among the Haitian slaves. Through revolution, the neophyte Black citizens proclaimed the first African and Latin American national state despite French warfare and white militant racism. In order to preserve its independence, the first successful slave revolution of the Christian era had to accept a gigantic debt to its former colonial masters. With French neocolonial protection, Haiti kept its limited sovereignty. Only after American slavery was abolished, could the United States recognize Haiti as a sovereign state in 1862. In the contemporary international hierarchy of national states, the Latin American ones did not have the highest ornamental ranking.

Except for the Haitian case, all the Latin American independence movements were led by neo-Europeans and for neo-Europeans. The Latin American independence took place at the time when Europe was in crisis, and England preached and promoted "free trade" around the world. The local resentments against the unfairness of the colonial system emerged when the metropolitan powers were in crises. It was the less oppressed who led the independence movement. They would appropriate for themselves the neophyte national states with all their democratic mythologies, and the nationalisms that flourished afterwards. From the outset, the independence movement became a *Criollo* project despite the fact that many Amerindians, Blacks and castes fought and died because of white promises and libertarian illusions. The births of Latin American nations like those of African and Asian states in the twentieth century were the result of forced European retreat. Latin America is the region of the Third World, which has the oldest post-independence period, and yet it still remains underdeveloped and not completely independent.

The bloody Haitian independence (1804), and the Indian rebellions of the eighteenth century encouraged a conservative spirit that favored the status quo among the Iberian American elites. Likewise, the *Criollos* observed the independence of United States and the French revolution for new possibilities. They were very prone to consider options that would allow them more free commerce. Above all, the *Criollos* sought corporate freedoms instead of individual liberties. Paradoxically, the *Criollo* intellectuals who adopted the slogans of the French revolution had a profound conservative scholastic formation and heritage.[49] The Catholic modernizers were inspired in the compassionate philosophy of Saint Thomas Aquinas (1226-74). From the entrails of the landed class imbibed in a feudal mentality, elites led an independence movement for the land owners and by the land owners. Only with the expansion of global capitalism, a dependent bourgeois class would emerge.

Indian and African slave rebellions occurred from the dawn of the European domination in the New World. But in Haiti, the French Revolution and the Napoleonic wars favored the emergence of the first Latin American national state. Unlike the Tupac Amaru rebellion, the Haitian slaves confronted a colonial state in crisis. The leader of the Haitian rebellion Toussaint Louverture (1743-1803) even intended to correct the mistakes of the French revolutionary process. Alas, Louverture was captured and died in a French dungeon.[50] Perceptively, the Colombian sociologist Orlando Fals Borda pleads for the historical recuperation of the Hatian revolution and its effect on the Latin American independence movement.[51] The Caribbean was a window to external political and intellectual movements in Latin America. The Napoleonic invasion of the Iberian Peninsula in 1807 eventually detonated the Iberian American emancipatory passions and the very cruel resentments of long ago. The resistance against the French invaders was led by the Seville Junta (May-September 1808), which united the Andalucian oligarchy with all its international connections. It was a conservative Junta, determined to maintain the corporate and monopolist system with all its errors and privileges.

The Spanish elites had three political parties in Cadiz: the Serviles, the Liberals, and the Americans (*Indianos*). The debates dealt with the struggle against Napoleon and the first European liberal constitution. At least in theory, the Spanish Constitution of 1812 eliminated the Indian tribute and other personal services. Wage earners would replace the neo-feudal obligations. However, those liberal slogans would only slowly become reality, and through violence during the next two centuries. The Constitutional debaters also discussed the abolition of Black slavery. But the Afro-

American slavery was not completely abolished until 1888 in Brazil.

When the Seville Junta was replaced by the Central Junta, the *Criollos* and *Indianos* became enthusiastic by its promise to liberalize trade. However, the replacement of the Central Junta by the Regency (pro-Fernando) and its flight to Cadiz where the traditional monopolist interests were the real authority, brought about the emergence of Revolutionary Juntas in Caracas (April 1810) and Buenos Aires (May 1810). The *Indianos* of Cadiz and Spain sided with the monarchical absolutism. The *Criollos* as well as Tupac Amaru II and the Indians before, began their revolutions in the name of the King. But Tupac Amaru under torture had to acknowledge loyalty until the very end of his agony. Despite their proclaimed loyalty to Fernando VII, the Venezuelan and Argentinean *Criollos* had already sparked the fire of the bloody independence wars that bled Spanish America for more than a decade. It was the *Criollos* at the Spanish American periphery who became the emancipatory vanguard.

When the sovereign Latin American nations were born, the neo-European patriots kept the Amerindians away from power. But the Amerindian dream of a national state partly flourished again in the distant Paraguayan hinterland. The *Mestizo* Paraguayan elites (1811-70) attempted to construct a native national state, which was independent from Western colonialism. This unique Paraguayan experiment occurred in the region where during colonial times, the Jesuits had attempted to build a nation with Inca and Christian conceptions of state formation. The Jesuits were temporarily overthrown by their white competitors in Paraguay and elsewhere. Postcolonial Paraguay was ultimately forced to accept international "free trade." Regional disputes and British neocolonial penetration led to war (1865-70) which forced Paraguay out of isolation.[52]

In response to European colonialism, Latin America was the first region of the Third World to attempt the construction of national states. The Latin American national states were directly or indirectly influenced by the Enlightenment as well as the French and American revolutions. Except for Brazil, Haiti and Mexico, all the Latin American elites opted for republicanism instead of monarchism after independence. In Latin America as in other regions of the Third World, European decolonization led to political boundaries, which did not necessarily coincide with ethnicity. The neo-European Latin American elites attempted to adopt and adapt metropolitan patterns of state building. Since whites were a minority at the time of Latin American independence, the "modernizers" encouraged European immigration to the detriment of the non-white majorities. The Argentine intellectual and "statesman" Domingo F. Sarmiento (1811-88) conceived "civilization" as the white colonizing of his country: "to populate [with whites] is to civilize" was his axiom. Sarmiento's pundits and the white settlers launched the Desert War (Guerra del desierto) which exterminated the Argentine Amerindians on the manner of the North American colonization.

The "discovery of America" coincides with the long-term process, which starts in the fifteenth century with the expansion of European colonialism outside that continent. In this macro-historical process, the only non-whites who escaped defeat were the Japanese. European colonialism functioned as an early form of geographical globalization. The ideology of colonialism was to conquer the world. Colonialism contributed to the so-called "primitive accumulation" of capital; it involved plunder and cruel exploitation in the periphery. The first great beneficiaries were the metropolitan merchants and conquerors. Imperialism, colonialism and neocolonialism became the midwives of Latin American and Third World nationalism.

At the time of the discovery of America, the economies of Spain and Portugal were beginning an unequal relationship with Western Europe. Spain exported iron, wool, wines and raw materials to Europe. Portugal imported grains, metallurgical products and salted fish in exchange for salt and African gold. Despite the Iberian agricultural-pastoral economy with its pre-capitalist social institutions, its geography, and navigational sophistication enabled the Iberians to become pioneers in establishing maritime colonies. The Iberian long-distance merchant trade during the fifteenth century consisted of the exchange of high-value small products. However, the massive entrance of precious metals into Iberia enabled Spain to import manufactured products at relatively cheap prices. But at the same time, Spain uningenuously destroyed its own infant industries. During the seventeenth century, the Iberian powers had fallen behind northwestern Europe. Moreover, Portugal and Spain lacked home markets and industries to absorb the wealth from their colonies.

The key products of mercantilist and imperial concern were precious metals. However, agriculture and cattle-raising would become more important for the Ibero-American economy. The ideology of mercantilist imperialism was that the colonies should produce raw materials or products needed in the metropolis. Likewise, the colonies should serve as a market for metropolitan goods. The Spanish American colonies partly played such a role during the sixteenth century, when tanned skins, dyes, and precious metals entered Spain in exchange for metropolitan products. Gradually, the economies of the New World and Spain began to compete with each other. By the end of the sixteenth century, both economies were practically producing the same items.

From the middle of the seventeenth century, England, with implicit collaboration of the Iberian elites, forced Spain and Portugal to lower the custom duties on British manufactured products. Thus, the Iberian oligopolists became big intermediaries and retailers. After mid seventeenth century, English, Dutch, French, and Italian merchants supplied up to 90% of Spanish American colonial imports.[53] To some extent, the West European nations imitated the English example in their commercial relations with Iberia and its colonies. The historic beneficiaries of the triangular trade were the northern Europeans and Anglo-Americans who participated in the three stages of the exchange.

Until the Bourbon Reforms of the eighteenth century, the Spanish trade was officially channeled through three Spanish American ports: Cartagena, Portobelo and Veracruz. Legal exchanges of limited European products for abundant precious metals and Spanish American coins took place in those ports. The commerce between Spain and its colonies was jointly administered by the House of

Trade and the Consulado (the guild of merchants) located in Seville until 1700 when it was moved to Cadiz. During most of the colonial period the House Trade and Consulado maintained their monopolies and privileges. The House of Trade was a state institution, but its members had very close relations with the Consulado; there were family, marriage and ethnic networks. The cozy relationship between these two institutions resulted in the control of trade, bureaucratic appointments, emigration and immigration to and from the colonies, and setting the dates when the Spanish fleets left for the colonies and returned. The Consulado also collected the *avería* or fee for military protection from merchant vessels that traded with the colonies.

During the age of the merchant warriors, the Spaniards from Manila made several projects to conquer China. In the pursuit of such a goal in 1595, they arrived at Pnom Penh and kidnapped and killed the local king before retreating in disaster. The Spanish expansion into the Philippine Islands was to be patterned after the Caribbean conquest, which extended itself to the subjugation of the Aztecs, Mayas and Incas in the Western Hemisphere. After the Spanish catastrophe in Cambodia, Spaniards (Indianos) concentrated in trading enterprises. Through Manila alone eight million kilos of silver were annually entering China by 1600.[54] It has been noted that between one third and 50% of all the bullion from the Ibero-American colonies ended up in the Far East. In the sixteenth century, Spanish and Portuguese trade promoted the production of sugar, textiles, porcelain, and metal wares in China for the overseas market. Mexican silver pesos were used in China until 1935.[55]

In the early nineteenth century, Alexander von Humboldt calculated that from 1492 to 1803, the Ibero-American mines had produced the equivalent of 5,706,700,000 pesos. More than 40,000 tons of silver alone were legally exported during the colonial period.[56] Brazil exported more than a thousand tons of gold in the eighteenth century. In that century, Brazil alone produced 80% of the gold production in the world. Brazilian gold financed England's war against Napoleon while Portugal became the fourth largest customer for British industries.

The Dependency School and the closely related System analysis[57] argue that from the long sixteenth century developed what has become the market economy, a core area or center, a semi-periphery or middle zone and a periphery. Both perspectives bring to discussion the historical role of the long-distance trade in the development of capitalism. The most central and enduring concept of what became the Dependency theory is the "unequal exchange." It means that in the long-run, the prices of industrial products rise while agricultural commodities and raw materials decrease in value. According to André Gunder Frank and Immanuel Wallerstein, "Latin America" became the first overseas "periphery" of the European world economy. Thus, Latin America's pioneering function was to supply primary goods for the expanding capitalism at the center. Latin American grains unlike those of Eastern Europe were not exported to the European core area. They were sold in local markets and to the mines and sugar plantations. Mines and plantations were the two main export enclaves of the colonial Latin American economy.

According to Immanuel Wallerstein, the trade among West European cities became the motor of mercantilist capitalism.Dependentist analysis asserts that the colonial transfers of value from the periphery to the metropolitan core were vital to the genesis of the capitalist system.[58] Colonial Latin America exported bullion, pearls, precious stones, indigo, cochineal, coffee, tobacco, cocoa and other tropical products. The French historian Fernand Braudel has asserted that Ibero-America participated in mercantilist capitalism.[59] The existence of precious metals in the Americas motivated and mobilized the most unlikely individuals to become *conquistadores*. In this sense, the conquest has not yet come to an end because Amerindians still have lands where gold, oil, uranium and even good soils for coca cultivation can be found. There is not doubt that the native owners of these resources will eventually be "civilized."

The profits of Latin American exports made their way to Europe and even the Far East. By the late sixteenth and early seventeenth centuries, the Spanish and Spanish American mints were producing the first "world currency."[60] And yet, the "periphery was peripheral" according to the British economic historian Patrick O'Brien. He calculates only in 7% the annual contribution of the mercantile periphery to the industrialization of the center during the *ancien régime*.[61] But as Braudel has noted: "Long-distance trade was the source of all rapid 'accumulation'. It controlled the world of the *ancien régime* and money was at its command."[62] Moreover, the business aristocracy of London, "at least before the railway era, consisted of East and West Indian families which drew their steady income from the dependencies."[63] Regardless of how much economic benefit the colonies brought to the metropolitan powers, the plunder, slavery and servitude that came along with colonialism are deeply intertwined with the present poverty and underdevelopment of Latin America.

The colonial plunder did not end with the collapse of colonialism. It continued with other and by other means. The European descendents as well as the native elites of the former colonies generally followed the colonial models of economic development. Neocolonialism became an indirect form of domination in which the local elites of the newly created national states functioned as the junior partners of the international market system. The economic hegemony by industrial powers over agricultural-extractive economies became more distinctive than direct political and military domination. Indeed, the metropolis changes its relationship with the former colonies, but it tries to maintain its domination. Neocolonialism grows, adapts and transforms itself along with the evolution of the international market system. In some cases, the new relations of international capital with the local elites began before the end of the colonial period. Although until 1898, Spain kept political and military control over Cuba, Anglo-American capital prevailed in the island. Cuban historians claim that Cuba was the first fully developed neo-colony.

CHAPTER III

THE POSTCOLONIAL PERIOD OF LATIN AMERICA

T he birth of Latin American nations like that of African and Asian national states during the twentieth century was the result of forced European retreat. Global crises at the Center gave the Periphery a chance to liberate itself. In an analogical manner, new nations and leaders came to the attention of the European cognoscenti. Their knowledge about the newly created nations was expanded. New peoples and cultures left the oblivion of anonymity. However, the majority of the twenty million inhabitants of the former Spanish, Portuguese and French empires continued to live with the same daily routines of colonial days. Despite rhetorical proclamations, republics without democracy were created. The great challenge for the leaders of the postcolonial period was to create national states and citizens in very heterogeneous societies divided by race, ethnicity, geography and socio-economic contrasts.

During the emancipatory wars, the Indians and dark-skinned masses had been forcefully drafted by both Royalist and patriot armies to do the killing and dying in elitist projects. In fact at the battle of Ayacucho (December 9, 1824) which has come to symbolize the final victory of the emancipatory forces over the Royalist armies there were more Amerindians fighting on the side of the colonizers than for the Liberators. Alas, the battle of Ayacucho was not the only case where more Indians fought on the side of the Crown than for the Liberators during the struggle for independence. Moreover, the leaders of the "new societies," both Conservatives and Liberals, did not envision any social restructuring that would relieve the downtrodden masses from the miseries of colonial oppression and exploitation.

The Haitian independence movement was the first and only successful slave revolution of the Christian era. It was the first great social revolution of the Western Hemisphere. The Haitian Revolution did inspire slaves and non-slaves to revolt. But as the Colombian sociologist Orlando Fals Borda has noted, from independence onwards the Latin American revolutions were led by the "anti-elites," that is, by socio-economic elites that were on the margins of political authority and/or military power. Thus, there is a struggle among elites as well as classes. Despite the many revolts of the post-independence period, "revolutions" have been mostly absent in Latin America. Furthermore, the Brazilian historian José Honório Rodrigues argued that in his country, the counterrevolution by the ruling elites and classes won.[1] During colonial times, the collaboration of the local elites was essential to the maintenance of metropolitan domination. After independence, the elites and anti-elites survived and thrived in tandem with the rise of neocolonialism. The elites and anti-elites confronted internal power struggles as well as relations and alliances with foreign powers.

The elitist background of revolutionaries also limited their efforts to restructure and improve their societies. The guidelines of reform were colored by what those elites considered to be the most appropriate to their countries and themselves. Certainly, they did not attempt to destroy themselves or their own social class. Both elites in the struggle to defend their interests and ideologies often articulated democratic ideals. To be sure, there was also idealism among elites and patriots. It was not an easy task to construct national states in a mosaic of "races" and diverse geography. However, some Latin American elites were more successful than others in modernizing their national states. Unlike the colonial state that promoted separate "republics" for whites and Indians, the elites of the neophyte sovereign nations advocated integrationist policies for all citizens. Despite the new sobriquets, the least "white" would remain at the bottom of the *pigmentocratic* societies as in colonial times. Rethinking citizenship and inclusion are the challenges that the Latin American elites still need to face.

The central issue is then, what did Latin Americans inherit from defeated Iberia and France? Agriculture and mining were in shambles, especially in countries where the struggles for independence had been more protracted. Although by 1800 the Spanish American colonies no longer had the virtual monopoly in the production of precious metals of earlier colonial days, Latin America still produced 90% of the world's silver. Moreover, the agricultural production for export, which had bloomed during the eighteenth century in the peripheral areas of the Spanish American empire had also been de-stabilized. In many areas, the decline in production had come about before the emancipatory wars had even begun. Much of this decline in production was caused by the Napoleonic wars which had disturbed the traditional trade routes. In addition, during the Napoleonic wars both civilians and the Church were forced by the Crown to grant loans that were never repaid. The revolutionary campaigns brought even more forced loans, and confiscations by Royalists and Patriots of property owned by civilians and the Church. Public works, projects and services either deteriorated or were abandoned for lack of funds. Fearing further losses the ranks of the affluent hid their liquid assets or smuggled their money to Cuba, Spain and Europe.[2]

The amount of specie and bullion that escaped Latin America during the emancipatory struggle is a very important question to consider but unfortunately very difficult to calculate. Scattered sources do reveal that the local "money markets" were virtually eliminated. For example, it has been reported that before revolutionary agitation started in Lima, "commercial" capital surpassed fifteen million dollars while immediately after independence it was less than a million.[3] Likewise, the British Consul in Lima Charles

Ricketts reported that between 1819 and 1825, British "men-of-war" alone had carried out from the city about 27 million pesos in gold and silver.[4] It is estimated that at least 100 million dollars in cash were smuggled out by Spanish merchants before they left Mexico.[5] The Peruvian and Mexican decapitalizations were the prototypes of other experiences throughout Latin America in the wake of independence. Moreover, from the perspective of the external debt it is important to remember that the outflow of local capital began before "foreign investments" came in. Thus, the mineral rich colonies which once inundated the world with bullion were suddenly in need of metallic currencies and foreign credits.

The European economy of the early nineteenth century was faced with a great shortage of precious metals for business transactions. In fact, Europe had been operating on paper money for two decades after the outbreak of the Napoleonic wars. Even before Latin American independence was consummated, foreign entrepreneurs had rushed into the region to speculate in land, mining, revolutionary campaigns and loans to the new governments. In the illusory golden bonanza, it was the British who took the speculating lead to the point that during the 1820s Latin America became the biggest recipient of British capital overseas. However, most of that capital was lost in heavy discount rates, commissions and embezzlements. Finally by 1826, the bubble burst and the Latin American governments defaulted payment on their loans and obligations.

The Latin American nations defaulted when they were unable to pay in cash or bullion. The defaulted debts were later refinanced at very unfavorable interest rates for Latin America. Only Brazil and Chile had a good credit rating in the international money markets right after the emancipatory period. Some of the defaulted obligations were eventually paid off when a bonanza resulting from the export of some natural resource occurred in a particular Latin American country. Most foreign claims against the Latin American nations were constantly refinanced by the technique of acquiring new loans to pay for old ones. Thus, we see the pathetic example of the Ecuadorian independence debt that could not be paid until

1974 when Ecuador's oil boom provided sufficient revenues to the government.[6] Certainly, it took Ecuador about 150 years to cancel its debt but this nation also paid interest throughout those years. Likewise, the birth of the first Latin American foreign debts began the region's insertion in the global financial system.

It was a mortgaged and debilitated fatherland that Latin Americans inherited along with independence. Several historians and economists have considered the British investments of the 1820s as a fiasco for British investors. It should be clarified that only in the "short run" those investments can be qualified as negative but on the "long run" they allowed England to become the most powerful foreign economic force in Latin America until World War I. Only Paraguay avoided foreign indebtedness by paying with hard cash for necessary imports. Despite the fact that individual British and foreign investors lost money or went broke by the Latin American default, England's nineteenth century investments in the region were built on the basis and terms of those first claims. A new wave of Latin American indebtedness blazed with modernization of transport and communications. Railroads were built with guaranteed interest payments regardless of whether they were profitable or not. Indeed, like the great majority of railroads built in the Third World during the nineteenth century, they were built at public risk for the benefit of private investment. Moreover, in Africa, Asia and Latin America, railroads, ports and infrastructure were developed to create a dependent economy. The modernization of infrastructures was mainly geared to the export of natural resources and agricultural crops.

As of December 1989, Latin America had a foreign debt of about 400 billion dollars, and Brazil was the biggest debtor. The Brazilian foreign debt amounted to 118 billion dollars; the debt had increased by 25% because of interest rates since 1985. Moreover, during the same period Brazil paid 69.7 billion dollars in interest rates and mortgage payments while receiving only 28.5 billion dollars in new loans and investments. Likewise, Latin America as a whole was paying about 50 billion dollars per annum, for the servicing of the foreign debt. Despite the fivefold multiplication in the Latin American GNP during the three decades after World War II, the increase depended on the export of commodities.[7] In the three decades after World War II, the Latin American rate of economic growth was about twice as in the United States and most of Western Europe.[8] It was before neo-liberal economics became the official orthodoxy.

The fact that Latin America exported more capital than it received in new investments and fresh loans led many observers to assert that the "foreign" debt could not be paid. Latin American economic nationalists as well as the right-wing ideologists of the Santa Fe Committee in the United States argued that the foreign debt was unpayable. While the former suggested its outright abrogation, the latter asserted that the foreign debt provided an opportunity to promote more free enterprise through "debt equity."[9] Debt equity allowed investors to buy "foreign-held" claims at a discount from creditors and then swap them at face value for national currency for investment in local enterprises. Recent American economic policy towards Latin America has supported debt equity conversion programs like the Brady plan and the "Initiative for the Americas." Some Latin American leaders have asserted that the foreign debt is the most perfected mechanism for the exploitation of the region's economies, and a fundamental obstacle for solving underdevelopment.

After the stagnant 1980s, neo-liberal opinion-makers predicted a very rosy picture for the last decade of the second millennium in Latin America.[10] Such optimism was based on the return of Latin American "flight capital" which bought privatized and prize-catch public properties from nearly bankrupt governments. But statistically, the Latin American "Booming Decade" registered an initial "plus" for the balance of payments.[11] Unfortunately, most return capital was in "portfolio investments" instead of direct entrepreneurial efforts designed to create sustainable development. The Latin American financial elites have traditionally benefited from such economic opportunities.

Unlike the contemporary Southeast Asian elites, most Latin American elites have not undertaken nationalist projects for the modernization and industrialization of their economies. Nevertheless, Latin American officials and articulators have long-complained that even if their economies should industrialize, the industrial nations are reluctant to open their markets. In their view, neo-liberals from the *North* have preached free trade for Latin America and the Third World while curtailing competitor textiles, steel, foodstuffs and "non-traditional" products from the *South*.[12] Perhaps if the United States had perceived a real Communist threat as in Southeast Asia, the "free-trade laws" would have been "favorably tilted" to promote an authoritarian capitalist modernization in Latin America.

Officially, the United States emerged as the biggest foreign source of credit and financing, thus replacing England's role during the nineteenth century. The role of native capital, which has acted as foreign investment under the neocolonial protection should be a top priority of Latinamericanist research. Such capital has been highly speculative, and it has gone in-and-out according to profitable cycles. In 1992, the president of Boston's International Bank noted: "Latin American flight capital has an active of over 250 billion dollars...It is bigger than the Citibank."[13] From independence onwards, most of Latin America became "a high credit risk" area for international creditors. Such a status meant high interest rates and outrageous cover-charges. A cumulative spiral of indebtedness has been unleashed which strikingly resembles the old system of debt peonage with all its trappings. Credits are granted on the terms of the rich. With a few exceptions, the native elites have been enthusiastic collaborators of foreign projects, which did not give priority to local self-sustainable development.

During World War II, Honduras, following the "advice" of the United States, declared war on Nazi Germany. While Honduras' contribution to the war effort was negligible, it did confiscate German investments and as a victorious nation became a charter-member of the United Nations. The defeated Germans were able to collect reparations from the victorious Honduras 34 years after the war had been concluded. The payment of 1.5 million dollars was a pre-requisite for further credits from West Germany. In addition,

West Germany loaned the money to Honduras so that the debt could be paid. The Honduran experience is not without parallels in the history of the Latin American foreign debt.

During colonial times, the colonies constantly had evaded Iberian limitations on trade with other nations. Independence meant even freer trade, which resulted in expanding purchases of industrial products, mostly from England. The Latin American fascination with British goods even led many to import fancy coffins for their own burials. The availability of cheap machine-made goods brought a rapid destruction of the local cottage industries and in particular the manufacture of textiles. Throughout the nineteenth century, the most significant neocolonial pressure was tariff policy, and England used its power to push for free trade policies in Latin America. "Dumping" made it cheaper to buy British textiles in Montevideo than in London. The English historian Eric J. Hobsbawm has noted that his country's textile industry was saved by Latin American imports during the first half of the nineteenth century because that region became its first great market abroad.[14] Despite some occasional efforts to shield local industries with protective tariffs, the competition was too overwhelming to stop the influx of industrial products.

The oldest and most successful effort by a Latin American nation in industrialization through "import-substitution" occurred in Paraguay during the dictatorship of Dr. José de Francia (1813-1840). It was import-substitution for local consumption. There were other abortive attempts in import-substitution in Latin America during the nineteenth century but the region was overexposed to European trade. The only way the Paraguayan experiment survived was by hermetically closing the frontiers of this land-locked nation located in the heart of South America. No other Latin American country had the natural geographic protection and the determination, which shielded Paraguay from the onslaught of Westernization. Protective tariffs enacted by Latin American nations were easily avoided through their extensive porous borders and with the connivance of corrupt officials. Smuggling has been an inrooted way of life from the earliest colonial days. Even today, there are Latin American countries where international smuggling plays a more significant role than international legal trade.

Unlike the Import-Substitution Industrialization (ISI) of East Asia, similar Latin American efforts did not find markets in the United States or the West. Latin American capital earnings still are mainly due to the export of unprocessed raw materials. Industrialization through import-substitution is something that gained its greatest historical momentum during the two world wars and the Great Depression when the North Atlantic economies were in crisis. Because of a small middle class and unavailable foreign demand, the Latin American import-substitution industrialization was based on a limited market for the consuming elites. The industrial growth in the post World War II period has been reinvigorated by the mass production of components and parts for foreign markets instead of local mass consumption. Unfortunately, dependent industrialization has not emphasized research development and technological transfers for a more self-sustaining economic modernization. With very few exceptions, recycling technology is minimal.

During colonial times the Spanish colonies paid for their contraband mostly with specie or bullion but with the increasing influx of foreign goods and the paralysis of mining, much of Latin America became further indebted. Due to the emancipatory upheaval, the annual Latin American production of precious metals was reduced to less than half from 1810 to 1830. It is only in Chile where the mining industry grew remarkably after the emancipatory wars. The gold production of New Granada or Colombia did not recover pre-emancipatory levels until the 1850s. A similar situation is observed in Mexico, Peru and Bolivia where silver production did not reach pre-emancipatory levels until the 1870s. Nevertheless, Latin America continued to produce more than 50% of the world's precious metals until the late 1840s.[15]

Paradoxically, the Latin American nations, which best survived the onslaught of European imports, credits and loans were the former peripheral areas of the Iberian empires. Unlike the former centers of Ibero-American colonization their success was not based in the export of precious metals but on the export of agricultural products, grains, meats and hides. These were products, which were in demand by the contemporary European economies. The massive foreign and local investments in the production of minerals, non-precious metals and export agriculture came about only during the last third of the nineteenth century. Large scale production required transport modernization, especially rail construction. A new wave of British and other foreign speculations and investments rushed into the region. Although railroads in the majority of Latin American nations were started by local capital, they were rapidly expanded and modernized by foreign credits. The "iron horse" soon became the most expensive technological import as well as the greatest cause of the foreign debt during the nineteenth century.

The Latin American economic growth of the post-independence period further reinforced the socio-economic power of the landed estate whose production was directed to foreign markets. Raw materials and agricultural products in wide scale were the major items of export. Such circumstances also hindered the growth of a rural middle class. The growth of urban middle sectors has been a spotty development, which was mainly limited to the Europeanized regions of Latin America. But despite the growth of urban centers, Latin America was controlled by the landholding aristocracy in alliance with entrepreneurial groups and foreign interests. The main challenger to England's economic influence was the United States, especially in Mexico, the Caribbean and Central America. By the early twentieth century, the United States had acquired virtual hegemony in the area north of Panama.

In the wake of independence, numerous political bosses known as *caudillos* emerged to fill the vacuum left by the demise of the colonial institutions and bureaucracy. The first guardians of "law and order" were former veterans of the emancipatory wars. Many of them had even served as officers of the royalist armies, both in Europe and the Americas. The British historian John Lynch argues that the *caudillos* flourished because they became "the necessary gendarmes" for elite survival.[16] Regardless of whether the *caudillos* came from military or civilian backgrounds, ultimately both of them came to defend their positions by armed means. Thus, from the outset of independence, governmental duties and the success of political cliques were safeguarded by armies. The *caudillos'* armies counted ballots and defeated their enemies. The birth and evolution of Latin American political parties are intimately connected with the emergence of permanent standing armies. A practical way for a politician to reach the rank of general was by revolting. Likewise, if a general wanted to enter politics he could revolt or run for political office. The pragmatic outcome was a symbiosis of politicians and soldiers who with the passing of time created the Latin American military heritage.

The Latin American ruling elites who emerged as the successors of Iberian bureaucrats proved to be inexperienced in restructuring the colonial institutions that hindered the modernization of their countries as sovereign states. More than 200 constitutions have been written since independence in an effort to promote a democratic, institutional and orderly functioning of society. However, Latin American history has been noted for its *caudillos*, dictatorships, corruption, and anarchy. The spinal problem has been that, in addition to the region's extreme socio-economic inequalities, its constitutions, laws and decrees have been inspired in foreign realities. The first Latin American constitutions were almost verbatim replicas to the *magna cartas* of France's First Republic and that of the United States. Several statutes and agrarian reform laws have provided for land divisions, universal education, and exempted soldiers from voting. Land divisions had the principle of creating a society of small farmers rather than latifundists. Excusing soldiers from voting was supposed to prevent their meddling in politics. But these laws, like the ones providing universal education without schools, were at best unrealistic and at worst deceitful. Thus, Latin America is still the land of the latifundia, the home of illiterates, and despite a general transition from military to civilian rule during the last two decades of the twentieth century, the region is not free of fear, emergency decrees, martial laws, incognito imprisonment and "extra-judicial executions" as well as para-military and terrorist violence.

The heroes of the emancipatory struggles were the first *caudillos* to lead their infant countries, provinces and regions through dictatorship. As the first *caudillos* died, were assassinated or exiled a new breed of political bosses came to lead their homelands. The new generation of *caudillos* included "doctores" and "generals" among their members; they could be corrupt or impeccably honest, benevolent or brutal, and clerical or anti-clerical. Their success depended on an alliance or intimidation of minor provincial *caudillos* and their defense of the landed aristocracy and privileged groups. *Caudillismo* with all its defects by the end of the nineteenth century had succeeded in centralizing the power of the Latin American republics, in diminishing the power of the provincial *caudillos* and that of the Church itself. Moreover, *caudillismo* in its greater dimension was deeply inter-related with the absence of democratic institutions and the emergence of the national state in Latin America.

During the late nineteenth century there was a feeling among the Latin American elites that the region's propensity to revolt could be eliminated if soldiers were promoted only for their professional merits, and were kept in the barracks mastering their military skills to defend the fatherland. Thus, Chile's hiring of German officers to train its army in 1885 was promptly imitated by Argentina and Bolivia while Brazil, Ecuador, Paraguay and Peru opted for French advisors. By the beginning of the twentieth century, United States military officers were performing similar tasks in the Caribbean and Central America. Until the rise of revolutionary Cuba, United States military missions acquired virtual monopoly in the training of the Latin American cadres. Unfortunately, the professionalization of soldiers neither stopped anarchy nor eliminated dictatorship. Moreover, military dictatorships became more efficient in repressing their opponents. Furthermore, the Army's bargaining power as a politically competing group and patriotic protector of the fatherland's integrity was increased.

The theory that the Army's professionalization would safeguard the growth of democracy is something that has never been proven in Latin America. On the contrary, it has reinforced the unjust control of society by the dominating elites and reactionary groups. Even more tragic is the fact that in recent times the Latin American armies have had better contacts with foreign powers than their own legal governments. For instance, when the democratically-elected Marxist government of Salvador Allende (1970-73) was cut off from American economic aid, the Chilean army continued to receive it. The American support for a non-democratic project is related by the then Secretary of State Henry Kissinger in the following terms: "I don't see why we have to let a country go Marxist just because its people are irresponsible."[17]

In Chile and Brazil of the nineteenth century, the rise of *caudillos* at the national level was eluded by the landholding aristocracies' support for a parliament in the first, and a European monarch in the latter. Both systems were successfully manipulated to the benefit of the elites, and when the Brazilian monarchy no longer served all the interests of the landed aristocrats they corresponded in a *quid pro quo* by refusing to lift a finger to prevent its overthrow by the Army. The Brazilian landholding classes in alliance with the emerging upper sectors of the urban centers supported the military, and when they found the military unsympathetic to their demands, a civilian presidency was welcomed. At any rate, whatever representative devices were created throughout Latin America, the landed aristocracy and its elitist allies used the electoral system to their own advantage. Thus, whether one scrutinizes the dictatorial Mexican system where Porfirio Diaz enjoyed the delicacies of being permanently reelected by overwhelming numbers or the Chilean parliamentary elections, one comes to the conclusion that to the socio-economic elite those differences in politics were differences that made no difference in its control of national life. The rise of the local oligarchies is intertwined with the evolution of the "soft" state. Although the "soft" state could acquire authoritarian political controls it was not allowed to develop an independent economic source of power. It was kept on the edge of bankruptcy by the ruling classes and elites.

The first major internal struggle of independent Latin America came about because of the political efforts by secular leaders to regulate the Church's power. As it has been noted, by the end of the colonial period, the Church had emerged as the biggest landholder and banking institution. In addition, the Church controlled education, public charity and most social services. During colonial times, the "royal patronage" had theoretically subordinated the Church to the Crown but in reality their similarity of interests permitted them to rule jointly as partners. After independence, the new governments claimed the right to the patronage whereas the Church claimed that the patronage had expired with the advent of independence. The Church had reluctantly endorsed the emancipatory struggle, mostly because it could do nothing to stop it. In fact, the Vatican refused to recognize the Spanish American independence until after the death of Ferdinand VII in 1834. Nevertheless, there were many idealist members of the lower clergy who fought and died in the emancipatory struggles. The intensity of the conflict between Church and state was avoided in Portuguese America, where the Church acknowledged its loyalty to the Braganza dynasty, then ruling Portugal and Brazil alike.

It was the Liberals who led the campaign to secularize society. This was a process which originated in the eighteenth century. From the very beginnings of party formation the issue that more clearly differentiated Liberals and Conservatives throughout Latin America was the Liberal opposition to Church power. Naturally, there were other issues that separated Conservatives and Liberals such as federalism versus centralism, and lower versus higher tariffs but those were controversies that were negotiable or inconsistently defended. By the dawn of the twentieth century, the Conservative and Liberal rulers had come to compromise on most of their differences about the status of the Church in the postcolonial society. Surely, the settlement of the religious question allowed the socio-economic elites and "anti-elites" to confront more effectively the revolutionary challenges from the lower classes, dark-skinned masses, ethnic and regional groups.

Occasionally it has been noted that in Latin America the Liberals were more sensitive to the plight of the Indians and the dark races, while Conservatives often favored monarchies in order to maintain the unjust status quo. By common sense, it can be accepted that there can be liberal monarchies and conservative republics but the record indicates that the Latin American monarchical systems were the last to abolish slavery: Puerto Rico (1873), Cuba (1886), and Brazil (1888). The republics of Mexico, Central America and Uruguay abolished slavery in their first decade of independence while the rest of Latin America did so by mid-nineteenth century. For sure, the slavers fought hard to protect their human property.

Ironically, it was the English monarchy and former slave-power, which became the most responsible outside force in the termination of slave imports from Africa. With the exception of Haiti, slavery lasted longer in the countries where slaves were more numerous and deemed vital for production in the local economies. Moreover, in countries like Peru and Cuba, the liberation of slaves was substituted with indentured Chinese coolies. By the close of the nineteenth century, *caudillos* and elites who claimed adherence to liberal ideology were on the rise but such a trend did not ameliorate the socio-economic conditions of the non-white masses. The legal termination of colonial bondages did not mean freedom from hard work with low pay for the lower classes.

Much of the bloodshed which was brought by Spanish American anarchy came as the result of religious conflicts, particularly in Mexico, Colombia, Ecuador and Central America. By the end of the nineteenth century, the Church throughout Latin America had lost part of its properties, control of the cemeteries, monopoly over education, and the right of clergymen to be tried by religious courts for common crimes. In addition, several nations had legalized civil marriages and freedom of religion. However, the Catholic Church survived as a very powerful institution into the twentieth century, and contemporary Latin America. By the close of the nineteenth century, Latin American society was more secularized than at its outset but the struggle for secularization had its ups and downs with much bloodshed among the contendants, and the exiling of prelates as well as the excommunication of politicians and rulers. Reconciliation and restoration of peace usually occurred when the Church accepted its diminished role, and the troubled nation signed a Concordat with the Vatican or officially dedicated the fatherland to the Sacred Heart of Jesus. But as late as 1955, the Church still had the audacity of ex-communicating the Argentinean president Juan D. Perón and his government. The Pope also ex-communicated the first Latin American communist head of state in 1962.

The anarchy engendered by religious conflicts was intensified by the latent regionalism and ethnicity, which were awakening during the independence period. Without the unifying symbol of the Crown and its bureaucracy, each region and province drifted apart. Influenced by the example of the United States, federalism became a much sought-out-solution by many Latin American leaders and interest groups. Bolívar's attempts to create first, Gran Colombia composed of Venezuela, Colombia, Panama and Ecuador was one of the most realistic efforts. In addition to Gran Colombia, Bolívar also wanted to form a Federation of the Andes by adding Peru and Bolivia to Gran Colombia. Prophetically, Bolívar felt that a divided Latin America would fall prey to the meddling of foreign powers and the United States. It was such preoccupation that led him to sponsor the first Pan American Congress, which met in Panama in 1826.

In spite of Bolívar's untiring efforts to promote Latin American unity and a supra-nationalism, he failed miserably. There were other abortive efforts by Latin American idealist leaders such as Francisco Morazán's Federation of Central America and Andrés de Santa Cruz's Peruvian-Bolivian Confederation. But why such failures? The basic reason was the inrooted regionalism fostered by the geographic separation of each region, province, nation and ethnic group. Perhaps one of the most difficult problems faced by the Latin American peoples throughout their history has been their struggle with their geographic diversity and ethnic differences. Latin America includes gigantic mountain ranges with permanently frozen tops, pleasant lowlands, tropical jungles, extensive deserts as well as swamps. Often, such geographic contrasts can be found within the boundaries of one single nation. According to geographers and others, Latin America is a "geographic problem area."

With very few exceptions during the nineteenth century, the concern of the Latin American elites for the indigenous cultures was limited to the literary writers. The *Mestizo* and *Pardo* cult of whitening suffocated the efforts to articulate an indigenous-ethnic consciousness. Paradoxically, it is in Paraguay, one of the most backward countries of the hemisphere, that Indian traditions were afforded the greatest respect. Although Paraguay was a *Mestizo-*country, it was more Indian than white in its *mentalité*, and soul; in short, in its *Indianidad*. It is in this isolated corner of the world that Indian culture survived best the onslaught of Western civilization. Paraguay is perhaps the only truly bilingual and bicultural country of the Americas where Guaraní and Spanish are spoken with almost equal fluency.

During the nineteenth century, the long struggle to obliterate the Indian cultures begun by the "Conquista" was pursued with a new tempo. Positivism and Social Darwinism provided further impetus to the historical tide of making the Americas a white man's country. The Indigenista and the ongoing "Indianist" movement throughout Indian America or Indo-America is something that does not gain momentum until the advent of the Mexican revolution of 1910. It is a process that has been nourished by the misery of the dark-skinned lower classes. Indeed, the Indianist movement has a great potential for growth because the Latin American masses are basically non-white.

Despite the fact that at the time of independence no more than one fifth of the Latin American population was white or nearly white, they strove to identify with the values of Western civilization and the white man. For the ruling elites, progress and virtue were not to find inspiration in Indian or African traditions. All efforts to encourage European immigration carried the conviction that the whitening of Latin America meant progress. But paradoxically, in spite of the Latin American elite's efforts to further the values of Western civilization, there has always existed an undercurrent of mistrust of the Anglo-Saxon world. The mildly disrespectful term *gringo*, used in Mexico and north of Panama to identify white United States citizens, is usually applied to all white foreigners in South America. Ironically, in the pigmentocratic society, the word *gringo* sometimes can be positive. Latin American hostility or perhaps frustration with the material "progress" of the non-Latin countries has naturally been directed against the powerful Yankee neighbor. The overwhelming presence of the United States has always been a reality that Latin American cultural nationalism had to confront throughout its modern history.

Latin Americans have long-understood what the United States can do against its enemies and allies as well. It should not surprise anyone that underneath the "good relations" between hemispheric allies there is a Latin American anti-Yankee feeling at the first scratch. Even Simón Bolívar had very strong suspicions of the United States. He noted: "The United States seemed to be destined by providence to plague the Americas with miseries in the name of liberty." Following that perceptive suspicion, the Latin American intellectuals of succeeding generations such as the Uruguayan José Rodó, the Argentinean Manuel Ugarte, the Brazilian Eduardo Prado, the Venezuelan Blanco Fombona, the Cuban José Martí and the Peruvian Ricardo Palma openly criticized Yankee materialism and its so-called liberal democratic way of life. American historians have been correct in attributing to Bolívar the primacy for Pan Americanism. But Bolívar's intentions were to exclude the United States from the Pan Americanist movement. The generous comments by the British historian John Lynch have sanctioned that Bolívar "admired, though not uncritically the progress of the United States."[18] It is more correct to say that Bolívar actually disliked the United States, though not uncritically.

The early aversion between Americans and Latin Americans was mutual. The American president John Adams (1797-1801), observed that to expect free governments in South America was as ridiculous as "to establish democracies among the birds, beasts and fishes." Racism and prejudices have been significant ingredients in the history of inter-American relations. Despite recent American adulatory rhetoric of fraternal intentions towards its Latin American neighbors, the latter still wait for the more dignified treatment accorded to Europeans and former "uncivilized" nations. Indeed, no Latin American government wants the risk of being branded as unfriendly to the United States. It is a public secret that even some Latin American right-wingers admire Fidel Castro for defying the United States.

If England and the United States had economic predominance in nineteenth century Latin America, culturally, France fascinated the local elites with gusto. The Latin American elites reacted against the former Iberian obscurantism and the polarization of the emancipatory struggles by assimilating French culture and Parisian tastes. Thus, we see that despite the long distances, not infrequently French cultural trends reached Latin America before Spain or Portugal. If Latin American erudites of colonial times were fond of writing poetry and prose in Latin, those of the nineteenth century wrote in French. There was always a permanent Latin American contingent of aspiring intellectuals, artists, and upper-class vagabonds living in the Parisian "Latin Quarter." Even though the Colombian publicist José M. Torres Caicedo is supposed to be the first to speak of "Latin America" in 1856, it was in the France of the nineteenth century that the former Ibero-American colonies and French-speaking peoples of the Western Hemisphere were christened "Latin American."

Indeed, it has been sarcastically noted that the Latin American elites preferred to talk Spanish or Portuguese with French accents instead of using their correct local intonations. Even the precursors and leaders of independence had been deeply impregnated by the French cultural and political currents of the eighteenth and nineteenth centuries. They were among the best of the best interpreters of European, and particularly French scholarship that the contemporary Latin American society had. Moreover, the French cultural policy was geared to promote the "Latin" identity among the former Ibero-American colonies. This policy was part of the French "civilizing" mission.[19] The Latin American elites were enthusiastic recruits and pundits of French culture.

In spite of some outstanding contributions, until the twentieth century, Latin American economic and political thought, like its literature, in the final analysis imitated European trends. Even the Venezuelan scholar Andrés Bello (1781-1865), who was one of the first to advocate for an independent Latin American intellectual thought, reorganized and directed the University of Chile on the French model. Certainly, much of this imitative process was not conscious and represented the struggles and frustrations for a peculiar modernization by an underdeveloped region surviving on the margins of Western civilization. It was the melodramatic confusion of an infant elite in search of identity in Europe and away from its own roots. The Latin American elites representing an underdeveloped region located far away from the power centers, which directed the main course of world history tried to imitate in the hope of achieving the economic success of the North Atlantic societies. By providence or design, Latin Americans always had the younger and former English colonies as permanent neighbors to remind themselves that perhaps their way of life, if not their race, had made them backward. The Latin American elites looked to France in psychological despair or as a source of inspiration to counteract the obvious modernization of the Anglo-Saxon world.

The most decisive external force in the evolution of Latin American events during the twentieth century has been the presence of a powerful Yankee neighbor. In Mexico, the Caribbean and Central America, the United States intrusions began much earlier and in some cases even before those countries had liberated themselves from European colonialism. In 1823, the American president James Monroe announced that the Americas were closed to colonization by European powers. This proclamation came at a time when there was a rumor that France was attempting to help her Spanish ally to reconquer its former American colonies. The proclamation by Monroe was generally ignored by the European powers for in those days the United States did not have the military capacity to prevent a massive invasion of the Americas. However, as American power expanded, the so-called "Monroe Doctrine" came to be used as a legal and ideological justification for Yankee interventionism in the Americas.

In 1904, President Theodore Roosevelt added an additional corollary to the "Monroe Doctrine" which self-imposed upon the United States a duty to intervene militarily in Latin America in order to forestall the intervention of European powers. To his Latin American neighbors, he offered the "carrot or the stick." But this corollary aroused a virulent Latin American nationalism, which even included governmental leaders. A United States congressional report has noted that from 1806 to 1933, Latin America had been subjected to military intervention by the United States 84 times.[20] During the 1930s, the United States in the spirit of the "Good Neighbor" policy renounced to its military interventionism in Latin America. But the United States continued to intervene through "undercover" operations, or openly when considered necessary, to "protect American lives" as was the case in the invasion of the Dominican Republic (April 1965). In a bizarre exercise of diplomacy, the United States asked the Organization of American States (OAS) for a *post facto* approval of such an invasion. In a scenario resembling a charade, the OAS granted permission. In brief, do what we say, or else.

At a moment when the Soviet Union was renouncing to military intervention in Eastern Europe and former satellites, American troops invaded Panama in December 1989, in order to capture General Manuel Antonio Noriega who in reality had been invented by Yankee foreign policy itself. The invasion took place only twelve days before the canal's administration was to go under Panamanian control. Despite the swift condemnation of the UN General Assembly noting that the invasion under code name "Just Cause" was a "flagrant violation of international law" the American action prevailed. The disintegration of the "Soviet threat" to Latin American "democracy" has encouraged the United States to search for another myth in order to maintain its hegemony in the region. The consequences of the American struggle against "narcotics" and "narco-terrorism" in foreign soil still awaits an honest and thorough analysis by historians and scholars. But much of it is a mockery with very little relationship to drug traffic. In the North Atlantic world, the crusades against Communism lost their mobilizing strength. Wars against all kinds of terrorism, fanatic nationalisms and drug traffic have no apparent end in sight. The "Cold War" continues in Latin America, and the war on drugs is the only one available for the American army to fight at the moment.

As the *Pax Americana* unfolded in the twentieth century, Yankee economic and cultural penetration in Latin America became more overbearing. Latin America developed as a caricature or poor imitation of its omnipresent neighbor. When the United States entered World War I, most of the Latin American nations either severed diplomatic relations or declared war against Germany. Only Argentina, El Salvador and Mexico remained officially neutral. During World War II, all the Latin American nations eventually declared war against the Axis powers. Even Argentina which had tried to remain neutral succumbed to American pressure and declared war in March 1945. Regardless of German wickedness, in both wars none of the Latin American nations dared to take the side of Germany. In both wars the Brazilians became the most active participants.

During World War II, Brazil sent more than twenty-five thousand troops to the Mediterranean front. In the last war, Mexico also sent an air squadron to the Far East. In both wars, the Latin American nations provided air and naval bases for the "Allies," confiscated "enemy" properties, and handed over alleged agents to the United States. However, the greatest Latin American contribution to the "war strategy" was made by providing vital raw materials, and agricultural products. The Latin American elites actually benefited from the high prices for their nations' exports. Moreover, the collaboration of the Latin American elites was rewarded with economic, military and technical aid from the United States. When the Cold War began, most of Latin America broke diplomatic relations with the Communist countries and persecuted local Communists. After the United States broke diplomatic relations with Communist Cuba all the Latin American nations, with exception of Mexico, followed the American example. By 1964, the United States had forced the Latin American governments to throw out Cuba from the OAS and all hemispheric organizations. The OAS was created at the initiative of the United States and it is based in Washington. But after the Cold War there have been growing efforts by Latin American governments to create an "Organization of American States" without the overwhelming presence of the United States.[21]

The doctrine of national security, the fear of "another Cuba," and the absurdity that the only foreign doctrines that are not foreign are those originating in the United States, have constituted venerated cults of the Latin American traditional elites. In a region where about half of the population lived in poverty, and at least 84 million were indigent,[22] the collapse of the "Evil Empire" made no difference in the need to redistribute wealth. Neo-liberalism and neo-colonialism have constituted neither affluent nor democratic alternatives to a continent that exports cheap raw materials and the products of cheap labor. The capitalist market economy with its "unequal exchange" has worked to the advantage of the Industrial World leaving most Latin Americans only with the illusions of theories that came from abroad. Latin American history has shown that the region was oppressed and exploited before Marxism was even dreamed. The broadcasting of the East-West conflict lost relevance with the "Communist" collapse but there is no guarantee that the *North-South* debate will find powerful and enthusiastic sponsors.

During colonial times, almost without exception, intellectual activity and literature were within the framework of colonial parameters and Catholic thought (Scholasticism). Independence increasingly brought French and Western intellectual and political trends in the battle of ideas. Right after independence, the movement of social protest came from the ranks of the Liberal party despite its elitist nature. Even before the middle of the nineteenth century, the utopian socialist theories of Saint Simon, Fourier and Proudhon were current among Latin American intellectuals and patriots. From the very beginning, the ideas of the *Communist Manifesto* were discussed by labor leaders, European immigrants and many intellectuals. Moreover, the scholar-revolutionary José Martí (1853-95) had pioneered the study of Karl Marx.[23] Learned men like the Peruvian Manuel Gonzales Prada (1848-1918) and the Mexican Andrés Molina Enriquez (1866-1940) also protested about the negative side of capitalist modernization.

From the late nineteenth century to the post World War I period, anarcho-syndicalism was fairly widespread among the working classes of several Latin American nations. As in Europe, Latin American anarcho-syndicalism was opposed to Marxist socialism but in the post World War I period, it lost ground to Marxist socialism. In recent times, "historical materialist" social analysis has even reached sectors within the clergy and the Army, although this is, of course, a minoritarian trend. With the advent of the twentieth century the traditional oligarchy confronted not only bourgeois demands to share power but growing proletarian assaults which regard social justice as an indispensable quality of democracy.

Coextensive and as a consequence of the Mexican Revolution of 1910, Latin American novelists, literary figures and scholars launched a virulent attack against the exploitation of the Indians and downtrodden masses. This movement (*indigenismo*) also made an effort to understand the Amerindian culture. Although the Andean *indigenismo* did not have the international resonance of its Mexican counterpart, it began earlier. The Chilean victory in the War of the Pacific (1879-83) sparked a crisis of identity among the defeated elites, which led to a concern for the Indians and non-white majorities. Among the most outstanding figures of this new Latin American social awareness are the Bolivian Alcides Arguedas, the Ecuadorian Jorge Icaza, the Mexicans Mariano Azuela, Gregorio López y Fuentes and Juan Rulfo as well as the Peruvians Clorinda Matto de Turner, Luis E. Valcarcel, César Vallejo, José Carlos Mariátegui and Ciro Alegría. More recently, the most prominent literary works from Latin America contain a profound cry of social protest. The vanguard of this tide has been led by the Cubans Alejo Carpentier and Nicolás Guillén, the Uruguayan Mario Benedetti, the Chilean Pablo Neruda, the Guatemalan Miguel Angel Asturias, the Colombian Gabriel García Márquez, the Brazilian Drumon de Andrade, the Peruvians José María Arguedas, Alfredo Bryce Echenique, Manuel Scorza and, even their compatriot Mario Vargas Llosa at the dawn of his literary career. This talented writer and Nobel laureate became a rabid anti-communist in 1980 and amidst the Latin American ideological disputes of the Cold War.

Social protest by creative intellectuals has not been without risks. As repeated reports by the Pen Club and humanitarian organizations have noted, the world's largest number of "disappearances" among writers have constantly taken place in Latin America.[24] Moreover, the contemporary Latin American death-toll for journalists is as high as those killed in the war-zones of the world. Talented writers like the Nobel laureate and former journalist Gabriel García Márquez articulate "magic realism" as well as denounce social injustice. Latin American writers, scholars and artists are struggling to survive and imagine the region's own future. Despite the authoritarian tradition of Latin America its cultural pioneers have been opening the path for political and cultural liberation. Nevertheless, their dream of life is deeply affected by the consumerism of "modern" and powerful societies in distant places. Not surprisingly, leftists and right-wingers alike have had an uncritical cult for the growth of industrial capacity.

Although the Latin American economy needs to modernize, it should not be just for the benefit of naked elitism and material growth. The prevailing Latin American social relations contradict the philosophy of progress and human dignity. Furthermore, the unrealistic goals of the ruling elites are to catch up with the material well-being of the Western World. In the main, there still is a lack of projects for alternative development. Likewise, we all need to assess very critically and very urgently the consequences of increasing productive capacity upon the environment and ecology. While the Amerindian understanding and respect for nature are being ignored, there is a disaster waiting to happen. Alas, it is the industrial world that is most responsible for the climate changes. Today, everything moves at a faster pace and the ecological degradation is part of such a process. Paradoxically, there is scientific research about meteorological warfare and the manipulation of the climate. Perhaps this plunder of the environment and nature could be the end of real history or at least the end of convenience in modern life. Ecology, economy and justice are global issues that, at the very least, need support from the Americas..

79

CHAPTER IV

LATIN AMERICAN WARS OF THE POSTCOLONIAL PERIOD

The Latin American wars of the post-independence period have a double-sided and inter-related nature with internal and external causants. These wars can be classified as external or internal wars even though they are not completely one or the other. It is a question of degree rather than quality. By the end of the second millennium, the primary concern of the Latin American countries was the question of internal wars. The major military confrontations among countries or national states had been almost eliminated, even though in 1969 there was a so-called "Football War" between El Salvador and Honduras, and thirteen years later in the "War of the Malvinas" Argentina was defeated by Great Britain. In the post World War II period Latin American societies were faced with a new ideological reason for militarization, that is, the doctrine of "national security" came to play a greater role than the doctrine of hemispheric defense.

After Fidel Castro gained control of the state in Cuba, the United States created military counterinsurgency programs, CIA covert operations as well as the "Alliance for Progress." It was a sweet and sour approach to reform neocolonial and socio-economic relations in Latin America. But the socio-political impact of the Cuban Revolution in the region marked a turning point in American and Latin American relations. The Cuban Revolution scared the wits out of the Latin American ruling elites. The Latin American elites and American foreign policy found a new momentum for convergence. An outcome of such development is that internal wars became a greater source of violence for the Latin American peoples. As the British victory over Argentina (1982) and the American invasions of the Dominican Republic (1965), Grenada (1983) as well as Panama (1989) demonstrated, the Latin American armies, with the exception of Cuba, were not prepared to fight external wars. Nuclear weapons are banned in Latin America.

When the problem of internal wars is discussed, it is important to differentiate between "guerrilla" warfare and terrorism. According to the British historian Simon Schama, the term "guerrilla" is a translation of "petit guerre" which originated in France (1793), when the armies of the "national state" were attacked by small peasant groups. Hit-and-run tactics, safe areas, and local sustenance are important parts of the framework. For certain, such praxis existed before the sobriquet "petit guerre" was invented. It follows that in order to call armed operations "guerrilla" activity instead of "terrorism" it is vital for their legitimacy that said actions enjoy popular support. Guerrilla warfare is the strategy of the less powerful. However, as recent history has shown, ideological factors often make the difference between terrorists and "Freedom Fighters." In the war against the enemies of the United States, the term "illegal combatant" was created for terrorists and guerrillas alike. Despite the collapse of the so-called "Evil Empire" there is no guarantee that the stressed search for a "Fifth Column" or "Sleeping Cell" will stop.

The Struggle for Stability and
Modernity in Mexico

When the viceroyalty of New Spain seceded from the Spanish Empire in 1822, it did so in the midst of wretched economic conditions.
Like in most of Latin America, the emancipatory and Napoleonic
wars had either dislocated or immobilized production not only for
internal consumption but for export as well. It is in Mexico like
Brazil and Peru where the monarchical sentiments were more
prominent during the emancipatory period. In the cases of Brazil
and Mexico, independence came about more as protest against the
liberalism of the Iberian Cortes (parliaments) than their monarchs.[1]
Although Mexico had been one of the first Spanish American
colonies to experience the turbulence arising from Napoleon's Iberian invasion, by 1822 the revolts begun more than a decade earlier
had been suffocated. The guerrillas operating in the southern and
western regions were a problem, but they did not have the support
of the social elite.

Augustín de Iturbide, a Creole aristocrat and military officer, was
chosen to eliminate the guerrillas as well as bring about conciliation
among Spanish and Mexican elites. With the support of the Conservative elements and the Army, Iturbide was installed as Augustín
I, Emperor of Mexico and the Central American provinces. The first
Mexican empire of the postcolonial period lasted about a year. Iturbide's failure to find a "modus vivendi" with the emerging provincial *caudillos* and to share power with the local elites brought the
collapse of his empire, which included within its borders California
and Texas in the north as well as Costa Rica in the south. Iturbide
had inherited an empty treasury, and diminishing government revenues. The monarchy's expensive extravagance lacked the funds
for its operation, and it did not have the symbolic loyalty given to
the Braganza dynasty in Brazil. Moreover, the Spanish and Mexican
elites preferred a "real" European prince.[2] The ineffectiveness of
the state created opportunities for the elites who called themselves
Liberals and Republicans to conspire with the Army and overthrow
the monarchy.

At this stage of Mexican and Latin American history, there were not yet full-fledged political parties but mere neophyte aggregations of elites and anti-elites. Many of them were intellectuals who had studied or lived in Europe. The Conservative forces from the elites comprised basically a negative pressure group, which proposed to maintain the status quo. They allied themselves with the Church, and constantly toyed with monarchical solutions in order to preserve their declining interests as well as "law and order." The most influential and perhaps the most liberal of the Conservatives, Lucas Alamán (1792-1853), proposed a constitutional monarchy like that of England but with Catholicism as the official religion— in short, a scholastic and Catholic modernity. He wanted to "modernize" the nation, and populate the northern frontier with white Catholics. When Alamán died in 1853, he was on the brink of creating a monarchy with the ubiquitous dictator Antonio de Santa Anna as an introductory transition. But it is not until Maximilian's execution in 1867 that Mexican Conservatives stopped dallying with monarchical schemes. The Conservatives wanted to keep the centralism of the colonial state in the hope of avoiding the emerging provincial *Caudillismo*. The Crown and the Church were to be united in the preservation of an orderly world. In the idea that only God and King could stop the anarchism of the turbulent masses, Liberals, Republicans, and even socialists were behind such reasoning.

It is within the ranks of the Mexican Liberal elites that we find the intellectuals who were most concerned with societal restructuring in order to modernize it. They advocated for the Church's subordination to the state, the abolition of corporate privileges, freedom of religion, and the alienation of lands in *mortmain*. To be sure, the rights of the Indians and castes were ignored by the Mexican political elites of every ideological inclination.

In the aftermath of Iturbide's downfall, internal conflicts for power brought much instability, and bloody confrontations. Likewise, the foreign debt acquired in order to finance the establishment of the neophyte national state was defaulted. Like in most of Latin America, the credit claims were held by the British. In addition, the American and British legations promoted further antagonism between the local political groupings by searching to advance their interests with the Liberals the former, and the Conservatives the latter. Nowhere in Latin America was the competition between the British and the Americans so intense, and so early as in Mexico. At first the British were the most powerful and opposed the American expansionism into Mexican territory. Likewise, Mexican rulers attempted to play the British against the Americans when granting commercial privileges, but the British managed to keep themselves neutral in order to preserve their economic interests.[3]

Behind the Liberal-Conservative confrontations was the shadow of General Santa Anna and his army. From 1829 to 1855, no other individual dominated Mexican politics as he did. Santa Anna (a former royal officer) was an opportunist provincial *caudillo* without many political convictions, who became bored by the intricacies of governmental administration. He preferred to exert his influence through his appointees or allies. Between 1832 and 1855, he served eleven times as president mostly on the banners of Conservativism and in absentia. The dictator lived in semi-retirement with his worldly pleasures in his hacienda, and occasionally returned with his soldiers to impose "law and order" whenever the fatherland was thought to be in crisis. During the age of Santa Anna, Mexico lost over one half of its territory to American expansionism through the independence of Texas (1836), the Mexican War (1846-48) or the War of the North American Invasion, and the *unrefusable* sale of La Mesilla Valley (1854). The United States used the "stick and carrot" towards Mexico, but Santa Anna and his coterie did obtain at least pocket-money from such a relationship. Likewise, California's "gold rush" had "escaped" to the United States. Moreover, Santa Anna frustrated the Liberal and idealist efforts to restructure the colonial institutions that retarded the nation's "modernization."

In the aftermath of the Mexican defeats by the powerful English-speaking neighbor, a new generation of militant and nationalist Liberals had emerged to challenge the power of Santa Anna and his corrupt coterie. The young Liberals constituted an internal developmentalist movement with grass-roots support that was known as the *Reforma* (reform). The *Reforma* leaders were determined to crush the political and economic power of the Church. In due course all corporate courts were abolished. A set of new laws provided that corporate lands were to be sold. Such laws were aimed against the Church, for it possessed about a third of the nation's cultivated territory. Those laws were intended to create a peasantry of small and free farmers, but like contemporary and analogous laws in Latin America such legislation was later distorted for the benefit of land speculators and political opportunists, and at the disadvantage of Indian communal lands. The Amerindian lands were parceled out for sale by the national state. In addition, the *Reforma* laws provided for religious freedom, and the separation of Church and state. Such laws became part of the Liberal constitution of 1857, which in theory persisted for the next sixty years.

The new *magna carta* brought a military confrontation between the government and the Church in alliance with its local and international supporters. The Pope Pius IX, in a typical response that characterized the Vatican's policy towards the secularization of Latin American societies, condemned the *Reforma* laws, and excommunicated the most important members of the Mexican government. By January of 1859, a bloody civil war had begun with two governments in power, one conservative, in Mexico City, and the Liberal on-the-run government under the leadership of Benito Juárez. Juárez was a full-blooded Indian lawyer with a mystical revolutionary zeal. This provincial figure would emerge as the foremost leader of Mexican liberalism during the nineteenth century. When the Conservatives and the Church were defeated in 1861, they searched for support in Europe and the Vatican. Juárez who had the sympathy of the United States government could not expect too much since the giant to the north itself was trying to survive its own civil war.

The Mexican government was bankrupt, but foreigners demanded payment of debts and interests. Many of those obligations had originated during the wars of independence. In December 1861, the Spanish, British and French navies blockaded the eastern seaports. The Spanish and British agreed to depart after the Mexican government promised payment "as soon as possible" but the French rejected Juárez's promises, and proceeded to invade Mexico. Thus, began the biggest European military intervention of a Latin American nation during the nineteenth century. After some internal and heroic resistance, the French army of over thirty thousand soldiers captured the capital by June 1863, and set up a native Conservative puppet regime. Such government immediately invited Napoleon III to nominate an emperor for Mexico. In many ways, the Mexican conflict between Church and state is symptomatic of the struggle for secularization, which occurred throughout Latin America during the nineteenth century. But nowhere did religion play such prominent role as a causant of internal and external wars as in Mexico.

France's foreign policy during this period was oriented to lead a Latin world, which included the underdeveloped "Latin American sisters." Napoleon chose the Archduke Maximilian of Austria, brother of Emperor Franz Josef. At the insistence of the imperial candidate some sort of plebiscite was conducted among the Mexicans by which the natives "unanimously" invited Maximilian to become their monarch. After receiving the Pope's blessing, Maximilian and his flamboyant wife Carlota departed for their new homeland. The royal couple immediately fell in love with this exotic country, and in a quixotic approach decided to impose a dreamland of stability and "progress." Railroads, factories, public works were planned. Maximilian wanted to rehabilitate the mining industry, and develop export agriculture. Foreign capital was encouraged "but only on terms that should be mutually beneficial to both Mexicans and foreigners." Indeed, the emperor intended to "modernize" his newly adopted fatherland.

From 1864 to 1865, it appeared as if the nation's second monarchical experiment would succeed, but Maximilian's dreams were operating out of context. The Church wanted to recuperate all its properties and privileges. The heart of the problem was that Maximilian came from a nation where the Crown did not tolerate the Church's domination of secular life. To the dismay of Conservatives and Clericals alike the emperor favored some of the most disliked Liberal laws. Furthermore, Maximilian wanted to bring some Liberals into his government. By European standards Mexican Conservativism was reactionary. Then, the French intended to recover all their financial claims, and grabbed whatever valuable resources they could find. On the other hand, after the conclusion of the American Civil War, filibusters, military equipment and supplies began to reach Juárez's resistance movement.

The warfare between the Liberals and Maximilian's forces was intensified with horrendous destruction and cruelty. Moreover, the growing Prussian menace to France's borders forced Napoleon III to pull his troops from Mexico. Napoleon also invited Maximilian to depart from Mexico but the Austrian emperor took himself most seriously, and remained to lead Conservatives and Clericals. True to his promises, courage, and foolishness Maximilian was captured in battle, and then shot with all the ceremonies of his monarchical rank on June 19, 1867. Juárez like the leaders of the triumphant liberalism felt that in order to stop the recurrent Conservative and Clerical support for monarchism, the second Mexican emperor like the first one had to be executed. Contemporary Latin America like Europe fought the battles between monarchism and republicanism, and the Liberals were the biggest defenders of the latter.

In the midst of economic crisis the victorious *Reforma* congress reassembled, and elected Juárez to a third presidential term. Revolutionary circumstances permitted the patriotic and peaceful dismissal of two thirds of the standing army without remuneration. Fiscal order was a major preoccupation of Juárez's administration. In addition, Mexico was faced by a virtual boycott from foreign investors and creditors. As the end of Juárez's term approached in 1871, his assistants Sebastián Lerdo de Tejada and Porfirio Díaz aspired to become the inheritors, but Juárez regarded himself indispensable. The Congress complied with his wishes by reelecting him once again. Díaz attempted a coup d'etat but the majority of the Army supported Juárez, and the revolt was quickly stopped. However, less than a year after Juárez's reelection he died. Juárez was succeeded by Lerdo de Tejada who remained in power until

1876, and, when he tried to get himself reelected a nation-wide revolt led by Díaz forced him to flee to the United States. Díaz had successfully revolted on the slogan of "effective suffrage and no reelection." Ironically, afterwards, he inaugurated the longest individual dictatorship of post independent Mexico. Only once did the presidential office avoid him.

Porfirio Díaz was born in 1830 in the state of Oaxaca. Don Porfirio was a Mestizo who distinguished himself as a brilliant officer in the struggle against the French invasion. After Juárez's death, Díaz fervently proclaimed himself the heir to the ideals of the great hero. Díaz was at heart a Conservative but conveniently chose to use the glories of liberalism, and the memory of Juárez for advancing his ambitions and "modernization." Díaz skillfully constructed a dictatorial apparatus that theoretically was based on the liberal constitution of 1857. He also brokered an alliance of national and regional elites. In each state, the Liberal party had a political machine which was directly answerable to Díaz himself.

The Congress became filled with obedient legislators who depended upon Díaz for their economic well being, and often their lives and liberty. Díaz spied upon anybody who was worth spying upon, and encouraged informers by doling out rewards and positions. Díaz was very astute in appointing military and police officers that he could dominate. They were often allowed to persecute their own personal enemies, and enrich themselves in exchange for their loyalty to *Porfirismo*. Corruption and prostitution flourished along with capitalist modernization. The system rewarded loyalty above all. It was built upon the slogan of *"pan o palo"* (the bread or the stick). Anyone who became too challenging could be eliminated by the *LeyFuga*, that is, shot while trying to escape arrest or prison.

Porfirismo's economic policy was geared to promote industrial development through "law and order." This project was led by the Minister of Finance José Limantour who was also the ideologist of an insider clique known as *Científicos*. They took as their intellectual mentor the French positivist philospher Auguste Comte (1798-1857). This very select group envisioned progress as the leadership of the white and nearly white elite over the Indian and Mestizo masses. In their ideological schemes, European culture and American technology must be imitated. They had a faith that science would solve all problems of society, and that it would civilize mankind. The elitist movement included Conservatives and Liberals. Moreover, such kind of positivist alliance was the prototype of similar alliances among the modernizing Latin American elites of the late nineteenth century. However, the religious factor was a deterrent to the collaboration among elites and anti-elites in the modernization of society, but the bloodiest battle fields were in Mexico and Colombia.

Prosperity and a peculiar modernization did come about, but only for the benefit of the local elites and their foreign allies. In seigniorial extravaganza, the dictator celebrated his last birthday in power by spending more than the nation's annual budget for education.[4] In a still agricultural economy by 1910, one half of all the rural population was controlled by the hacienda, and only 3% of them owned any land. Fifteen oligarchic families owned more than 300 thousand acres of land each. Furthermore, 90% of all the villages in the Mexican central plateau had lost their lands to speculators. By the turn of the nineteenth century, the national budget was balanced, foreign and native investors were buying haciendas, mines, and were building railroads, telegraph and telephone lines. Finally in 1900, when some of the world's richest oil pools were "discovered" within Mexican territory, Americans and Englishmen rushed to buy the subsoil rights of the republic. By then, the Church had also regained some of its power, although never to the extent of pre-*Reforma* days.

As Mexico moved from the nineteenth into the twentieth century, nothing seemed to have preoccupied the ruling elites in regard to the collapse of the system that had increased their power and affluence. The Díaz regime meant a "golden era" for foreign capitalism, especially American and British. Díaz became the "darling" of American investors despite their initial conflicts with the dictator. President Theodore Roosevelt politely acknowledged Díaz's goodwill by referring to him as "the greatest living statesman." But sardonically Don Porfirio was prone to lament his relations with his northern neighbor in the following terms: "Poor Mexico so far from God and yet so close to the United States." Quite perceptively, the American historian John Mason Hart noted that under *Porfirismo*, the American elites "tested a variety of approaches they have since used to extend their power and influence" around the world.[5]

The basic preoccupation of Díaz's biggest beneficiaries was how to continue their bonanza without Díaz. Everything seemed to be well in all fronts until 1908 when Don Porfirio granted an interview to the American journalist James Creelman in which Díaz addressed himself to a United States audience, and inadvertently stated that he hoped that in due time Mexico would develop a two-party system, and that he considered not running in the election of 1910. Creelman went back to the United States, and wrote a praising article about "the greatest man of the hemisphere," Porfirio Díaz. However, the contents of the interview filtered into Mexico triggering a political storm.

The decisive figure who synthesized the explosive discontent against *Porfirismo* was a man from the whitest landed elite, Francisco I. Madero. He was born in 1873, in Coahuila, and had been educated in France and the United States. Madero was an engineer by profession, but a mystic spiritualist and vegetarian in his daily life. Underrated by Díaz, Madero was allowed to run for president. He travelled virtually undisturbed throughout the country creating surprising excitement and agitation. When the votes were counted by Díaz's political machine, the Dictator received over a million votes while Madero obtained less than two hundred. Alas, ballot-counting remains as a constant struggle in the course of postcolonial Mexican history.

Crying fraud, Madero escaped to the United States border where he organized a revolt. Madero's platform was mainly concerned with political reform, and a few vague references to social justice. In the meantime, in southern Mexico a charismatic peasant Emiliano Zapata led the discontented peons against the hacienda owners under the slogan of "Land and Liberty." In the state of Chihuahua,

91

the intrepid Mestizo Pancho Villa led an army of revolutionaries, cowboys and bandits. With everything going down the drain, Díaz fled for Europe in May 1911. This was the beginning of the first and bloodiest Latin American internal war and revolution of the twentieth century.

With the departure of Díaz, a national euphoria was unleashed which culminated in the election of Madero to the presidency five months later in the freest elections of the nation's history. Madero's reluctance to undertake agrarian and labor reforms had brought unrest in many sectors of the lower classes. The biggest sources of instability were the continuance of armed campaigns by his former allies, Villa and Zapata. In addition, the professional army, and Díaz's followers conspired to prevent the disruption of the socio-economic order created by *Porfirismo*. Madero's indiscreet comments against American and foreign imperialism put the American ambassador Henry Lane Wilson on the warpath. The confluence of those internal and external conflicts engulfed the nation in a decade of violence, bloodshed, famine, and disease that diminished the Mexican population of fifteen million by at least one million.

Madero's inability to quell the revolutionary unrest brought the feeling among the endangered elites and their foreign allies that Madero had to be replaced. A conspiracy between the Army and the American ambassador resulted in a coup d'etat and the cold-blooded assassination of the president and vice president in February 1913. However, the American involvement in those murders was not the main determinant in the outcome of the Mexican Revolution. The emergence of the sinister figure, General Victoriano Huerta as the head of state was more than the United States had bargained for. Moreover, Huerta began to favor British interests over those of the United States. The American search of a replacement for Huerta brought aid to Huerta's enemies and the American invasion of Veracruz. Huerta finally fled to Europe in July 1914.

Huerta's departure brought another round of civil war in which Villa and Zapata fought against the American favorite, Venustiano Carranza. Carranza's pledge to build a constitutional government brought a wide fauna of followers who became known as *Consti-*

tutionalistas. It was Carranza's commitment to a constitution that attracted leftist intellectuals who tagged along with his armies. The creators of the "socialist" constitution of 1917 sanctioned measures for the abolition of the latifundia, and the elimination of Clerical and foreign domination of the "national state." In the final analysis, all property belonged to the state, including subsoil rights such as mineral and oil deposits. The protection of the urban and rural proletariat was guaranteed by the right of workers to organize themselves. Limits on working hours were proclaimed as well as the abolition of debt peonage. Provisions for the preservation and enlargement of the Indian communal lands were passed. The neofeudal relations that had bound *hacendados* and peons for centuries were to be gradually ended afterwards. It was a revolutionary and idealist effort from above as well as a nationalist project.

The Mexican nation was also comprised of significant reactionary forces that enjoyed the encouragement of the neighboring Yankee colossus and a Scholastic tradition. The aristocrat Carranza represented the forces of reaction, and he did not intend to enforce the radicalism of the new *magna carta*. A revolt was led by one of Carranza's former supporters, General Alvaro Obregón. When Carranza attempted to flee with the national treasury he was caught and executed. Obregón was a former revolutionary hero who called himself a socialist. The revolutionary project of confiscating oil and mining interests brought a most reactionary alliance between the Church, Clericals, and American companies against what was referred as the "Bolshevist" government. The United States withheld recognition of Obregón's administration until he informally promised to spare American investments from confiscation. The treatment of the Church as an enemy of the revolution brought a polarization of society on religious grounds. Thus, a popular and armed movement known as the *Cristero* revolt (the revolt for Jesus Christ) engulfed the nation in another bloodbath during the 1920s. Through terrorist actions, the *Cristeros* killed innocent civilians, teachers, women and children. It was a mosaic of revolutions, "counter revolutions" and civil wars. In this period of terrible violence, ordinary people fought against the state and its army.[6]

Obregón himself was assassinated by a Catholic fanatic on July 17, 1928.

With the death of Obregón, Mexico gradually made the transition from individualist to institutionalized authoritarianism in which the emergent bourgeoisie played the most prominent role. In 1929, the National Revolutionary Party (PNR) was created. The political establishment that evolved from this "revolutionary" elite has had the suspected virtue of never loosing an election until the very end of the twentieth century. Originally, the neophyte party was a coalition of "revolutionary generals" and organized labor. The party changed name on two occasions, and from 1946, it became known as the Institutional Revolutionary Party (PRI). The name alterations reflected not only leadership changes but institutional efforts to increase the grass-roots support for the Mexican Revolution.

The election of Lázaro Cárdenas to the presidency (1934-40) brought a new tempo in revolutionary change. Cárdenas, a charismatic leader from the Revolution's military campaigns represented the advent of young activists who were repulsed by the corruption of the old "revolutionary generals." Many of Cárdenas' followers and protégés openly claimed to be Marxists. The Great Depression had brought economic chaos in Mexico as well as an upsurge of Mexican socialism. Moreover, the Mexican experiment managed to captivate not only local but Latin American leftists as well. During the Cárdenas administration, Latin American and European leftists of every shade flocked into Mexico. About half a million Spanish Republicans were to find sanctuary in Mexico thenceforth.

Cárdenas set out to revolutionize the nation by his commitment to enforce the constitution of 1917. With militant zeal, there was a search for the creation of a "new society" and a "new revolutionary citizen." Cárdenas felt that the factories should be controlled by the workers, and wholeheartedly supported them in their struggle against their employers. The Confederation of Mexican Workers (CTM) and the National Confederation of Peasants (CNC) became the official recipients of governmental patronage, and the anointed organizers of the industrial and rural proletariat. More than 49 mil-

94

lion acres of land were distributed to the peasants and the communal *ejidos*. It represented more than twice the amount of land distributed by all previous "revolutionary" presidents. The workers were given the management of the nation's railroads. A protracted dispute between the CTM and the oil companies (owned mostly by British and American interests) gave Cárdenas the excuse to nationalize the oil industry in 1938. Despite American and British threats, Cárdenas ignored them and created PEMEX (the Mexican state monopoly for the oil industry). The bold nationalization of the oil industry without foreign reprisal was due, in great part, to the American and British preoccupation with Nazi Germany. The United States wished a "united continent" on the eventuality of another world war.

Cárdenas' legal and peaceful departure from the presidency meant the decline of socialist revolutionary fervor. Mexican political commentators have long debated about why Cárdenas chose Manuel Avila Camacho instead of the leftist Francisco J. Mujica as his successor. It seems that the local political class truly feared an American invasion if more socialist reforms were encouraged in Mexico. Due to the determined and early American hostility against the Mexican Revolution, the fears of the native ruling elites were not without reason. The peculiar Mexican modernization in the post Cárdenas years has been along capitalist guidelines, and in close collaboration with its Yankee neighbor.

Although until 1991, the law provided for a Mexican-majority ownership (51%) of all enterprises, foreign investors reappeared through native fronts and partners. Most of these irregularities occurred with the tacit consent of the Mexican government. Moreover, the United States continued to be the biggest buyer of Mexican exports as well as its biggest source of imports. Land distribution has ceased; worker benefits and public welfare have grown at weak rates. Likewise, the undercapitalized minifundio had become a major obstacle to the growth of agricultural production. In 1991, the Mexican government legislated that the minifundistas could sell their lands, thus, creating the possibility for the latifundia's official rebirth (agribusiness) under the pretext of efficiency and modernization. Gradually, the constitution's socialistic stipulations were replaced by capitalistic priorities in the spirit of neo-liberalism.

The Mexican wealthiest elite approaches 5% of the population. The upper 20% of the population owned about 55% of the national wealth (1990). According to *FORBES* magazine, Mexico ranked fourth among countries with multimillionaires (1993). The top family clans are closely interconnected with multinational financial interests. The family clans of Emilio Azcárraga, Jerónimo Arango, Bernardo Garza Sada, Eugenio Garza Lagüera, Claudio González, Adrián Sada, Fernando Senderos, Carlos Slim,[7] Lorenzo Servitje and Marcelo Zambrano manage entrepreneurial and financial empires in the multibillionaire-dollar class.[8] They were also asked to contribute with more than 25 million dollars each for the reelection campaigns of the PRI.[9] The peculiar modernization of society launched by the "revolutionary generals" promoted an expansion of capitalism. It is true that many Mexican aristocrats were killed or fled the country during the Revolution, but the contemporary Mexican elites have not lost their pedigree and links to those "revolutionary generals" who created the twentieth century's Latin American capitalist version of the one-party system.

It came as a shock to many Latin American cognocenti when, the CIA defector Philip Agee listed President Luis Echevarría (1970-76) along with other Latin American leaders as CIA agents or former informators. While Echevarría was president he engaged in pompous nationalistic rhetoric and leftist Third World causes but as the former head of security (Gobernación), he co-ordinated "national security" with the United States intelligence agencies. However, only Cuba has been the lasting exception to this quid pro quo of Latin American-United States relations. Moreover, in October 1968, Echevarría directed the assault on student demonstrators which caused at least 400 casualties (Tlatelolco Massacre). During his presidential term, he continued the suppression of leftist agitators, urban terrorism, and rural guerrillas. Thousands of troops hunted down the legendary Lucio Cabañas (1938-74) and his followers (Party of the Poor) until they were wiped out in the mountains of Guerrero. Since 1967, Cabañas had led guerrilla activities in the state of Guerrero.

In the post Echevarría years, the Left has achieved greater vitality, and so-called "criminals" deserving the appellation of "political prisoners" were released. In 1978, the oldest Latin American Communist party (1921) was legalized after being driven underground since Cárdenas left office. Moreover, a dissident movement emerged from the PRI's own ranks. They founded the Democratic Revolutionary Party (PRD). A return to revolutionary and democratic ideals as well as the end of nepotism and corruption constituted their basic manifesto.[10] It is claimed that the PRD's candidate Cuauhtémoc Cárdenas (son of Lázaro) won the presidential election in 1988. But since the "state ruling party" counted the most expensive Latin American ballots, the opposition had to wait for a more impartial counting in the elections of 2000. Amnesty International and Americas' Watch have constantly reported that police brutality and torture in Mexico are among the worst in Latin America. The *mordida* (bribe), corruption, criminality and human rights violations continue to plague Mexican society and democracy.

Mexico has a special relationship with its almost omnipresent neighbor to the North. Occasionally, Mexico has tried to develop a more independent foreign policy. During the last stages of the Nicaraguan civil war (1979), Mexico together with other Latin American nations were successful in subtly neutralizing the American efforts to intervene militarily in defense of the "Old Nicaragua." Despite the American preponderance over its nearest "backyard," Mexico was the only Latin American nation that refused to break diplomatic relations with Communist Cuba, and for many years it became the only link between Latin America and the island. Even after the collapse of Soviet aid to Cuba, Mexico in a disguised and silent way continued to collaborate with the island. After all, the nearest neighbors of the "backyard" have experienced in flesh and blood the rage of Yankee interventionism long before the "evil empire" or the war on terrorism was invented.

Until the year 2000, the official rhetoric emanating from the PRI was that the party would continue to institutionalize the ideals of the Mexican Revolution. It is germane to note that in the aftermath of the Mexican Revolution, a political system developed with more stability than Italy or France in the twentieth century; it was a record unmatched in the non-communist world. Presidential candidates were chosen through the *dedazo* (pointing of the finger by the incumbent). Only few countries in Latin America entrusted their presidents with as much power as Mexico. The Supreme Court routinely dismissed constitutional challenges to executive decrees. The Army was under civilian and bureaucratic control. The military were co-opted by allowing them to play a major role in the political process and the PRI. With the decline of the PRI, the military is diversifying its alliances with emerging political forces, including the conservative National Action Party (PAN).

With growing slums, chronic inflation, unemployment,[11] and about 25% of the population living in extreme poverty,[12] many students of the Mexican Revolution wondered whether the revolution was dead or dying. In fact, commentators christened Carlos Salinas' neo-liberal government (1988-94) as "neoporfirismo." In 1992, President Salinas declared that the Mexican Revolution was over. The succeeding governments have further promoted neo-liberal economic policies and Americanization. Likewise, whatever the nature of internal conflicts, Mexicans will always have to consider the powerful external factor played by the Yankee neighbor. Not surprisingly, many Mexicans equate modernity with Americanization. Injustice and poverty constitute important ingredients of the Mexican model for economic development. Peace, stability, and a peculiar modernization have taken place without utopian theories. However, the "Mexicanidad" (Mexicaness) will remain as the most permanent cultural legacy and identity of the Mexican Revolution.

From 1980 to 1990, the United States went through economic expansion while Latin America suffered a decade of recession. With the exception of Chile and Colombia, the Latin American per capita income declined by about 10% during that decade. However, at a moment when the "foreign debt" had become 400 billion dollars (1989), the prestigious American publication *Foreign Affairs*[13] reported that the Latin American elites had invested 325 billion dollars in the United States alone. The Mexican national state was the first to be overwhelmed by the foreign debt. Because of lower prices, the world's fourth oil producer suddenly had become the most indebted "developing nation." After its virtual bankruptcy in 1982, the "Neighbor South of the Border" was aided with new American loans, investments and lower tariffs. The International Monetary Fund (IMF) required monetary devaluation, reduction of public expenses, wage freezing, and deregulation of prices. The foreign debt's service-payments were formally linked to the Mexican ability to pay. Despite constitutional restrictions, the Mexican modernization was being rapidly integrated into the American economy even before the creation of the North American Free Trade Association (NAFTA) in 1994. Mexico gradually obtained a privileged status within the system of unequal exchanges between the American industrial-complex and the underdeveloped Latin America.

By the end of the twentieth century, the United States had two Latin American neighbors who claimed to enjoy democracy, Mexico and Cuba. Of the former, Mario Vargas Llosa (1990) remarked that it was "the perfect dictatorship because it was camouflaged so as not to look like one." In the "magic realism" of Mexican democracy, candidates were paid to run against the ruling elite in order to legitimize the formality of political pluralism. As for Cuba, Fidel Castro refused to give up the proletarian dictatorship or "egalitarian democracy." Mexico thrived as a Third World capitalist society and one-party rule with the implicit support of the United States while Cuba has survived despite the most fantastic Yankee hostility. To Western observers, Cuba remains as a mutant of a dying system. But Cuban revolutionary change did not begin as a Communist conspiracy. It followed the only available alternative that Latin American countries had when they challenged the neocolonialist nerve-center. The utopian experiments, which failed in the Soviet Union and Eastern Europe, were not exactly copied by the island. However, for a decade (1975-85) the Cuban struggle for modernization and social justice attempted to copy the Soviet model with almost catastrophic results. Rectifications are taking place, and a Marxist socialist experiment is still an ongoing project in Cuba. The island is still a Third World nation, but in some categories of human achievement it equals or surpasses the most advanced industrial nations.

During the decade of the 1980s, Western observers described the Cuban modernization as a "show case" which was costing the former Soviet Union up to five billion dollars per year. At the height of the Cold War it was argued that the Soviet Union's special relationship with Cuba was comparable to the annual three billion dollars that the United States was giving to Israel. Before the collapse of the trade arrangements with the Soviet bloc, Cuba claimed that the elimination of the "unequal exchange" between the low-priced exports of the Third World and the expensive industrial goods had occurred. Thus, a fair price was paid for Cuban commodities despite the price fluctuations on the international market.

With the collapse of "Communism" the "Unequal Exchange" was introduced into the economic relations of the former Soviet Union and the island. For example, under their pre-1989 trade arrangements Cuba exchanged one ton of sugar for 4.5 tons of Soviet oil; by 1992 the ratio had reached one ton of sugar for 1.4 tons in oil.[14] The greatest challenge to the Cuban Revolution was whether it could continue to thrive without the co-operation and trade relations based on "Marxist-Leninist principles and proletarian internationalism." As for the "Mexican democracy," the United States is gradually incorporating it at a slightly better status than the other nations of the "backyard." Moreover, Mexicans, in this case, would rather switch than fight. After all, the Mexican GNP was only as big as that of New Jersey by the close of the twentieth century.

The Caribbean:
From Columbus to Castro

It can be noted that while the Caribbean nations speak several European languages, they also constitute the most africanized group of nations in the Americas. Most of the Caribbean Indians were exterminated during the first century of European colonization. The Caribbean depopulation and the European settlers' needs for cheap labor brought the importation of African slaves. It is true that Indians from the American mainland, especially from Yucatan, continued to be brought in for plantation work even after independence. Asian indenture workers were also brought in fewer numbers by the European colonial powers. But the prevailing ethnicity and races of the Caribbean are in the first place African and then European. The Caribbean is the Latin American region where the great majority of American armed interventions have taken place.

After the "discovery" of America in 1492, the Caribbean Sea was incorporated into the long-distance trade, which was emerging along with European mercantilism. The Caribbean was quickly internationalized and globalized by the European powers. It served as a staging platform for the conquest of the American mainland as well as transnational trade. It was a transit and confrontational zone for colonial empires. The Caribbean with its port cities and trade routes emerged as an American Mediterranean. It became an essential part of the so-called triangular trade. Industrial products and black slaves were exchanged for precious metals and tropical products. It was a capitalist-slavist system linked to the emerging global world. The Caribbean was the part of Latin America, which first entered the peripheral capitalism. By the close of the second millennium (with the Cuban exception) the Caribbean was silently and gradually being absorbed by the North American economy on the latter's terms. Some Western articulators have asserted that because different colonial powers ruled the islands, "fragmented" identities were promoted among the neophyte *Caribbeans*. However, the Caribbean islanders share the history of slavery, plantation agriculture and their struggle for liberation. The Cuban historian

101

Manuel Moreno Fraginals argued that all the Caribbean slaves were subjected to the eradication of their cultures and ethnic roots in order to facilitate their utilization as cheap labor. But the Caribbeans faced by cultural domination responded through cultural resistance with very concrete classist characteristics regardless of their pigmentation.[15]

The island of *Hispaniola* (Haiti and the Dominican Republic) as well as Cuba, constitute the two largest islands of the Caribbean. Both islands were among the first "discovered" and conquered American territories, which culminated in the Spanish colonization of the continent. Therefore, those islands served as refuelling stations, smuggling centers, and occasionally were raided by pirates and foreign powers. After 1697, the Spanish crown formally recognized France's domination of western Hispaniola. By then, Spain had lost Jamaica and most of the smaller islands to other European colonial states. During the eighteenth century, with the use of black slaves, Haiti was transformed into the richest sugar colony in the Caribbean and the world. Before the advent of the French revolution, Haiti produced two thirds of all the sugar consumed in the world, and it was the world's main coffee producer. It was the production of some 2,000 plantations. The income of Haitian planters was far superior to that of the British planters in the Caribbean.[16] In Cuba and Santo Domingo, tobacco, coffee, sugar, hides and woods were produced, but they did not reach the profitability of the mineral rich colonies of the continent or the sugar and coffee plantations of Haiti.

Although small in size and population, Hispaniola and Cuba have the importance of having engendered the first and the last independence movements of Latin America. By the end of the eighteenth century, Haiti or Saint Dominique had about a half million black slaves and over seventy thousand free white or nearly white inhabitants. Haiti was the most prosperous colony of the French Empire. The French Revolution had a very unsettling impact among the Haitians. At the outset, mobilization was restricted to the white and Mulatto elites. By August 1791, the slaves had become so agitated that the entire process culminated in one of the bloodiest Latin American revolutions of all times. The conflict became a class and racial war in which nearly all the white population was either killed or forced to escape to the neighboring colonies. Most planters fled to Cuba, the United States and Jamaica. The few German and Polish volunteers who had fought on the side of the revolutionaries remained only after they were officially proclaimed to be Black.

In 1793, Haiti became the first country to abolish black slavery in the Americas. The former black slave Toussaint Louverture (1743-1803) emerged as the leader and authority in the virtually independent colony. Louvertoure had become a very literate landholder who professed Catholicism and Voudou as well as membership in a Masonic lodge. In 1801, Louverture distributed a constitution, which granted equal protection to all citizens regardless of color and prohibited slavery for ever. Louverture was the great conciliator who advocated for Haitian economic development with the technical contribution of whites as well as paid labor.[17] Haiti had been too profitable for France to tolerate its de facto emancipation. In 1802, Napoleon I sent an expeditionary force of over twenty thousand soldiers who managed to dupe and capture Louverture, whereupon he was sent to die in a French dungeon. The French treachery intensified the resistance against the colonial state, thus increasing the butchery, disease and death that virtually exterminated the reconquering armies. The white settlers were slaughtered in the struggle to create a Haitian national state.

By January 1, 1804, Haiti proclaimed its independence and became entirely free from European rule. For nearly two decades after independence the nation was torn apart by a fratricidal civil war between the defenders of monarchical and republican systems. The republicans emerged victorious under the leadership of Alexandre Pétion, a Mulatto who had been educated in France. The sanctuary Pétion gave to Simón Bolívar when he escaped from Spanish persecution during a regression in his emancipatory campaigns was of great significance to the liberation of South America, and the struggle to abolish black slavery in Venezuela. After Pétion's death in 1818, his successors completed the pacification of the country. Moreover, after some fifty thousand Spanish-speaking Dominicans proclaimed their independence from Spain, they were also incorporated into the neophyte Black republic. Indeed, Haiti was the first Black postcolonial state of the modern world.

The Haitian neophyte elites dreamed about restoring the colonial prosperity and from 1822 to 1844, the island of Hispaniola was unified. The first major problem to the Haitian national state comprised of foreign threats to its independence. Haiti's most powerful "neighbors" (France, England, Spain and the United States) refused to recognize the independent Black republic. Citizenship in independent Haiti was "by reason of being human." The United States and the European powers considered Haiti a bad example to their slaves in neighboring areas. Haitian independence was considered to be an inspiration to slaves and Blacks from the United States and the Caribbean who struggled against slavery and colonialism. The United States, the biggest threat, did not recognize Haitian independence until 1862, after it had abolished slavery in its own territory.

Haitian leaders in a deliberate effort to preserve their independence and obtain better concessions from powerful foreigners attempted to maneuver one power against another when granting them special privileges in their country. Thus, only when Haiti agreed to pay the outrageous sum of 150 million francs for damages to French property during the emancipatory campaigns, did France recognize Haitian independence in 1825. The last Haitian payment was made in 1947. Following the French diplomatic recognition, other European nations swiftly recognized Haitian independence. Although foreigners could not legally own any land until 1918, they bypassed this limitation by marrying Haitians and establishing purchasing houses for local exports. In the immediate post-independence period, France emerged as the most dominant foreign economic force, but by the late nineteenth century German interests took the lead. By 1914, Germany controlled approximately 80% of Haitian foreign trade, and by then Haiti had become the biggest center of German investments in the Caribbean.

In the post-independence period, a Mulatto elite emerged as the dominant socio-economic force. In essence, it was the pigmento-cratic system of colonial days that survived. Paradoxically, the whiteness of one's skin became a major determinant of success in the new society. It is true that in Haiti there were poor Mulattos and rich Blacks but nowhere in Latin America was the political affiliation of the ruling elites so determined by the shade one's skin. But an old Haitian proverb asserted that "a Black with money is a Mulatto and a Mulatto without money is a Black." The Mulatto ethnicity was francophile in tastes and culture. This trend was, however, reversed by the American occupation of Haiti (1915-34). As David Nicholls has noted, to the American troops all Haitians, both Blacks and Mulattos, were "Niggers."[18] Except for the modernization of the compliant National Guard, the American occupation kept intact the archaic socio-economic structures that had historically ruled Haiti.[19]

In many ways, the opposition to Yankee occupation forced Haitians of different shades to forget their complexions and historical prejudices. Moreover, the election of the populist Dr. Francois Duvalier (1957) institutionalized the official glorification of "négritude" (blackness) and the Black culture. It was a reaction against the values of the colonial experience and Mulatto rule. After three decades of Duvalierist dynastic dictatorship, a "new rich" Black elite emerged. The Mulatto tycoon class stayed out of politics and prospered even more through entrepreneurship. When the leftist and dark-skinned Jean-Bertrand Aristide was democratically elected president in 1990, both pigmentocratic elites plotted and bankrolled a military coup the following year. Moreover, the United States constantly supported these elites while sabotaging Aristide. Although the Clinton administration restituted Aristide, the managers of American foreign policy on the ground were only interested in maintaining the status quo. Aristide claimed afterwards: "In 1994, Clinton needed a foreign policy victory, and a return to democracy in Haiti offered him that opportunity."[20] Bill Clinton recalled, "As president, I worked to end a violent military dictatorship and to restore Haiti's elected president."[21] Be that as it may, the United States still calls the crucial shots in this wounded nation.

From early post-independence, Haitian internal and external problems alike led to political instability, dictatorship and foreign intervention. The political machine, which claimed its roots in the illustrious Alexandre Pétion, came under strong attack for its authoritarianism during the early 1840s. The outcome of agitation and chaos was the final independence of Santo Domingo in 1844, and three years later the emergence of the illiterate Faustin I as emperor of the French-speaking islanders. Although he was a former black slave, he was brought to power by the Mulatto elite, which expected to manipulate him. Unfortunately for his backers, the emperor had some ideas of grandeur and proceeded to exterminate his suspected unfaithful subalterns. Faustin's rage against the Spanish-speaking Dominicans was even greater.

In order to discourage Haitian aggression, the Dominicans searched for reentry into the Spanish colonial empire, and in 1861 Santo Domingo became a Spanish Captaincy-General. While the United States was struggling with its own civil war, there was a revival of French and Spanish efforts to regain their former colonial domination in the Western Hemisphere. Thus, Santo Domingo played only a strategic role on the more far-reaching plans of the Spanish government. Santo Domingo was inundated with Spanish soldiers, bureaucrats and priests. The Spanish government in the spirit of the times could not settle for anything less than the policies of old colonial days. The outcome was revolts, assassinations of Spanish officials, and boycott of the Crown's policies. Finally, in frustration and defeat, Spain withdrew in 1865.

In the meantime, after the downfall of Faustin I in 1859, Haiti was organized into a republic, but as usual the succeeding presidents came and left by violence. At the outset of the last quarter of the nineteenth century, annual sugar production reached only one third of what it used to be in the years before independence. Haiti lost its leadership in export agriculture because of production for local consumption, deforestation, soil degradation and the competition by sugar plantations in Cuba, the British and Dutch Caribbean. However, during the last decade of the nineteenth century, German and French commercial houses stimulated the growth of sugar and coffee exports. The railroad, telegraph and telephone as well as modern docks, bridges and roads were built. The elites prospered in alliance with foreign interests, while the governments became indebted from credits extended by foreigners to undertake the public works that lubricated the growth of the export economy. Such a process of financing was so abused that defaults occurred, and there was the ominous threat that the nation would be invaded by foreign powers in defense of their citizens' investments. Finally, at a time when Europe was at war and the United States was launching military expeditions to reassert its hegemony in Mexico, Central America and the Caribbean, Haiti was also assaulted.

The incidents that provoked the American intervention are very telling of the way in which the United States exercised its growing status in the Caribbean and Central America. The National City Bank of New York had acquired a controlling share in the National Bank of Haiti, which operated as the country's treasurer. When it was discovered by the government that the bank was secretly shipping some of its gold assets to the United States, an open confrontation between the Haitian government and the bank occurred. In tandem, a French company which was building a railroad with the financial backing of the National Bank went broke. Consequently, the government nationalized both the bank and the railroad. The critics of the then ruling president, Vilbrun G. Sam, accused him of collusion with the defaulting concerns. In a moment of despair, the president found asylum in the French Embassy, only to be dragged out by the incited mob, which brutally butchered him in public. With France at war to reprove the insult, the United States took over Haiti under the pretense that the Germans could use local instability to gain a foothold in the Americas.[22] In July 1915, the United States marines occupied Haiti and imposed "law and order."

The Dominican Republic in no less dramatic circumstances had already fallen under American occupation by 1904. The Dominican Republic although less populous than Haiti, comprised two thirds of Hispaniola's total territory. During the last third of the nineteenth century, the cultivation of sugar for export increased. Much of this development was due to the entrepreneurial activities of exiled

Cuban planters who exported their sugar to the United States and Europe. As in the case of Haiti, the ruling aristocracy with foreign connections became the greatest beneficiary while the government became indebted with loans that provided for some necessary infrastructures and profits for corrupt politicians. The excuse that triggered the American intervention was the perennial inability of the Dominican government to service or pay its foreign debts.

When in the judgement of the American president Theodore Roosevelt, there was a danger that several European powers would assist their citizens in collecting their defaulted claims; American troops invaded the Dominican Republic. This was the beginning of an occupation that lasted for the next two decades. With the revenues from the custom-houses, the United States paid in the proportion of 55% for the creditors, and the remaining for the management of the Dominican government. Since the government's revenues were insufficient to finance its infrastructure and administrative costs, American loans were extended. The forceful American presence in the Dominican Republic can be understood by the fact that this little nation had already become a major producer of sugar for the United States market, and the Yankee fear that hostile European powers could acquire naval bases on the route to the Panama Canal. It was in the Dominican Republic where the United States first abandoned a reactionary Latin American ally (Rafael Trujillo) for fear of "Another Cuba."[23] By the close of the twentieth century, the former Hispaniola as well as other smaller Caribbean islands remained as semi-independent Commonwealth members or territories of the North Atlantic economy.

Cuba was the biggest and the most important Caribbean island to any imperial power that controlled it. When Spain was in control of the American mainland colonies, Cuba served as the most significant station en route between Europe and the other colonies. Cuba was also a place where Spanish legislation for the other colonies was first tested or experimented. Although during colonial times, coffee, tobacco, and cattle were raised, by the late eighteenth century those activities began to lose their primacy to the swift rise of sugar for export. However, Cuba's greatest value to Spain before the independence of the mainland Spanish American colonies was strategic. When the Haitian slave revolts occurred, many of the surviving white planters fled to Cuba. The stories of Black terror, which they brought, scared the white Cubans who looked to the Spanish crown as a guarantor of their security. Thus, when the emancipatory movements of the Spanish American mainland broke out, Cuba like Puerto Rico remained relatively calm and thereafter served again as a sanctuary for about twenty thousand Spaniards and Royalists who fled from the former colonies. In essence, when Cuba was being Africanized by the growth of Black slavery, the island became suddenly bleached and europeanized by the influx of reactionary white settlers who escaped from the collapsing French and Spanish empires.

The royalist make-up of the Cuban elites won for Cuba the title of "my ever faithful island" from the Spanish king, Ferdinand VII. By the same token, Ferdinand abolished a number of state monopolies, granted royal lands to Creoles and fleeing refugees, and liberalized international trade. This new economic liberalism, plus the international demand for sugar created by the collapse of Haitian exports after its independence, brought a period of booming economic growth. The expansion of Cuban sugar plantations permitted the introduction of the first steam engine (1820) and the first railroad (1835) in Latin America and Spain itself. It was the fourth in the world. By mid-nineteenth century, the Cuban sugar industry had become the most important and most modernized in the world. The rapid growth of sugar cultivation, however, brought drastic changes of land use that shook up the political power of the coffee and tobacco growers.

In the midst of the economic and political instability, Spain maintained a para-military authoritarianism. However, during the 1830s, an undercurrent of Liberal and romantic protest against Spanish colonialism was led by Cuban intellectuals. Among the outstanding figures of this movement were Félix Varela, José Antonio Saco, José María Heredia and the Mulatto "Plácido." In addition, Cuban prosperity and strategic location brought the attention of the United States. From President Thomas Jefferson

(1801-09) onwards, American politicians aimed at annexing Cuba into the United States. Throughout the 1840s and 1950s, further efforts were made by American and Cuban opponents of Spanish rule to bring Cuba into the Union but the north-south slave conflict of the United States prevented the consummation of such endeavors. After the American Civil War, new efforts were made by Cubans and Americans to bring the island into the United States.

It is in the post Civil War period that a new generation of Cuban patriots advocated independence while rejecting annexation to the United States. Such revolutionary ferment culminated in the "Ten Years' War" (1868-78) against Spain. From this emancipatory campaign led by "Gentlemen Revolutionaries" until the final expulsion of the Spanish in 1898, Cuba became the battleground of intermittent and internecine warfare, and bloody repressions by Spain. Unfortunately, the expulsion of the Spaniards did not constitute the island's liberation from imperialism. The increasing penetration of American capital in the Cuban and Puerto Rican sugar industry during the last third of the nineteenth century had brought the American "sugar lobby" to advocate the extension of American governmental hegemony over Cuba. The American economic penetration coincided with the revival of "Manifest Destiny" and United States expansionism beyond the continent. Thus, when all the Cuban independentist revolutionary groups operating inside and outside Cuba united and launched a massive military campaign against Spanish rule, the United States solidarity and militant nationalism manifested itself by participating in the so-called "Spanish American War."

But which incident triggered the American revival of "Manifest Destiny"? The United States had sent the battleship "Maine" to Havana in order to guarantee the security of its citizens residing in the island. On February 15, 1898, the "Maine" blew up, killing 266 tripulants. As to who blew up the vessel and the mostly Black crew is still a mystery. The American public was agitated and mobilized by another broadcast example of Spanish tyranny. President William McKinley noted that after having consulted with God in the middle of the night, he had decided that a declaration of war against the Spanish tyrants was the most proper course of action.[24] Within three months the decadent Spanish imperialism was ingloriously defeated not only in Cuba but in Puerto Rico, the Philippine islands and Guam. The outcome of all the revolutionary efforts by Cuban patriots to liberate their homeland was obscured by the military intervention of the nascent Yankee imperialism.

It was the American general Leonard Wood who first ruled the last emancipated Spanish American colony, and it was the United States that designed the entire governmental apparatus for the million and a half Cubans. Furthermore, the United States refused to evacuate Cuba until the Platt Amendment, which made Cuba a "protectorate," was accepted. The Platt Amendment provided that the United States had the right to intervene in Cuba to preserve the island's independence, and no Cuban government could make treaties with foreign nations that would impair its sovereignty! Furthermore, the United States had the right to buy or lease local property for naval bases as well as intervene to protect life, property and individual liberty. After forcing the Cuban elites to accept the American demands, the United States left the management of the island under the direction of its loyal president Tomás Estrada Palma. Thus, before the decline of British imperialism in Latin America during World War I, the United States was already the greatest inheritor of Spanish supremacy in the Caribbean, Mexico and Central America. Consistent with the geopolitical traditions of imperialist control, the Yankee colossus began its hegemonic expansion among its nearest neighbors.

Perhaps no other Latin American nation reached the level of americanization as that of pre-Communist Cuba. What was called the "War of Independence" by the Cubans became the "Spanish-American War" in American historiography. American historiography has devoted many efforts to analyzing whether economic or strategic reasons brought on the so-called "Spanish-American War." Even before the advent of Castro's revolution, local historians disagreed with their United States' colleagues for the way in which the war was looked at. The great majority of Cuban intellectuals of every ideology felt that their independence had been snatched away by the United States under false pretences. More-over, this perception originated with José Martí, the father of the independentist movement from Spain as well as the United States.

Even when the independence from Spain was not yet accom-plished, Martí noted: "I lived inside the monster [the United States] and I know its entrails...Every day I am in danger of giving my life for my country and for my duty to prevent in time, with the inde-pendence of Cuba, the expansion of the United States into the An-tilles and over all our lands of America."

As was the case in much of the Caribbean and Central America, economic and strategic factors coincided and complemented each other under the "Pax-Americana." In the twentieth century, to-gether with Panama, Cuba emerged as the biggest American strate-gic military base for Latin America. Moreover, Cuba has the unique peculiarity of being the only Communist nation to have an American military base within its territory. Indeed, communism eventually became an instrument in the defense of Cuban national identity and sovereignty.

As in most of Latin America the two world wars actually bene-fited the ruling elites with high international prices for sugar, ba-nanas, tobacco and other raw materials. During both world wars, Cuba followed the United States as an ally. However, the economic dislocations of the inter-war period, and the Great Depression ac-celerated political discontent and social unrest. Until 1934, when the United States in the spirit of the "Good Neighbor" policy re-linquished its "protectorship," Cuba had been faithfully ruled by both civilian and military dictators. Except for the occasional in-terruptions by American military interventions, the duties of gov-ernment were carried out by politicians who like their Latin American counterparts called themselves Conservatives or Liber-als. The leadership of both political groupings came from the socio-economic elites. The last politician of the "old order," the Liberal Gerardo Machado (1925-33) became one of the most abhorrent dictators of Latin America. Intellectuals, university students and labor groups were ruthlessly repressed. Occasionally, the American press horrified its readers by reports that political prisoners were being thrown alive to shark-infested waters. Machado was a psychopath who could charm his neocolonial sponsors and the native elites.

The economic destabilization of the Great Depression culminated in the collapse of *Machadismo*. Through popular revolt and with the mediation of the United States, Machado was forced to go into exile on August 12, 1933. Cuba suffered a year of turmoil, conspiracies, and the possibility of revolution in which Fulgencio Batista emerged as the local strong man. For the next seven years, Cuba was led by seven different presidents but it was the Army, which ruled under the leadership of Colonel Batista. Batista was an intrepid sergeant who purged the upper echelons of the Army and promoted himself to colonel. Between September 4, 1933 and January 14, 1934, Sergeant Batista deposed two presidents. Moreover, he suffocated the *Auténtico* movement, which attempted moderate democratic reforms. At the early stages of his political career, Batista opted for a populist rhetoric and cultivated the support of organized labor, socialist groups and the Communist party. It must be remembered that during the decade of the thirties, Latin American rulers from Mexico's Cárdenas to the colonels of Paraguay and Bolivia were nationalizing or attempting to confiscate foreign companies with virulent popular support. In 1940, Cuba was given a constitution with socialist overtones, and Batista was formally elected to a four-year presidential term.

Batista was the stereotype of the dictators who were propped up by the United States throughout the Caribbean and Central America during the inter-war period as the United States withdrew its troops, and renounced its military interventionism. American-trained native officers remained to defend the economic, political and military interests of the United States in the region. Criticism by the American news-media to the brutality of the new surrogates found a nonchalant defense by President Franklin Roosevelt who pointed out that although this neophyte breed of dictators was a bunch of "sons of the bitches, they were our sons of the bitches."[25] While Batista was officially visiting the United States, Roosevelt urged him not to run for reelection in 1944. Thus, Batista peacefully left the presidency and for the next eight years the civilian politicians who had risen along with Batista after the fall of Machado steered the nation. With the support of the Army, Batista returned by coup on March 10, 1952. Batista came to restrain the political unrest which had proliferated in Cuba as it did in Latin America of the post World War II period.

Batista replaced a corrupt democracy for a more corrupt dictatorship. According to contemporary Cuban folklore for Batista existed two social classes: torturable and untorturable. The working classes were among the most marginalized in Latin America. In the view of the Cuban-American historian Louis Pérez, such a condition was due to the intimate relationship between the American government and the Cuban elites who prevented the working classes from entering the liberal democratic process.[26] The main challenger to his autocracy was the young lawyer Fidel Castro. As a student and member of the Orthodox party as well as scion of the social elite, Castro had survived the repression launched against the advocates of radical change. The position of the Communist party during this period was that "conditions were not ripe for an armed uprising." Thus, in a quid pro quo some sort of "detente" existed between Batista and the Communists. On the other hand, the Orthodox party had been founded in 1947, and it was a middle class movement with socialist overtones but anti-Communist. Its main platform was a demand for constitutional rule, and the termination of political corruption. After all, Cuba was a "banana republic" with all the legal trappings of a modern, bourgeois and decent society.

On July 26, 1953, Castro and some 150 young revolutionaries attempted to capture the Moncada Fort, in the city of Santiago. The Communist party accused the perpetrators of being adventurers with gangster-like methods. It was a premature attempt in which most of the participants were killed, while the survivors received long prison terms. The survivors founded the "July 26th Movement" under Castro's leadership. After having received amnesty, and lived in exile Castro and other revolutionaries returned in December 1956 to the mountains of eastern Cuba. After two years of guerrilla warfare and popular uprisings, Batista fled with the National Treasury on January 1, 1959.[27] A last minute coup was attempted against Batista by the professional army but as in Nicaragua, years later, it was a grass-roots revolutionary movement that had brought victory.

Social and political change were to be supervised by the July 26th Movement's directorate. Among Castro's followers, a plethora of political ideologies were current. Castro did not declare himself publicly to be a Communist until December 1961.[28] By then, Castro had survived counter revolutionary sabotage, joint-assassination attempts by the CIA and Mafia, an economic blockade, and the ill-fated American sponsored invasion in Bay of Pigs (April 17, 1961). The CIA continued to sabotage Cuba, and attempted the elimination of Castro and his revolutionary cadres through "Operation Mongoose" even after the October Missile Crisis (1962). Unlike in other Latin American revolutions, the dependent Cuban bourgeoisie and oligarchy also left the country. The Cuban exile project has lost many battles, but some extremist *émigrés* continued to operate through "Alpha 66."

The American commentators of the Cuban Revolution have spent many pages pondering whether Castro was a Communist at the start of his political career or the United States made him one. Perhaps a more fruitful dialogue would be to consider whether radical social change is possible despite American support for the elites that have historically ruled Latin America. Although, Castro's ideological formation included Marxism at the time of the Bay of Pigs invasion, the revolution's program was not socialist; it was one of national liberation. Unlike the coups sponsored by the Soviet Union in Eastern Europe, the Cuban Revolution was also a nationalist movement against the United States. The Cuban Revolution was an autochthonous nationalist and patriotic struggle against injustice and foreign humiliations. It was also a struggle for Cuban identity. Moreover, in the beginning the Soviet leadership was reluctant to support Castro because the Cuban Communist party had not led the struggle against Batista. In the Kremlin there was a feeling that the Cuban Revolution de-legitimized the Soviet leadership as a generator of revolutionary social change.[29]

For the sake of the historical record, it should be noted that before the downfall of Batista, sugar, the nation's biggest source of income was owned by the local elites in alliance with American interests. Only 1.5% of all landowners controlled 46% of the total area of the country. Sugar exports almost entirely went to the United States under the status of "most favored nation." The United States had become the island's exclusive supplier of industrial products. About 90% of the telephone and electrical services were owned by American companies. In addition, Cuba fulfilled the role of many border towns in northern Mexico. It was a place for illegal activities or otherwise not permitted in the United States. Bars, casinos, hotels and brothels attracted American tourists and servicemen from neighboring bases. Havana was nicknamed the "Las Vegas of the Caribbean." The likes of Lucky Luciano, Frank Costello, Meyer Lansky, and other "mafiosi" had interests in the tropical bonanza. American dollars and Cuban pesos circulated legally and freely at the same value.

Although economists have noted that Cuba before Castro had one of the highest "per capita incomes" of Latin America, it was also the land of extreme poverty. Illiteracy reached 43%. Despite the fact that Cubans had doubled in numbers between the 1920s and the 1950s, a smaller percentage of school-age children were enrolled in schools in 1950 than in 1925. Moreover, 95% of the children in rural areas were suffering from diseases caused by parasites. According to the 1953 census, about 85% of the rural population had no electricity or running water, and over 90% had no baths or showers. In a population of six million, there were over half a million permanently unemployed, and 100,000 prostitutes survived in the sweet island of pleasure.

Since the victory of the Cuban Revolution, the island has found its goals constantly sabotaged by the most powerful nation on the globe. Moreover, the American confrontation with the USSR over Cuba led to the possibility of nuclear holocaust (October 1962). Whatever progress has been made in building socialism, it has ensued despite the United States. With the conniving assistance of the powerful Cuban-American lobby, the American government insisted that the former "Soviet Union" and East European nations forsake Cuba if they wanted foreign aid. Due to the fact that the Eastern Bloc nations constituted 83% of Cuban foreign trade, their governmental changes caused not only the end of subsidies but trade as well. Indeed, Cuba was subjected to a double economic blockade at the end of the Cold War.

The American economic blockade upon the island included fax, telephone,[30] mail, travel restrictions, "international" credits, technological transfers and medicines. Foreign companies, which trade with Cuba, run the risk of being kept out of the American market. Although there have been negotiations between Washington and Moscow, the United States has refused to make peace with the little island which has challenged the Pax-Americana. Moreover, Castro's solidarity with the Third World in the spirit of "proletarian internationalism" intensified the crisis with the United States. Cuba is in fact a very small country whose "dangerous" significance and dictatorial qualities have been broadcast and orchestrated by the United States.

The asymmetric interests between rich and poor nations are brought to focus in the relations between Cuba and the United States. As long as unequal economic exchanges exist, the Cuban position will maintain its global relevance. With limited resources the Cuban revolutionary cadres pretend to articulate the cause of the underdeveloped world. Concrete examples of the Cuban "internationalist solidarity" have been seen not only in Latin America but in Africa and Asia as well. For example, over twenty-five thousand students from the Third World studied with scholarships in Cuba by the end of the twentieth century. There is a self-imposed mentality, that their struggle is the same as that of the poor exploited masses from Latin America and the Third World. However, Cuban "solidarity" has been classified as adventurism by the United States. Alas, the recalcitrant little island has managed to avoid "humanitarian" military intervention by foreign powers.

Fidel tried to lead a bureaucratic and personal revolution, which redistributed private and state resources to the lower classes under the aegis of the Communist party. This was a high-wire-act in which Fidel emerged as the prime mover. It has been noted that he was the Revolution's worst critic. The eradication of several social vices and slums were accomplished. The island has the lowest infant mortality rate[31] as well as the longest life expectancy in Latin America and the Third World. Cuban infant mortality is even lower than in the United States. Massive efforts in education, health, housing, and economic diversification are underway. Radical changes have not been made without sacrifices, mistakes, and the individual loss of freedoms and libertine tastes. Fidel himself admitted with unusual candor that revolutionary enthusiasm caused the idea of skipping stages in the road to building socialism. The Cuban leadership is conducting an orderly retreat from "self-evident" truths and the idea that they knew what was "socialism" or how to construct it. Conditions on the ground demanded an updating of theoretical and ideological inadequacies.

There is a trend to market economics within contemporary world Communism, and "Cuban socialism" is also debating and acting on "rectificación." It is the intention of the Cuban leadership to proceed with its own rectifications. So far, and not without arrogance, the American government has made clear what changes it wants inside the island and how are they to be carried out. Likewise, the Cuban regime fears that any concessions will lead to a counter-revolution directly controlled by the United States or through the Cuban-Americans. While compromises may promote peace, the former President George Bush (the older) expressed his vision of the "Pax-Americana" and the neo-liberal market utopia in the following terms: "We look forward to the day when not only are the Americas the first fully democratic hemisphere but when all are equal partners in a free-trade zone stretching from the port of Anchorage to Tierra del Fuego" (July 1990).

The United States and Cuba are telling each other that they will not back one inch from their ideological tenets. The nations are located 160 kilometers apart, and neither of them can move away from the neighborhood. Apparently, free markets are coming to the island only if they should be conditioned by Cuban socialism. The theory that "markets are not inconsistent with socialism" will have to be proven. Although, the Cuban government is avoiding the use of labels for its structural economic changes, the state intends to keep control of the financial system. Moreover, China, Russia, and Venezuela have become the island's biggest trading partners (2008). For a small country without important natural resources like Cuba, it is vital to trade in the international market, but its possibilities were systematically curtailed by the United States. Despite critical mumblings from European and other capitalist powers, the United States passed the Helms-Burton Law (1996), which in fact prohibited the world from trading with the island. Apparently, it does not matter that the United Nations General Assembly has already condemned the American economic embargo on more than one occasion.

Security restrictions and curtailment of liberties constitute important aspects in the Cuban strategy against the American bullying tactics and sabotage. If we discounted the long-lines and the scarcity of luxury and consumer goods after thirty-one years of revolution, Cuba had achieved the highest Latin American standard of living. Despite the shortages affecting the island when the Soviet Union was collapsing, the American publication *Time* admitted that Cubans were "the healthiest and best-educated younger class in Latin America."[32] By the end of the twentieth century, one out of fifteen Cubans had a college degree. The island is one of the top four nations in biotechnology and biogenetics in the world. The Cuban model distributes scarcities and benefits among the entire population. However, the toughest rationing and austerity measures since the early 1960s took place after the collapse of the Soviet Union. If Cuba is an egalitarian democracy its mobilization made it look like a dictatorship to its bourgeois critics and other opponents during that "special revolutionary period." Although revolutionary policy tolerates criticism under the slogan "everything within the *Revolution* and nothing against it," Cuba has only one news media.

When the Soviet Union collapsed (1991), there were already over 70,000 private small farms operating along with co-operatives and state farms. After three revolutionary decades, the industrial sector had risen from virtually nothing to 30% of the Cuban economy.[33] Material along with "moral" or social incentives was official policy. In order to obtain profits and efficiency for the socialist model, free movement of labor as well as mixed ventures with foreign capital in tourism, industry and technological research have been promoted. In order to eliminate the "black market," the free circulation of American dollars was sanctioned since 1993.[34] Triangular trade has partially neutralized the American blockade but the most disruptive external factor was the cut-off of Soviet oil, raw materials and components which until 1990 constituted 70% of Cuban foreign trade. For an energy-starved economy, the refusal to supply the final components to complete the atomic plant in Cienfuegos was the culmination of the new trade terms started by *Perestroika*. It is estimated that during 1991-93, the GNP shrank by over 30%. This economic decline failed to destroy the Cuban Revolution.

Apart from its internal socio-economic system, Cuba has dared to challenge American hegemony more than any other Latin American nation. Paradoxically, the encouragement of Cubans to exile themselves in the United States served as a safety-valve to the political pressure against the Cuban Revolution. It created a very weak internal political opposition. A survey by Florida International University (1991) showed that 79% of the Cuban-Americans in the Miami area favored American support for an armed rebellion to overthrow Castro, but only 25% wished to return to their native country. In a swashbuckling display of braggadocio, Castro answered to the Cuban-American pretensions in the following terms: "I would rather see our bones fertilizing the earth than see ourselves converted into another Miami." If everything collapsed, the Cuban vanguard had the "zero option" which meant that people should move from the city to the countryside in order to resist. In a way, such an alternative has already taken place with home-grown vegetables, chickens and other backyard poultry. Likewise, thousands of bulls, horses, mules, and bicycles replaced cars, buses, trucks and tractors. But Cuba needs to improve the productive process.

The great Cuban problem was that it first structured its productive capacity to the needs of American capitalism, and afterwards to interdependence with the Communist Bloc. The collapse of East European socialism placed the little island in the necessity of restructuring again in order to satisfy local needs with its own natural resources. It was a painful struggle against time. Cubans kept their spirits high with an incredible sense of humor. In the midst of the crisis, the Cuban poet Pablo Armando Fernández predicted that Cuba's resistance and disobedience would convert her into some sort of *"CimarrónIsland"* or lonely runaway slave.[35] Cubans are music lovers and they sing and dance constantly. Music is everywhere and from wall-to-wall. Faced by an unrelenting American thrust, the Cuban government considers itself in a state of war. The Cuban siege mentality and the deficiency in individual liberties were not independent of the American efforts to overthrow the eradicators of the Batista establishment. Indeed, the Cuban problem is also an American tragedy that has caused self-inflicted wounds.

The United States and Cuba need a dialogue without the eerie Cold War mentality. The first step consists in approaching the Cubans with the necessary respect to establish a common ground for discussion because Cubans and Americans do not need to be enemies. American policy towards Cuba also needs to liberate itself from the reactionary Cuban-American National Foundation (CANF). Apparently its hard-core members are more American than the Americans themselves. Those self-serving attitudes are not conductive to peace or the definition of what is democratic. Despite their vociferous nationalistic claims, those Cuban-Americans have divided loyalties. Ironically, they are becoming nationalists without a nation.

In the aftermath of the failed coup against Mikhail Gorvachev (August 1991), Boris Yeltsin answered to an American TV audience that "it would have been better if the communist experiment had been conducted in some small country to make it clear that it was only a utopian idea, although a beautiful idea." On the small Cuban island, a socialist dream is being experimented with, within which the ideas of "Ché" Guevara still survive in the efforts to form the new socialist man. The Cuban leadership preaches a dialectical inter-relation between "socialist patriotism" and "proletarian internationalism." Personal sacrifices and hopes of a better future still maintain discipline against internal and external pressures. With such convictions they survived both the American economic blockade and the cut-off from the former Soviet bloc nations. However, Cuba is beginning to flourish and increasingly disregards the forceful opinions of its giant neighbor to the North.

Although Cuba is not a paradise on earth, the likelihood that "socialism" is not an impossible Cuban dream is still an obsession for the United States policy makers. Bureaucratic favoritism and inefficiency (*sociolismo*) and individualistic egoisms are problems to be solved inside the island. The rectifications agenda asserts that development is to take place through the reduction of inefficient *sociolist* workers and their reassignment to more productive tasks as well as individual entrepreneurship. In the words of Raúl Castro: "We have to erase for ever the notion that Cuba is the only country in the world in which people can live without working."[36] However, popular support for the state and the elite or vanguard has been nurtured through the provision of education, health care, housing accommodations and employment.

Unlike the changes attempted in the Soviet Union, the Cuban rectifications are taking place under the political guidance of united revolutionary cadres, as well as approximately four million Rapid-Reaction Brigades to nip conspiracies in the bud. While the United States wants a "transition period" to democracy, the ideologists of the Cuban Revolution articulate for "a continuity process of thinking and action."[37] According to the Cuban-American and Harvard academic Jorge Domínguez, Fidel believed that in the long-range, Cuban and American interests were incompatible but nevertheless Fidel combined "strategic and tactical abilities rarely surpassed among world leaders."[38] If the heirs to the Cuban Revolution continue Fidel's pragmatism, its uniqueness will prevail. The great challenge of the Cuban Revolution is to make a transition from "revolutionary" doctrines to post-revolutionary conditions.

CHAPTER V

THE BATTLE
FOR CENTRAL AMERICA

D uring the colonial period, Central America was administered through the Captaincy-General of Guatemala whose million and a half people were mostly Indians and Mestizos. Less than 10% were white, and most of them lived in Costa Rica. In geographical terms Central America extends from the Panamanian isthmus in the south to the Tehuantepec isthmus in the north (in southern Mexico). Politically, during colonial times and the nineteenth century, Central America comprised modern Guatemala, El Salvador, Honduras, Nicaragua and Costa Rica. After Panama seceded from Colombia in 1903, the concept of Central America broadened to include Panama. In colonial days, Central America was a relatively backward region of the Spanish empire which survived on its subsistence agriculture, the production of indigo for export, and subsidies from New Spain. When Mexico proclaimed its independence, the Spanish Captain-General of Guatemala in connivance with the Central American elites joined Mexico as a province of Iturbide's monarchy. And when Iturbide was overthrown, the Federation of Central America minus the province of Chiapas seceded. Much of the conflict between Mexico and

Guatemala during the post-independence period has been based on the dispute over this border province.

In the Federation of Central America, the biggest and most Indian province, Guatemala, emerged as the leading force, and for a while the center of government. However, due to the diverse Central American geography and ethnicity, these mini-states were often more isolated from each other than from the outside world. Geographical apartness and ethnic factors hindered the political crystallization of a united national state. The issues that separated the quarrelsome clusters of Liberals and Conservatives throughout Latin America were also present in Central America. As in Mexico, the British and American "diplomatic" policy was for the former to side with Conservatives, and the latter with Liberals. It is in Central America where we see the rise of the largest number of small *caudillos* who in due time were euphemistically nick-named "generals" by their subjects. Indeed, the disruption of the Spanish bureaucratic apparatus was replaced by mini-*caudillos* who Balkanized Central America. Noting such a process of political and regional disintegration, Domingo Sarmiento (1811-88), the Argentine statesman and contemporary student of *caudillismo* in his own country remarked: "Central America has made a sovereign state out of each hamlet."

By the close of the nineteenth century, the national or bigger *caudillos* had subdued the smaller provincial *caudillos* throughout Latin America, thus creating the basis for the emergence of modern national states. In Central America a super *caudillo* or charismatic leader capable of imposing a big "national state" did not emerge as it had been the experience in most of Latin America. Moreover, the region's isthmian geography subjected it to relentless hegemonic efforts of the United States and the European powers that wanted to build an inter-oceanic canal. Such external factors intensified the regional and ethnic tendencies within Central America. But Central America did have idealist leaders and patriots who, despite internal and external hindrances, attempted to create viable federal republics of semi-autonomous provinces. Perhaps the most noteworthy of those early leaders was the Honduran Liberal Francisco Morazán (1799-1842). Morazán and his followers dominated Central American politics until 1839. Like contemporary Latin American liberalism, the Liberals in Central America felt that in order to eliminate the colonial heritage, the power of the Church had to be curtailed in politics, the economy and education. Accordingly, the Liberals and Morazán began the systematic banishment of the most anti-Liberal clergy, including the Archbishop. In addition, religious properties were confiscated; the tithes, burials inside the church, and many religious holidays were abolished. The legalization of religious liberty, civil marriages and divorce also occurred.

Branded as heretics by the Church, the Liberals were challenged and attacked throughout Central America. When Morazán's second presidential term was about to end in 1839, all the provinces except El Salvador had left the Federation of Central America, although the fiction of union was preserved until Guatemala formally seceded in 1847. Moreover, Morazán was overthrown by the illiterate Mestizo Rafael Carrera who represented the most reactionary Central American conservatism.[1] The advent of Carrera meant not only a reactionary period, but it accelerated the disintegration of the former colonial Guatemalan province. The Federation of Central America had become too closely associated with liberalism for the Conservatives to support it. Thus, Carrera permitted Costa Rica and Nicaragua to go their own ways. There were other Central American heads of state such as the Guatemalan Justo Rufino Barrios (1873-85), the Hondurian Marco Aurelio Soto (1876-83), and the Nicaraguan José Santos Zelaya (1893-1909), who made sincere but abortive efforts to reunite Central America.

The Guatemalan Carrera as the *caudillo* of the biggest Central American nation still had a hegemonic influence among neighboring countries, especially in El Salvador and Honduras. In the style of contemporary Latin American landowning *caudillos*, the patriarch ruled from semi-retirement in his hacienda until his natural death in 1865. Carrera's dictatorship did bring enforced internal peace, but Guatemala like most of contemporary Central America was characterized by its subsistence economy and religious fanaticism. Although the Mestizo Carrera did attempt to protect Indians and their cultures, his paternalism was limited by the pigmento-cratic socio-economic system. In the final analysis, Carrera was an instrument of the landholding oligarchy and the Church; both were loyal to the autocrat and they also feared his mercurial temper. Caucasoid Costa Rica, ethnically different and geographically distant, more effectively resisted Carrera and even dared to have Liberals as presidents most of the time.

Nicaragua was also a troublesome state to Guatemalan hegemonic ambitions. Two rival cities polarized the regional political tendencies in Nicaragua: Conservative Granada and Liberal León. With the aid of Guatemala the Conservatives were usually in control. Although under Conservative rule (1857-93) the Nicaraguan elites of opposing ideologies agreed on the promotion of agriculture and mining for export.[2] Due to the "gold-rush" colonization of California during the 1850s, it became easier and cheaper to travel by way of Nicaragua than crossing the North American West. Suddenly, international priorities upset the internal status quo. British and American entrepreneurs came to operate the profitable steamship lines from Nicaraguan ports on the Caribbean and the Pacific Ocean. Before long, the Yankee entrepreneur Cornelius Vanderbilt became the most successful monopolist of this traffic.

By 1855, the adventurer William Walker from Tennessee with a number of his fellow countrymen, and in alliance with the Liberals from León, seized control of Nicaragua. Walker, as self-proclaimed president and dictator was concerned with profits from the Nicaraguan route. Although his government became diplomatically recognized by the United States, Walker was trying to drive Vanderbilt out of business, and to that goal he was not a match for the more resourceful Vanderbilt. Vanderbilt skilfully manipulated and bribed an alliance with Carrera and the Costa Rican Liberal elites. Such an alliance, plus Vanderbilt's powerful mercenary army, defeated the Tennessean intruder. Walker was ousted in 1857, and three years later when trying to rally support for his schemes, he was captured and executed. By the late nineteenth century, the intensity of Conservative-Liberal conflicts increased and was distorted by British and American support for the *caudillos* who promised more advantageous concessions in the construction of an interoceanic canal.

With the death of Carrera, the power of the Conservatives became impaired and finally by 1873, a Liberal became president. He was Justo R. Barrios, a Creole aristocrat who was killed in battle (1885) when trying to unify Central America. After the tragic demise of Barrios, he was mostly succeeded by Liberals until 1920. Barrios was in a sense the prototype of Liberal dictators and "modernizers" who emerged throughout Central America by the close of the nineteenth century. They attempted to secularize society and accelerate the region's integration into the world economy by the rapid exploitation of natural resources and agricultural production for the export market. Foreign ideas, technology and investments were welcomed with rhetorical adulation in the promotion of what was to become the new materialist and Positivist age. However, according to René Reeves, the modernizing policies that promoted the development of the export economy already began during Conservative rule.[3] Moreover, the Liberal modernization excluded the Guatemalan indigenous population, which still constitutes the overwhelming majority. The heritage of ethnic exclusion has not ended in Guatemala.

With the exception of Costa Rica, Central America has been the most backward region of the Americas. These nations of "generals" and peasants have been branded with the epitaph of "banana republics" par excellence. Not without dislocations, these nations' economies were transformed from subsistence diversified agriculture to highly modernized export monocultures. It was a patchwork transformation in which the greatest beneficiaries were the ubiquitous United Fruit Company from the United States, and the landed elite who was quicker to ally and adjust itself with the new sponsors of production. Moreover, the greatest contrasts of social extremes are found in the ethnically different Costa Rica (white) and Guatemala (Amerindian). In the rest of Central America, the socio-economic gaps have more regional variations and origins.[4]

Perhaps the Central American country that benefited most from the development of an export economy was Costa Rica. It has often been noted that Costa Rica does not seem to belong to the region, and it has even been euphemistically nick-named together with Uruguay, as a "Switzerland" of the Americas. Costa Rica from colonial times onwards had the advantages of being "racially more homogeneous" (i.e., in Caucasian terms) and geographically confined to a relatively small area. Most of Costa Rica's inhabitants had come from northern Spain during the colonial period. The Indians were pushed aside, and only few African slaves were imported for the small farms that were developed. After independence, the public lands were parcelled out without the existence of Indian masses to be dispossessed. Certainly, large plantations also developed, but the exploitation among social classes was tempered by the fact that it was inflicted among whites themselves.

Costa Rica was the first and most successful Central American country to cultivate coffee and then bananas for the export market. With its increasing foreign income from exports, Costa Rica enjoyed greater affluence than its neighbors. There was relatively sufficient fiscal revenue to finance infrastructures and education that benefited a larger percentage of the population as well as whetting the palate of corrupt politicians. Costa Rican affluence gave the ruling elites a chance to foster more libertarian structures as well as finance a class society at minimum costs. Software productions as well as the tourist industry are the newest economic enclaves sponsored by the local elites and their foreign partners. Costa Rica is not only a big producer of bananas, coffee, lumber and sugar, but it also has rich natural resources of gold, copper, mercury and other minerals. In addition, a significant light industry has developed from the outset of the twentieth century. It is the wealthiest Central American nation.

Except for the brief dictatorship of Fedérico Tinoco (1917-19), and the short civil war of 1948, Costa Rica has been ruled by constitutional governments elected in relatively free elections. Even during the 1930s when dictatorial regimes were revitalized throughout Latin America, Costa Rica was ruled by constitutional governments which were only mildly authoritarian. In the depth of the

Great Depression, the reformist National Republican Party (PNR) was elected (1932) on the promise to eliminate the nation's social problems without Communist solutions. This party controlled the presidency until 1948.

During the PNR's rule, a program of social welfare and reform was carried out. The rights of organized labor, a social security system, and income taxes were enacted. However, from the early 1940s, middle class leftists and Communists achieved moderate influence in governmental policy. The outcome of the growing cooperation between leftists and the PNR accelerated social reform. Likewise, the growing power of leftists brought about political polarization. Thus, at the strongly contested presidential election of 1948, the opposition candidate Otilio Ulate, representing the extremely anti-Communist forces, claimed victory. The PNR annulled the elections and arrested Ulate as well as other political figures. For two months, the nation was plagued by bloody clashes of diverse political groups ranging from the reactionary-Right to the Communists. Over 3,000 people were killed. With the diplomatic mediation of the United States and Mexico, anti-Communist moderates and Conservatives emerged as the victors of this brief civil war.

In the new elections of December 1948, Ulate's National Union Party (PUN) won. Moreover, as the result of the political events after the civil war, the Army and the Communist party were proscribed. Thus, Costa Rica became the only Latin American nation that had more teachers than soldiers. In the post civil war period, the Conservative PUN and the National Liberation Party (PLN) have alternated the presidency. The PLN is ideologically aligned with the Christian Democratic movements of Europe and Latin America. Costa Rica remained as an island of political stability and moderate social reform, and it has created some sort of welfare capitalism, although poverty is still a national problem. Minority leftist parties, including the Communists have been legalized since 1970. They constituted a powerful critical voice in favor of radical but non-violent social change. In 1977, Costa Rica and Cuba resumed diplomatic relations after a sixteen-year break. Within the context of the *Pax Americana* and the Cold War in Latin America, Costa Rica was allowed to become one of the most neutral nations.

Unlike the interruption to American hegemony in Mexico by the revolution of 1910, the outset of the twentieth century in Central America was characterized by the militant solidification of United States interests. The creation of the artificial Panamanian nation was the first official installment of the Yankee penetration in the region. Panama emerged as a "sovereign" state because President Theodore Roosevelt (1901-08) became impatient with the objections made by the Colombian congress to the American request for an isthmian canal route. The American interest in the Colombian province of Panama originated with the railroad across the isthmus built by Bostonian entrepreneurs (1848-55) in order to transport settlers bound for California. Furthermore, the United States and Britain signed the Clayton-Bulwer Treaty (1850) by which they pledged themselves to the neutrality of any inter-oceanic canal built across Central America.

Since the 1820s, the Dutch had negotiated to build a canal through Nicaragua, but it was the French who began construction of the inter-oceanic canal during the 1880s under the entrepreneurship of Ferdinand de Lesseps. Partly because of the Anglo-American financial boycott, French entrepreneurs were unable to finance the construction of the Panama Canal. Confronted by financial problems the French sold out to American financiers. When the Colombian congress refused to grant permanent territorial and sovereignty transfers, the United States and the Panamanian provincial elites conspired on an emancipatory revolt. On November 3, 1903, the insurrection broke out. Accordingly, the American navy prevented the Colombian troops from landing in Panama to quell the rebellion, and the United States government immediately recognized Panama as an independent and sovereign nation. Two weeks after its independence, Panama signed the Hay-Bunau-Varilla Treaty with the United States providing for the construction of the canal, and the creation of a ten-mile-wide canal zone to be administered by the United States "as if it were sovereign."

The United States paid the neophyte republic ten million dollars for its concessions, and it promised to pay 250,000 dollars annually in rent for the use of the Canal Zone. Rent payments were periodically increased to compensate for the devaluation of the dollar. The Panama Canal was opened to traffic in 1914. Likewise, the United States claimed Panama like Cuba as protectorates until 1936. As in other places in Central America and the Caribbean subjected to American occupation during the early twentieth century, a police system known as the *Guardia Nacional* (National Guard) was created. The *Guardia Nacional* helped the United States to "maintain law and order" in the neophyte "banana republics."

Nowhere in Latin America was the level of American political, economic and military domination as high as in Panama. Every president of this small nation had to avoid the antagonism of Uncle Sam. Nationalist leaders such as Arnulfo Arias remained in office (1940) only a few months; others were not allowed to take office because of United States disapproval. Panama is a country whose economy was based on the rent from the canal, and supplying food and labor to the American civil and military installations. Within those facilities the United States operated one of the biggest military bases in the world and trained the elite military cadres of Latin America. Since the 1930s, Panama has been trying to develop a light industry, but it has been more successful in becoming the home for "mail box" corporations, and in providing tax shelters for foreign shipping companies that register under the Panamanian flag. Thus, on paper Panama appears as the possessor of one of the biggest merchant marines in the world.

Tropical Panama has also emerged as an odd mixture of Switzerland and Las Vegas with its banking facilities, brothels, casinos and other similar entertaining accommodations for fun-loving and affluent Latin Americans, and foreign visitors. Panama has a free enterprise system resembling Singapore, Taiwan and other capitalist spots within the Third World. Panama is a nation, which did not even have its own currency, the American dollar being the official medium of exchange. Due to local nationalist pressure and bloody riots, as well as Latin American solidarity, the United States in 1978 agreed to return the canal and its facilities to the Panamanian nation by the onset of the twentieth century. However, precautions and provisions were made to the effect that the promised transfer would not constitute a "threat to the security and interests of the United States." The overthrow of General Manuel Antonio Noriega (December 1989) and the subsequent dismantling of the *GuardiaNacional* insured that the only military force capable of protecting the "navigation freedom" through the canal is the American army. It is in Panama where the formal and informal hegemony of the United States over a Latin American country became a most obvious affair.

Where the Revolution Lost

By the dawn of the twentieth century, Guatemala had emerged as a coffee producer for the export market. By 1914, more than 85% of the nation's foreign income came from coffee. Guatemala was ruled under the banners of liberalism by the ruthless dictator Manuel Estrada Cabrera from 1898 to 1920. During this extensive dictatorship, the biggest areas of investment were in sugar and banana plantations whose production was for export. The greatest beneficiary of the expansion in export agriculture was the United Fruit Company, which after its foundation in 1899 by the American entrepreneur Minor C. Keith in Costa Rica, gradually expanded its holdings throughout Central America, the Caribbean and northern South America. Tired of Estrada Cabrera's iron-fist dictatorship, a group of civilian aristocrats and military officers led a conspiracy that culminated in his overthrow by April 1920. Three months later, the civilian aristocrat Carlos Herrera was elected president in the first free elections of Guatemalan history.

Unfortunately, there was only a brief interlude of free political activity. Herrera was deposed by his fellow conspirators and generals after three months of civilian government. Afterwards, the nation was ruled by alternating military officers but by 1931, the sinister General Jorge Ubico emerged as the dominant figure. Ubico was a man who openly admired Hitler, and he was extremely anti-Communist, anti-labor, and anti-intellectual. His enemies were subjected to periodic purges, imprisonment, executions and assassinations. The press and intellectuals were silenced, and the discussion of social problems was prohibited. Ubico publicly acknowledged that he had no friends—"only domesticated enemies." He was an insecure tyrant that saw ghosts everywhere and tried to repress them.

Underneath the superficial stability of Ubico's Guatemala, sporadic agitation surfaced from the early 1940s. Intellectuals, university students, professors, labor leaders and some military officers joined forces and conspired. By July 1944, the country had been paralyzed by labor strikes and barricades. Ubico fled to the United States, and a military junta took over. However, the junta's attempts to remain permanently in power brought an armed revolt of civilians and young officers that culminated in the establishment of a "Revolutionary Junta" which ruled until March 1945. The "Revolutionary Junta" handed over the government to the democratically elected Dr. Juan J. Arévalo. During a decade, Guatemala was governed by legitimately elected leaders for the first time in its history. The Government was for the majority of the population rather than the oligarchy.

Arévalo was the leader of the newly created Revolutionary Action Party (PAR) which represented a coalition of professional groups, intellectuals, students, workers and young officers. Arévalo was an exiled philosophy professor who had lived and taught in Argentina. He claimed to be socialist and was determined to socialize Guatemalan society through democratic means. A socialistic constitution resembling the Mexican constitution of 1917 was immediately drafted. With state support, urban and rural workers were organized. Freedom of the press was respected, and political exiles returned to build "the new Guatemala." A diverse fauna of Latin American leftists also flocked into Guatemala to participate in the "Guatemalan road to socialism." The Communist party and other leftist groups were allowed to organize. Educational programs for children and adults were created in order to eliminate the staggering 75% illiteracy. Despite the popularity of Arévalo's government, it was boycotted by the local elites and foreign companies as well as small militant leftist groups who advocated more drastic changes.

In the elections of 1950, the official candidate Colonel Jacobo Arbenz was elected by an overwhelming majority. The advent of Arbenz to the presidency meant a more radical turn to the Left, and closer diplomatic relations with the Communist countries. Likewise, local Marxist leaders acquired significant political influence, both formally and informally.[5] The nationalization of the extensive landholdings owned by the United Fruit Company solidified the alliance between local reactionary groups and foreign interests despite the fact that at least in the beginning, a few opulent members of the bourgeoisie openly co-operated with Marxist officials. Unfortunately, the Guatemalan experiment was taking place at the height of the Cold War, and at a time when none in the "backyard" neighborhood dared to say "no" to Uncle Sam. Moreover, the agrarian reform also produced disorder in the countryside because of class, group and ethnic interests.[6] The traditional elites feared that the revolutionary genie would get out of the bottle.

The administration of Dwight Eisenhower (1953-61) was determined to remove "the first Communist foothold in the Americas." Financial credits and technical aid were suspended to the Guatemalan dependent economy, and when news that the Swedish ship *Alfhem* had carried Czechoslovakian arms to Guatemala was publicized by American newspapers, the United States government claimed that it had no choice but to intervene. Accordingly, a CIA-trained army under the command of the exiled General Carlos Castillo Armas invaded Guatemala from Honduran and Nicaraguan bases in May 1954. With strategic sectors of the Army standing aside to allow the march of the invaders, the government and the resistance quickly collapsed and fled. Arbenz had committed the error of making revolutionary changes while leaving the professional army intact. On July 8, Castillo Armas became provisional president, and in a pre-arranged plebiscite three months later he legalized his presidency.

After the successful CIA-covert operation, generous economic and military aid from the United States returned Guatemala to the status quo. The Communist party and all types of leftist groups were disbanded, and the National Committee for the Defense against Communism was set up. The United Fruit Company and other foreign and local landowners recovered virtually all their lands, amounting to 1.5 million acres. An agrarian reform law was passed in 1956 providing that only "idle lands" (*tierrasbaldías*) could be distributed to the peasants. A new constitution severely restricted the rights of organized labor. Guatemalan governments of the post Arévalo-Arbenz period have been controlled by crusading generals and militarized civilians determined to uproot any trace of Communism from their country. Indeed, a murderous strategy to eliminate leftist insurgency was undertaken by the state.[7]

Despite the Christian Democratic rule of Venicio Cerezo (1986-91) and the Pentecostal Jorge Serrano (1991-93), power conflicts among the Guatemalan ruling elites oscillated between "anti-Communist" and "more anti-Communist" military officers. When in May 1993, the corrupt Serrano government briefly attempted to create a civilian dictatorship; it did so with support of the military. The seesawing-power-grabs that resulted in the parliamentary election of the former human-rights ombudsman Ramiro de León Carpio were also supervised by the armed forces. Behind this political establishment of nearly white people which rules an Indian majority (about 70%), there is the socio-economic fact that 3% of the population owned 60% of the national wealth. By the end of the twentieth century, the top 6% of the population possessed 62% of the arable lands. The Landed aristocracy is of ancient pedigree. The landed oligarchy and the industrial elites are intimately related by marriage and business.[8] The so-called Guatemalan democracy is hierarchical and racist. It is a nation in which 34% of the population survives on less than two dollars per day.

From the early 1960s, leftist guerrilla activity became intermittent, and the indiscriminate repression against Indians by para-military groups was successful in limiting revolutionary activity. Nowhere in the Americas were Indians persecuted and alienated with so much violence. The power apparatus used psychologists, pastors and priests in order to launch a spiritual crusade for the bodies, minds and souls of the ancient Mayas' descendants. It was estimated that since the overthrow of Arbenz, over a million people live as refugees inside and outside the nation, 200,000 were killed, and over 40,000 disappeared. The majority of the victims were Maya Indians. According to the Truth Commission of the United Nations, 80% of the killings were committed by the Guatemalan army (1960-96). During the Guatemalan civil war, the military in collaboration with the CIA experimented on models of counterinsurgency and low-intensity warfare.

Opium cultivation in the "emergency areas" converted Guatemala into one of the largest Latin American producers. Indeed, Guatemalan counterinsurgency warfare was intimately intertwined with the struggle against and for narcotics.[9] Peace was signed with the mediation of the United Nations. Until very recently, Guatemala was a country where political prisoners were almost non-existent: prospective political prisoners were simply executed or assassinated. In the aftermath of the civil war, political and criminal murders have continued. Over 40 suspected criminals were lynched by the outraged crowds in the year 2009 alone. The drug traffic has further increased the daily violence, which confronts life in Guatemala. In the year 2006 alone, 5,800 murders took place. It was the highest per capita in Latin America.

The awarding of the Nobel Peace Prize to Rigoberta Menchú (1992) bestowed on her some personal protection, but Guatemala is a mined battlefield for those who have tried to shake the oligarchy's power or have unprotected lives. By the dawn of the twenty-first century, some twelve families owned the most fertile Guatemalan lands. Their physical safety is guaranteed by private and state protection. Menchú must also face the omen of racism and *machismo*. The criminals who were responsible for the genocide against the Maya peasants are still at large. Nevertheless, Menchú has proclaimed her dream to become the first Amerindian president of Guatemala. The Mayas have not yet liberated themselves from the nightmares of European and neo-European colonization. If Menchú is to emulate Nelson Mandela, a miracle would help.

The Agonizing Nicaraguan Alternative

Through revolution, the Liberal leader José Santos Zelaya over-threw the Conservatives and the traditional oligarchy in 1893. For the next sixteen years, the new dictator tried to secularize Nicaraguan society and curtail American and British meddling in Nicaragua and other Central American countries. Zelaya led a na-tionalist project of modernization based on coffee production for export. The Nicaraguan efforts against foreign penetration and American mining companies invited the United States to take the war-path. Due to American manipulations and threats of military invasion, Zelaya's own lieutenants replaced him in 1909 in order to appease the Yankee rage. After a year of turmoil and economic crisis, Zelaya's own followers were removed by the Conservatives with American and British help. The landed estate and mine own-ers became the recipients of governmental favors. The Conserva-tives recognized the foreign debt, restored the Church to most of its former privileged status, and placed themselves under the pro-tection of the United States. Likewise, the United States loaned Nicaragua 15 million dollars to solve its financial problems and pay its creditors. But since the Liberals continued to agitate against the new American protégés, American marines landed in 1912 and remained for over two decades.

In 1916, the Bryan-Chamorro Treaty gave the United States the perpetual right to build an inter-oceanic canal across Nicaragua as well as ninety-nine year leases for military bases. In exchange, Nicaragua received three million dollars for the payment of its for-eign debt. However, the provisions of the treaty were not fully en-forced because the neighboring countries of El Salvador, Honduras and Costa Rica protested, claiming that the proposed canal in-fringed on their territorial rights. In addition, the completion of the Panama Canal postponed the need for a new canal for an indefinite time. During the period of the American occupation, United States economic interests consolidated their leadership over other foreign investments faster than in any other Central American nation.

The final departure of the United States marines came after they had created a well-disciplined and well-equipped Guardia Nacional under the command of Anastacio Somoza García. The most difficult task faced by the Guardia Nacional during the 1930s was the suppression of guerrilla warfare led by Augusto Sandino. Sandino was a socialist who like many of his Latin American contemporaries had fought in the Mexican Revolution of 1910. Although he had never claimed to be a Marxist, among his followers were found a wide range of Marxists, anti-imperialists and leftist nationalists. In due course, the Guardia Nacional invited Sandino for peaceful negotiations and then treacherously showered him with bullets in 1934. With the death of Sandino, the extensive Somoza family consolidated its power with grateful and generous amounts of economic and military aid from the United States.

Until Anastacio Somoza Jr. was expelled from Nicaragua on July 17, 1979, the Somozas ruled their country directly or through puppets as if it were a giant hacienda. It was a very successful entrepreneurial venture for the Somoza clan. To be sure, there were the subtle formalities of elections, a congress and a judiciary system. The Somozas claimed to be members of the Liberal party, and enlisted their bureaucratic officials, employees and patronized clients as voters and supporters. It is estimated that by the end of the Somoza dictatorship over a third of all the nation's resources were owned by the first family. In alliance with American capital, the Somozas developed Nicaragua for themselves. Until September 1978, Nicaragua had the best international credit-rating in all of Latin America. The nation exported cotton, coffee, bananas, sugar and beef. The United States became its biggest buyer and source of imports. The Somozas also invested in industry, commerce and mining, both in Nicaragua and abroad. The Somozas are a multinational entrepreneurial clan.

The Somozas' dictatorship was ruthless and violent, especially against leftists. The Conservative party as well as the Church was allowed to operate and cooperate. The Sandinistas were virtually extinguished until they reorganized in July 1961 under the leadership of Carlos Fonseca Amador. The Somozas' economic and political monopolies also had the consequence of alienating members of the socio-economic elite who were forced to sell out their businesses, driven into penury or suffered confiscation. The Somozas had the first option on any enterprise that had a profitable future. Their power monopoly became the biggest source of capital accumulation. Survival in life and success in social, economic and political activities required the benevolence of the Somozas. The earthquake that killed over ten thousand people and virtually destroyed Managua on December 23, 1972, not only sharpened the misery of the poor but caused destitution among many members of the middle and upper classes. Moreover, American and foreign aid for the reconstruction of the ravaged capital city and its victims was unscrupulously used for the reconstruction and expansion of the Somozas' enterprises. Protests came from every social level, and the Sandinistas capitalized on the new wave of discontent.

By early 1978, the Sandinistas with considerable popular support were launching guerrilla attacks throughout the nation. It is estimated that during the last year of Somocismo approximately 40,000 people died in a struggle, which crossed class and ideological boundaries. The United States attempted to thwart the Sandinista victories by armed intervention under the guise of an OAS peace keeping force, and then by proposing that a broad coalition government which included "moderate" members of the Guardia Nacional should replace the last Somoza. The new government was ideologically pluralist but the new army responsible for national security was of Sandinista orientation. Not since the victory of Fidel Castro in Cuba had a popular armed movement been able to defeat a professional army.

The Nicaraguan Revolution had transcendental significance in the struggle for radical social change in Latin America. Moreover, the survival of Nicaragua as a non-aligned nation became a test case on whether United States' foreign policy could adjust to the realities of Latin American revolutionary social change. The great Nicaraguan tragedy came about because the Sandinistas tried to develop a mixed-economy without American supervision. The camouflaged war against Nicaragua was brought to an "end" with the mediation of the Nobel laureate and Costa Rican president

Oscar Arias. The Guatemalan President Vinizio Cerezo also played a significant role in defusing the confrontation between Nicaragua and the United States. The diplomatic negotiation of the sobriqueted Arias Plan frustrated the militant efforts of American War Hawks and arms dealers who advocated a final military solution to the Nicaraguan problem. But, above all, it was the Sandinistas' willingness to risk being voted out of office that defused the Yankee rage.

Despite the desperate efforts of Ronald Reagan (1981-89) to crush the Sandinistas during his two presidential terms, the two freest elections in Nicaraguan history took place in 1984 and 1990. Moreover, those elections took place in the midst of warfare conditions. The war caused almost 60,000 casualties and more than 500,000 refugees. It took half the national budget, produced the worst Latin American and world inflation, and made Nicaragua one of the poorest nations in the planet. It is estimated that the war destroyed more than 18 billion dollars worth of Nicaraguan infrastructure.[10] Under all the democratic formalities, the leader of the political opposition (UNO), the victorious Violeta Chamorro, was handed over the government after the second Sandinista elections. The demobilization of the Contras or Reagan's "Freedom Fighters," and the reconstruction of a war-devastated Nicaragua were the biggest challenges for the first non-Sandinista president. The struggle against Somoza and the subsequent undeclared war with American foreign policy caused about one hundred thousand Nicaraguan deaths. For a nation of 3.5 million people the price to change its unjust social structure was almost traumatically inhuman.

The Sandinista leadership left the control of the government, and it was unprepared to play the role of a democratic opposition. With internal peace, the Sandinistas had an opportunity to earn grassroots support for their cause without the benefit of governmental patronage. They attempted to defend the revolutionary changes from the political opposition. In defeat, the Sandinistas had a chance to create a new revolutionary paradigm for social change in the region. Mrs. Chamorro's electoral victory can be easily explained by the fact that the Nicaraguan people were tired by ten miserable years of war against the United States. In addition, the United States Congress officially allotted 9 million dollars for covert electoral support to the anti-Sandinista political opposition. At least 600,000 dollars of those funds were channelled through CIA operations. But as the Mexican writer Jorge G. Castañeda noted, it was "the most shattering setback the Latin left has suffered since Salvador Allende's overthrow by the military in Chile in 1973."[11]

Despite Reagan's efforts to portray Nicaragua as a communist enclave in Central America, the nation's government was never one of peasants and workers. It was loosely patterned after the European Social Democratic model, and it encouraged the development of a mixed economy, political pluralism, and non-alignment. In fact, it was Swedish and Swedish-trained economists who had helped to design the Sandinista tax-system. Moreover, Nicaragua became the biggest recipient of Swedish foreign aid in Latin America. The Nicaraguan Revolution also incorporated the ideas of Sandino, Mariátegui, the Liberation Theology and other anti-imperialists. The efforts to restructure once again the model of economic development in the neo-liberal perspective by Mrs. Chamorro brought a new chaos to the nation. Unemployment reached the unprecedented 60% within three years of her rule. Internal and external political vindictiveness did not foretell a peaceful way out from revolutionary socio-political policies to normalcy.

At a time when the United States was fetching former protégés like General Noriega to American justice, the Central American nations found their possibilities for maneuvering very slim. In its traditional backyard, the United States is of the very strong opinion that peace and conflict should be regulated in accordance with American law. Apparently, it does not matter that the International Court of Justice in The Hague declared the United States in contempt and violation of international law for conducting a dirty war against Nicaragua.[12] The mass media lost its interest in the Nicaraguan story and other world events dominated the news.

Although Nicaragua became a virtual charity case, the Sandinista project is still alive. But the Sandinistas understand in their minds and own skins the consequences of angering the United States. Fear is still on the making even among non-Sandinistas. The United States demanded that the Sandinistas give up control of the Army[13] if Nicaragua was to receive financial aid and collaboration. Moreover, the Nicaraguan army complained that the American strategy was deliberately designed to "de-stabilize" even a non-Sandinista government in order to eliminate the last Sandinista vestiges.[14]

At least 10% of the Central American population fled the region during the period of political violence (1980-90). It has been noted that many of those refugees landed in the United States. The conflictive Central American events are interchanged impulses in Central and North America.[15] Defusing those conflicts demands reciprocal understandings and compromises even though the unawareness of the conundrum by the American people may be the biggest obstacle to overcome. Nicaraguans will rather switch than fight. Their history has taught them the tragic consequences of unleashing the Yankee rage. But the Sandinista return to power is a high-wire performance of compromises with the United States. The Sandinistas are not trying to pick up a fight with powerful nations; they prefer their generosity in order to solve Nicaragua's underdevelopment. Nicaragua has become one of Latin America's most aid-dependent nations.[16]

The Persistent Salvadorians

Although El Salvador has the smallest territory of Central America, it is the most populous country after Guatemala. From 1898 to 1931, the presidency was under the control of fourteen elitist families among which the Carlos Melendez family was the most prominent in maintaining "law and order." Those families matured into bigger clans, and they still constitute the most dominant force in national life. With the collapse of coffee markets (the nation's biggest export) brought about by the Great Depression, economic crisis inundated El Salvador. In addition, El Salvador was the most industrialized Central American nation. Thus, social unrest affected the urban proletariat as well as the peasants. The local Communist party agitated and mobilized under the leadership of Farabundo Martí (1893-1932). Like Augusto Sandino, Martí was an intellectual who had participated in the campaigns of the Mexican Revolution. A coup d'etat by General Maximiliano Hernández Martínez, director of the military academy, took place in December 1931. The maestro of the *mano dura* (iron-fist), as Hernández Martínez was known, launched a bloody crusade against Communism. It has been estimated that during the year 1932 alone approximately thirty thousand people were killed, and one of them was Martí.

During the dozen years of the Hernández Martínez dictatorship, over one fourth of the population fled him and from poverty. The majority went to Honduras, Central America, and everywhere else. The "Football War" and the internal violence of attrition (1980-92) were intimately related to the repressive crusade that Hernández Martínez could not finish. Moreover, he inaugurated a new militaristic era in which his successors were former officers or civilians with very close links to the Army. Like many of his Latin American dictatorial contemporaries, Hernández Martínez became a great admirer of European fascism and maintained close relations with the fascist powers until the American entrance into World War II. Political agitation against the system was led by student groups, professors and labor unions. With striking resemblance, and not independent from the Guatemalan political crisis, Hernández Martínez was overthrown after a nation-wide strike in April 1944.

As in Guatemala, the participation of middle class political groups with "non-Communist" perceptions was tolerated but such democratization did not alter the control of national life by the traditional elites. Despite the high density of the Salvadorian population, 95% of the arable land was controlled by 5% of the population (1979). Likewise, fourteen families owned an estimated 60% of the arable land, and they show no sign of giving it up. The ratios of land ownership, and the explosive demographic growth have been some of the most serious sources of Salvadorian internal and external conflicts in the twentieth century.

The so-called *Football War*, which took place in July 1969 between El Salvador and neighboring Honduras, is directly related to the explosive Salvadorian population growth. Historically, the industrious and landless Salvadorians have migrated throughout Central America in search of land and economic opportunity. Most Salvadorians moved to the relatively under-populated Honduras. Honduras was some kind of safety-valve for land hungry Salvadorians. The relative success of Salvadorian immigrants, which during the 1960s constituted approximately 3% of the Honduran population, had created much friction and made them scapegoats for national frustrations. In addition, there was a boundary dispute over loosely defined borders, which periodically created much tension between the two nations. Violence between these countries climaxed in 1969 during the World Cup football play-offs in which El Salvador won. In response, Hondurans savagely attacked Salvadorian immigrants, causing them to flee by the thousands. The Salvadorian government demanded reparations on behalf of its persecuted population and broke diplomatic ties. After military clashes and air raids on the border areas, the Salvadorian army invaded Honduras, and reached within 100 kilometers of Tegucigalpa on July 14. Four days later, the OAS arranged for a cease-fire. The "Football War" was a primitive little war in which the bulk of the fighting was done by machete-wielding peasants from two "banana republics."

The return of about two hundred thousand Salvadorians to their homeland increased the social tensions and dislocations among the landless peasants. From 1980 to 1992, over seventy-five thousand people were killed. El Salvador concluded a bloody civil war, which has not yet been televised in all its brutality for the awareness of the outside world. The ruling elites faced the greatest challenge to their historic control of national life. The fear of "another Cuba" or "a new Nicaragua" caused the United States to support those elites and their military establishments in all their brutality. Until the outbreak of the civil war, the Salvadorian oligarchy usually replaced the incumbent governments by state coups.

In 1993, the Salvadorian government granted amnesty to all military officers involved in war crimes. The United States tried to encourage a "moderate" government that would defuse one of the most confrontational Central American spots. Unfortunately, there was not a middle sector in the Salvadorian political scene. The adversaries just did not trust each other. A strategic equilibrium of forces supposedly existed. Negotiations took place at the highest levels of international diplomacy by elites and vanguards, but the Salvadorian majority suffered unmitigated violence. In this struggle, American foreign policy was of the utmost importance in the blood bath's duration. It is clear that the forces that killed Archbishop Oscar Romero (1980), priests, teachers, and other innocent people could not have remained in power without the help of the Reagan and Bush (the elder) administrations.[17]

During the 12 years of the Reagan and Bush administrations, more than six billion dollars were given to the Salvadorian government. El Salvador emerged as a human laboratory where post-Vietnam counterinsurgency military operations were tested. The Army's clean-up of parasitic criminals who thrived on the civil war remained as a major unsolved task. The Death-Squads continued to assassinate and intimidate people. Despite the strongest denials by the Reagan-Bush I administrations, declassified documents reveal that both knew who were the leaders of the Death Squads.[18] Defusing internal conflicts is also a question of how the United States wants to deal with its nearest "backyards." Likewise, the United Nations promised investments in the Salvadorian lower classes because the local elites were not planning to give up their traditional resources and privileges. When the civil war officially ended, 1.4% of the landowners owned over 50% of the agricultural lands. Unfortunately, no reconciliation took place after the civil war. Nobody forgave anybody.

One of the most tragic side-effects of the Salvadorian civil war resulted in the rise of the *Maras* (young criminal gangs). Many of them were children of former exiles who survived in American slums while escaping the Salvadorian bloodbath. With plenty weapons left from the civil war, social polarization and violence are on the rise. In 2006 alone, 3,726 murders were related to the *Maras* and common delinquency.[19] Two years later, El Salvador reached the world's highest murder rate. The Maras have evolved into a transnational criminal organization in Central America. Can a lasting peace come about without the elimination of social misery? The Salvadorian masses still survive despite unfulfilled promises while the traditional elites are still flourishing and reinventing themselves with well broadcast populist rhetoric. By the same token, until Mauricio Funes' presidential election in 2009, the former guerrillas (FMLN) had failed to provide a political alternative to the ruling oligarchy. Funes was elected despite the open opposition of the American Ambassador. But internally, Funes faces the antagonism of the Salvadorian oligarchy and the "extreme Left." Demons and angels aside, the Salvadorian nation has to construct and reconstruct its structural and social predicaments after a brutal civil war. Salvadorians are intelligent and diligent people.

The Cheapest Banana Republic

Honduras still is the most backward nation of Central America, and together with Bolivia, Haiti and Paraguay have the lowest per capita incomes of Latin America. Since most of its legal foreign exchange earnings come from banana exports, Honduras is a banana republic par excellence. Other major exports are coffee, tobacco and lumber. The political developments of this nation from the outset of the twentieth century are closely intertwined with those of its neighbors. Until 1933, *caudillos* that called themselves Liberals and Conservatives alternated in the presidential office by either limited elections or armed revolt. By election, General Tiburcio Carías Andino was made president with the blessings of the United States in 1933. He was the leader of the National Party, which was the name taken by the Conservatives in the early 1920s. For sixteen years Carías Andino ruled by dictatorial methods in the style of his Central American contemporaries. Carías Andino retired voluntarily but made sure that his protégé, General Juan Manuel Galvez was elected. The National Party and the Army ruled until 1957 with the anti-leftist vehemence of Carías Andino.

In the Honduran democratic mirage, the way Liberals and Conservatives (Nationalists) vote is almost by reason of family tradition. Honduras' political economy is dominated by about ten oligarchic families and their clients. The Honduran *caudillos* and their families still rule in semi-feudal style, and in close collaboration with the United States. Most Honduran exports and imports are to and from the United States. The Honduran government granted the CIA training bases for the overthrow of the Arbenz government in Guatemala, the Cuban revolution (on Cisne Island), and the Sandinistas in Nicaragua.

A turning point took place in 1957, when the charismatic Liberal Dr. Ramón Villeda Morales was elected despite military hostility. His government represented a victory for the "democratic left." Moreover, Villeda Morales pledged his support for land reform, revision of government contracts with the United Fruit Company, and respect of workers' rights. His agrarian reform would have affected the lands of the American company. Villeda Morales undertook a moderate campaign to ameliorate the social conditions of the poor but the traditional landed elites feared and opposed his reformist policies. In October 1963, General Oswaldo López Arellano noted that national security was endangered by Communist infiltrators and overthrew Villeda Morales. Villeda Morales had been a local dreamer who believed in the rhetoric of John F. Kennedy.

In the aftermath of Villeda Morales' dismissal and the "Alliance for Progress" which encouraged land reforms for Latin America, the Honduran rulers decreed an agrarian law that provided for land redistribution. The United Fruit Company and the local elites were exempted. Distribution was to be from uncultivated public territory (*tierrasbaldías*), and only for Honduran nationals. Thus, the social pressure was brought upon the peasants of different ethnic backgrounds. Under those circumstances the "Football War" broke out in which the Salvadorian minority was massacred. At least five thousand died or were killed while the material damages were incalculable. With the advent of the Sandinistas in neighboring Nicaragua, the United States encouraged the election of civilian presidents in Honduras but the Army was revitalized with very generous military aid. The most modern Central American air force was donated to the nation.[20] Overnight, the country became a military base for the *Contras* and their American advisors in the war against Nicaragua.

Honduras became an important component in the American strategy to maintain its hegemony in the isthmus. In addition to banana income, the Hondurans received foreign currency for providing "pleasing" services to the United States. The American Embassy was a well-connected and important power factor in the internal management of this neo-feudal, patriarchal and conservative banana republic. After the United States succeeded in suffocating the Nicaraguan revolutionary process, the newly founded Honduran bonanza returned to the exclusive reliance on the export of cheap bananas for survival. But the containment of the Nicaraguan Revolution and the Central American insurgencies also affected the Honduran lower classes. Hondurans were awakening from lethargy to a changing world and an almost defeated Central America.

Although Honduras produced exceptional visionary leaders like Francisco Morazán and Villeda Morales, the Honduran elites have shown only modest ambitions. As President Rafael Callejas (1990-94) noted in 1990: "We want to be a banana republic in a positive way. We want to produce the best bananas in the world." Of all the Central American nations, Honduras is the most dependent on the export-enclaves sponsored by multi-national corporations. The local elites have accumulated their wealth by collaborating with the enclave economy and in the import business.

Honduras left the "benign neglect" of American foreign policy when the Contras' covert operations required a geographical stage for action. Guerrilla warfare and violence reached a new stage in the twilight of the Nicaraguan political process. The *Recontras* and the *Recompas* were born, and the United States required the non-Sandinista Nicaraguan government to accept financial and technical aid against drug smuggling and other priorities. The American war against drugs in foreign territory replaced the threat of the "Evil Empire" with another myth. The brand-new Honduran air force participates with great enthusiasm in the "anti-drug" surveillance operations of the United States. In the meanwhile Tegucigalpa has become one of the most violent and crime-ridden cities in the Western Hemisphere. Hondurans have even imitated and refined the activities of the Salvadorian *Maras*. Honduras used to accept aid, charity and donations from anybody regardless of race, color, ideology or interests.

When President Manuel Zelaya tried to organize a plebiscite for a constitutional amendment that would have also allowed his re-election and drastic social changes, the head of the Army forcefully dismissed him on June 28, 2009. Almost two years later, Zelaya was allowed to return as a civilian with the ironic mediation of Colombia and Venezuela. Zelaya had been offering Liberal-Social Democratic solutions to local socio-economic problems. However, popular mobilizations, which demand power-sharing, are still taking place in Honduras. The local oligarchy pretends to maintain the status quo in a changing Honduras and a more defying Latin America. In the meantime, seven out of ten Hondurans live in poverty. The Hondurans and Central Americans have a chance to collaborate or antagonize the United States, but the Andean booming export will continue as long as there is a demand in the *North*. The promise and tragedy of Central America is that it is geographically located in a transit area. The powerful and intimidating drug cartels have arrived at Central America. Like in other places, they bribe politicians; buy newspapers and whatever they wish. Approximately 150,000 Latin Americans are killed annually because of the drug traffic. Indeed, trafficking has become a threat to the entire socio-political system.

In the wake of the Iran-Contras scandal, the American writer Gore Vidal questioned if anybody dared to ask what cargo American planes brought on their return from Honduras and Central America. It was cocaine.[21] Furthermore, the Nobel laureate Paul Krugman has asserted: "One of [Bill] Clinton's biggest mistakes was not airing what really happened in the Iran-Contra. And then, the Iran-Contra guys come back to do it all over again."[22] Apparently, the struggles against "communism" in Central America have come to an end, but the wars against trafficking have found new battlefields outside the consuming markets. However, the battle-front has not yet reached the laundering of criminal profits and financial safe-heavens. According to the United Nations (2010), Honduras, Guatemala and El Salvador are the most affected by the cocaine traffic. They also have the highest percentage of homicides in the world because of trafficking. Life and death have become cheap and Dantesque in Honduras.

The United States is determined to maintain its omnipresence in the Central American region as long as it remains balkanized and without its own initiatives. The details and consequences of American foreign policy in Central America should be understood by the majority of the American people. They are part of the problem as well as the solution; democratic transparency is in order. In the meanwhile, "benign neglect" covers-up the selfish interests of those few who have traditionally taken most advantage. Before the "Evil Empire" was invented, imperialist blocks mobilized themselves and fought to defend their colonies and areas of influence. In post independent times, neocolonialism made Latin America north of Panama especially significant to the United States. The small Central American states have limited resources in the struggle against organized crime, and the region is for the taking by powerful interests. Upon demand, the Honduran elites are willing to provide the cheapest services and delicious bananas while international charity mitigates the endurance of the status quo. Hondurans and Central Americans would do well to redeem the initiatives of the patriot Francisco Morazán.

CHAPTER VI

THE ANDEAN REGION: THE LIBERATOR'S DREAMS

S imón Bolívar once had the ambition that a federation of Andean nations would become a superpower that could hinder the United States from plaguing "the Americas with miseries in the name of liberty." In the 1960s, Ché Guevara dreamed about making the Andes a new Sierra Maestra that would liberate Latin America from American imperialism. Bolívar and Ché were the rebel children of the white elites who have ruled Latin America since independence. Both conspired against their origins and social class. They attempted to create new societies despite common contemporary wisdom and socio-economic forces, which traditionally created "law and order." For sure, Bolívar, Ché, and their followers left many unfulfilled dreams. But Andeans and Latin Americans continue to have dreams and nightmares in their quest for modernization and democracy. In the Andean nations, over 80% of the rural populations are poor. Furthermore, in Bolivia, Ecuador, and Peru, 80% of the Amerindians are poor and more than 50% of them live in extreme poverty.[1]

Venezuela, Colombia, Ecuador, Peru, and Bolivia were emancipated by Bolívar, and thus, those countries have been often referred to as the Bolivarian nations. In 1825, when Bolívar became president of all these newly liberated national states, he advocated for "Federation of the Andes" composed of semi-autonomous republics. The unity of these Andean countries was never consummated, and the illusions faded as soon as the Spanish armies were defeated. When Bolívar died five years later, his followers had been deposed, and he had resigned from his Colombian stronghold. Bolívar lived to have the glory of seeing Alto Peru christened after him as Bolivia. Bolívar also lived long enough to witness the disintegration of his dearest dreams. Bolívar died bitter and disillusioned. Only a month before his death, and on his way to self-exile, the Liberator confessed: "America is ungovernable for us...he who serves a revolution ploughs the sea...the only thing that can be done in America is to emigrate." In the aftermath of Bolívar's death, the Andean nations further drifted away from any unifying goals. In reality, they became more distant than had been during colonial days.

Since immigration was meager in the aftermath of independence, most Andean inhabitants are descendants of the Indian, white, and Black ancestors from colonial and Amerindian days. The discovery of Venezuelan oil in the twentieth century brought many European and non-European immigrants, but relatively little racial or ethnic variation has resulted. All the Andean nations contain large non-white majorities steered by white and nearly white minorities. Moreover, countries like Ecuador, Peru, and Bolivia constitute the core of indigenous South America. At least since late colonial days, Indians are minorities only in Colombia and Venezuela.

The Andean nations are crossed by the biggest South American mountain range and are adjacent to the tropical Amazon basin. All these Andean nations used to have a seacoast. Chile took away the Bolivian coast. The loss of Bolivian territory remains a recurrent source of tensions between these two nations. It was not until the 1960s that a search for economic integration among the Andean elites brought about the idea of a common market or Andean Pact. The Andean Pact became the Community of Andean Nations (CAN) in 1991. However, full-grown and coordinated economic development among the Andean nations still remains an unfulfilled dream. The overwhelming force of geography unavoidably ties them into the future. The efforts of the Andean nations to generate more autonomous and integrated economic development are filled with adulatory rhetoric to the Bolivarian schemes. Ironically, Venezuela under the leadership of Hugo Chávez, a self-proclaimed follower of Bolivarian ideals, left the CAN in 2006.[2] However, Chávez attempted to develop the more inclusive and more revolutionary Bolivarian Alternative of the Americas (ALBA). Moreover, the ALBA still is defiant to the hegemony of the United States in Latin America.

The Venezuelan Connection

During colonial times, Caracas was the start of the mule trail known as the *camino real*, which ran for more than two thousand miles, linking Bogotá, Quito, and Lima. Caracas was an Andean window into the Caribbean and was receptive to the influence of foreign ideas and revolutionary trends. It is in the margins of New Granada's viceroyalty that one of the most genuine emancipatory movements was led by Francisco Miranda, and afterwards by Bolívar. During the Napoleonic wars, Venezuelans were among the earliest participants in the Ibero-American resistance to Napoleonic imperialism. As successor to Miranda, Bolívar continued the Venezuelan and Andean emancipatory struggle. At the beginning of the Spanish colonial period, the Andean region was under the jurisdiction of the Peruvian viceroyalty and the Lima establishment. With the advent of the eighteenth-century Bourbon reforms, two more viceroyalties were created, New Granada and La Plata. The first included modern-day Colombia with Panama, as well as the Captaincy of Venezuela and the Ecuadorian Presidency. The viceroyalty of La Plata took away from the Peruvian viceroyalty, Alto Peru (Bolivia), Paraguay, and parts of present-day Chile and Argentina.

In 1821, while still struggling for independence, the federal republic of Gran Colombia was created with Venezuelan, New

Granadan, and Ecuadorian territories. The newly created national state was ruled by President Bolívar. Unfortunately, as soon as the Spanish armies had been dislodged, conflicts arose over the centralizing efforts of the Bogotá government. As long as Bolívar headed the central government, there existed a simulacrum of unity; but in reality, local *caudillos*, aided by their diverse and distant geographic apartness as well as poor communication facilities, steered the provinces away from each other. In 1829, when Bolívar was fighting for his own political survival as head of Colombia proper, his former lieutenant José Antonio Páez revolted and became the first Venezuelan president. Páez was a charismatic Mestizo who dominated Venezuelan politics from 1819 to 1847. Oftentimes, in the style of Santa Anna and Rafael Carrera, his power was exercised from semi-retirement, but with the loyalty of his *Llanero* (rustic cowboy) army. Páez's daring activities during the emancipatory wars made him a national hero, and when Bolívar was away in the Andean military campaigns, Páez became the actual ruler of Venezuela.

In Venezuela, the landed elite, in alliance with small merchant groups, constituted the dominating class. They have been portrayed as the agrarian and commercial bourgeoisie.[3] Like the other Latin American elites and anti-elites, they were divided among groups that called themselves Liberals and Conservatives. During his first administration (1831-35), Páez tried to rule with an Olympian detachment by appointing Conservatives and Liberals to the government. His first formal presidency was a relatively peaceful and prosperous one. Even European immigrants were briefly attracted. Religious toleration and freedom of the press were permitted. Agricultural production was restored to pre-emancipatory days. Foreign trade flourished due to exports, which had already been increasing during the late colonial period. Venezuela exported hides, cotton, indigo and cacao. In addition, a virtual export boom in coffee was taking place during the 1830s and early 1840s. The income from exports was sufficient to pay for the national debt incurred during the independence wars. Because of Liberal pressure, Páez withdrew many privileges from the Church and disbanded several monasteries. In Venezuelan historiography, Páez's downfall symbolizes a transition from Liberal to Conservative oligarchies.

From 1847 to 1861, when Páez was forced out of power by his former Liberal allies, the nation went through intermittent political instability. During this period, the Liberals managed to gain firmer control and significant reforms were imposed that promoted social secularization and completed the final abolition of black slavery. As in much of Spanish America, this was a time when bloody confrontations between Liberals and Conservatives intensified. The so-called Federal War (1859-63) in which about 200,000 people died, broke out. In the midst of this civil war, Páez returned from retirement as an unmitigated Conservative in 1861. His earlier associations with the Liberals were abandoned, and he became a strong advocate of Conservative rule. However, the winds of change were impregnated with Liberal agitation, and two years later he was overthrown.

After Páez's downfall, the nation almost disintegrated by the Conservative-Liberal power struggles until the Liberal *caudillo* Antonio Guzmán Blanco captured Caracas in 1870. Guzmán Blanco was a well-educated white aristocrat who enjoyed oligarchical support and the veneration of the masses. He was a persistent survivor. Like Colombia's Rafael Núñez, he was called the "Regenerador." The Liberal rhetoric was set aside, and Guzmán Blanco ruled as an autocrat at home or from abroad until 1889. Moreover, Guzmán Blanco exiled the Archbishop, disbanded the religious orders, confiscated their holdings, secularized cemeteries, legalized civil marriages and sanctioned complete religious toleration.

The charismatic Guzmán Blanco did succeed in providing peace and prosperity for the ruling elites. The increasing Venezuelan prosperity was based on the exports of coffee, cacao and sugar. The export economy's rapid growth also dislocated the political power of the Llanero group, which failed to adjust its production for the international market. Following Guzmán Blanco's disappearance from Venezuelan politics and his convenient retirement in Paris, the nation went through numerous political disturbances until General Joaquín Crespo, a former protégé of the Regenerador, captured

Caracas and prolonged Liberal rule until 1898.

The administration of Crespo was plagued by a dispute with England over a boundary line between British Guiana and Venezuela. When rumors circulated during the 1890s that the area in question contained immense gold deposits, Britain, of course, wanted jurisdiction over the gold-bearing lands. Diplomatic pronouncements and popular demonstrations throughout Latin America expressed solidarity with Venezuela. The boundary dispute brought American mediation, which, however, acceded to most of the British demands. More significantly for Latin America, the American Secretary of State Richard Olney reinvoked the Monroe Doctrine, informing the European superpowers that: "Today the United States is practically sovereign on this continent, and its fiat is law upon the subjects to which it confines its interposition."

Since the 1890s, foreign merchants, especially English, German, Italian and American, had subjected Venezuela to increasing penetration. The growth of European interests in Venezuela was in tandem to the growing American penetration in the Caribbean and Central America. In 1902, the English, German and Italian navies blockaded the Venezuelan coast in retaliation for the government's refusal to accept the exaggerated debt claims; the United States again intervened as a mediator. Although the foreign claims were scaled down, Venezuela was forced to pay. Moreover, the American mediatory participation had the same effect of analogous actions in the Caribbean and Central America. That is, the American mediatory protection had the aftermath of placing the United States as the leading external force in this resourceful and strategic geography. The discovery of the immense Venezuelan oil pools in 1914 paved the way for the complete victory of the Americans over their European counterparts. Coffee, cocoa and beef exports were drastically replaced by oil. While in 1920 agricultural exports constituted 96%, 45 years later they had decreased to 1.5%; by then, oil reached 91% of the total exports. Oil set the pace for the nation's economy, politics, social dynamism, and culture.

From 1899 to 1945, Venezuela was ruled by ruthless para-military dictatorships. During this period, all the national rulers came from the western Táchira province, the land of coffee plantations and cattle ranches. Juan Vicente Gómez was one of the shrewdest and most unique Latin American dictators. He ruled directly and indirectly for at least 27 years (1908-35). With plenty oil revenues, this *caudillo* paid Venezuela's foreign obligations and avoided Western takeovers. Gómez also crushed or bribed his local enemies. The landed elite prospered and diversified in alliance with foreign oil companies. The Venezuelan elite became one of the richest in Latin America, and it was closely associated with American interests. The biggest foreign inroads were made by Standard Oil and the Rockefeller group, which also invested in mining, land holdings, banking and industry. Although the main beneficiaries of the oil exploitation and its subsidiary enterprises were multinational corporations and the local elites, the new economic dynamism attracted thousands of European and Latin American immigrants. The most numerous were Italians, Portuguese, Spaniards and Colombians. Moreover, the oil wealth shielded Venezuela from the financial nightmare created by the Great Depression.

Like most of Latin America during the post-World War I period, Venezuela was affected by labor, student and Marxist agitation. A coalition of progressive civilians and young officers attempted to overthrow the oligarchy in 1928. The challengers, known as the "Generation of 1928," were defeated, persecuted, jailed, killed, and exiled. Their grass-roots struggle became a rallying force that gave origin to the political parties of the post-World War II period. The most powerful offsprings were Acción Democrática (AD), the Communists, and other Marxist parties. The AD became the main modernizer from the "Democratic Left." The AD was ideologically aligned with the European and Latin American Social Democratic movement.

In 1945, the AD, in alliance with moderate and leftist groups as well as members of the armed forces, overthrew the government by revolution. For the next three years, the Acción Democrática ruled with the intent of transforming Venezuela into a quasi-socialist society. The oil companies were forced to pay 50% of their profits to the state. With this new income, the government built schools, hospitals, low-cost housing and irrigation projects. Labor was granted the right to organize. Efforts were made to pass an agrarian reform law, reduce the Army and create a people's militia. In 1947, the approval of a new constitution and the nation's first free elections took place. The new president, Rómulo Gallegos, lasted only nine months in office. Gallegos and his followers were the victims of a reactionary army coup in connivance with the oil companies and the oligarchy. For the next ten years, Venezuela was ruled by a ruthless military dictatorship that searched for "Communists" behind every bush. The leading figure of the new military dictatorship was General Marcos Pérez Jiménez from Táchira. His government was a period of wholesale corruption in which oil revenues created large fortunes for government officials.

Pérez Jiménez built extravagant futuristic and government buildings, highways and boulevards as well as several low-cost apartment buildings. Army officers emerged as privileged entrepreneurs. A sophisticated spy network protected the new order. But in January 1958, an air force revolt spread into civilian riots, shoot-outs and labor strikes. A last-minute coup by the armed forces allowed Pérez Jiménez to flee, and prevented the consummation of a leftist revolution. Free elections were announced and Rómulo Betancourt, the AD's leader, was elected to the presidency. Until the rise of Hugo Chávez, the post-Pérez Jiménez dictatorship was an era dominated by the AD and the more right-wing oriented COPEI (Committee Organized for Independent Elections) or the Christian Social party. Both parties became the new political oligarchy. During the 1960s, the AD purged its Marxist members. Betancourt, a former Communist himself, launched a crusade against Communism. The first decade of the AD's rule was plagued by leftist and state terrorism. Political compromise and the legalization of Communists and other leftists in 1969 followed this decade of attrition.

In 1974, the Venezuelan government nationalized the oil industry, and with its bountiful oil revenues proclaimed the intention of freeing the nation from underdevelopment. The latter was easier said than done. While the corrupt state became indebted, local capitalists moved their funds abroad. In 1989, the Venezuelan foreign debt reached 29 billion dollars, but at the same time, Venezuelans had publically about 58 billion dollars in American banks.[4] During the last quarter of the twentieth century, Venezuela received over $300 billion for energy exports which benefited, in the main, a few hundred oligarchic families, corrupt politicians and their foreign allies.

Oil still remains the biggest source of Venezuelan foreign income. Until the ALBA policies, the government had not confronted poverty, which affects most Venezuelans. Although Venezuela had one of the highest Latin American per capita incomes, about 50% of the population survived under the United Nations' "poverty-level" by the close of the twentieth century. Food riots, attempted military coups against the Democratic Action president Carlos An-drés Pérez (1974-79, 1989-93), and his resignation in May 1993 revealed the fragility of rich, unjust and corrupt Latin American elites. The subsequent reelection of the veteran politician Rafael Caldera (1993-98) to the presidency as coalition-leader for seventeen parties (*Convergencia*) marked the end of the two-party monopoly that had ruled Venezuela for 35 years. Caldera's chaotic rule was the prelude to the nationalist Bolivarian movement, which intends to overhaul Venezuelan society. It is a leftist project with grass-roots support and very challenging consequences for Latin America.

The "Doctores" of Colombia

In Colombia, Francisco de Santander became vice president and exercised power while Bolívar was campaigning for the liberation of the Andes. Colombia's internal affairs had been disturbed from the very start of Bolívar's departure to Peru. Bolívar's participation in the Peruvian campaigns distracted his schemes for Gran Colombia. The proto-Liberal clusters had undertaken opposition to Bolívar's growing dictatorial and centralization efforts. It was the Venezuelan resentment of being steered from Bogotá that brought the Liberator back from Peru in 1826. Furthermore, Santander was no longer an obedient partner, but a challenging figure with his own political ambitions. Back in Bogotá, Bolívar apparently solved his differences with Santander and then moved to Venezuela, where Páez was persuaded to remain within Gran Colombia. After returning to Bogotá in September 1827, Bolívar tried and failed to give Colombia a constitution similar to the ones created for Bolivia and Peru. Bolívar undertook dictatorial powers only to provoke an almost successful assassination plot that implicated Santander himself. Fourteen alleged conspirators were executed, and Santander was eventually exiled.

As soon as Bolívar had left Peru, his followers were overthrown. The neophyte regime claimed Ecuador as Peruvian territory and invaded it. Although the Peruvian armies were repelled, the nations that had been liberated by Bolívar were rapidly growing apart. Finally, in December 1829, Páez again withdrew Venezuela from Gran Colombia. Soon after, Ecuador also broke away. Disappointed and ill, Bolívar resigned in March 1830. On his way to self-banishment, the Liberator suddenly died in Santa Marta (Colombia), nine months later.

With Bolívar's demise and the departure of Venezuela and Ecuador from Gran Colombia, the republic emerged with the name of New Granada. After Santander's return from exile in 1832, the nation went through a period of constructive peace. One of his biggest tasks was settling the foreign debt, caused by the emancipatory wars and owed mostly to the British. Venezuela and Ecuador agreed to pay one half of the total debt, while New Granada assumed the other half. In his efforts to modernize the nation, Santander built institutions of higher learning, elementary schools, and introduced Jeremy Bentham's utilitarian philosophy in education. Although Santander cannot be labelled very easily as a Conservative or Liberal, he wanted to curb the Church's power while promoting a more secular society. This is, however, a struggle that engaged Conservatives and Liberals for most of their post-independence history. Perhaps no other Latin American nation compares with Colombia in its religious intensity. Even in the last decade of the second millennium, Colombians were the most frequent churchgoers in Latin America.

Colombia has been further fragmented by its awkward geography of mountains, jungles and valleys, which kept the provinces as isolated from the outside world as from one another. Yet, the struggles between those who wanted regional autonomy and those who favored a centralized republic were not mere expressions of self-interest and search for power. It is in Colombia where ideology, passions and doctrines played a greater role than in most places of the then contemporary Latin America. Ideologies and images became bloody issues in the internecine-armed confrontations. If Central America is the land of "generals," Colombia belongs to the "doctores." Perhaps, it can be noted that they composed beautiful poems, liked to speak Spanish with Castillian purity, and debated all philosophical themes, but in real life the "doctores" were just as bloody as if not worse than, the "generals." The Colombian poet María Mercedes Carranza claimed that this suffering nation "could mitigate its pain and perhaps cure itself with the effects of poetry."

When independence came, Colombia was about 90% rural. The best lands were held by the white or nearly white latifundists. On the haciendas the labor force was a combination of sharecroppers, renters, day workers and temporary help contracted on different conditions. The debt peonage of other Andean countries and the black slavery of Venezuelan cocoa plantations were rare in the Colombian labor systems. Colombia was from the outset the most Mestizo country of the Andean region. *Resguardos* (communal ethnic lands) were not as important as in Peru or Bolivia since Indians constituted less than 25% of the population, most of them living in Boyacá, Cundinamarca and the Southwest. Due to the Free Birth Law of 1821 and sales to Peru, black slaves were almost nonexistent thirty years later when slavery became completely abolished. In the end, only 20,000 black slaves could be liberated. Most slaves worked in the western gold mines and the Caucan sugar plantations. There were numerous small farmers, especially in the northwestern (Antioquia) and northeastern regions of the nation;

together with the Indian communities, they accounted for the production of most of the food crops.[5]

The 1840s were times of proto-Conservative ascendancy and prosperity brought by tobacco cultivation for export. This decade witnessed the rise of the ubiquitous General Tomás C. de Mosquera, who served as a Conservative president from 1845 to 1849. As a hero of the emancipatory wars and oligarch, he remained in the background after his term expired. This *caudillo* was a nightmare that haunted both Conservatives and Liberals alike. The first Mosquera administration was a time of enlightened despotism. Technological education was supported, and geographical surveys of natural resources were conducted. Great efforts were made to modernize the nation and its transportation system. When Mosquera's first term was over, the nation was agitated by a Liberal revival and the European revolutions of 1848-1849. As in France, many Colombians were concerned with libertarian and socialistic ideals. Intellectuals, artisans, shopkeepers and students created "democratic clubs." When it came time to choose a successor for Mosquera, the Congress found itself under pressure by agitators from the galleries and the street mobs who demanded the election of a Liberal president. Fearing for their lives, the congressmen elected the populist Liberal José Hilario López.

With the rise of the Liberals to power, drastic anti-clerical legislation was enforced. Church courts and the tithes were abolished. Separation of Church and state, religious toleration and divorce were legalized. The Archbishop, the Jesuits and many priests were exiled. In the libertarian and socialistic spirit of radical Liberalism, black slavery and the death penalty were abolished. But afterwards, radical Liberalism was gradually co-opted by the ruling classes. In exchange, Liberalism supported a mixture of seigniorial and bourgeois social dominance. Except for the period between 1857 and 1861, the Liberals ruled until 1885, when a civil war drove them from power until 1930.

Colombia has always been a difficult country to govern regardless of which party controlled the presidency. Under the second Mosquera presidency (1861-64), the most ultra-Liberal constitution of 1863 was created. It sanctioned a federal republic known as the United States of Colombia. No other contemporary Latin American *magna carta* granted so many sovereign and individual rights to its provinces and citizens. The fear of dictatorship and the patriarchal Mosquera had led the constitutional drafters to sanction a two-year presidential term without possibility for immediate reelection.

The Liberal constitution and program promoted instability. Anarchic conditions fostered within the Liberal party a movement known as the *Regeneración*, led by Rafael Núñez. The *Regenerador* became president for a second time in 1884. This time, he became the advocate of strong centralized rule and rejected the radicalism and anti-clericalism of the Liberals. With the help of the Conservatives, he pushed aside his Liberal partners and gave the nation a Conservative constitution, which lasted until 1991. The former position of the Church was restored, and reconciliatory Concordats between Colombia and the Vatican were signed. Directly or indirectly, Núñez ruled until his death in 1894. By the time of the Regenerator's death, the Conservatives had taken firm control. Only the world's economic depression of the 1930s would bring them down. But the Liberals did not give up without bloodshed, and as the turn of the century came, they made their last effort to regain power through the "War of the One Thousand Days." Some historians have claimed that it was the bloodiest Latin American war of the nineteenth century.

As the last third of the nineteenth century began, the nation's first export crop collapsed. Colombian tobacco was driven out of competition by cheaper brands from Japan, then available in the international market. Colombian planters shifted for a while to indigo production, but the crop that became king was coffee. The Colombian soils and mountainous topography were perfectly suited for the production of the highest quality coffee beans in the world. In 1991, the value of Colombian coffee even surpassed Brazil's larger coffee production. Although the biggest beneficiaries of coffee cultivation were the landed elites, small producers also benefited.

In the aftermath of the "War of the Thousand Days" (1899-

1903), in which approximately 100,000 people were killed, the Liberals were granted some minority representation until they gained control of the government in 1930. Although this civil war led to a Conservative-Liberal rapprochement, only five months after internal peace had arrived, the nation was traumatized by the American-sponsored independence of its Panamanian province. It was not until 1922 that American-Colombian relations were normalized, after the United States paid 25 million dollars in exchange for Colombian recognition of Panamanian independence. The settlement of the dispute opened the gates for American investments. During the 1920s, Americans invested approximately two billion dollars in government bonds, mining, oil, banking, agriculture and industry. This decade of foreign and local entrepreneurial activity was known as the "Dance of the Millions." The 1920s were times of dramatic economic dynamism and prosperity for the local elites and their foreign partners. The United States became Colombia's leading exporter and importer. Coffee, bananas, sugar, rubber, gold, lead, platinum and emeralds flowed to the United States. But coffee remained the nation's biggest source of foreign income.

With the advent of the Great Depression, political and economic crisis reached Colombia. The Liberals were elected in 1930, and they ruled for the next sixteen years. The Great Depression was short-lived in Colombia. In the meanwhile, the Liberals briefly experimented with government-financed jobs and projects. Some sort of agrarian reform was actually enacted. The local economic depression was brief, because there was a high demand for Colombian exports. With foreign supplies of industrial goods curtailed, the pace of import-substitution was accelerated, especially in Antioquia.

By the end of World War II, Colombia experienced grass-roots political agitation in the urban and rural areas. A powerful left-wing sector within the Liberal party had emerged under the charismatic leadership of the Mestizo Jorge E. Gaitán. Gaitán and *Gaitanismo* challenged the oligarchy and the rule of the two-party system. From the mid nineteenth century, the Colombian oligarchy had reduced its internal power struggles to Liberal and Conservative politics. *Gaitanismo* demanded "real democracy" and social justice.[6]

Gaitán's multi-class movement had the support of the labor unions, Communists and socialists. A "Red Scare" divided the Liberals, resulting in the election of the Conservative Mariano Ospina Pérez in 1946. The return of the Conservatives to the presidency in alliance with right-wing Liberals brought a new momentum in political polarization and leftist defiance.

While the Inter-American Conference was meeting, Gaitán was shot in broad daylight in downtown Bogotá on April 9, 1948. A suspected assassin was immediately cut to pieces by the enraged bystanders. A violent rampage by Gaitán's followers and others plagued the capital city for several days. This upheaval became known as the *bogotazo*. Although nobody officially knows who ordered the death of Gaitán, the oligarchy with its allies, clients and employees brutally repressed Gaitan's followers in the aftermath of the *bogotazo*. The *bogotazo* marks the official beginning of a chronic civil war, which in the following decade claimed at least 200,000 lives. At the outset, it was a civil war between Conservatives and Liberals, but the hostilities soon degenerated into a merciless genocide which bypassed political ideology or class warfare. Over two million peasants fled the rural terrorism to swell the urban slums. This tragic period has been christened the *Violencia*. However, the massacre of peasants started before Gaitán was murdered.

Under martial laws, reactionary right-wingers were strengthened, and in the elections of 1948 the unopposed Conservative candidate Laureano Gómez was elected. In the same year, the adolescent peasant Pedro Marín (1932-2008) founded the oldest Latin American guerrilla force in reaction to the repression by the landed oligarchy. His guerrillas eventually became the FARC (Fuerzas Armadas Revolucionarias de Colombia). In due course, the FARC developed as the armed branch of the local communist party, which was under Soviet influence. Gómez was a strong admirer of Spanish fascism; Colombians called him "the monster." His government gathered the most reactionary forces in a holy crusade against Communism. "Gómez's life spanned the era in which Colombian society became increasingly individualized and violent."[7] Gómez's struggle against Communism was manifested in punitive actions against local leftists and Colombian foreign policy as well. Colombia became the only Latin American nation that sent troops to fight on the side of the United States in Korea.

When Gómez could no longer manage his presidential duties because of quasi-paranoia and other health disorders, he was deposed by General Gustavo Rojas Pinilla on June 13, 1953. Rojas Pinilla's populist efforts to extend his military dictatorship brought reconciliation between the Conservative and Liberal "doctores" in 1957. Thenceforth, the National Front was created. This coalition provided for alternating the presidency as well as executive appointments between the two parties every four years until 1978. Such a political arrangement survived until the rise of Alvaro Uribe. It succeeded in containing the struggle for grass-roots social reform. The National Front agreement also left Colombia with unresolved socio-economic problems that still haunt the nation. Nowhere in Latin America had the Liberal-Conservative power monopoly reached the sophisticated levels of Colombian politics and pedigree. For example, in 1974, the three leading presidential candidates were children of former presidents. Indeed, the Liberal-Conservative party-politics was more the exquisite result of a hereditary cultural tradition than class conflicts or democratic institutions.

Since the late 1940s, Colombia has been ruled by an intermittent state of siege, extra-judicial executions, and with the most apathetic electorate in Latin America. Guerrilla warfare, urban terrorism and violence are still rampant despite amnesties and treaties. Colombian cities are probably the most crime-ridden in Latin America. In 1986, the greatest Colombian cause of death was homicide. Nowhere in Latin America is the sight of destitute children (*gamines*) as pathetic as in Colombia. By the end of the twentieth century, six children were killed by para-military and criminal violence every day. It was the biggest number in Latin America. Yet Colombia is a mineral and oil-rich country, which is also endowed with abundant fertile soils that produce bananas, coca-leaves, coffee, cotton, flowers, marijuana, opium, sugar and tobacco. But many of these lands are fiercely and unabatedly disputed.

Although Colombia has developed a significant light industry, over 70% of its official foreign income still comes from coffee. Behind the official economy, "informal" capitalism dynamically thrives on an illegal foreign income that probably surpasses the coffee earnings. Colombia has become the main artery and dealer of South American illegal drug exports. A "new rich" or "emergent" class has developed and, with ready cash in hand, is diversifying into legal enterprises. The legal economy grew by 6.8% in 2006.[8] A new "Dance of the Millions" based on the cocaine industry has begun. The drug traffic is a growing virus which has penetrated the most exclusive niches of Colombian society. The Colombian exotic garden of *cumbias* and "magic realism" has become the third most populous Latin American nation. Despite the "Medellín Cartel" and other cartels, most Colombians are law-abiding citizens who work hard for their daily bread. The Colombian struggle against poverty, ignorance, dependency and underdevelopment has a genuine touch of collective genius.

The Ecuadorians

The province of Quito was coveted by both Colombia and Peru. In 1830, the Creole elites chose Bolívar's lieutenant, Venezuelan-born Juan J. Flores, as the *caudillo* to guarantee their interests and sovereignty. The neophyte national state located in the middle of the planet was christened the Republic of Ecuador. Flores proclaimed himself a Conservative. Although the great majority of Ecuadorians were Amerindians, the Indian tribute was maintained until 1857. Like in Peru and Bolivia, the maintenance of the Indian tribute made the excluded "citizens" the only payers of personal taxes. In addition to the Liberal-Conservative struggles, the most significant source of instability was the regional conflict between Quito and coastal Guayaquil. The antagonism between both cities came to typify the *caudillismo* and regionalism which has characterized most Ecuadorian political history in the post-independence period. Flores overcame this difficulty by agreeing to alternate the presidential office with the Liberal Vicente Rocafuerte from

Guayaquil. The arrangement was arbitrarily terminated by Flores when he completed his second presidency.

The Liberals revolted and forced Flores to resign in 1845. For the next fifteen years, the Liberals were not very successful in holding power or maintaining stability. The efforts to secularize society were convulsive. Furthermore, the republic was threatened by Spanish efforts of re-conquest as well as Peruvian invasions. But by 1860, Flores and the Conservatives captured Guayaquil. The death of the old *caudillo* brought his young protégé Gabriel García Moreno to the presidency the following year. This was the return of Conservative rule, which lasted until 1895. But ideologically, García Moreno promoted a Catholic modernity. He was a white aristocrat from Quito who had been educated at the University of Paris and cultivated the reputation of a towering genius for himself.

Until his death, García Moreno was the most dominant political force in the nation. Upon his return to Ecuador, he became a science professor and chancellor of Quito University. Like the illiterate Rafael Carrera from Guatemala, the intellectual García Moreno was a relentless Catholic fanatic. He was determined to eliminate the anti-clerical Liberal virus. This *caudillo* claimed to be a man of God and his persecutions were in God's name. The nation was officially dedicated to the Sacred Heart of Jesus, and a very close alliance with the Vatican was inaugurated. The Jesuits returned from exile, and together with other religious orders overhauled the entire educational system in order to create the most authoritarian theocracy of the Americas. García Moreno's fear that the nation would be contaminated by the Western world led him to close Ecuadorian borders in the style of Paraguay's José de Francia. As in Paraguay, the drastic elimination of foreign economic penetration allowed the local industries to flourish. However, political stability and native industrial development were accompanied by a nearly insane repression of Liberals. García Moreno's policies also engendered strong passions among young Liberals who conspired against and finally butchered the tyrant in 1875.

With García Moreno's death, anti-clericalism was tempered.

The Liberals, however, continued to conspire. Finally, by revolt in 1895, the Liberals under the leadership of General Eloy Alfaro were brought to power. Alfaro refused to pay the foreign debt and most extraordinarily negotiated a moratorium with British creditors. For the next fifteen years, this strong man controlled the nation, occupying the presidency from 1895 to 1901 and again from 1906 to 1911. The following year, Alfaro was assassinated in a style reminiscent of García Moreno's death, but the Liberals held the government until 1925. Influenced by the writings of the Ecuadorian philosopher Juan Montalvo (1832-89), the Liberals began the gradual secularization of society. The Liberal plans included efforts to modernize and end the protracted national isolation. Because of international demand, cacao became the most successful earner of foreign exchange; its export value increased by more than 700% from 1870 to 1920.[9] Since most cocoa was produced in the coastal region, the conflict between the central government and Guayaquil intensified. The latter collected the export taxes while the former consumed and distributed the revenues according to its own priorities.[10] By the turn of the nineteenth century, Ecuadorian economic growth remained relatively lethargic. Ecuador was among the most backward countries of the continent.

As exports fell during the 1920s, the Ecuadorian economy fell into deep crisis. The demands for the development of internal markets[11] remained as mere projects and desperate fantasies. Like in most of Latin America, the Ecuadorian post-World War I period was affected by labor and leftist agitation. The massacre of some 2,000 workers and their families in the streets of Guayaquil (November 15, 1922) was the climax of the confrontational times. In 1924, the Liberal intellectual Gonzálo Córdoba was elected to a four-year presidential term with leftist and labor support. His government intended to reduce the power of the landed aristocracy as well as guarantee Labor's rights and provide land reform and basic social services. Córdoba's "radicalism" alarmed the most reactionary elite, and in less than a year his "chaotic" government was overthrown by a "progressive" military coup.

With the advent of the Great Depression, the world demand for cacao decreased, and Ecuadorian socio-political unrest gained new momentum. During the economic crisis, the rise of the populist Dr. José M. Velasco Ibarra became the most outstanding political phenomenon for the ensuing four decades. Between 1934 and 1972, he was elected to the presidency five times. Likewise, all his short-lived administrations were terminated by military coups. Velasco Ibarra was a distinguished jurist from the traditional elite who began his political career as a Conservative. However, Velasco Ibarra attempted to modernize society and contain social pressures through policies that included collaboration with Communists, socialists and organized labor. His style and policies had striking similarities with those of the Brazilian Getulio Vargas and the Argentinean Juan D. Perón. Velasco Ibarra became the most vibrant articulator of Ecuadorian nationalism, neutralist foreign policy and anti-Yankee feelings. Velasco Ibarra's foreign policies represented an unsuccessful attempt by a small Latin American nation, which envisioned a "third alternative." Latin American neutralism without Yankee sponsorship has been a restricted illusion.

The Ecuadorian nationalism of the Velasco Ibarra era has been characterized not only by its anti-Americanism but its anti-Peruvianism as well. A boundary conflict dating back to the immediate post-independence period climaxed in the Peruvian-Ecuadorian War of 1941. After the Peruvian army reached the outskirts of Quito, the United States mediated. As the result of the American mediation, a peace treaty was signed in Rio de Janeiro (1942) by which Ecuador relinquished its claims to the Amazonian region.[12] Ecuadorian claims to the Amazonian region have persisted, and they have constituted an intermittent source of tensions between the two Andean nations. Much of Velasco Ibarra's political success was based on his demagogic rhetoric that promised to recover the fatherland's lost territories.

Velasco Ibarra's last government was plagued by instability, leftist agitation and fears of the traditional aristocracy that the entire fabric of society was in danger. As so often happened, the Army intervened and overthrew the most successful master spinner of Ecuadorian politics in 1972. Unlike previous military coups, this

170

time the Army pledged to remain in power and bring about revolutionary social transformations. The new junta, like its Peruvian counterpart, supposedly represented the nationalist and "leftist military." But like all the Latin American leftist military movements, they began in conspiracy and were ended by conspiracy. Movements such as the leftist military, which began in Peru in 1968, were the victims of counter coups by officers themselves.

After much civilian pressure and the proddings of the United States, the Army was persuaded to permit free elections. In 1979, the civilian populist Jaime Roldós, who represented the Concentration of Popular Forces (CFP), was inaugurated after a free election in which illiterates were allowed to vote for the first time. Ideologically, the CFP was aligned with European and Latin American Christian Democracy. The Communists and other leftist parties were legalized and granted minority status. Political pluralism and civilian governments became the style of oligarchic control in the little republic. Despite the undemocratic social structure, Ecuadorian Indians have been able to negotiate on their own terms better than in any other Andean nation.[13]

Ecuador continues as an exporter of agricultural products such as bananas, coffee, rice and cacao. Ecuador modernized its underdevelopment by becoming the largest producer of bananas in the world. Alas, most Ecuadorian bananas, like those from Latin America, are patronized by companies based in the United States. Since 1972, Ecuador has become a major oil producer. The new oil income revitalized state finances and the incipient light industry. But the fact remains that the nation's newly found oil wealth has primarily benefited the ruling elites and their foreign partners. Ecuador is also a transit route and staging post in the Andean cocaine industry. Ecuador had very close economic and military links with the United States. Until the rise of Rafael Correa, it did not matter whether the Ecuadorian Left or Right won in local elections; as in Central America, the United States claims geopolitical interests in Ecuador. Correa's expulsion of the American naval base from Manta affects the United States' global network of geopolitical-military assets.

From Silver to Coca

During most of the colonial period, the fabulously silver-rich Alto Peru (Bolivia) had been a province in the Peruvian viceroyalty. From 1776 to 1811, Alto Peru was incorporated into the viceroyalty of La Plata. In the wake of the nineteenth century, Peru and Argentina sought to control the Bolivian elites, but they resented Spanish rule just as much as interference by their South American big neighbors. The Bolivian elites could not settle for anything less than complete independence. When Bolívar's armies consummated Peruvian independence, they pursued their liberating mission into Alto Peru under the command of the Venezuelan Antonio José Sucre. The local leaders, in gratitude and in tactical convenience, renamed their land as the Republic of Bolívar and placed themselves under the Liberator's protection by electing him president for life. An honor of this nature could not, of course, be rejected by the man who was to lead the Federation of the Andes. In a gala reminiscent of those of Roman emperors, the hero was welcomed in the new republic. He gave the neophyte Bolivians eloquent speeches and a constitution that was also adopted by Peru; it was to serve as a model for the other Andean nations. Installing General Sucre as his vice president, Bolívar left Bolivia in early 1826. But as the plans for the Federation of the Andes began to crumble, the Bolivians became hostile to Sucre and his foreign soldiers. The Bolivian elites and the Church resented the financial burden of Sucre's army; an unsuccessful attempt on his life was made. Disenchanted and unable to stop the oncoming anarchy, Sucre left the country in 1828.

With the departure of Sucre, the quarrelsome national assembly eventually chose General Andrés de Santa Cruz as president. He was a very capable and honest Mestizo who had become a hero during the emancipatory wars. By benevolent dictatorship he ruled almost peacefully. Santa Cruz gave his country a new constitution, reorganized the administrative and tax systems, built schools and expanded higher education. Unfortunately, Santa Cruz was a man of great dreams who wanted to revive the glories of the past. By 1836, he had succeeded in organizing the Peruvian-Bolivian Confederation, and he expected Ecuador to join the alliance later on. The confederation's neighbors were, of course, displeased with the neophyte realm. A Chilean expedition invaded and virtually annihilated Santa Cruz's army by 1839. In defeat, his authority was reproached, and he fled to Europe. With his departure, the Peruvian-Bolivian Confederation disintegrated. Bolivia fell into the hands of less capable *caudillos* while the *Criollo* elite launched a final assault on the Indian community lands, which until 1846 still sustained 51% of the total population. The Indian tribute was kept until the 1870s. Although the Bolivian hacienda expanded at the Indians' expense in the Cochabamba province, it also became fragmented due to the abolition of entails (*mayorazgo*), land sales, and ecological changes. The rise of numerous small landholders in Cochabamba is intimately related to such a process.[14]

Perhaps the worst *caudillo* to rule Bolivia during the nineteenth century was Mariano Melgarejo (1818-71), who presided over the nation from 1864 to 1871. This frightening Mestizo general rose to power through violence and ruled with brutality. The "barbarian caudillo" was the very incarnation of brute violence. From the 1850s onwards, Bolivia was plagued by urban and rural unrest. The Bolivian mines, which once upon a time inundated Europe with silver, were often deserted. It was not until 1872 that silver production reached pre-independence levels, and then under British control. There were no factories, and agricultural production provided only for local subsistence needs. In addition, the educated elites of the two biggest cities, Liberal La Paz and Conservative Sucre, were constantly struggling to impose their hegemony upon the nation. The local oligarchies felt that order was necessary, and the alcoholic Melgarejo was tough enough to promote free trade and eliminate corporatist ownership. He was popular with the soldiers, and the rest were too intimidated to challenge the self-proclaimed "most illustrious man of the century."

Frequently, Melgarejo invited his friends to the presidential palace for drinking parties, which could end in fistfights, shooting duels, and casualties. On one occasion, Melgarejo, after being annoyed by the British ambassador, tied him on a donkey to be spat at and ridiculed through the streets of La Paz. After this outrageous insult, it is reported that Queen Victoria crossed Bolivia off the map, exclaiming, "Bolivia no longer exists." But Melgarejo did bring some prosperity to himself and his followers by selling Indian communal lands, granting mining concessions to foreigners and nitrate privileges to Chileans. Melgarejo's tyranny and volcanic personality inspired conspiracies from the least expected quarters. After the dictator tried to stop a rebellion, he escaped to Peru where an assassin's bullets killed him in 1871. The tyrant's downfall was followed by a sequence of less spectacular *caudillos*. Like their Peruvian counterparts, they blundered when dealing with the Chilean and British ambitions to the nitrate lands. With less glory than their Peruvian allies, the Bolivians were defeated, and their homeland was converted into an isolated country without a seacoast.

In the War of the Pacific's aftermath, the Conservative oligarchy overthrew the military (1884). A period of civilian administration was started in which the Conservatives ruled until 1899. Conservative power was based in Sucre, the former center of Spanish colonization. It was led by a faction known as *Constitucionalistas* for their avowed loyalty to constitutional principles. Prosperity had returned to the elites by the reopening of silver mines and the discoveries of lead, copper and tin deposits. Rubber was also being exploited in the Bolivian Amazonian region. Roads and railroads were built, including the Oruro-Antofagasta line, which gave Bolivia an outlet to the Pacific through Chile.

When the Conservatives tried to make Sucre the nation's permanent capital in 1899, they triggered a Liberal and Indian revolt. In the aftermath of the War of the Pacific, most community Indians had lost their lands. They expected some justice and compensation. After the Liberals captured the government, they betrayed their Indian allies. The Indians were savagely repressed and thereafter further marginalized from power. Liberals and Republicans controlled the presidency for the following three decades, but the mining oligarchy that emerged after the War of the Pacific called the shots.

The first third of the twentieth century was characterized by dramatic growth in tin mining. The Patiño and Aramayo families, in alliance with English, American and Argentinean partners, became the greatest beneficiaries. With the advent of the Great Depression, political and economic crisis also reached Bolivia. In June 1930, the last Republican president, Hernando Siles, was overthrown in a military coup. During the 1930s, the tempo of military coups increased due to a socio-economic crisis and the intermittent border dispute with Paraguay. The so-called "Chaco War" was officially fought between 1932 and 1935, but from the late 1920s on border skirmishes were periodic occurrences. The great dispute was over the 1,000,000 square miles of territory in the Gran Chaco, which, although uninhabited, was reputed to be rich in oil. After at least 52,000 Bolivians and 36,000 Paraguayans were killed in action, Argentina mediated and persuaded the belligerents to sign a peace treaty in which Paraguay gained most of the disputed territory. Ironically, with the passing of time, geologists realized that the hydrocarbons were located in the territories left to Bolivia.

In the Bolivian defeat's aftermath, a group of nationalist officers and civilians (The Chaco Generation) led by Colonel Germán Busch took the government. They advocated for the nationalization of the mining industry and a socialist state. In an effort to neutralize American and British influence, this nationalist generation cultivated the goodwill of Nazi Germany. However, in August 1939, it was officially announced that Busch had committed suicide. The myth still prevails that the mining oligarchy ordered the death of the young hero. Busch's successors toned down their anti-British and anti-American policies and agreed to supply them with all the lead, copper, tungsten, tin and silver needed for the war effort against Germany.

Busch's followers continued to organize, agitate and conspire under the leadership of Dr. Victor Paz Estenssoro. Paz Estenssoro was a distinguished jurist who organized the MNR (National Revolutionary Movement). From 1943 to 1946, the MNR played a significant role in the government of General Guadalberto Villaroel. In the aftermath of World War II, falling prices for Bolivian minerals brought economic crisis and a chance for reactionary officers to crush the Villaroel regime. The MNR was also driven underground, but through revolution it captured the government in April 1952. The MNR was a multi-class coalition of reformers, nationalists and Marxists. The MNR instituted universal suffrage and replaced the Army with a workers' militia. The MNR nationalized the mining industry and conducted a radical agrarian reform that divided two thirds of the arable land among the peasants. Prior to the MNR's revolution, 6% owned 92% of the cultivated lands. However, the agrarian reform divided the land in the western region and bypassed the east. The outcome eventually resulted in *minifundios* in the former and agribusiness in the latter.

Paz Estenssoro's first presidential year was a time of revolutionary social change, but mineral exports depended on foreign trains, ships and refineries for reaching the international market. In June 1953, Milton Eisenhower, the brother of the American president, visited Paz Estenssoro and gave him an ultimatum and an alternative. In exchange for financial aid and the avoidance of an economic blockade, Bolivia was to welcome foreign investors, "free enterprise" and an American military mission to train the Bolivian army. It was an offer that Paz Estenssoro could not refuse. For the ensuing seven years, Bolivia was granted more economic aid (over 150 million dollars) than any Latin American nation. Furthermore, Bolivia was specifically prohibited from accepting economic aid from Communist countries.[15] The professional army was modernized with the latest military gadgets, while the workers' militia kept its antiquated rifles. American technical experts and military advisors poured into Bolivia while American funds were used to compensate dispossessed property owners. Americans were allowed to infiltrate the Army's command structure and promote "counterinsurgency" training.[16]

Bolivia inherited a dilapidated mining industry which had seen its best days during World War II, when the Far Eastern mines were under Japanese control. The profits from cheap minerals and cheap labor had left Bolivia long ago. The biggest "Tin Baron," Simón Patiño, himself left Bolivia in 1943, and never returned. His family settled in the United States and Europe, and it remains one of the richest clans in the world. Patiño's oldest son diversified the family's assets with the help of the Rothchild clan, in which he became a partner through business and marriage. But the Patiños are not different from many rich emigrants that the Bolivian mines have produced throughout their history. When the booms were over, they left with their money to live somewhere else.

The MNR remained in the government by constitutional means until 1964, when the Army overthrew it. Manipulated elections and coups did not stop in the fragmented Bolivian society and geography. During the sixties, the tempo of guerrilla warfare was accelerated throughout Latin America and Bolivia. Ché Guevara's capture, and his summary execution on October 9, 1967, became one of the most successful "counterinsurgency" victories for the Bolivian army and its American advisers. From 1970 to 1971, the leftist and nationalist General José Torres attempted to bring revolutionary changes in collaboration with Marxist groups and labor unions, but he was also overthrown by a military conspiracy. In July 1980, the 190th military coup since independence occurred when the president-elect, Hernán Siles Suazo, was on the brink of being inaugurated. Siles Suazo had organized a coalition government that included leftist members of the MNR, Marxists and labor groups.

Unstable international prices, obsolete equipment and managerial corruption yielded chronic inefficiency and indebtedness in the mining industry. Bolivia has become an exporter of oil, natural gas and agricultural products to Brazil and Argentina. Cocaine production had become the most booming business of the Bolivian informal economy. The drug industry had also created a generation of "new rich." In fact, the 190th military coup led by General Luis García Mesa (1980-81), was conducted with open financial support and connivance of the cocaine mafias. The "cocaine generals" lasted less than a year, but the war on drugs has not yet been won due to internal and international interests. It is a capitalist enterprise of the worst kind.

The "drug cartels" are not the only ones who have benefited

from the Andean cocaine boom. The aggregate impact goes beyond the region, transit routes or staging-posts. Alternative development and crop-substitution have been ritualistically underfunded, and, perhaps, misunderstood by the United States. As former Peruvian President Alberto Fujimori (1990-2000) noted: The cocaine economy is "a problem which has been imposed on us from abroad, because the production of coca and its transformation into cocaine are a consequence of the demand in foreign markets, particularly the United States."[17] From 1982 until the rise of the Amerindian Evo Morales, the Bolivian ritual elections in which rightist and leftist elites collaborated and compromised returned. Under neo-liberalism, the formal and informal economies experienced a new dynamism, which benefited mostly the local elites and their foreign partners. Nevertheless, the majority of the 6.4 million Bolivians remained among the poorest in Latin America. Of the 2.7 million rural Indians, 97% barely survived at the "poverty-level" by the end of the twentieth century.

The Peruvian Military Society

Although the independence of Peru was proclaimed in 1821, the emancipatory struggle was not completed until Bolívar's victory over the royalist forces in Ayacucho, three and a half years later. Finally, the last Spanish military stronghold in South America was crushed. Bolívar's preoccupation with his Federation of the Andes led him to create laws and institutions in Peru and Alto Peru that would serve as prototypes for his project. Catholicism remained as the official religion, but the Liberal Spanish laws of 1812 were kept. The Bolivian constitution of 1825, which provided for a life-long presidential term, was extended to Peru one year later. The Congress was to assist the Executive on legislative matters and the supervision of educational and moral standards. Although the indigenous ethnic groups constituted the overwhelming majority of the population, they had become legally invisible. After the Andean revolts of the 1780s, the Spanish crown had eliminated Indian intellectuals, and systematically curtailed the opportunities to educate natives. Thus, at the birth of the republic, there were no longer Indian leaders and sages who could force the *Criollo* elites to negotiate ethnic rights. The Indian tribute and black slavery prevailed until mid-nineteenth century. In the republic that excluded and discriminated Iagainst ndians, they were the only ones who paid personal taxes. Indeed, the socio-economic and ethno-cultural structures were extremely unfavorable for the emergence of a political democracy.

After being elected president, Bolívar placed his vice president in charge and left for Gran Colombia. Only four months after Bolívar's departure, his supporters were overthrown, and then the new regime attempted to reconquer the claimed colonial provinces of Quito and Alto Peru. During the first decades after independence, there was a frustrating obsession among the local elites with bringing those former provinces within the orbit of the Peruvian national state. Such a struggle was rejected by Ecuadorian and Bolivian regionalism, as well as by Colombian and Chilean fears of a Peruvian super power.

No other country in the Americas has had the military tradition that has plagued Peruvian history. While in post-independence Spanish America conflicts raged between Conservatives and Liberals, in Peru the disputes engaged militarists and *Civilistas* (those favoring civilian rule). To be sure, there were civilians and military who called themselves Conservatives and Liberals. The militarist age was begun by former veterans from the emancipatory wars and officers of the Spanish royal army. Although some officers had certain inclinations to acquaint themselves with the contemporary intellectual currents, on the whole, they were dull men without issues except maintaining life as it had been during colonial times.

After independence remained a lingering vice-regal arrogance among the ruling elites. The military leaders maintained their power monopoly by a series of alliances with the regional oligarchies. However, the system was based on constitutional and legal subtleties that provided for a republic based on free and democratic elections. On balance, the military prevented demagogues from establishing a monarchy, a theocracy or the carnage that characterized the Liberal-Conservative struggles in Mexico or Colombia. When the military handed the government over to the civilians for the first time in 1872, ecclesiastical courts, the tithes and holding lands in *mortmain* had been terminated. But religious freedom and the separation of Church and state had not been sanctioned.

One general who deserves special attention is the much revered national hero Ramón Castilla (1797-1867). He ruled as president on two occasions (1845-51, 1855-60). He was a Mestizo and self-educated officer of plebeian origins who had achieved distinction in the emancipatory campaigns. Castilla ruled during prosperous times brought about by guano exports.[18] Historiographic assertions have noted that this *caudillo* was an honest man who expected his subalterns to have similar scruples. With the newly acquired revenues, the debt of the independence war was paid to the British, and new equipment was bought from England for the Army and Navy. Castilla also used the new fiscal revenues to build schools, roads, harbors, bridges, aqueducts and one of the first South American railroads. He encouraged European immigration, but only a few Chinese indentured workers were lured to Peru. Under Liberal pressure, black slavery and the Indian tribute were abolished. Although personally anti-clerical, he made only modest efforts to challenge the Church. Castilla was fearful of the rampages caused by the Liberal-Conservative struggles in other Spanish American countries. Castilla believed in "law and order" and before leaving the presidency, a new constitution was promulgated that remained in force for the next sixty years.

The post-Castilla decade was a period of extravagant government spending in infrastructure for the export market. The construction of the highest and most expensive railroad in the world (Lima—La Oroya) was begun.[19] Other transportation facilities and public works were being undertaken at exaggerated costs. A new boom was beginning to take place in the nitrate-bearing deserts of southern Peru. It was like a "gold rush" with local and foreign entrepreneurs prospecting in a previously ignored region. Until the War of the Pacific (1879-83), Peru became the world's biggest nitrate producer and exporter. The 1860s were also times of waste, corruption and heavy borrowing from foreigners.

By 1869, the government regarded the public debt as unmanageable, and it granted to the French-Jewish merchant Auguste Dreyfus the exclusive right to market guano abroad. In exchange, Dreyfus would service the consolidated foreign debts of the government. This arrangement worked well only for a few years, when guano prices were high. It later caused the nation very serious regrets. The extravagant decade was further complicated by Spanish efforts to reconquer Ecuador, Chile and Peru, whose ports were blockaded and bombarded. Such actions came in the wake of new European expansionism in the Third World and Latin America. On this occasion, these three South American nations collaborated and repelled the Spanish aggression. Moreover, Peru retaliated against Spain by recognizing and aiding the Cuban exile government operating in New York.

In 1872, the first *Civilista* president, Manuel Pardo, was inaugurated after a tumultuous election in which several civilians and military officers were assassinated, including the outgoing president José Balta. Pardo came from one of the most illustrious and affluent white families. The Civilistas had a national project for economic and political modernization along the contemporary Western visions of progress. The Civilista modernization included railroad construction, tax reforms, administrative professionalization, educational promotion and agriculture for export. Pardo believed that the state, civil society and local private capital were indispensable for the realization of the Peruvian national state. But Pardo faced revolts and assassination attempts by militarists. In response, the Civilistas reduced the armed forces and prevented their modernization.

The Civilistas could hardly have chosen a worse moment for reducing military expenses because an armed conflict with Chile over the nitrate region was already imminent. The Civilista nationalization of the nitrates in the southern frontier and its "secret" alliance with Bolivia made Peru vulnerable to powerful foreign interests. Civilista rule was further tarnished by the sudden fall of the guano prices in the international market. Dreyfus was unable to raise money in Peru or abroad, and his financial schemes caused very much local antagonism. By late 1875, the nation suspended payment on most of its foreign debts.

In the midst of financial crisis, the military returned to lead Peru into its biggest external war in postcolonial times.

Although the "War of the Pacific" may be easily blamed on Chilean expansionism, the Peruvian pseudo vice-royal delusions did not prevent the catastrophe. With the hope of replacing the diminishing guano income, the Peruvian government licensed American and French entrepreneurs to join local investors in prospecting the southern nitrate fields. However, the Chileans, under laissez-faire economic policies and with British financial interests, were already exploiting Bolivian nitrates. Furthermore, Peru "secretly" instigated Bolivia to curb the growth of Chilean holdings in Bolivian territory. When in late 1878 Bolivia tried to collect higher taxes on nitrate production, the Chilean companies protested and obtained military protection from their government. After Peru refused the Chilean demands to cancel its "secret" defense treaty with Bolivia, Chile declared war. By April 1879, Chile was at war with both Bolivia and Peru.

Peruvians and Bolivians were no match for the Chilean army, which had been training with German equipment for at least a decade prior to the war's outbreak. The most modern weapons of the world were put to use. Yet, it cannot be said that Chile was prepared for war, as some historians have claimed. The problem was that Bolivia and Peru were totally unprepared. In less than a year, the Bolivians were defeated and lost their seacoast. By January 1881, the Chileans captured Lima despite some heroic efforts to defend the capital. Thereafter, the nation was subjected to a brutal occupation. After futile and nearly suicidal attacks by some Peruvians to repel the aggressors, Peru signed the Peace of Ancón. Accordingly, Peru lost the nitrate provinces of Tarapacá in perpetuity and Tacna and Arica for at least ten years. The Chileans plundered whatever valuables could be hauled away, even the vine-stocks from Peruvian viniculture. The Peruvian elites had been abruptly awakened from their vice-royal delusions by the agony of defeat.

Barnes & Noble Booksellers #2932
395 Route 3 East
Clifton, NJ 07014
973-779-5500

STR:2932 REG:004 TRN:9873 CSHR:Lisa L

People's History of Latin America
  9781558765788   T1
  (1 @ 24.95)   24.95

Subtotal   24.95
Sales Tax T1 (6.875%)   1.72
TOTAL   26.67
CASH   40.00
CASH CHANGE   13.33-

A MEMBER WOULD HAVE SAVED   2.50

Thanks for shopping at
Barnes & Noble

101.44A   08/06/2017 11:00AM

CUSTOMER COPY

applicable warranty.

Returns or exchanges will not be permitted (i) after 14 days or without receipt or (ii) for product not carried by Barnes & Noble or Barnes & Noble.com.

Policy on receipt may appear in two sections.

Return Policy

With a sales receipt or Barnes & Noble.com packing slip, a full refund in the original form of payment will be issued from any Barnes & Noble Booksellers store for returns of undamaged NOOKs, new and unread books, and unopened and undamaged music CDs, DVDs, vinyl records, toys/games and audio books made within 14 days of purchase from a Barnes & Noble Booksellers store or Barnes & Noble.com with the below exceptions:

A store credit for the purchase price will be issued (i) for purchases made by check less than 7 days prior to the date of return, (ii) when a gift receipt is presented within 60 days of purchase, (iii) for textbooks, (iv) when the original tender is PayPal, or (v) for products purchased at Barnes & Noble College bookstores that are listed for sale in the Barnes & Noble Booksellers inventory management system.

Opened music CDs, DVDs, vinyl records, audio books may not be returned, and can be exchanged only for the same title and only if defective. NOOKS purchased from other retailers or seller are returnable only to the retailer or seller from which they are purchased, pursuant to such retailer's or seller's return policy. Magazines, newspapers, eBooks, digital downloads, and used books are not returnable or exchangeable. Defective NOOKs may be exchanged at the store in accordance with the applicable warranty.

Returns or exchanges will not be permitted (i) after 14 days or without receipt or (ii) for product not carried by Barnes & Noble or Barnes & Noble.com.

If anything was gained by Peru, it was those numerous heroes who today give names to streets, boulevards, monuments, institutions and other symbols that constitute Peruvian nationalism and identity. The war with Chile had its heroes and cowards, but the remembrance of heroism has had its official sponsors. It is interesting to note that during the naval campaigns, the Chileans discovered a much glorified young hero, the officer Arturo Prat, who, while boarding an enemy ship, leaped to his death with enough time to harangue his compatriots to fight for the fatherland. The Peruvians more than matched Prat's heroism through the young lieutenant Alfonso Ugarte, who, while protecting his flag from Chilean captors, also jumped from a high cliff to his death with sufficient time to incite his compatriots to save the national honor. Without tape recorders, movie cameras or impartial witnesses, the dramatic actions of both heroes have been used as patriotic examples in their own countries. However, to this day in Peru and Chile, it is an example of the popular "black humor" to note that the last words pronounced by their respective heroes were: "Don't push me!...etc...etc!"

In the defeat's aftermath, some rebellious Peruvian intellectuals began to question the national identity. The "Indian problem" came into discussion. The *Indianidad* was discovered by non-Indians and the hegemonic culture. For the first time, the nation was told that its strongest cultural and ethnic components were not Spanish but Indian. Local intellectuals brought the entire Peruvian territory, rather than Lima or the few Europeanized centers, into focus. The ideological roots of Peruvian *indigenismo* go back to this identity crisis. Furthermore, anarchist and syndicalist ideologies also made their appearance in the Peruvian territory.

After the "War of the Pacific", the Army in alliance with the Civilistas ruled for a decade. But in the midst of the national identity crisis, new political forces began to coalesce. In 1895, the patrician Nicolás de Piérola led a group of discontented army officers, Civilistas and the urban masses in a populist coalition known as the Democratic Party. Through revolution, Piérola defeated the Army. The charismatic Piérola had become a man of alleged democratic inclinations who also wanted to curtail oligarchic power. Piérola was the populist angel of the *ancien régime*. He granted voting rights to all literate male adults, and established direct electoral suffrage. Pierola was not a thief and died almost in poverty. However, during the three and a half decades after the war with Chile, the foundations of the contemporary oligarchic state were created in Peru.[20]

Piérola's administration brought freedom of the press, peace and prosperity for the local elites. By the turn of the nineteenth century, Peru had regained international credit by mortgaging its railroads through the Grace Contract (1890). British concessionaires had obtained control of the nation's mining centers and richest oil pools. Just as in the Brazilian Amazon basin, in the Peruvian jungle the extraction of rubber for export was harvesting large fortunes. Amazonian Indians were hunted down and virtually enslaved in the rubber collection. The northern Peruvian coast was transformed from diversified subsistence agriculture to a modernized sugar monoculture for export. Certainly, there was great dynamism in elitist local capitalism with foreign sponsorship. But the great majority of the nation's three million inhabitants lived in untold misery. At least 75% of them were Indians.

In 1919, the aristocrat Augusto B. Leguía returned to the presidency for a second time and remained in office for the ensuing eleven years. Leguía started his political career as a Civilista, and as such, he had been president from 1908 to 1912. After World War I, conflicts within the oligarchy allowed Leguía to organize an anti-Civilista coalition with grass-roots support. Once again in the presidency, when he was confronted by Civilista and leftist agitation, he opted for a quasi-corporatist dictatorship and right-wing populism. Leguía ruled as a *caudillo* in alliance with sectors of the traditional elite and the Church. The Church was liberated from the state patronage, and Leguía attempted to consecrate the fatherland to the Sacred Heart of Jesus. Moreover, the Church's economic power was left untouched. Leguía paid lip-service to the Indian culture and gave speeches in Quechua. Leguía attempted a modernization from above that favored the urban middle classes.

Leguía's aim was to create a "New Fatherland" of progress and order. With enforced political stability, American investments poured in unprecedented quantities and took the lead over British holdings. The public debt was also multiplied by more than ten times. Minerals, oil, cotton and sugar flowed out of the country in order to pay for the new foreign credits. In order to contain proletarian demands, Leguía instituted a system that provided for the arbitration of labor conflicts and accident insurance for workers. The insurance coverage for workers was operated by private companies with state subsidies. Leguía's biggest obsession was the construction of roads. He created a permanent labor corvée, which forced the unemployed and vagrants to work for minimum wages in road construction and other public projects. Males with full-time jobs were required to pay the salary of one day's work per month for their substitutes. Leguía's grandiose dreams were crushed by the Great Depression. Perhaps no other Latin American nation was affected as deeply by the Great Depression as Peru. In the midst of economic crisis, wholesale bankruptcies occurred. Acute social unrest caused the Army to overthrow the government in August 1930. For the next fifty years, the military became preponderant, ruling directly for a total of thirty years.

During Leguía's dictatorship, two grass-roots political movements developed under the surface of the official society. José Carlos Mariátegui led the Communists, while Haya De La Torre founded the Popular Revolutionary American Alliance (APRA). Both intended to take over the government by elections or by force. The latter conceived a populist multi-class and a nationalist alliance against the oligarchy and imperialism. Mariátegui advocated for the construction of Peruvian socialism based on its own reality. Mariátegui with Italian Antonio Gramsci, became the first two foreign theoretical critics of Bolshevik orthodoxy. The Peruvian historian Pablo Macera asserted that Peru was definitely the most advanced South American nation in political ideology during the late 1920s.[21] The APRA party developed a program for Peru and Latin America as well. At its outset, Aprismo captivated revolutionary support throughout the region. After the APRA attempted to take the government by a revolt in July 1932, it was violently persecuted and outlawed. Moreover, the indiscriminate execution of officers by the *Apristas* during the revolt brought the official military vow that the APRA would never be allowed to take the government. The ghost of that promise haunted the APRA until Alan García's first election (1985-90).

During World War II, the APRA leadership convinced the United States, as well as the Peruvian civilian elites, that the party had dropped its anti-American stance and radicalism. Without its own presidential candidate, the APRA was allowed to participate in the elections of 1945. The candidate favored by the Apristas, Dr. José L. Bustamante, won an overwhelming victory. Bustamante's reformist coalition granted the APRA a minority representation in the Cabinet. The Congress under the Aprista majority pushed for social welfare laws and labor rights. But the APRA lacked the military power to enforce its programs. In addition, the APRA's "radicalism" brought a reactionary boycott in the Congress and Cabinet. In a climate of political polarization and civilian violence, the APRA and some navy units unsuccessfully revolted in October 1948. After the bloody repression of the rebels, General Manuel Odría ruled like right-wing military dictatorships in Venezuela (Pérez Jiménez) and Colombia (Rojas Pinilla). Haya De La Torre found asylum in the Colombian Embassy for five years before being allowed to leave Peru. De La Torre was allowed to return in 1957, when the country was again under civilian rule. Until his death twenty-two years later, he collaborated with the most reactionary civilian and military groups. In the 1980s, the APRA emerged as the biggest political party, and it had allied itself with the international Social Democratic movement.

In the 1950s, civilian politicians as well as military ideologists had concluded that Peruvian society must modernize in order to avoid "Communist" solutions. A former Aprista, Fernando Belaúnde, founded the reformist party Popular Action (AP) with support from the lower and middle classes and the progressive high-bourgeoisie. Belaúnde felt that all citizens must be activated in popular and communal action to integrate the fatherland by building roads, schools and public works. Likewise, the nationalist military leaders felt that "counterinsurgency" must be accompanied by a modernization in which the Army should be a promoter of progressive social change. Moreover, they were very critical of the archaic Peruvian land tenure system.[22] In 1963, Belaúnde was elected to the presidency with euphoric enthusiasm to reform and modernize the nation. Although the *Aprismo* and the AP had many points of ideological convergence, the former in alliance with the most reactionary forces sabotaged Belaúnde's programs in the Congress. In addition, the AP's electoral campaign had promised to confiscate the American oil company IPC within one hundred days. It was easier said than done. Belaúnde's government was characterized by flagrant corruption, peasant agitation and guerrilla warfare.

On October 3, 1968, General Juan Velasco overthrew Belaúnde, and for the ensuing seven years attempted to revolutionize the nation from the top. Radical agrarian reform virtually eliminated the power of the landed aristocracy and the agrarian bourgeoisie. The nationalization of banks, mines, factories, oil companies, the fishing industry and newspapers gave the state more than 50% ownership in all means of production. Worker's profit-sharing plans were started. Adult education and the reorientation of school literature with nationalist ideals were emphasized. The Communist party was legalized, and diplomatic relations were reestablished with Cuba and the former Soviet bloc nations. The Soviet Union granted Peru economic and military aid on very generous terms. During the Velasco years, Peru became a very articulate standard-bearer of the non-aligned nations. A massive propaganda campaign described "the Peruvian revolution" as neither communist nor capitalist, but rather as "socialist, humanist and pluralist."

The Peruvian military of the Velasco years was successful in cultivating local and foreign supporters. Moreover, Bolivian and Ecuadorian military officers launched coups that followed the steps of the Peruvian experiment. The "Leftist" Peruvian army, like their Andean counterparts, also brought the boycott from local and international capitalists.[23] Likewise, democratic slogans became essential ingredients in the containment of a nationalist experiment. The United States and international financial institutions drastically reduced loans and credits to Peru. Foreign creditors nearly bankrupted the debt-ridden Peruvian economy by demanding payments on the foreign debt. At a time when Velasco's inner clique was planning to renounce the foreign debt and adopt even more anticapitalist policies, a bloodless military coup overthrew him. Velasco's effort with all its ideals to revolutionize Peru was a project that was never completely consummated. It was stopped in the middle of the road by military officers themselves.

Although Velasco attempted to incorporate many APRA modernizing projects, he faced relentless opposition by the APRA leadership. From Velasco's downfall until Belaúnde's reelection (1980), the new military administration purged Velasquista officers, abolished or ignored the most socialistic policies and opened the nation to free-wheeling capitalism. Belaúnde pledged to "undo the wrong-doings of Velasco's rule." The neo-Civilistas returned to steer the business of Peru. All non-violent Marxist and right-wing political parties alike were legalized. Afterwards, the APRA as well as the political outsider Alberto Fujimori were allowed to govern by the military. However, the Army in its historic role remains in the background as the final judge of when the fatherland is in danger and deserves its direct management.

When, in 1990, the traditional elites and anti-elites expected the overwhelming election of the famous writer Mario Vargas Llosa, the once humble Japanese-Peruvian Alberto Fujimori surprised conventional wisdom and won. He had no party structure or oligarchic support. This cunning populist was a master of anti-politics who cultivated those who had lost faith in traditional politics and institutions. With the support of sectors within the intelligence services, Fujimori acted as the representative of the non-white majorities who had been historically sidelined. About 60% of the Peruvian population lived below the "poverty level," and yet, despite Fujimori's austere monetarist economic policies, bureaucratic pruning and the cut-off in public spending, he maintained overwhelming popular support. It is, perhaps, because Fujimori appeared in chaotic times of guerrilla warfare and most flagrant public corruption.

When the Aprismo was elected to govern in its own right (1985-90), it had lost its early idealism and already learned the traditional kleptomania of other rulers. Fujimori gave hope and illusions to those tired of Aprismo who were ready to believe in anything other than Maoist rule or "the Twelve Apostles" (i.e., the oligarchic leaders). Fujimori's modernization ambitions strikingly resembled the dictatorial trajectory to more pluralist governance followed by the "newly industrialized" Southeast Asian countries. But Fujimori's regime did not industrialize or democratize. According to an American periodical, Fujimori enforced "a U.S.-approved democracy plus the power of a virtual dictator."[24] But in the Peruvian magic realism of politics, the APRA leader Alan García returned as a born-again neo-liberal to the presidency in 2006. This eloquent rhetorician ruled mostly by decree and corruption. Eventually, García brought the ideological and political suicide of his party.

Fujimori's power-base was the intelligence apparatus and the Army. Fujimori intended to rule Peru like an enterprise, and his administration was hierarchic and corrupt. The Peruvian army had its own historic ambitions, which were not entirely different from Fujimori's economic nationalism and modernizing schemes. Their biggest reason to collaborate had been the struggle against the Tupac Amaru and Sendero Luminoso guerrillas, especially the latter. Peru's future depended very much on the course of this internal war. Of all the contemporary Latin American insurgency movements, none had incited so much violence for Marxism-Leninism's sake. After Mao, the Senderist leader Abimael Guzmán represented to his followers the "Fourth Sword" of the Communist revolution. However, his capture in 1992 destroyed Sendero's aura of invincibility. But Sendero was only a horror in a beautiful country with many horrors. During the last two decades of the twentieth century, nearly 70,000 Peruvians were killed in political violence. The frightful violence had an ethnic, racial and socio-economic character. The great majority of the casualties were non-white peasants who were victimized by the guerrillas and state repression; 79%

of the victims lived in rural areas and 75% spoke indigenous languages.[25]

The Eurocentric Peruvian elites who gladly display their pedigree by claiming as many European grandparents one can claim were shocked by a proud and astute non-white president. The rule of Fujimori, which included non-white governance at all political levels was a major departure from the pigmentocratic Peruvian tradition. Racism and class exploitation have been intimately intertwined from the outset of Peru's European history. The elites' white-philomania has hindered the development of national capitalism and a more egalitarian modernization. It is necessary that the traditional ruling elites ask themselves why the *Senderist* tragedy emerged in Peru instead of somewhere else in Latin America. In the confusing search of identity, some Peruvians looked at Europe, while others found "illumination" in Maoist China. The ruling elites could begin by moving their minds, souls and money from Europe or Miami to Peru. After all, in terms of the so-called "national bourgeoisie," Peru is among the most underdeveloped in Latin America.[26] The historian Manuel Burga has asserted that the Peruvian twentieth century was a century of useless and unintended efforts with perverse results.[27] Indeed, Peru continues to be a geography of "lost opportunities" and unfulfilled dreams.

The presidential election of Commandant Ollanta Humala (2011-) reminds us that military officers still aspire to liberate the fatherland from its past nightmares. He had proclaimed his admiration for General Juan Velasco. Humala has the challenge of conducting structural changes that include and benefit all Peruvian citizens. Structural relations can only change slowly or by revolution. Many had branded Humala as a follower of Hugo Chávez, while others claimed he was inspired by Brazil's Lula da Silva. But in post-Cold War times, the nationalist Humala will find his own way according to conditions on the ground. The Latin American winds of change are in the making and the Andean nations are part of such a process. Peru is an important strategic asset for the American presence in the Andean region. However, Humala intends to join the biggest South American common market (*Merco-

sur) and make Peru a Brazilian strategic partner. Among all the Andean nations, Colombia remains the only one at the neo-liberal stage. In the other Andean nations, the state is emerging as an active actor and is gradually moving away from the American model.

CHAPTER VII

FROM SOUTHERN CONE TO ABC POWERS

The "Southern Cone" of Latin America geographically includes Chile, Argentina, Uruguay and Paraguay. The first three countries have the lowest "poverty level" in South America, but even so, it still affected over 30% of their populations by the end of the twentieth century. These nations are located in the most temperate zone of Latin America. With the exception of Paraguay, these are the Spanish American countries that became the most Europeanized in the postcolonial period. The two biggest nations of the Southern Cone, Chile and Argentina, together with Brazil, have often been referred to as the "ABC powers." Such an image relates to their geographic proximity, economic vitality and hegemony in the region. Although Brazil received numerous European immigrants, it also remains an Africanized nation. During colonial times, these countries were sparsely populated and more backward than Peru or Mexico. Until recently, the relations of the Southern Cone nations and the ABC powers intertwined more as the result of conflicts than cultural similarities or collaboration. That has particularly been the case with Argentina, Brazil, Uruguay and Paraguay. The Andean Mountains and Chile's location along the

Pacific coast isolated this nation from involvement in the Argentine-Brazilian conflicts over the Platine region. Chile and Argentina have had boundary disputes from independence onwards, but outright war has been averted despite a history of difficult tensions.

It has been on the margins of the former Iberian viceroyalties that the most difficult disputes occurred during the nineteenth century. Colonization and the exploitation of natural resources became the most serious causes of war. In the Southern Cone, like in the United States-Mexican border disputes, the loosely defined national boundaries were concluded on favorable terms for the nations that had received the largest number of white immigrants, "the more civilized nations." Moreover, the Indian "pacification" of the United States and the Argentinean-Chilean southern frontiers were strikingly similar. Historically, the Indians of Latin America had been decimated by gunpowder, overwork, diseases and miscegenation. In the American West, as in the Argentinean-Chilean southern frontier of the nineteenth century, miscegenation was almost bypassed. The extermination of Indians was too dynamic to permit sexual and gender approaches to the confrontation of two different "races."

In the last decade of the twentieth century, all the Southern Cone and ABC nations had elected governments, which conducted neoliberal economic policies in collaboration with the International Monetary Fund (IMF) and the World Bank. During the 1980s, their military dictators gradually transferred governance to civilian authority. At the height of the anti-Communist crusade, the military collaborated across international boundaries to eliminate insurgents and dissidents under the sobriquet " Operation Condor."[1] For sure, the traditional ruling elites remained secure in command of national affairs. Furthermore, they proclaimed their faith in free elections, political pluralism and democracy. Prosperity for the lower classes remains distant. But by the dawn of the twenty-first century, popular and mostly peaceful mobilizations are again on the march.

Brazil is a country with about 195 million inhabitants (2010). From the mid-twentieth century on, Brazil changed from predominantly rural to overwhelmingly urban. This nation is one of the richest in the world, and yet income distribution is the most un-equal in Latin America and the planet. The top 5% own 75% of the national wealth; 2% own 60% of all agricultural land; 60% of the population live under the United Nations' "poverty level." There are 12 million homeless children, and four of them were as-sassinated everyday.[2] With over 500,000 child-prostitutes, Brazil was the tragic first in Latin America.[3] In 1989, the young Fernando Collor de Melo was democratically elected president on an anti-corruption crusade. The flamboyant "Mr. Clean" proved to be one of the most venal politicians in the nation's history. Before Collor completed the third year in office, his government was virtually paralyzed and the traditional elites had to remove him from the presidency. Corruption has not ended. The masses were certainly losing faith in the Brazilian political class. Then, Lula da Silva of the Workers Party (PT), with grass-roots support, appeared as the most radical alternative and non-traditional politician for the mul-tifaceted and labyrinthine Brazilian society. His goal was demo-cratic socialism. Lula's presidential election (2002-10) revealed that the struggle to bring structural changes by peaceful means is a slow process. Reactionary forces defend their interests and mo-nopolies. But the PT and Lula's successors remain committed to a democratic process, which includes social justice and solidarity.

Once upon a time, a global cliché noted "rich as an Argentine" and the natives claimed to eat steak every day; but in 1989, the Radical president Raul Alfonsín left five months before his term was over because of food riots, hunger, and hyperinflation. Alas, one of the greatest food-baskets of the world continues to have food riots. The incoming Peronist president Carlos Menem pledged a return to prosperity and the good old days. Menem accelerated the amnesty to the "dirty war" veterans and reversed the entire Peronist ideology, claiming that the financial chaos required "surgery without anaesthesia." While in office, Alfonsín faced con-stant Peronist opposition as well as 13 nation-wide labor strikes.

Menem's policies and populist rhetoric avoided the workers' up-heaval. Presidential decrees outlawed strikes in "essential indus-tries" and labor unions were forced to negotiate contracts on a company-by-company basis rather than through nation-wide terms. Reduction of the bureaucracy and social welfare programs as well as privatizations of state properties enticed the return of capital investments to the legendary Argentina. As soon as Menem became president, he informed the United States that Argentina "wanted to be on very friendly terms with the most important country in the world."[4] Argentina exchanged its historic antagonism for an eager-to-please attitude, throwing itself on the American doorstep. In 1991, Argentina officially left the Non-Alignment Movement. Peronism's changed international loyalty and its fight against corruption remained within the magic pedigree of Argentinean politics. Menem's administration was a Latin American prototype of candidates who during election campaigns promise exactly the opposite of their intended actions.

In 1979, the Chilean sociologist Fernando Dahse reported that in his country, the five largest financial clans controlled two-thirds of the 250 largest companies. Very little has changed since then. Chile had emerged as a widely acclaimed model of how authoritarian stability and neo-liberal economics could promote capitalistic development. Moreover, during his dictatorship Augusto Pinochet never had less than 34% approval in opinion polls. Alas, Chile had the highest Latin American GNP growth during the last decade of the twentieth century. The "economic miracle" had also reduced the "poverty level" of the population from 42% (1989) to 32% (1992). However, the "poverty level"[5] was only 28.5% in 1969.

The price Chileans had to endure for the "economic miracle" is painfully realized when unnamed graves, clandestine cemeteries and corruption rings like the "Cutufa" from dictatorial days were occasionally discovered. It should surprise no one that the former president, General Pinochet (1915-2006), travelled all over the world representing Chilean military enterprises without asking permission from the civilian authorities. After Pinochet was briefly arrested for crimes against humanity in England, his travelling was curtailed and his foreign bank accounts were frozen. But the Chilean writer Ariel Dorfman acidly noted the lament after

Pinochet's death among one third of his countrymen, who were "still justifying his crimes, still rejoicing that the general overthrew Salvador Allende."[6] Moreover, two decades after the end of Pinochet's dictatorship, Chileans elected the right-wing billionaire Sebastián Piñera to the presidency.

The Parliamentary Mirage

Chile had been a Spanish colony, which developed almost as an antithesis of the Peruvian colonization process. During most of the colonial period, Chile was a backward frontier province that survived on royal subsidies from Peru. There were no fabulous amounts of gold and silver like those that attracted so many conquistadores to Peru. Chile produced mainly dry meats, olives, grains and wines for local consumption and the mining centers of the Peruvian viceroyalty. However, Chile was revitalized by a large influx of Northern Spaniards and particularly Basque immigrants during the eighteenth century. As a consequence, by the end of the colonial era, Chile was flourishing without royal subsidies. It was a prosperity that was controlled by some sixty landed families. Most Chileans were Mestizos with a high percentage of white blood in their veins. They were concentrated in the fertile Central Valley and were relatively homogeneous in their ethnic make-up. Since most of the Araucanians who had not been acculturated were then living to the south of the Bío Bío River, class exploitation did not have a strong racial basis. With such a socio-economic background, the republic began its rather unique political evolution among its neighbors.

For about five years after independence, Chile was ruled by the hero and Supreme Director Bernardo O'Higgins (1818-23). Like Bolívar and José de San Martín, O'Higgins felt that Spanish power had to be completely crushed in Peru in order to insure the independence of the already liberated South American republics. Because of such a conviction, O'Higgins supported San Martín's emancipatory campaigns in Peru despite the costs and criticism by many of his compatriots. In his efforts to modernize the nation, he

supported education by building new schools and importing foreign teachers. Irrigation projects were started, roads were paved
and port facilities improved.

O'Higgins opened the nation to foreign trade and welcomed European immigration. Like most contemporary Spanish American
rulers, he tried to regulate the power of the Church, which wanted
to keep its colonial privileges without pledging the type of loyalty
it had given to the Crown. The conflict between the Church and
O'Higgins became so intense that he exiled the Bishop of Santiago
only to increase the wrath of Clericals and Conservatives. More
significantly, the landed aristocracy resented the high taxes required by O'Higgins' modernization endeavors. Although O'Higgins considered himself a Liberal, he aspired to centralize the
nation and become an enlightened despot. Unfortunately, he ruled
in a vacuum, devoid of the aristocracy's social support. Finally, the
Army joined the malcontents and revolted. O'Higgins escaped to
Peru by early 1823.

O'Higgins' departure was followed by seven anarchical years
in which the Conservatives and Liberals seized and left power
through violence. It was an interlude of bloodshed, criminality,
instability and Indian revolts. If anything noble was accomplished
during this violent period, it was the abolition of black slavery. It
was also a time of attrition in which both doctrinaire Liberals and
Conservatives alike were decimated. Finally, a confrontation of
forces came about on the banks of the Lircay River in which the
Liberals were completely defeated. After this bloodbath, the Conservatives ruled the nation under relative peace for the ensuing
ninety-five years. It is true that the Liberals continued to exist and
debate, but generally they or their ideas were assimilated into the
Conservative Party. In many ways, the Liberals served as the voice
of innovation, which permitted the landed oligarchy and the urban
political machines to preserve their power. Such a political strategy
provided an almost unique evolutionary process of unhindered
functional government, something very uncommon in Latin American history.

The man who was most responsible for the Conservative ascendancy was the patrician and entrepreneur Diego Portales. From 1830 to 1837, he was most often without any official governmental post, but from his home in Valparaiso his views were heard and heeded by the ruling politicians. His political perceptions guided the Conservative strategy in the manipulation of national politics. Portales felt that the landed aristocracy and the big merchants must unite in order to control the turbulent masses and the Army. Although Portales was an atheist, he felt that religion and the Church were necessary as a constraint on the impulsiveness of the lower classes. Consequently, the state and the Church must be allied in the propagation of order and progress. Furthermore, the nation must be opened to foreign trade and maintain its good credit by recognizing the foreign debt.

Portales' economic ideology also included nationalist policies by which the government was to protect local industries and develop a merchant marine.[7] Before Portales left political office, he removed his real and suspected enemies from the bureaucracy and staffed it with Conservatives and loyal supplicants. Portales reduced the regular army and created the national militia, which became directly answerable to the political bosses of each province. In addition, Portales was very concerned with preventing the political re-unification of Peru and Bolivia. It is due to his insistence that Chile invaded the Peruvian-Bolivian Confederation and dissolved it.

A group of army officers attempted unsuccessfully to overthrow the Conservatives in 1837. The rebels were soundly defeated but only after they had assassinated Portales. His death made him an overnight martyr, to be invoked as a civic symbol by the bearers of authority. In life and in death, Portales proved to be an influential figure. In the wake of the Conservative ascendancy, the Constitution of 1833 was drafted and kept in force until 1925. It was centralist and authoritarian. The new *magna carta* provided for a five-year presidency and eligibility for immediate reelection. The Executive and the Congress shared authority. The President could veto legislation, appoint the Cabinet and controlled the political machinery. Suffrage was by indirect vote and limited to literate male property owners. Furthermore, Catholicism became the official religion.

With the legacy of Portales and Conservative rule, Chile experienced booming prosperity with the best credit rating in Latin America. Silver, copper and coal deposits were discovered. Aided by the proximity between embarking ports and mining centers, Chile became the only Spanish American country that increased its mining production in the aftermath of independence. In fact, by mid-nineteenth century Chile had already become the world's largest producer of copper. Like in most of Latin American mining history, the basic purpose of Chilean mining development was for export. Wheat production for the export market increased with the "gold rush" in California and Australia. German settlers opened lands for agriculture and cattle ranching in southern Chile. Furthermore, Valparaiso emerged as the largest Latin American port on the Pacific and the biggest British commercial entrepot for the South American West Coast nations. Education also flourished, especially after the 1840s. Schools of agriculture, engineering, sciences, seamanship, fine arts and music were founded. In 1842, the National University of Chile was reorganized on the French model, and the Venezuelan erudite Andrés Bello directed it. Moreover, during these peaceful years numerous South American exiles and particularly Argentineans, served as professors and teachers in Chilean academic institutions. In this Catholic society there was a relative freedom of debate on the issues of secularization and modernization, which had important consequences on the Chilean political evolution.[8] Santiago became a major Latin American intellectual center.

During the 1850s, when Chile was presided over by Manuel Montt (1851-61), like everywhere else in Spanish America, the Liberals agitated, conspired and revolted. To be sure, they were efficiently repressed, but Montt and his coterie, aware of the anarchy and bloodshed befalling among the Latin American republics, decided to adopt and adapt many Liberal programs. It was time for adjustments if the basic fabric of society was to be preserved undisturbed in the main lines. There was economic prosperity, and a *nouveau riche* entrepreneurial class had emerged in the urban and mining centers. They were demanding more political power from the landed aristocracy. Montt cautiously engineered the transition to the modernizing society. In 1857, he allied himself with the moderate Conservatives and the job-seeking Liberals in organizing the National party, which gave him firmer control of the Conservative political machine. The neophyte political organization was in essence Conservative, but it recognized the need for gradual change.

Chilean and foreign historians alike have disagreed on whether the Conservatives or the Liberals predominated in the government after Montt's reforms. However, the socio-economic conditions of the lower classes were basically unaffected by the internal power struggles among the elites and anti-elites. The constraint of the landed aristocracy and the secularization of the state were to be promoted gradually. Montt sponsored the abolition of the primogeniture laws in order to encourage the latifundia's division. Modest credits were provided for tenant farmers who wanted to buy their plots from their landlords. As for the Church, a gradual severance of its power was started, and within the next three decades, legislation was enacted which provided for the abolition of tithes, the secularization of cemeteries, religious toleration for non-Catholics, and the recognition of civil marriages. Despite those reforms, the Church remained rich and powerful. Chilean secularization went as far as in most of Latin America without the drastic "Mexican-style" revolutionary laws, which brought political backlashes and annulled those accomplishments.

The decades following the mid-nineteenth century were of booming growth. The railroad, telegraph and steam navigation became firmly established. The development of the southern lands and the exploitation of mining and nitrates expanded production for export. The new economic dynamism gradually abandoned the protectionism of Portalean ideology. *Laissez-faire* became the orthodoxy, which suffocated the local infant industries. Mono-productivity for export under the aegis of British capital, became the overwhelming tendency. Likewise, the Congress gradually gained a degree of power in the decision-making process. Underneath the development in representative politics, the military was also becoming a growing establishment due to its success in the repulsion of Spanish naval attacks during the 1860s, the victorious Chilean outcome in the War of the Pacific (1879-83), and the final suppression of the Araucanian revolts in the 1880s.

In the War of the Pacific's aftermath, the executive authority gradually lost control of the Conservative political machine, which culminated in a congressional power confrontation with President José Balmaceda (1886-91). In addition, Balmaceda wanted to revive the Portalean protectionism and prevent foreign monopolies with their local allies from seizing public nitrate lands. Faced by pressure in 1890, Balmaceda bowed to the congressional demand that the Cabinet be held responsible for the legislative branch. But while the Congress was adjourned, the president replaced the Cabinet with one more congenial to his policies. In January 1891, the Congress responded by deposing Balmaceda and then fleeing to the north with naval support. With the help of sectors in the Army, Balmaceda remained eight months as dictator in Santiago. However, when the Congress, with the aid of the German military training mission and the Army, pressed for a total confrontation, Balmaceda was abandoned. The president fled to the Argentine Embassy, where he committed suicide. A nationalist bourgeois revolution from above had failed, causing nearly 10,000 deaths.[9]

Balmaceda's downfall brought a new age of political history in which the executive branch lost much power. For the next 30 years, the nation was transformed from a strong presidential system to a parliamentary republic more similar to European models than those in Latin America. The new system provided that a congressional majority should elect Cabinet members and that all government officials must be answerable to the Congress rather than the President. The President also lost the right to appoint provincial governors. The Congress legislated that towns throughout the nation must elect their own local governments.

Although Chile by the turn of the nineteenth century had made outstanding democratic gains and had increased its territory by one third with nitrate lands, only a small minority shared the benefits of political *modernity* and the newly acquired wealth. The nitrate income was so great that little taxation was necessary outside this sector. The nation was rich enough to undertake numerous modernization projects. More significantly, the most democratic Latin American republican system was structured to promote corruption. In the parliamentary republic, aspirants to congressional seats paid very high costs for their election, ostensibly to serve the fatherland without pay. Obviously, they served the possessing elites better than the great majority of the fatherland's offspring. For as much income as the nitrates and minerals brought to Chile, virtually nothing was provided for the welfare programs of the masses.

Under *laissez-faire* economics, the country developed some small industries geared to local consumption, but the overwhelming nature of growth was nitrates for export. Moreover, because of the dramatic growth of the nitrate industry, England became a monopolistic force in the national economy. Before the War of the Pacific, English capital controlled only 13% of nitrate production. The Chilean victory over Peru and Bolivia signalled a rush by local and foreign companies to exploit nitrates; English capital led the scramble. By 1895, English companies controlled 60% of the production. In addition, nitrates were transported in English ships, and almost exclusively sold in the international market via London.

On the verge of the twentieth century, the Chilean nation was vibrant with economic dynamism based on its nitrate income. American investments in copper mining had increased the nation's dependency. An urban middle class and proletariat had emerged under the parliamentary system but the traditional aristocracy remained supreme through partisan vote-counting and blatant bribery. However, the export economy had also generated a very active proletariat, which mobilized itself together with other classes in search of better working conditions as well as political and social reform. In 1887, the Democratic Party was founded with a program, which included a defense of workers' rights. This front included many socialist and nationalist militants. One of the most brilliant ideologists, Luis E. Recabarren broke away and founded the Socialist Labor Movement in 1912. A decade later, it became the Communist party. Chilean organized labor had the earliest evolution under Marxist leadership and ideology in South America. Chilean and Argentinean labor movements became classic Latin American counterpoints in their evolution. The latter's anarcho-syndicalist origins ultimately unfolded into corporatist and right-wing nationalism.[10]

The conclusion of World War I was accompanied by the collapse of the market for Chilean nitrates, which had been subjected to decreased demand and competition from cheaper chemical substitutes. In addition, copper prices were unstable and declining. In 1920, the charismatic Arturo Alessandri was barely elected by a coalition of the middle and Liberal upper classes, on the promise of terminating the corrupt parliamentarism and reinstating a strong presidency. He also promised a social security system, state control of banking and a progressive labor code. Despite the fact that only 50% of the population was literate and merely 8% voted, Chile had one of the most active political populations in Latin America. Although Alessandri's supporters had a majority in the chamber of deputies, the oligarchy's domination of the senate prevented him from fulfilling his campaign promises. With the support of reformist sectors in the Army, a new presidential constitution was enacted in 1925. Having achieved his promised reform, Alessandri resigned and ultimately was replaced by General Carlos Ibañez, who ruled as a dictator until July 1931. Ibañez was brought down by nation-wide strikes and the social unrest caused by the Great Depression. Ibañez's downfall was followed by a series of turbulent and short-lived governments that included a "Socialist Republic" which lasted only twelve days. Chile was one of the hardest hit by the Great Depression in Latin America.

In the midst of army, naval and civilian coups and counter coups, Alessandri was reelected in 1932 to serve a six-year presidential term. Despite the growing democratic socialistic tendencies among Chileans, Alessandri's return in the depth of economic depression signalled a sharp turn to the right and the unmitigated repression of Communists and socialists. Alessandri had become an admirer of Italian fascism as a solution to local socio-economic problems. Behind the constitutional protocols that regulated the relationship between the president and Congress, the military powers of the Executive were increased by the creation of the Republican Militia.

Alessandri's second administration made some concessions to the labor movement, but the power of the opulent elites was preserved. However, he was not the oligarchy's "darling." Such a reward was bestowed on the enigmatic General Ibañez, who in 1938 unsuccessfully attempted a coup with the connivance of the local Nazi party. Under a state of siege and the probability of a further shift to the right, the center-left Radical party emerged as the biggest political group. This party included an odd combination of moderate Conservatives and non-Marxist leftists. Moreover, the Radical party was willing to accommodate itself with Marxist groups in order to control the government. A Popular Front was created in the style of León Blum's French coalition, and it succeeded in keeping the presidency in Radical hands from 1938 to 1952. The election of the Popular Front brought for the first time an alliance between the proletariat and the middle classes against the elite. The Popular Front brought a new era of social welfare legislation, state capitalism and industrialization.

With the conclusion of World War II, the low prices and diminishing demand for Chilean exports resulted in economic instability and social unrest. Political polarization and rumors of Communist subversion in the wake of the Cold War prompted a break between the Radical party and its Marxist allies. The government outlawed the Communist party, exiled many of its members to the frigid south and broke diplomatic relations with the Soviet bloc nations in 1948. The Communist party remained illegal for the next decade, but it continued to operate underground and through other parties.

In the elections of 1952, General Ibañez was brought to power by a coalition of right-wing forces. His government, like that of his successor Jorge Alessandri, son of the former president, kept the presidency in reactionary hands until 1964. However, this period of rightist upsurge was paralleled by the growth of two new political coalitions that advocated for drastic social change: one under the aegis of the Christian Democrat Eduardo Frei Montalva, and the other led by the Marxist Salvador Allende. Promising a "revolution in liberty," Frei Montalva was elected to the presidency in 1964. He pledged himself to revolutionary socio-economic change within the context of "democratic capitalism." The first great task of Frei Montalva's administration was the "chileanization" of the Gran Minería, owned by American multinational companies and responsible for approximately 85% of the copper production, the nation's biggest source of foreign income.

Chileanization allowed the government to buy 51% of the affected mines as well as receive between 25% and 33% ownership on new private mining ventures. In exchange, taxes were lowered in order to encourage greater production and private investments. Frei Montalva devised an agrarian reform law, which provided for the nationalization of all land holdings larger than 80 hectares. Despite massive credits from the United States, the mining sector remained under foreign control. Only limited amounts of land had been granted to the peasantry by the end of the Frei Montalva administration. Yet Chile's relative prosperity had fostered one of the most literate populations and advanced social welfare systems in the world. Chilean industry was also among the most outstanding in Latin America. The problem was that Frei Montalva's program had failed to live up to the expectations it had created among one of the most politicized populations of the world.

In the election of 1970, Allende's leftist coalition, the Unidad Popular (UP), received only 36% of the votes. But the UP's victory had the unprecedented distinction of electing in free elections a Marxist president for the first time in national world history. Although Chile had a rather low rate of illiteracy (16%), it was the first time that illiterates were legally permitted to vote. The UP coalition included Radicals, Communists, socialists and other minor Marxist groups. Moreover, the Christian Democratic candidate, on a quite radical platform, had received 28% of the votes.

Hence, in the Chilean parliamentary tradition the possibilities for democratic revolutionary change seemed feasible in the wake of Allende's victory. The first year of Allende's government was a successful one. The copper industry was expropriated and land distribution to the peasantry was accelerated. Most of the iron, automobile assembly and textile industries were brought under state ownership. The rates of inflation and unemployment were lowered.

The local and foreign cognoscenti were full of praise for the "Chilean road to socialism." Marxists from all over Latin America and the world flocked to observe and participate in this exciting revolutionary carnival. But Chile had a sizeable reactionary population, which had the connivance of powerful elements within the government, the press and the armed forces, as well as the unmitigated support of the Richard Nixon administration. The United States and international credit institutions subjected Chile to an economic blockade. Spare parts for Chilean factories, food imports, medical supplies and other American imports on which the Chilean economy had come to depend were delayed or suspended. Nixon gave direct orders to his "crisis team" in charge of Chile: "to make its economy scream."

Allende's third year in the government was characterized by near economic paralysis and rampant inflation, and yet in the congressional elections of March 1973, his coalition improved its percentage over the previous presidential elections. The American sabotage of Allende's government also involved CIA undercover operations with the labor unions and local enemies of the government. The bloody military coup that brought General Pinochet to power on September 11, 1973 had the logistical support of the American navy, which conducted maneuvers on the Chilean coast under the code epithet "Operation Cousin Sam." In a TV interview with the British journalist David Frost in 1977, Nixon revealed that the American conspiracy against Allende's government came about because "international communism [by] using Cuba and Chile as bases was trying to transform all of Latin America into a big bloody sandwich." Moreover, in the aftermath of the coup, the War Hawks in the American Congress noted that the Chilean generals had taught the United States a lesson on how to deal with communism.

Perhaps the only way in which Allende's government could have survived local and foreign intrigues would have been by the establishment of a leftist dictatorship. Obviously, the struggle for Latin American social change and modernization is not a neutral affair. With massive investments from private American capital and some monetarist policies of the "Chicago School of Economics," Chile became, in the words of the Nobel laureate Milton Freeman, "the economic miracle of the century." The process of nationalization was reversed, and the workers' gains of the previous four decades were wiped out. Chile officially aimed to become the nation with the lowest taxes in the world. Inflation was lowered from 500% (1973) to 30% (1980), and production increased. For almost seventeen years, Pinochet imposed upon Chile one of the most repressive political systems in the world and forced about a million nationals to leave their homeland for political and economic reasons. Possibly the most refined and legalized police apparatus dedicated to the extinction of Marxism was devised and tested. About 32,000 Chileans were murdered by Pinochet's dictatorship. Civilian rule returned, but the Army is still a privileged institution in a country, which maintains the basic social injustices common to most of Latin America.

Argentina: The Port and the Pampa

The viceroyalty of La Plata was one of the first colonies to become independent as well as escape the Spanish efforts of reconquest. After 1810, Argentina officially remained a colony, but in reality Spain had lost control. When Spain was launching a major effort to reconquer its newly emancipated Spanish American colonies, Argentina proclaimed itself independent on July 9, 1816. With the break-up of the Spanish bureaucracy, political instability became endemic. The basic source of trouble was the conflict between the interior provinces and Buenos Aires, which with its strategic location collected import and export taxes. Likewise, the *Porteños* (people from the city of Buenos Aires) had little interest in buying wines, textiles and other goods produced in the inland country, for they could be obtained from Europe more cheaply. Furthermore, independence from Spain had brought a breakdown in trade relations with Alto Peru.

During the first half of the nineteenth century, the Argentinean interior underwent a reorientation of its economy away from Alto Peru and towards Buenos Aires and the Atlantic World. In addition, there was the ideological political dilemma, which debated on whether the nation should be a centralist or federal republic. The Liberals or Unitarios, who came mostly from the europeanized capital, associated themselves with the movement for centralization, while their Conservative opponents became the Federalists. As long as the threat of Spanish reconquest or Portuguese-Brazilian aggression prevailed in the 1820s, all the provinces collaborated with each other.

Perhaps the most significant figure in the early aftermath of independence was the Creole Bernardo Rivadavia, who served as minister of state for Buenos Aires as well as foreign minister for all the Argentine provinces until 1824. From 1826 to 1827, he also served as president for all the provinces. Rivadavia felt that the nation should modernize along the lines of a European society, and that it should be populated by European immigrants. His goals included the establishment of a unitary republic in which Buenos Aires was to be the center of authority. The acquisition of European credits, investments and technology should be encouraged. As in most of Latin America, it was England who made the biggest inroads in providing loans at outrageous interest rates. Furthermore, Rivadavia abolished the tithes and the ecclesiastical courts, secularized the cemeteries and closed several monasteries. In order to fill the vacuum left by the Church in social welfare and charity, Rivadavia created philanthropic societies operated with public and private funds. He expanded government support for education, public works and port facilities. Unfortunately, he represented ideas, not interests.

Rivadavia's attempt to draft a centralizing constitution and his official recognition of Brazilian hegemony over Uruguay brought repudiation for his modernization schemes. Rivadavia's disclaim of the Brazilian agreement did not stop the nation-wide antipathy for his government, and he ultimately went into exile in Europe. The conflict between Argentina and Brazil, and that of Buenos Aires and the interior provinces, continued in the post-Rivadavia days; in the first case, England forced the two underdeveloped South American giants to accept an independent Uruguay as a buffer country. The conflict between Buenos Aires and the other provinces was to linger on as a more enduring predicament until the advent of the *caudillo* of *caudillos* Juan Manuel de Rosas.

For nearly a quarter of a century, Rosas ruled by reactionary dictatorship, proto-nationalism and informal centralization. Rosas was a former entrepreneur from the white propertied classes who had accumulated his wealth in cattle ranching and slaughter-houses. From 1829 to 1831, and again from 1835 to 1852, he was governor of Buenos Aires, but as head of the Federalist Party and through informal alliances with the provincial political bosses he controlled Argentina. Rosas was a ruthless *caudillo* who led the smaller *caudillos* against the politicians of Buenos Aires and the Liberal ideologists. Ostensibly, Rosas represented federalist principles. In reality, he centralized the nation through terror methods and his private *gaucho* army. Rosas killed, jailed, and exiled his enemies. Thousands of the nation's intellectuals fled to neighboring countries from where they mobilized repugnance against one of the most brutal contemporary Latin American dictatorships. Rosas' autocracy was supported by the landed aristocracy and the Church. The lower classes worshiped their *caudillo*.

Rosas was an isolationist who wanted to keep Argentina free from European influence, ideas and immigrants. The only contact Rosas wanted with Europeans was the sale of salted meats and hides. His isolationist policies brought Argentina into constant conflicts with the British. In 1833, Britain captured the Islas Malvinas (Falkland Islands) and converted them into refuelling stations for its navy, shippers and whalers while obtaining control of the Atlantic-Pacific Sea route. Further conflict with Britain occurred with Rosas' efforts to bring Uruguay under Argentinean rule. Likewise, the British were using Uruguay as a spearhead to open the whole La Plata estuary to international trade. In addition, Uruguay exported nearly the same products as Argentina, and Montevideo functioned as a free port for European industrial products. Moreover, from 1838 to 1848, the British and French navies unsuccessfully attempted to blockade Buenos Aires. Rosas failed to capture Uruguay, but the conflict with the British and French increased his popularity among Argentine nationalists.

Rosas' international conflicts as well as the swift expansion of livestock-raising had prompted an internal debate among gaucho leaders who had come to think that the nation could benefit by greater economic intercourse with Europeans. The leader of the conspiracy was Justo Urquiza, governor of Entre Ríos. His province was to benefit greatly by opening the Plata estuary to foreign trade. When Urquiza challenged his former protector and boss, most of the smaller *caudillos* joined him against Rosas. Furthermore, all the political enemies who were underground or in exile rushed to Entre Ríos to train for battle against the tyrant. Finally, by February 1852, the armies of Rosas and Urquiza fought at Monte Caseros. Rosas was defeated and fled to Europe.

Urquiza, like Rosas, was a man to be feared. Urquiza considered himself a Federalist, but wanted all the provinces to share equally in the custom duties collected in Buenos Aires. Urquiza was opposed by the Liberals who insisted on a centrally controlled nation led by Buenos Aires. Moreover, many politicians from Buenos Aires wanted to detach their province from the "barbarian" interior provinces and the "Federal *caudillos*." Urquiza was forced to call a constitutional convention, which met in Santa Fe in late 1852. Under the guidance of the Liberal ideas proposed by the philosopher Juan Bautista Alberti, the convention met and drafted a constitution similar to that of the United States. "Alberti combined a liberal vision of statehood and historiography into a brand of constitutionalism...to create new ideological identities."[11]

With a new constitution and plentiful fertile lands, Argentina welcomed European trade and immigrants. The neo-European nation boomed by exporting salted meats, hides, tallow, wool and wheat. Argentina produced what European industrial growth needed. Despite the successful Argentinean debut to world intercourse, the interior provinces continued to struggle for economic aegis with Buenos Aires. Urquiza counterattacked Porteño dominance by favoring the Paraná River port of Rosario with low taxes on international trade. The success of Rosario brought further conflicts between Buenos Aires and the provinces, which were rerouting their trade through the new international port. Finally, under the military command of the historian Bartolomé Mitre, the Porteños defeated Urquiza and the "Gauchocracia" in late 1861. A year later, the Constitution of 1852 was amended to provide further centralization of power. It can be said that after the confrontation between Urquiza and Mitre, the unification of Argentina was accomplished. Afterwards, the nation was ruled by presidents who reinforced the domination of Buenos Aires. It was an alliance of the landed aristocracy and the export-import dealers of Buenos Aires who nominated and elected the official candidates. Such a political dynasty became known as the National Autonomist Party, and as the century passed, it became the Conservative party. It had the suspected virtue of winning every presidential election until 1916.

Concurrent to the rising supremacy of Buenos Aires and centralization, Argentina developed in booming leaps. Railroads were built throughout the country, and by the turn of the nineteenth century, Argentina had the greatest railroad mileage in Latin America. Although the basic purpose of the rail lines was to develop the export economy, they also rendered considerable services for local markets, and immigrants to the hinterlands. Of all the railroads built in Latin America, it is in Argentina where they had the greatest public use.[12] After the mid-nineteenth century, the doors to European immigration were enthusiastically opened, and the European annual arrivals increased from 6,000 in 1860 to a peak of 200,000 in 1890. Despite the latifundia, Argentina was a big country with abundant fertile soils where virtually anything that was planted blossomed. The remaining Indian inhabitants were pushed aside, as in the American West and southern Chile. The nation added wheat, corn, wool and mutton to its fast-growing exports. When refrigerated ships were introduced in the 1870s, the meat industry was revolutionized.

The fertile soils enabled Argentina to produce staples at lower cost than the international market prices, thus fetching surplus value in the form of differential rent from buyer to seller.[13] From the 1880s until the Great Depression, Argentina experienced its golden age of agricultural exports. Argentina was gradually bleached by increasing arrivals of Spanish, Italian, German and other European settlers. The Homestead Act of 1884 opened the newly conquered Indian lands to European immigrants. Thus, a country which, by the end of the Spanish colonial period, had fewer than a million inhabitants comprising mostly Mestizos and Mulattos by 1914 had eight million Argentineans who claimed to be white. Native arrogance claimed that Argentina was the whitest country south of Canada. However, the old dark-skinned amalgam of Indians, Blacks and whites (*cabecitas negras*) were the majority in the lower classes, especially in the rural interior. This ethnic and racial element still persists even though the official myth maintains that the *cabecitas negras* are immigrants from other Latin American countries.

By the turn of the nineteenth century, Argentina had a per capita income similar to that of the United States and higher than those of England, Germany or France. Before World War I, Argentina had become one of the richest countries in the world.[14] Argentina had become a leading world exporter of staples through private entrepreneurship.[15] By then, it was possible for European migrant workers known as the *Golondrinas* (swallows) to come to Argentina during the harvests, and just a two-week salary covered their round-trip tickets. Abroad, the Argentinian "cattle barons," like the Cuban "sugar kings," were the most famous entrepreneurs and voluptuous vacationers from Latin America. Buenos Aires became an elegant city with paved streets, beautiful parks and boulevards. Local perceptions christened the capital city the Paris of South America. Buenos Aires set the fashions and cultural trends in South America. Furthermore, together with Uruguay, Argentina

achieved the highest literacy rate in Latin America and the Hispanic world.

Indeed, Argentina had become a white immigrant's land in
which at least one fourth of the national wealth was in the hands
of foreigners who did not consider themselves immigrants. The
largest group of these Europeans consisted of English entrepreneurs who operated strategic service industries such as banking,
insurance, shipping and railroads. As long as the needed services
were provided by English and European efficiency, the Argentine
"cattle barons" were happy with their bountiful income from their
exports. However, long-term economic underdevelopment was
being unwittingly promoted. Since affluent Argentines could import relatively cheap European industrial products, there was no
great thirst to industrialize or begin import-substitution schemes.
Urban sectors engaged in low-level industries such as tailoring,
blacksmithing, wineries, bakeries, tanneries and food-packing. The
Argentinean economic structure permitted foreigners and foreign
interests to siphon off very easily the wealth made in the service
industries. Thus, unlike the United States or Australia, Argentina
failed to industrialize despite its high per capita income.

The election and government of Bartolomé Mitre as president
(1862-68) personified the triumph of Argentinean nascent nationalism. It was the crystalization of a process that had been in gesta-
tion since Rosas' days. It was the ideological victory of the forces,
which advocated the formation of a united country with European
perspectives. But provincial isolationist sentiment remained in the
interior, and the Paraguayan dictator Francisco Solano López intended to benefit from the anti-Porteño antipathy in order to settle
Paraguay's disputed borders. After López invaded claimed-Argen-
tinean territory, Argentina joined Brazil and Uruguay in the war
against Paraguay. The so-called War of the Triple Alliance (1865-
70) was the bloodiest and biggest Latin American war of the nineteenth century. Mitre himself led the Argentinean armies in the
style of campaigns against local gaucho leaders. When he left the
presidency to his hand-picked candidate Faustino Sarmiento, the
nation was still at war.

Sarmiento pursued the war until the Paraguayans were completely defeated and humiliated. However, what made him one of the greatest presidents in Argentinean history was his concern with education. The "school master president" had been an educator in his country, and then in Chile while exiled during the Rosas' dictatorship. In Chile, Sarmiento had become a devoted collaborator of President Manuel Montt's educational programs. Montt had sent him to study European and American one education. Of all the foreign educational systems, the American one impressed him most, and when Sarmiento came to power in Argentina he instituted Yankee pedagogical methods. The "school master president" overhauled the entire educational system and attempted to provide primary education in every village. Even after Sarmiento left the presidency, he continued to work in his life-time obsession of educating Argentina. Through his direct efforts or influence were created teacher-training colleges, vocational institutes and schools for the handicapped. He founded the faculties of mining, agriculture as well as naval and military sciences. When Sarmiento left office, his hand-picked Minister of Education Nicolás Avellaneda succeeded him.

From the mid-nineteenth century onward, the Conservatives took the reigns of power. Unlike most Spanish American nations, Argentina did not go through the violent confrontations between Church and state. Although the Conservatives ruled and Catholicism was the official religion, the constitution was gradually amended to accommodate the immigrants of different creeds. During the 1880s, civil marriages were legalized and the clergy was prohibited from teaching religion in the public schools. The Church continued to be influential, but in a country with so many fertile lands her large landholdings did not cause too much antagonism.

Unlike Chilean parliamentarism, congressional power was curtailed before the nineteenth century came to an end by a strong-willed president who had the support of the national oligarchy. He was General Julio Roca, who served as president from 1880 to 1886 and was reelected in 1898. Roca was a national hero who had gained his reputation by killing Indians (solving "the Indian problem") and opening new lands for white colonization.

Why did the Argentinean oligarchy fear parliamentarism? First of all, unlike Chile, the Argentinean population was widely dispersed, and there existed a strong tradition of local government. A strong congress would have given the local political bosses great leverage in counting ballots. Furthermore, Argentina had a large foreign-born population, which during the 1880s was being organized by radical leaders. By 1890, the charismatic intellectual Leandro Além founded the Radical Civic Union (UNCR) with overwhelming immigrant support. Historians have described Além as a quixotic figure who was "reminiscent of the romantic French revolutionaries of 1830 or 1848."[16] His new political movement, supported by mainly urban middle sectors, advocated drastic changes, which threatened the oligarchy's power. In crisis, the oligarchy patched up its internal differences and kept away the centrist "Radicals" from the presidency until 1916. In that year, the charismatic Hipólito Yrigoyen was elected despite oligarchic opposition.

Yrigoyen was the nephew, protégé and ideological heir to Além. The Radicals had agitated and unsuccessfully revolted in 1893 and 1905. However, through their threats and militancy they had pushed for extensive electoral legislation between 1910 and 1913. These reforms provided for universal male suffrage and secret ballots. Under the new set of rules, the Radicals kept the presidency until September 1930, when in the depth of the Great Depression, the Army, for the first time since 1861, overthrew a legitimate government. Thenceforth, officers were to repeat this procedure in 1943, 1955, 1962, 1966 and 1976. While the Radicals were in the government, they succeeded in creating a state petroleum monopoly (YPF), taking few measures to protect the nascent industry and enacting social legislation that included a six-day work week, minimum wages, arbitration of labor conflicts and the abolition of child labor. Although those reforms added up to some sort of bourgeois revolution, the economic power of the oligarchy was preserved virtually intact. The traditional landed elite had learned to survive, grow and even diversify despite Radical rule. The military coup brought the Conservatives and the oligarchy to the government for almost thirteen years.

The curtailment of exports and imports brought by the Great Depression also accelerated the process of import-substitution in the already most industrialized Latin American nation. Because of its affluence, Argentina was the only South American nation that did not default on its international debts during the Great Depression.[17] But the industrial census of 1935 revealed that almost half of Argentine industrial capital was in foreign hands, particularly British. Moreover, by the Roca-Rucinam Treaty of 1933, Argentina had agreed to protect British investments from confiscation as well as import British products virtually without taxation. In exchange, Britain would maintain the prevailing import levels of Argentinean frozen meats, wool and grains, which had come under intensive competition by imports from its Commonwealth.

The return of the Conservatives to the government meant a re-strengthening of economic links with England. When World War II broke out, the Conservatives were pressured by the British and the Americans to join them against the Axis powers. But due to pro-German sentiments within the Army and widespread nationalist feelings, Argentina remained neutral. When it became apparent that a very pro-British Conservative candidate would be elected to the presidency, the generals overthrew the civilian government in June 1943. Behind the generals, there was a group of populist and nationalist colonels led by Juan D. Perón.

As Minister of Labor and with support from sectors in the Army, the newly promoted General Perón organized a grass-roots political movement among the lower classes known as *Justicialismo* or Peronism. It was a corporatist and populist project from the Right. It claimed to be neither Communist nor capitalist. In the presidential elections (1946), as the official candidate of the Army and Labor, Perón won comfortably. It was a cross-class coalition that brought Peronism to the government. With the help of his charismatic wife Eva, Perón mobilized the *descamisado* (shirtless) masses from above. Eva was a reputed former prostitute and actress. Peronism promised a middle-class standard of living to the working classes.

A massive mobilization campaign of workers (male and female) was launched, especially in the urban areas. Labor unions were granted higher wages, shorter working hours, paid vacations, safeguards against accidents and old age, free medical care and improved housing. But labor was not independent from Peronism.

Women obtained the right to vote. The president's wife headed a private and government-supported system of charity. Perón nationalized practically all the banks, insurance companies, means of communication and transport, public service facilities, mineral and oil resources. The state also purchased a merchant marine abroad. Perón undertook a massive industrialization program in an attempt to make Argentina economically independent. The Argentine Institute for the Promotion of Exchange (IAPI) became the state intermediary in the sale and purchase of exports and imports. The IAPI set a series of monetary exchange rates, which favored industry while paying lower rates for agricultural and meat exports. With the IAPI's income, the government imported capital goods for the industrialization programs. And by 1955, Argentina was already manufacturing 99% of all consumer goods used in the nation.[18] However, the development of heavy industry remained meager.

The Peronist rhetoric and praxis were nationalist, anti-British and anti-American. However, the most reactionary nationalists never dominated Peronism.[19] During World War II, Argentina had managed to declare war against the Axis powers with only enough time to join the United Nations as a charter member. In reality, Argentina had refused to collaborate with the United States and the Allies in the search for Nazi agents, criminals, scientists and millionaire refugees. Before Francisco Franco and the United States reconciled themselves, Argentina was the main link between isolated Spain and Spanish America. At the height of the Cold War, Argentina maintained diplomatic and economic relations with the Soviet bloc nations, and allowed the Communist party to operate legally.

The ambitious Peronist industrialization goals and independentist foreign policy were based on the large accumulation of hard currency from Argentine exports during World War II. But inflation and public financial problems had been caused by the post-war decline in prices for exports, the flight of native capital, the massive import of capital goods, the dependence on foreign fuels the payments for nationalized foreign assets, near full employment, and the cost of social welfare. Moreover, Perón was faced by a boycott from cattle ranchers and agricultural magnates, who deliberately reduced production levels. Perón's government was forced to borrow money from the United States and the international financial institutions. Such a change in policy was, of course, exploited by his political enemies, which included the most reactionary elements within the oligarchy, the clergy and the Army as well as the Communist party.

The main source of conflict between the Peronists and Communists was their mutual struggle to control organized labor. Peronism advocated for national unity regardless of class or ethnicity. At the outset of Perón's rise to power, he received support from the clergy, but as he moved to eliminate religious influence in the schools and politics as well as legalize divorce, a conflict culminated in the Papal excommunication of Perón and his government in June 1955. However, it was a coup led by the reactionary General Pedro Aramburu that crushed Peronism three months later. Perón fled from Argentina, and eventually established his headquarters in Spain. From Madrid, Perón continued to direct his followers against the military and civilian alliances that ruled Argentina for the next eighteen years.

It can be asserted that during the first Peronist dictatorship, Argentina industrialized, diversified its production and improved living conditions for the lower classes, but injured the landed elite and lowered its exports. An increasing share of the national income went to salary- and wage-earners, as opposed to profits and capital gains. Socio-economic rewards were distributed in favor of the lower classes and lower middle classes.[20] Peronism was a subtle dictatorship in which all political parties were legal; the Congress and Judiciary were allowed to operate while Perón set the limits of opposition. When the press became recalcitrant to his blandishments or threats, he handed the newspapers to his loyalists. Despite the disdainful comment by Henry Kissinger that "Argentina was a dagger pointed at the Antarctic," much of the American hostility to Perón was based on the historic rivalry between the two nations. By the late nineteenth century, Argentina had become the most articulate critic and challenger of American imperialism in Latin America. Since then, American foreign policy was deliberately designed to strengthen Brazil as a counterbalancing force in South America.[21] Thus, Brazil benefited from the American containment of Argentina.

Perón's departure meant a return to a free market-oriented economy, the revival of the traditional economic sectors, a curtailment of proletarian benefits and the welcoming of multinational corporations, especially American oil companies. The heavy industries fell under growing foreign control.[22] Perón's removal also meant a suppression of his followers. But generals and civilian politicians found out that if they expected to rule, an accommodation with Peronism was necessary. Moreover, leftist Peronist groups faced with constant repression allied themselves with Marxists in militant and terrorist activities during the 1960s. Under such chaotic conditions, sectors in the Army led by General Alejandro Lanusse (a scion of the oligarchy) felt that the only figure who could bring peace to the nation was the charismatic Perón. In 1973, the leader returned on his own terms, which included the election of his new wife Isabel as vice president.[23] For over a year, Perón succeeded in bringing a semblance of peace to his country.

The attempts to continue Peronism without Perón after his death completely misfired. President Isabel Perón was unable to reconcile leftist and right-wing Peronists. The tempo of violence and the struggle to control the government by different Peronist factions increased. Political anarchy was brought to an end by a military coup on March 24, 1976. The military restoration of "law and order" was swift and bloody. It has been estimated that at least 20,000 "enemies of the state" were eliminated by the armed forces and para-military groups. The brunt of official persecution was endured by the *Montoneros* (leftist Peronists) and other Marxist groups. However, the Argentine Communist party was spared from the barbarities committed against other suspects. The apparent reason for the survival of the Communist party was its refusal to support the terrorist activities of other Marxists,[24] and the fact that Argentina was one of the biggest trading partners of the former Soviet Union in Latin America.

After having completed the brutal elimination of the internal opposition, the military attempted to recover the Falkland Islands from England in 1982. For the military, it was an unfortunate miscalculation of the British will to defend an outpost of their former empire. The Argentinean army expected to have American support for its collaboration in the "secret" war against Nicaragua. Other priorities caused the United States to prefer its British ally. Argentina was soundly routed and humiliated, but in the wake of the catastrophe, the civilians were allowed to compete for the government. The dictatorship's demise was also influenced by the economic stagnation and the crisis of legitimacy affecting the military regime.[25] Once again, the Radicals were elected a year after the military defeat. However, the Radicals' failure to provide solutions for the economic prostration and the legacy of military mismanagement and deindustrialization paved the road for the return of Peronism under the right-wing leadership of Carlos Menem six years later. The party's new leadership had reversed the most sacred tenets of *Justicialismo*, and neo-liberalism became the newest illusion that would make the nation great once again.

Menem proclaimed that Argentina was no longer a Third World power, and that the country's future was in the company and solidarity of the industrial nations. Such verbosity must remain within the framework of Latin American magic realism for the time being. From the Spanish philosopher José Ortega y Gasset (1883-1955) onwards, it has been repeatedly asserted that the young Argentinean country of immigrants and emigrants had nationalists without a nation. Despite the Argentinean beliefs about their country as a European nation, Argentina suffers the classic ills of Latin American underdevelopment. Certainly, the Argentinean elites have disdained nationalist projects to liberate the whole country from underdevelopment despite abundant resources. It has been relatively easy for the Argentinean elites to move to more profitable places when local conditions became difficult. Perhaps with the passing of time the neophyte nationalists will realize that there is a nation to build in Argentina. However, Peronism still attempts to mobilize women and the Argentinean masses in a nationalist project.

As Argentina ended the second millennium, it did so with one of the most industrialized Latin American economies. Argentina is an exporter of meats and grains who also exports industrial products, from toothpaste to nuclear technology. Furthermore, Argentina and Brazil had become the biggest South American economies sponsoring *Mercosur*, the common market for their adjacent region. Argentina had the largest Latin American middle class, but the "Villa Miseria" and rural poverty persisted with all their wretchedness. It is estimated that over 30% of the Argentinean population survived on incomes below the "poverty level" by the end of the twentieth century. Peronism, as in the days of its founder's exile, continues to survive, grow and adapt without "the general." For the sake of economic recovery, the Argentinean elites encouraged a "dialogue" between civilians and the Army. However, it should not be forgotten that one of the most politicized Latin American armies does not intend to lose its grip on the way in which the fatherland is to be modernized and defended.

The Obsessive Hinterland

In 1811, the Paraguayan republic emerged as an independent entity apart from Spain and Argentina alike. This isolated country was inhabited by about a quarter of a million Indians and Mestizos. The Paraguayans lived from subsistence-agriculture and their exports of *yerba mate* tea. After Paraguay had become one of the first centers of Spanish colonization during the sixteenth century, it was virtually abandoned to its own devices. Aided by its remote geographic location and ecology, Paraguay developed a unique culture. During colonial days, Paraguay was at first part of the Peruvian viceroyalty. After 1776, it was attached to the newly created viceroyalty of La Plata. Furthermore, the Jesuits operated within Paraguay an almost theocratic society of about 100,000 Indians. With the increasing Brazilian and Argentinean penetration in the colonial era's final days, the Paraguayan hinterland began to lose its geographic remoteness, but the Paraguayans fought back and rejected the "civilizing" encroachments.

By 1814, Dr. José de Francia became absolute dictator and ruled until his natural death, twenty-six years later. Francia was a Guaraní-speaking white lawyer and mystic intellectual of impeccable honesty who became an outstanding figure during the emancipatory struggle. The benevolent and ideological *caudillo* ruled his country like a hacienda; he was the law and the state. Like Argentina's Rosas, he did not wish his countrymen to have any contacts with the outside world, except for exporting native products. The *caudillo* barred foreigners and their publications from entering his country. Paraguay avoided diplomatic relations with European and Latin American countries as well. Francia was obsessed with maintaining the Paraguayan identity. In order to promote national identity, Francia's idiosyncrasy even extended to advising dark-skinned Paraguayans to marry light-skinned ones, and vice versa.

Since the Plata River estuary was the only easy way of communication with the outside world, Paraguay's independence was actually protected by its remoteness. The autocratic Francia wanted to create a self-sufficient society and, consequently, encouraged small industries and cultivation of new crops for local consumption. Without foreign competition, the growth of the textile industry became the most remarkable accomplishment. Local artisans supplied the basic needs of a rustic society. Francia's rule was characterized by its material progress and social peace. Paraguayans respected and feared the patriarchal *caudillo*. The opposition against his paternalism was ruthlessly silenced. The entire apparatus of government was controlled through his own personal appointees in the courts, the Army, the police and the tax-collecting agencies.

When Francia died, the Congress elected Carlos Antonio López

223

and Mariano Alonso to share the executive power for a three-year period (1841-44). López emerged as the strongest figure and became the absolute dictator until his death in 1862. His style and political control was similar to that of Francia. But unlike Francia, López tried to modernize the country with the help of foreigners. Prosperity brought regular steamboat service in the Platine estuary and the construction of a railroad. Schools were built and foreign literature was tolerated.

When Carlos Antonio López died, his son Francisco Solano López succeeded him. Solano López was a man of grandiose illusions. With the increasing income from export taxes, modernization projects were undertaken as well as the creation of the biggest standing army in South America. Francisco Solano López, like previous Paraguayan rulers, feared the expanding European and neo-European penetration of their territory. However, from independence up to 1865, the isolated Paraguayan "native" modernization had provided a better life for its citizens than was the case in other Latin American nations, while avoiding the foreign debt to British neocolonialism. The Paraguayan economic development was based on the collaboration of state and private capital in entrepreneurial ventures. Some American experts have labeled the Paraguayan developmental experience "socialism."[26]

From the outset of independence, Paraguay had been threatened by Brazilian and Argentinean claims over its loosely delimited borders. Moreover, Argentina wanted control of navigation in the Plata estuary. Solano López was interested in a favorable settlement of his country's borders as well as playing an important international role in the Plata region. The greatest threat to his hegemonic ambitions was Brazil's intermittent interference in Uruguayan internal affairs. The excuse for belligerency occurred in late 1864, when Brazil invaded Uruguay in order to install a political faction of its preference. The Brazilian refusal to depart at Paraguay's ultimatum brought a declaration of war and the invasion of the Brazilian Mato Grosso region by Paraguayan troops. Furthermore, Solano López intended to occupy Uruguay and southern Brazil (Rio Grande do Sul). Such a maneuver necessitated the crossing of claimed

Argentinean territory. After Argentina's refusal to collaborate, Solano López also declared war against that nation. Thus began the so-called War of the Triple Alliance or Paraguayan War, which pitted the combined armies of Brazil, Uruguay and Argentina against Paraguay.

The conflict dragged on for over five years of brutal warfare, in which soldiers and civilians were decimated by epidemics and guns. From the outset, the Paraguayan troops were unsuccessful, but their opponents insisted on absolute victory. When Solano López's armies were destroyed, he undertook guerrilla warfare. His fear of being betrayed unleashed a series of executions in which his own relatives became victims. Finally, by March 1, 1870, the autocrat was killed in battle. By then, more than half of all Paraguayans had been killed or died from epidemics. Only 9% of the 220,000 remaining people were male adults. Paraguay's territory was reduced by about 88,000 square kilometers, and Brazil became the biggest beneficiary. Brazil was granted the disputed lands of northern Paraguay. Argentina received the former Jesuit mission area to the east of the Paraná River. Navigation in the Plata estuary came under Argentinean domination. Until 1876, Paraguay was occupied and sexually mated by the victorious armies. It is not by accident that Paraguayan women were the last to be granted voting rights in Latin America (1961). Alas, Paraguay has one of the world's highest death-rates among teenage girls because of unwanted pregnancies.

An indirect consequence of the Paraguayan War was the recognition of Uruguayan and Paraguayan independence as buffer states by Argentina and Brazil. Finally, Paraguay was opened to the globalization process and neocolonialism. While the nation was still under foreign occupation, a few surviving intellectuals gathered and drafted the Constitution of 1870, which remained in force for the next seventy years. The new legal foundation was supposed to prevent the rise of dictators and limited the presidential term to four years without the possibility of immediate reelection.

From within the remnants of the possessing elites, General Bernardino Caballero emerged as the most powerful figure to lead the reconstruction of the war-ravaged country. In 1874, Caballero founded the Colorado (Conservative) Party, which became the most influential political organization of the post-war period. It remained in control of the presidency until 1904, when it fell by popular revolt. Caballero served as president from 1882 to 1886 and exercised great influence through the political machine of the Colorado party until his death (1892). According to the American historian Harris G. Warren, the greatest accomplishment of Colorado rule was that it prevented Argentina and Brazil from partitioning Paraguay.[27] The Colorado party also fabricated the iconographic figure of Francisco Solano López in the Paraguayan struggle against foreign domination.[28]

Although, in the aftermath of the Paraguayan War, Argentina had to content itself with a smaller land acquisition than Brazil, Argentineans emerged as the most powerful foreigners in Paraguay. Argentinean entrepreneurs and British credits developed lumber mills, sugar plantations, cotton, tobacco, rice and fruit farms for the export market. The peasants were reduced to near-serfdom and agriculture for local markets was neglected.[29] Perceptively, the English historian Eric Hobsbawm has noted: "The Paraguayan War may be best regarded as part of the integration of the River Plate basin into the British world economy [which] forced Paraguay out of the self-sufficiency."[30] By the same token, Solano López remains a symbol of Paraguayan patriotism. In the aftermath of the Paraguayan War, a railroad that linked Asunción with the Platine estuary, from where steamboats and barges crossed to Argentina, was completed in 1885. During the last quarter of the nineteenth century, the land-locked nation accelerated its acquisition of gadgets from the industrial world. Although rail and telegraph mileage increased as steamers multiplied, Paraguay had become one of the most backward nations in the hemisphere.

After the Liberal revolt of 1904, the victors managed to hold the presidency for the next 32 years. But in the wake of the Paraguayan victory over Bolivia in the Chaco War (1932-35), the Liberals were overthrown by an army coup led by Colonel Rafael Franco on February 17, 1936. Franco was a hero of the Chaco War, and he led a movement of young officers and civilians who called themselves Febreristas. The Febreristas took their name from the fact that they had overthrown the Liberals in the month of February. The Febreristas were populists who attempted to create a "New Paraguay" through some sort of native socialism. They advocated for land reform and actually distributed over five million acres of public lands during their 18 months in power. An eight-hour workday and labor's right to unionize were sanctioned. But the possibilities of more radical change brought a military coup with the connivance of the Liberal party. However, the Febrerista program had created a new perspective of local politics, and succeeding governments attempted to incorporate some Febrerista tenets into their political platforms.

The new alliance between the Army and the Liberals resulted in the further political ascendancy of military officers at the expense of their civilian allies. This situation became prevalent especially after General Higinio Moríñigo became president in September 1940. Moríñigo ruled as a ruthless *caudillo* for the next eight years, but in order to give his government some legitimacy, he revived the nearly defunct Colorado party by doling out bureaucratic jobs. Moríñigo's strength was the Army, while the Colorado party provided the conservative ideology of "law and order."

During World War II, Paraguay prospered by exporting coffee, cotton, sugar, beef and forest products to the United States. In an effort to contain the Argentinean control of about 75% of all foreign interests in Paraguay, the United States granted military, technical and economic aid to Moríñigo. But with the end of the war, a decline in the demand for Paraguayan exports brought serious dislocations to the economy as well as political unrest. From March to August 1947, a bloody civil war was unleashed in which Moríñigo, the Colorados or Conservatives and the most reactionary elements of the Army defeated the Febreristas, Liberals, Communists and leftist officers. As a result of the civil war, the Conservative Party was revitalized and prevailed in the nomination of a civilian successor to Moríñigo. The Colorado party dominated the succeeding six years of political life; however, conflicts between

227

its civilian and military leaders had brought much instability.

Finally by July 1954, General Alfredo Stroessner inaugurated his election as president. He became one of the most reelected and durable anti-Communist dictators of the world until his son-in-law General Andrés Rodríguez exiled the patriarch in February 1989. Stroessner was the typical Paraguayan and Latin American dictator who fits the portrayal by Gabriel García Márquez and Augusto Roa Bastos as having "an irrepressible passion to endure" and yet dying or losing anyway. Stroessner required professionals and bureaucrats who hoped for a good future to join the Colorado party. Surveillance dominated every aspect of life. Stroessner was a descendant of German immigrants who protected Dr. Josef Mengele and other runaway Nazi criminals. Because of the Cold War, the United States tolerated his brutality, eccentricities and stage-managed elections.

Stroessner's inheritors promised free elections and political pluralism. A more just distribution of the nation's resources was not included in the democratic scheme by the most kindred Latin American elite. Paraguay remained the only Latin American country to still vote in the United Nations for the American economic embargo against Communist Cuba until the very end of the twentieth century. A modern security apparatus and generous American military aid also defend the local elites. Since the early 1940s, there has been increasing penetration by Brazilian enterprises. In the mirage of Latin American interests, the Paraguayan geography is becoming a strategic component of the Brazilian "near abroad."

Paraguay has become one of the least industrialized Latin American nations, and although involved in agribusiness, it remains nearly pastoral. Paraguay's inland location has allowed this hermit nation to live almost indifferent to world trends. Likewise, the Paraguayan geographic remoteness has allowed the local elites to develop one of the most sophisticated and diversified South American smuggling centers. Politicians, entrepreneurs and crooks are nearly the same actors. Until very recently, the voices of dissent were systematically killed, endured long prison terms or fled to neighboring countries. About a million Paraguayans live abroad for political or economic reasons. The cozy relationship between the Army, the Colorado party and the bureaucracy are dictatorial heritages with which democratic activists will have to contend for years to come.

When the Liberation Theologian Fernando Lugo challenged the ruling elites and became a presidential candidate, he was suspended by the Vatican. His election to the presidency on April 20, 2008 was intended to end over six decades of Colorado autocracy as well as challenge American hegemony. By the end of Colorado rule, one percent of the population controlled 77% of the agricultural lands and over 40% lived in poverty. Although acknowledging that plantation magnates and peasants had legitimate rights, Lugo was elected on the promise to redistribute land, provide jobs and end corruption. He was boycotted from the beginning and eventually deposed by the employees of the oligarchy. The Paraguayan elites have returned with their old theology and incapacity, to reform the status quo.

The Swiss Illusion

Uruguay is the smallest South American republic with 116,094 square kilometers (about 1/4 the size of Sweden). If Paraguay had to struggle for its independence with Spain and Argentina, Uruguay had as additional claimants to its sovereignty Portugal and Brazil. Since 1810, about 70,000 Uruguayans (most of European descent) have been the participants and victims in the vexations of independence campaigns and foreign domination efforts. Finally, by 1828, and under British forceful mediation, Brazil and Argentina agreed to respect the independence of Uruguay. Ever since, both South American powers have struggled to establish their hegemony upon this little country. However, it was Britain that emerged as the most influential power in Uruguay. Before World War I, Britain had invested over 46 million pounds in Uruguay, and it controlled its railroads, infrastructure and foreign debt.[31]

In 1830, a constitutional convention drafted a *magna carta* that remained in effect until 1919. It provided for a four-year presidency without possibility of immediate reelection. The president was elected by the General Assembly, which was composed of the chamber of senators and deputies. The right to vote was granted to every literate male. During the 1830s, more than two thirds of the population lived in Montevideo and the coastal area. The rural interior was sparsely inhabited, and it sustained immense herds of wild cattle. In many ways, Uruguay resembled a miniature Argentina. As in Argentina, there existed a great economic and cultural cleavage between the rustic countryside and the port city of Montevideo. Thus, from the 1830s onwards, we discern the evolution of two major political parties: the Blancos (Conservatives) and the Colorados (Liberals). Their differences and adherents resembled the general pattern of Latin American politics.

The first Uruguayan president was General Fructuoso Rivera. He had fought for national sovereignty together with the "first patriot" José Artigas. After independence he led a revolt, which arranged for his proper constitutional election. When his four-year term expired, Rivera handed the government to General Manuel Oribe, who eventually became the leader of the Conservative party. However, Rivera intended to remain in control of the provincial armies. Finally, by 1836, Rivera revolted in the name of Liberalism. The conflict was further fuelled by the economic and military aid provided by Argentina's Rosas to the Conservatives. Oribe managed to complete his presidential term, but by then (1839-51) the intermittent conflicts between Liberals and Conservatives had intensified. This fratricidal period is known as the "Great War." With the help of the British and French navies, Rivera and the Colorados usually occupied Montevideo, while the interior was controlled by the Blancos or Conservatives with Rosas' support.

Montevideo became more Europeanized and intellectually active. Like contemporary Chile, Montevideo became a refugee center for Argentinean intellectuals who escaped Rosas' persecutions. Public and private education was revitalized with the collaboration of Argentinean exiles as well as educated European immigrants. The most outstanding economic development of the "Great War" period was Montevideo's growth as a duty-free port. Montevideo's prosperity was based on the handling of exports produced in the interior and the smuggling of European industrial products into the Platine region. Rosas' defeat with Uruguayan participation and the struggles against Brazilian invasions (1850s-1860s), plus the fact that the nation was dragged into the Paraguayan War, convinced the Liberal and Conservative elites alike that foreign entanglements occurred regardless of which party was in power.

In an effort to eliminate internal conflicts and external threats, from the 1850s onwards several politicians advocated the "politics of fusion," which meant some representation for the party that was out of office. Furthermore, after mid-century, the Colorados had rapidly grown through immigration and urbanization. The Blancos feared obliteration and constantly revolted. Finally, by 1872, the Blancos agreed to demobilize their armies in exchange for 500,000 pesos and the right to appoint the prefects (political bosses) in four of the 13 provinces. Such a political arrangement permitted the Liberals to rule the nation until 1959 as well as evade intervention by Brazil or Argentina. The tempo of internal conflicts was lowered, but since the marginalization of the Conservatives from the presidency was not a voluntary role, they continued to conspire. The last Blanco effort to capture the presidency by force occurred in 1904, when its leader Aparicio Saraiva was killed in battle. Thereafter, a new age of Uruguayan politics was inaugurated by Colorado and Blanco efforts to create what used to be known as Latin America's Switzerland.

By 1900, Uruguay's population had reached the one million mark as the result of European immigration and natural growth. During the last third of the nineteenth century, the politics of compromise prevailed, and under those peaceful conditions the economy bloomed, in many ways like the Argentinean modernization process. Likewise, Uruguay's high literacy rate had become comparable only to that of Argentina in the Iberian world. If Paraguay has been the Latin American nation most underexposed to European influence, Uruguay has had the opposite fate.

Before the advent of the Great Depression, José Batlle (1856-

1929) was the most influential statesman in shaping the Uruguayan political system. He was the son of a former president and was educated in Uruguay and Europe. At the dawn of the twentieth century, Batlle emerged as the Colorados' leader and, on two occasions, the president of the republic (1903-07, 1911-15). As chief ideologist of the majority party, his influence prevailed while in office and out of it. Batlle was an economic nationalist. Moreover, he felt that the biggest source of political instability as well as dictatorship was the presidential system. Batlle and his followers set out to create a plural executive patterned after that of Switzerland. Thus, the Constitution of 1917 provided for a plural executive office (Colegiado). The presidency was to be shared by the nine members of the Administrative National Council. The minority party (i.e., Conservative) was guaranteed one-third representation in both the Council and the bicameral parliament. Universal male suffrage was also legislated.

For the ruling elites, the age of Batlle was one of unmitigated prosperity based on exports of wool, grains, meats and South American banking. Likewise, the nation's bountiful resources financed one of the most advanced social welfare programs in the world. Labor was granted the right to organize, a minimum wage, an eight-hour work-day and a six-day work week, old-age pension, unemployment compensation and accident insurance. The underprivileged and mothers were guaranteed free medical care. Although Batlle was no feminist, he believed that women, like the proletariat, children, the poor and weak, had to be protected in what has been called the "paternalist" modernization.[32]

The death of Batlle coincided with the outbreak of the Great Depression. Uruguay lost one of its greatest leaders as well as its export markets. Exports declined by more than 80%, causing widespread bankruptcies, unemployment and near collapse of the social welfare system. The leadership of the Colorado party fell into the hands of the dictatorial Gabriel Terra. In 1930, Terra was elected to a four-year presidential term. But faced with social and political unrest, he allied himself with the Army and dissolved the Council and Parliament. In 1934, Terra gave the nation a new constitution that restored the single presidency and got himself reelected. Terra ruled by decree and used unprecedented repression to contain social and political unrest. When Terra's term was over, he was succeeded by his brother-in-law, General Alfredo Baldomir.

The late 1930s brought a revival of the economy. Trade was expanded with Brazil, Germany and the United States. Moreover, the advent of World War II brought a boom to Uruguayan exports. Like Argentina, Uruguay accumulated much foreign currency during the war. State revenues were used to revitalize the social welfare system, the infrastructure and purchase the British-owned railways. The booming demand for Uruguayan exports continued even after the war was over because of British and American hostility towards comparable products from Perón's Argentina. The outbreak of the Korean War revitalized furthermore the export of Uruguayan commodities. Under prosperous conditions the nation was returned to the plural executive system in 1951. It lasted a decade and a half.

The collapse of the wool market in 1957, as well as declining prices for other Uruguayan exports, brought social unrest. Inflation, unemployment and disclosures of corruption in the bureaucratic system further discredited the leadership of the Colorado party. After almost 93 years, the Blanco party obtained a majority vote in the elections of 1958. For the next eight years the Blancos ruled in a stagnating economy. The majority of Uruguayans came to realize that the Colorado and Blanco governments made very little difference for the elitist socio-economic domination of the nation. The so-called ideological parties (i.e., mostly Marxists) felt excluded from any meaningful role in the power monopoly exercised by the two traditional parties. The suspension of diplomatic relations with Cuba and the increasing collaboration between the Blanco administration and the United States further alienated labor unions, students and intellectuals. In 1966, the Colorados and the single presidency were returned under the leadership of General Oscar Gestido.

The late 1960s and early 1970s were characterized by growing social unrest. Moreover, urban guerrillas who called themselves

Tupamaros, in memory of the Inca martyr Tupac Amaru II, virtually immobilized the government. With the connivance of the Colorado leadership, a military coup brought a fanatical crusade against "communism" in February 1973. Murder, torture and the abrogation of the most basic human rights became a way of life in the former showcase of Latin American political and social democracy. Four years after the military took over, Uruguay achieved the world's record number of political prisoners per capita; that is, some 5,000 prisoners out of a total 2,763,964 people. More than 500,000 Uruguayans fled their country because of the "dirty war" and for economic reasons. The tragic Uruguayan experience demonstrates that one of the most "harmonious" societies of the planet can regress to barbarity when economic crisis arrives.

The mismanagement and near collapse of the Uruguayan economy brought demands from the traditional elites for political change. In 1985, the military allowed plebiscitary elections in which the Blanco and Colorado parties presented together only one presidential candidate. Amnesty for the crimes of the "dirty war" was a pre-condition before the military handed over the government to the civilians once again. Two decades later, the first former *Tupamaro*, Tabaré Vásquez, was elected president. By then, the *Tupamaro* dreams about a socialist future were more concerned with market values and compromises with the defeated political opposition. His *Tupamaro* successor, José Mujica; advanced further in the same political and economic direction. Since mid-nineteenth century, the Uruguayan elites have had a history of political compromises when facing internal and external pressures. Indeed, the structural changes from neo-liberal conditions need the Uruguayan institutional assets for a peaceful transition. Uruguayans do know, literally in flesh and blood, that they do not need another "dirty war." But the new *Tupamaros* still have the audacity of imagining a different future and correcting previous mistakes.

The Awakening Giant

Brazil's transition from colony to sovereign nation was accomplished without much change. The emancipatory struggles, which brought so much bloodshed, destruction and political polarization throughout the Spanish Empire, were avoided in Portuguese America. In 1822, when Brazil became independent, it not only had an emperor in Pedro I, but the monarch was a Braganza born in Portugal. The relatively peaceful transition allowed the Brazilian nationalist elites to develop at a higher pace of material growth than most of its neighbors.

Within the Latin American context, Brazil was a backward geography with some 3.5 million inhabitants at the time of independence. More than a million Brazilians were black slaves and an equally approximate number were Indians, Mulattos and mixed races. Indeed, they were the backbone in the Brazilian slavist mode of production. Over half a million were white or nearly white. They constituted the top of the pyramidal ruling elite. Their power was concentrated in the northeastern sugar and cotton plantations and the southern cattle ranches, as well as in commerce, mining and the bureaucracy. Although there was much antipathy between Portuguese and Brazilian whites, their differences were not between the rich and the downtrodden. It was a conflict of elites and anti-elites.

Pedro I led the newly emancipated colony to believe that he was very concerned with the political modernization of his realm. He surrounded himself with distinguished Portuguese and Creole advisors. His most influential confidant became the Brazilian-born intellectual Bonifacio Andrada, who represented the native elites. Pedro and Andrada seemed to agree on the conception that the nation should pattern itself after the most modernizing European monarchies. In 1823, a constitutional convention was summoned under which Liberal and Republican influences demanded more power than Pedro had envisioned. The outcome was a confrontation in which Andrada and other important Creoles had to flee into exile. With the most Liberal opposition dismissed, Pedro redrafted

235

the constitutional proposals into a document that remained in force until the monarchy collapsed in 1889. According to the constitution, the emperor was granted the "moderator power," which placed him above politics and gave him absolutist prerogatives. The monarch could veto judicial and legislative decisions as well as dismiss parliament at his will. He also appointed the provincial governors. As in colonial times, Catholicism remained the official religion, and under the emperor's patronage.

Between 1825 and 1828, Brazil negotiated agreements with England that recognized its independence and established low tariffs for English products. England persuaded its junior Portuguese partner to accept Brazilian independence. England also forced Brazil to acquiesce to the termination of slave imports by 1831 and help Portugal pay its debt to the British. Brazil and Argentina alike were compelled by the British to honor Uruguayan independence. The relative peace of Pedro's rule was disturbed by Republican and secessionist revolts in the northeast, but with the services of mercenary troops and the private navy of the Scottish fortune-hunter Lord Thomas Cochrane, the movement was quelled.[33]

As Pedro's autocracy reached its seventh year, it was faced by mounting Liberal and Republican agitation. Pedro, like his father João VI, had attempted to ignore the Brazilian rural aristocracy, which, until the Portuguese monarchy fled to Brazil (1808) from Napoleon, had been a very influential local force. When Pedro's father died in 1826, he renounced to the Portuguese throne and appointed his infant daughter María da Gloria as queen. However, Pedro's brother Miguel overthrew María. Pedro's protracted and expensive involvement in the Portuguese civil war brought greater defiance at home. Furthermore, he was also blamed for allowing the rise of Uruguay as an independent national state. When the Liberals and several army units demanded that Pedro's reactionary Portuguese advisors resign, the emperor suddenly abdicated in favor of his five-year old son Pedro de Alcantara and left for Portugal, where he fought to reinstate his daughter as queen. In the meantime, a three-man regency was created to govern Brazil until the new emperor became of age.

Pedro's departure gave the native aristocrats a greater chance to manipulate the government in their favor. Unfortunately, they were divided and quarrelsome. Their economic and regional differences were further impaired by ideological divisions. The Liberals wanted federalism and secularization, while the Conservatives wanted to preserve a centralized monarchical system with close links to the Church. During the regency (1831-40), there were slave revolts, military uprisings and mass demonstrations as well as secessionist movements in Pará, Maranhão, Minas Gerais and Rio Grande do Sul. Moreover, there was an undercurrent revival of Republicanism, especially in the south. In an effort to appease the landed aristocracy, the principal regent Diego Feijó, a Liberal priest, granted more powers to the elected provincial legislatures in 1834. A year later, the three-man regency was replaced by the sole authority of Feijó. His power monopoly lasted only two years. Perhaps the most significant factor in his downfall was his inability to quell the secessionist movement in Rio Grande do Sul, which had become a Republican cause. In a desperate effort to save the monarchy and the fragmentation of the Brazilian national state, the Conservative and Liberal elites united forces and declared the fourteen-year old Pedro the official emperor.

The adolescent Pedro II proved to be a pragmatic ruler who succeeded in pitting local politicians for his patronage. By 1848, the Army under the monarchist Marshal de Caixas suppressed the Rio Grande do Sul secessionist movement despite its heroic efforts, which had the sympathies and participation of many foreign volunteers like the Italian Guiseppe Garibaldi.[34] Furthermore, Pedro II tamed the struggles between Conservatives and Liberals by astutely alternating them in the Cabinet. During the monarch's long regime, the differences among Conservatives and Liberals were virtually obliterated. Both groups supported the monarchy with all its ornamental trappings. They were socially conservative and intensely anti-democratic. Their aspiration was to reconcile order and progress, and the status quo with modernization. Pedro's power was based on his alliance with the landed aristocracy, whom his father and grandfather had alienated. With an artistic touch, the

237

emperor courted and delighted the large landholders by granting titles of nobility and appointments to high bureaucratic positions.

Like Argentina after the mid-nineteenth century, Brazil experienced unmitigated economic growth. However, Brazil was a country of wider ethnic, racial, economic and geographic contrasts. Railroads, telegraph lines, steamboats, mills and rustic factories were built, mostly as intertwining appendages to the rapid growth of coffee cultivation for export in the central and southern regions. European immigrants arrived in increasing numbers to profit from the Brazilian economic opportunities and peculiar modernization. About four million Europeans migrated to Brazil during the first century of independence. As was the case in most of Latin America, British capital became the most prominent foreign financing source. Likewise, until World War I, England remained the biggest supplier of imports to Brazil.

Like Sarmiento in Argentina, Pedro II wanted to educate his people. He was obsessed with "civilizing" Brazil. The "school master emperor" made sincere efforts to modernize education, and hired American and European educators to innovate the empire's pedagogical system. Although a law in 1850 made primary school attendance compulsory for non-slave children, there were not enough facilities or personnel to carry out this fantasy. Through private philanthropy, efforts were made to build new schools, buy books and even provide scholarships for students to study in the United States and Europe. But by the end of the nineteenth century, no more than 15% of the total people were literate.

By most contemporary standards, Pedro's long rule was a successful one, and yet he was swiftly replaced by a republican system in November 1889. There was no bloodshed or any resistance behind the change. Despite Pedro's popularity, he was only an instrument of elitist control in which not more than 2% of the people voted. The Army was the most significant in Pedro's downfall. From the outset of his rule, Pedro had deliberately kept the military in the background. However, the Paraguayan War (1865-70) brought the Army into prominence as well as disturbed the sociopolitical harmony of the system. Moreover, the war had caused over 50,000 casualties in a struggle that came to be seen as the emperor's own crusade. Yet after the bloody victory, the Army was virtually dismantled and pushed into obscurity. As long as Marshal Caixas was alive, the Army was restrained. With his death in 1880, a new generation of politicized officers was promoted, many of them influenced by republican ideas. Furthermore, the upper echelons wanted a share in political power, and when the emperor appointed a premier distasteful to them, they conspired with the Republicans and overthrew the monarchy.

The landed aristocracy's failure to prevent the downfall of its illustrious and magnanimous emperor is deeply rooted in the structural transformation of the nation's socio-economy after mid-nineteenth century. The metamorphosis came slowly but it had a cumulative effect, which eroded the patriarchal base of Brazilian society, especially in the northeastern region. As the result of British pressure and naval patrols, the import of slaves was terminated in the 1850s. Henceforth, a virulent abolitionist movement thrived throughout the urban centers with the emperor's tacit consent. Finally, while the emperor was in Europe (1888), his daughter Isabel liberated more than 600,000 slaves without compensation to the owners. This decision most severely injured the royalist sugar and cotton planters of the northeast. The expansionist southern coffee planters were never very strong supporters of the monarchy. Their growing affluence had come to thrive mostly on free immigrant labor. Moreover, slaves escaped from the coffee plantations and disturbed production. Thus, it was not difficult for the large landholders to forsake the emperor. Abolition simply precipitated the fall of the monarchy.

Brazil was not plagued by the big crisis between Church and state that affected most of Latin America in the aftermath of independence. In the 1820s, Buenos Aires and Brazil were the first in Latin America that dared to introduce freedom of public worship. In Portuguese America, as in Argentina, the Church was relatively weak and its wealth was in land. Since both Brazil and Argentina had plenty of fertile lands, anti-clerical sentiment could not be mobilized as easily as in Mexico or other Spanish American republics.

The establishment of a Brazilian monarchy of the same dynasty as in Portugal after independence also facilitated the continuation of the royal patronage. Despite the relatively smooth relations between Church and state, Pedro had alienated the most reactionary clergymen by his tolerance of Protestants, Jews and Masons.

In 1872, a crisis came about because several bishops launched a public campaign against the Masonic lodges, ordering all faithful Catholics to condemn or forsake them. Such an order brought an open clash between secular and religious forces since the Masonry had a long honorable tradition in Brazil. Furthermore, many intellectuals were self-proclaimed Masons, and Pedro II was suspected of being one. The emperor considered the clerical pronouncements against the Masonry unlawful Church interference and saw that the transgressing bishops were prosecuted and jailed. Although the bishops did not serve their full sentences, the Church had been alienated. Many clergymen came to think of the royal patronage as unnecessary governmental interference in religious affairs. Henceforth, a receptiveness developed in many religious quarters to Republican promises of ending the patronage system. Moreover, anti-clericals also became fearful of Church designs, especially since the heir-to-be Princess Isabel was a reputed Papal loyalist. But as the Brazilian historian Emilia Viotti has perceptively noted: "Republicans were more concerned to emancipate society from the Church than to emancipate the Church from the State."[35]

The structural socio-economic changes and Pedro's non-political decisions during the last days of his rule hastened the monarchy's demise. Pedro had gradually lost his historic allies without developing new sources of support. The clients of royal patronage had also lost their incentives.[36] The Army succeeded because the traditional forces, which usually supported the monarchy, had failed their emperor in a moment of crisis. It was the Army that, in reality, guaranteed the enforcement of the emperor's "moderator power." It was in Brazil where the professional army made possible the peaceful transition from colony to independent monarchy and from monarchy to republic. With the emperor's departure, the

Army struggled to legitimize its inheritance of the "moderator power." The transition from monarchy to republic was not a major break with the past. The planters and merchants with their clients preserved the oligarchic system nearly intact.

While the intellectuals debated on the theoretical foundations of the new republic, the Army took over. The Army's salaries were increased, and the ranks invaded all levels of the bureaucracy and profitable ventures. The military increased its power-grip by an alliance with the socio-economic elites of Rio de Janeiro and São Paulo. Under the slogan of "order and progress," Deodoro da Fonseca declared the United States of Brazil a federal republic that provided for the separation of Church and state, suffrage for all literate males and a four-year presidency without immediate re-election. A hand-picked congress formally elected Fonseca to the presidency. But Fonseca and the civilian politicians had different ideas as to how the republic should be governed. Fonseca was a very authoritarian officer who intended to command the country as he ordered his soldiers.

Federalism became a misnomer, for out of 20 states only the biggest (São Paulo, Minas Gerais and Rio Grande do Sul) had any degree of sovereignty. Moreover, the Congress intended to legislate. When the legislators delayed the president's budget, his troops invaded their chamber and forcefully unseated them. Fonseca's high-handed methods caused a national uproar, forcing him to resign only two years after his assault on the monarchy. The vice president, Marshal Floriano Peixoto, another leader in the conspiracy that abolished the monarchy, succeeded him. During his rule, there were naval insurrections, monarchist revolts and riots. In addition, inflation and the mismanagement of public funds convinced the regional oligarchies that military officers should remain in the barracks. When Peixoto's term was over, they elected a civilian. This was the beginning of non-military rule, which lasted until 1910. Except for a short military interlude (1910-14), civilians from São Paulo and Minas Gerais ruled until 1930 because of a tacit understanding between the oligarchies of both states to alternate the presidency.

By 1900, all major revolts had been quelled, including a syn-cretistic popular movement in the interior of the backward north-east. The mystic and charismatic leader Antonio Counselheiro launched a military crusade to exterminate the godless republic in favor of Jesus and the monarchy. The revolt and movement for Jesus hardly received any support outside its region (Bahía state), but it took the Army more than three years (1893-97) and much bloodshed to eradicate it. In many ways, such a conflict represented the bloody confrontation between the traditional and modernizing world. With order restored and British financial backing, the Brazil-ian territory was guided into capitalist prosperity, for the nation had most of the rubber that the industrial world demanded, and coffee exports were just as important revenue-earners. Sugar, cotton, wood, tobacco and hides were also exported in significant quanti-ties. Although the political influence of the sugar and cotton planters had declined, their tax payments were significant. How-ever, the balance of economic power had shifted from the northeast to the central and southern states.

Until 1930, an alliance of civilian politicians and entrepreneurs from the two most powerful states (São Paulo, Minas Gerais) was able to curb the growing powers of the Army. But in 1910, the Army forced the candidacy and consequent election of Marshal Hermes da Fonseca, the nephew of the first president. His govern-ment coincided with the collapse of the rubber boom and lower coffee prices. After Fonseca's unhappy period, the Army was dis-credited and remained in the background. The return to civilian rule was concomitant with the outbreak of World War I. The ruling elites' sympathies were with the Allies, Brazil's biggest trading partners. When several Brazilian ships were sunk by German sub-marines, Brazil declared war on Germany in October 1917, thus becoming the only South American nation that declared war against the Central Powers. World War I brought high prices for Brazilian exports and accelerated import-substitution industrialization.

After World War I, falling prices for local exports and the renewed competition faced by the infant industries from foreign competitors brought serious economic dislocations. Social unrest

242

challenged the rule of the regional oligarchies. During the early 1920s, a movement of young officers (*Tenentes*) and civilians advocated for drastic social and political changes. One of the most important leaders of this movement was Captain Luis Prestes, who in 1924 led unsuccessful uprisings in São Paulo and Rio Grande do Sul. After his defeat, Prestes became a leader of the Communist party. Behind the military, political and social agitation of the "roaring twenties," there was rapid economic growth, particularly in São Paulo. São Paulo, as the largest coffee producer and most industrialized state, had become the home of the most powerful regional plutocracy. Brazil produced 70% of the world's coffee. Coffee also constituted about 72% of Brazilian exports. But the advent of the Great Depression was immediately felt in Brazil and São Paulo. Coffee prices dropped to less than one third of what they had been, and the lines of credit were interrupted. The coffee oligarchy was seriously injured.

When in the elections of 1930 the Paulista political machine attempted to maintain its control of the presidency for another four-year term, a nation-wide revolt was led by the governor of Rio Grande do Sul, Dr. Getulio Vargas. With the help of the Army, Vargas was installed as provisional president. Due to emergency conditions and personal manipulations, this political maverick ruled as a dictator for the next fifteen years. Vargas inaugurated a new political era by centralizing the entire bureaucratic system, crushing the traditional political machines and subsidizing industrial production. A shift from external to internal stimulants of growth was promoted. Vargas shifted the direction of political and cultural nationalism to "developmental nationalism." Vargas and his followers argued that the only way Brazil could become truly independent was through industrialization and modernization. Ever since, generations of Brazilian nationalists bickered as to whether a basically socialist or capitalist economy was to be promoted.[37]

Vargas gave Brazil decrees, martial laws and constitutions that attempted to create a corporatist and nationalist society called the New State (1937-45). Industrialization in which private and state capital would participate became a major concern of his govern-

243

ment. Organized labor was granted minimum wages, shorter working days, pension benefits, accident insurance, free medical care, cheap restaurants and low-cost housing. Literate women were enfranchised and public education was popularized. Indeed, Vargas was an economic nationalist who attempted to diminish American and British influence by courting and increasing trade with Nazi Germany. Thus, during much of the 1930s, Germany replaced England as Brazil's second biggest trading partner. But American threats and rewards to Vargas' "adventurism" kept Brazil distant from the fascist powers. Only a month after the United States entered World War II, Brazil joined the Allies.

Vargas and Perón in Argentina were economic nationalists who intended to industrialize their nations with state support. Although Vargas' dictatorship had much affinity with European fascism, his policies were a response to local conditions. Moreover, Vargas repressed the "ideological" fascists who identified themselves with European models. With the Army's loyalty, Vargas suppressed revolts by the Paulistas (1932), Communists (1935) and the *Integralistas* or Fascists (1938). He was the master politician with a silver tongue who played one extremist group against the other. Gradually, the Army and Vargas came to depend on each other in a quest for a nationalist modernization.

As World War II reached its conclusion, the voices of opposition clamored for free elections. With pressure from the United States and the Army, Vargas promised elections in April 1945. In a carnival-like atmosphere celebrating the victory over fascism, political amnesty was granted to all politicians, diplomatic relations with the Soviet Union were established and the Communist party was legalized. Vargas very reluctantly agreed not to run in the promised elections. In order to make sure that his pledge was fulfilled, the Army and the American Embassy forced him to resign. In the freest elections in national history, the two major candidates were military officers. The victor was General Eurico Dutra, Vargas' former War Minister and last-minute endorsee. For the first time in the nation's history, women were allowed to vote, which was a contemporary Latin American privilege practised only in Cuba and Uruguay.

Dutra was the candidate for the newly created Social Democratic Party (PSD), which represented urban, middle-class and bureaucratic interests. The PSD was created by Vargas during the last days of his dictatorship, when elections had become inevitable. Moreover, Vargas also founded the PTB (Partido Trabalhista Brasileiro) or Brazilian Labor Party, which appealed to the proletariat, nationalists and leftists. In the last stages of the election campaign, the PTB supported Dutra. Of the many political parties founded after World War II, three played significant roles until the military coup in 1964: the PSD, PTB and UND (National Democratic Union) or Conservatives.

President Dutra was a man of reactionary tendencies who in earlier days had openly admired Nazi Germany. His strongest supporters were the upper classes, the Army and the Church. His foreign policy was very closely co-ordinated with the United States. With the outbreak of the Cold War, Dutra broke diplomatic relations with the Soviet Union and outlawed the Communist party. By 1947, the foreign currency accumulated during World War II had been depleted in the import of capital goods, industrial products, oil and the purchase of the British-owned railroads. Fortunately, the United States was willing to reward Dutra's loyalty with new credits to solve the deficits. Moreover, Brazil became the biggest Latin American recipient of American and other foreign investments in the post-World War II period. The Brazilian attraction for foreign investment has been its abundance of cheap labor and every sort of natural resource. Through private enterprise and government subsidies, Brazil has developed the biggest Latin American industrial complex.

In the post-World War II period, a process of democratization ensued in which the Brazilian masses became more politically active. Moreover, the Constitution of 1946 created a federal republic in which the presidential office was downgraded and the possibility for immediate reelection was eliminated. The president and the vice president were to be elected on separate tickets, and they could be from different parties. All literate adults were enfranchised, and all elections were to be by popular vote. During the Dutra administration, Vargas spent his time reorganizing and expanding his party, the PTB. In 1950, Vargas was elected by an overwhelming majority as a candidate for the PTB, with the support of the Marxist left. Opposition from the traditional elites, the most reactionary sectors in the Army and the United States plagued Vargas' return to the government. The restrictions imposed by Vargas on the multinational corporations' profits brought a break with the World Bank. Vargas refused the American "invitation" to participate in the Korean War. He attempted to develop a neutralist foreign policy. Through his Labor Minister João Goulart, an effort was made to mobilize the proletariat. But, after Vargas was accused of intriguing to create some sort of local Peronism, the most reactionary leaders of the Army, including General Dutra, demanded his resignation. Instead, Vargas chose to commit suicide on August 24, 1954.

After Vargas' death, Goulart undertook the leadership of the PTB and the mobilization of the lower classes. With grass-roots support, Goulart was twice elected vice president, and when President Janio Quadros of the UND resigned in 1961, he reached the presidency. Goulart was a populist aristocrat who mobilized the masses and permitted Marxist activists to join in the "politization" campaign. Among his goals were: A neutralist foreign policy, restrictions on multinational corporations and the expansion of trade with Communist countries and the Third World.[38] But during Goulart's administration, American short-term credits and foreign investments dried up, leading to near economic chaos. Finally, on March 30, 1964, the Army, with the logistical support of the American navy under code operation "Brother Sam," overthrew the president. Unlike previous military interventions, on this occasion the generals came committed to institutionalize their rule and safeguard the fatherland from the "Communist menace." Their repression was selectively brutal.[39] Although the military dictatorship repressed local leftists, Brazil expanded its trade with the Communist nations.

Brazil was the first to be subjected to the technocratic and military administration, which flourished throughout Latin America for over two decades. In spite of its neo-liberal rhetoric, the military launched an industrialization agenda in which the state became a prime mover. The motivation to industrialize was the desire to reduce Brazilian dependence on the industrial nations and make Brazil a "great power." Manufactured goods rose from 20% of exports in 1968 to 57% in 1980.[40] Brazil has the most extensive industrial *Research and Development* (*R&D*) program in Latin America, and it has become a technology recycler.[41] The nation exports instruments, shoes, textiles, machine tools, cars, air planes and oil-exploration technology. Before the military left the government in 1985, they had converted Brazil into the first arms manufacturer of the Third World. Brazil's import-substitution industrialization has also been hastened by a growing internal market. The "economic miracle" has benefited, above all, private capital.

Coffee, although important, was relegated to fourth or fifth place as an earner of foreign exchange. The elites also made Brazil an emerging agribusiness power. When the industrialization process nearly resulted in a dictatorial state capitalism, the economic and political elites demanded a civilian government and neo-liberal economic policies. However, among the "world's forty democracies," the Brazilian military retained the most prerogatives.[42] The military continues to diversify, bureaucratize and modernize under the privileged mantle of "National Security." But the Latin American and Brazilian military strategists and ideologists have anticipated that unless internal socio-economic problems are solved, the near future will be "a new form of Fascism."[43] It does appear that the road to militarize Latin American societies is shorter than the one to civilize the military. Fortunately, Brazil does have many patriots and educated cadres who believe in a better future for most of its citizens.

From mid-1970s, Brazilian foreign policy gradually pulled away from its subservience to the United States. A neutralist policy of "responsible pragmatism" is emerging along a search for new trading partners in Europe, the former Communist nations, Africa, Asia and Latin America. Although Brazil is one of the hungriest nations, Brazilian agribusiness is one of the world's biggest food exporters.

247

Brazil has not yet liberated itself from dependence; it has only modernized its dependency. Despite recent changes, Brazilian structures still delay real changes. But lately, sectors of the Brazilian elite are beginning to search for their own model of modernization and are making Brazil a "major nation" of the world. The Brazilian state, after the charismatic President Lula (2002-10), is no longer willing to be taken for granted by the industrial powers and their local allies. The election of the former guerrilla fighter and "convicted terrorist" Dilma Rousseff as president of Brazil (2011–) is a new watershed in Latin America's political and gender history. In Brazil, as in Uruguay, former guerrillas have become heads of state. However, peaceful changes of structural conditions can only come about slowly. Ironically, Brazil, which was historically propped up by the United States to contain Argentina, has emerged as the biggest challenge to American hegemony in South America.

CHAPTER VIII

LATIN AMERICA AFTER THE COLD WAR

T he American hegemonic shadow has been a constant menace of, or "protection" for, the elites and peoples of Latin America. The so-called "backyard" has strategic resources as well as geopolitical significance. Moreover, the United States is the only outside power with military influence in Latin America, even though Europe, Japan and China are great investors. Latin American nationalism and patriotism have been searching for alternative socio-economic models and powerful allies throughout the "independence period." Latin American political leaders, patriots and idealists have different ideas and passions about the future of their region. They are constantly reinventing themselves within local and global contexts. One of them, Fidel Castro, noted that although there were no two identical socialist processes, "China has become the most concrete and promising hope and best example for all the countries of the Third World."[1]

At least in the short term, "socialism" without equality is being promoted by the Chinese Communist Party for the sake of China's rebirth as a great nation. Unlike the Soviet reversion from communism, the Chinese retreat from Maoism was a well-organized retreat. After the Cold War, American foreign policy south of the Rio Grande was concerned with "drug wars," military cooperation and the enforcement of neo-liberal economic policies. The war against narcotics and terrorism involves American interventions through "undercover" operations. Unilaterally and annually, the United States decides which Latin American nations deserve "certification" for their efforts against the illegal drug trade. Furthermore, the United States can politically isolate itself from the rest of the world but not from Latin America. American isolationism and interventionism are not contradictory discourse categories in Latin America's geographic reality. Moreover, American hegemony in the region has been constructed with the collaboration, and even passionate pleasure, of the local elites. However, with the development of non-American economic interests in the region, the Latin American elites are keeping their options open.

China has emerged as a major commodity buyer and another type of trading partner. From 2000 to 2006, Chinese investments in Latin America increased fivefold to $70 billion annually. During the first decade of the third millennium, the trade between China and Latin America increased from less than $15 billion to $183 billion per year. Moreover, China is conducting currency swaps in Latin America, which bypass the traditional role of the dollar for international trade. China and Latin America are also diversifying their trade in commodities as well as coordinating exchanges in services and processed goods.[2] China's entrepreneurial drift is relentless. Perceptively, the political scientist He Li asserts that China "represents an attractive alternative...because Beijing respects sovereignty of Latin American nations, not meddling in their affairs and certainly not dictating their policies."[3] Although Chinese exports to Latin America are only one-third of those by the United States, China has already become the biggest trading partner of Brazil, Chile and Peru.[4] For sure, multi-polarity is on the march in the global scene. But Latin America is not China's global or regional priority.

At the time when Latin American governments had budget deficits during their economic crises of the 1980s, the United States

urged Latin America to privatize according to the recommendations of the IMF and the World Bank. The reforms were conducted
without regard to social costs and "social justice." Thus, the IMF
policies in Latin America were enforced by elites who delivered
the opposite of what they promised before getting elected. For example, in Peru, after two years of neo-liberal economic policies
and broken promises, only 8% of the population approved the democratically elected government of President Alejandro Toledo
(2001-06). Although the Peruvian economy was growing faster
than most of its Latin American neighbors, it was not creating
many job opportunities or fairly distributing the benefits of growth.
Furthermore, the fiscal revenues from the Peruvian exports were
enough only to pay the interest on the foreign debt instead of the
principal.[5] While in 2007 the Peruvian economy was growing by
a record high 8.3%, nearly 30% of the children under four years
old suffered chronic malnutrition.[6] Most of them were Amerindians
and non-whites. Toledo was the first self-proclaimed "Indian" who
became Peru's head of state, but he was not a president for the
Amerindians or downtrodden.

The overall economic growth for Latin America during the first
decade of the twenty-first century was due mostly to high commodity prices. More than 70% of Latin American exports were primary or partially processed natural resources. Current Latin
American economic growth is not enough to solve the region's underdevelopment or overcome its structural relationship with the industrial world in the foreseeable future. The Latin American
neo-liberal privatizations of the late twentieth century were supposed to bring development as well as eliminate the foreign debt.
In essence, state monopolies were corruptly transformed into private monopolies. From 1985 to 2001, the Latin American foreign
debt increased from $300 billion to $750 billion. However, from
1992 to 1999, Latin America paid $913 billion on debt-servicing
charges alone. The foreign debt was consuming 56% of the region's export income.

According to United Nations figures, 39% of Latin America's
people were poor in 1980, while two decades later it had become

44%. Until the late 1990s, the success of the neo-corporatist Chilean economy was cited as proof that neo-liberal economic policies were the answer to the Latin American underdevelopment. But according to the American economist Paul Krugman, "Chile's success has not been replicated."[7] Moreover, about 70% of the Latin American labor force remained informally employed.[8] A backlash against the neo-liberal economic policies from the last decades of the twentieth century is underway throughout Latin America. However, neo-liberal economic policies still are being enforced by ruling elites, especially in Colombia, Mexico, Peru, Chile and most of Central America. Alas, the backlash finally reached Peru with the presidential election of Ollanta Humala (2011). Thus, Latin American governments and politicians ideologically range from those who visualize a neo-liberal future to the articulators of a new socialism for the twenty-first century. Nevertheless, in Latin America's underdeveloped political institutions and the strong military establishment, drastic changes can come anytime. There are latent conditions for state coups.

Some articulators of capitalism have asserted that the battle for the Latin American soul "is between liberal democrats—left and right—and authoritarian populists."[9] Pragmatic leftist movements took over governments in free elections, from Argentina to Bolivia, Brazil, Ecuador, Uruguay, Venezuela, Nicaragua, Paraguay, El Salvador and even Peru. Moreover, constitutional assemblies have been elected with the sole purpose of changing the law and to recuperate national resources from corporate capital. This process is on a fast-track in Venezuela, Bolivia and Ecuador. The latest coups in Honduras and Paraguay were right-wing and corrupt efforts to stop such a trend.

Until the WTO conference in Cancún (September 10-14, 2003) the Quadrilateral Group (United States, EU, Canada and Japan) dominated its scheduling, agenda and decisions. The meeting of the WTO at Cancún was a failure because the Third World nations rejected the systemic proposals of the industrial nations. According to the American government, Brazil and India led the rebellion at Cancún. Indeed, it was an Asian-Latin American collaboration that sabotaged the festivities. The then "Group of Twenty-One" (G-21) openly accused the industrial nations of being morally untrustworthy for advocating free trade while subsidizing their own agriculture.[10] Within a month after the Cancún confrontation, the United States pressured Colombia, Peru, Costa Rica, Guatemala and El Salvador to leave the G-21. They were threatened with exclusion from bilateral trade with the United States. Likewise, the George W. Bush administration forced upon the hemisphere's most underdeveloped and dependent region the Central American Free Trade Agreement (CAFTA), which opened its markets to American products without reciprocal concessions. The CAFTA promotes the unequal exchange among the most underdeveloped Central America nations.

Brazil and Mexico are the two largest Latin American economies, and are currently attempting to follow different paths in economic development and international politics. Because of his market economics and austere fiscal policies, Western analysts placed the Brazilian President Lula on the "left of the center," while the American Marxist scholar James Petras labeled him as a neoliberal social democrat.[11] Unlike the Mexican establishment, the Brazilian elites refuse to accept the American version of free trade. Brazilian nationalism aims to make Brazil a regional power with a strategic tilt away from American foreign policy. Lula is a former factory worker who was democratically elected as the leader of a capitalist society in the periphery of the global system. Lula was a pragmatic politician with a social conscience who attempted to correct the deformations caused by dependent capitalist expansion. However, social democrats and neo-liberals as well as leftist radicals challenged Lula's policies. His struggle for social justice and modernization gave the State an active role without antagonizing entrepreneurship and philanthropic capitalism. Until the end of his rule, Lula considered himself a man of the Left. On the other hand, the Mexican President Felipe Calderón (2006-12) assured investors that while other countries and Latin America were confiscating foreign properties, "we are thinking about how to guarantee further investments in our country."[12] But Lula's struggle for social justice and modernization had the open support of very powerful Brazilian entrepreneurs and patriots.

Latin America is the region where class differences are the biggest in the world. Except for sub-Saharan Africa, Latin America had the world's lowest per capita income growth from 1970 to 2006.[13] If Africa is the poorest region of the Third World, Latin America is the most unequal society of the world. Brazil still is the single worst in this category. In 1976, one percent of the Brazilian population held 20% of the nation's worth; about a quarter of a century later, 10% held about 50% of the country's wealth.[14] At least 23% of the Brazilian people live in poverty,[15] despite the recent economic upsurge. Although Lula's first presidential term was characterized by disclosures of corruption, the so-called "Teflon president" was untouched. Lula promised to clean up corruption in his party, but this is a problem that affects the wheeling-dealing political and business culture of the biggest Latin American economy. The so-called "man of the people" was more successful in reducing poverty than curtailing political corruption. Among Lula's efforts to ameliorate the greatest income gap of the world are state subsidies (*bolsa familia*) for needy families. This program requires reciprocal performance from the recipient families, which includes the obligatory school attendance of their children. Education and reeducation were Lula's major priorities for modernization. Over 50 million Brazilians were benefited by Lula's multiple subsidies.

The wheeling-dealing Brazilian capitalism has made its gated cities with posh neighborhoods and check controls among the most crime-ridden in Latin America. The Brazilian growing markets for protection and private guards have not scared away foreign capital. However, in the year 2005, about 4,500 murders took place in Rio de Janeiro alone. Despite the near social meltdown, the global media describes Brazil as one of the most successful capitalist "emerging markets" in the world. Brazil's GNP grew by 3.8% in 2006. But with the help of creative accounting and financial engineering, the growth became 4.3%. Such a "magic realism" and synergy coincided with the timely reelection of President Lula. Despite taxes on financial flows, the growing Brazilian economy has become a favorite magnet for foreign investment. Lula's government guaranteed private property and foreign investment. Brazil aims to expand production and exports with state subsidies.[16] Brazilian exports to new customers reduced its dependence on the United States market to 13% (2008). The levels of Brazilian trade with China, Asia, Latin America, Africa and Europe are rapidly increasing.

The democratic election of Lula to the Brazilian presidency represented one of the most genuine and pragmatic Latin American acculturations of Leftist theories to the Latin American reality and market economy after the Cold War. Likewise, since the late 1990s, Brazilian policy-makers had increasingly disregarded the neo-liberal recommendations of the IMF in the modernization process. In Lula's world, competent governance was also a struggle against underdevelopment. Lula's pundits have been influenced by the Liberation Theology and Paulo Freire's ideas on popular education.[17] The Liberation Theology takes Dependency as its official source of economic analysis. Thus, there is an ongoing reevaluation of many Dependency premises by Lula's cadres and followers. Short of a revolution, the corrections of structural injustices and underdevelopment remain as the challenges to be solved by Lula's successors. Lula ended his presidency with a greater than 82% approval/popularity rate.

The arrival of Bush the younger to the White House created many positive expectations among the Latin American elites, especially in Mexico. After the state dinner offered by the American president to his Mexican colleague Vicente Fox, many rosy predictions were made about the future of American-Latin American relations. Bush asserted that the United States had "no more important relationship in the world than with Mexico." The North American Free Trade Association (NAFTA) and the Free Trade Association of the Americas (FTAA) were to become future neo-liberal prototypes of modernization and *laissez faire* in the Western Hemisphere. Mexican taxes (about 10%) have become lower than the average tax-level among all the Latin American nations[18] as well as Brazil. The United States failed to deliver. The American slogans of "Democracy, free trade and cooperation" have lost supporters in Latin America. On balance, neo-liberalism has won and lost in Latin America.

Mexico, as well as Latin America, is becoming more politically and economically divided. The almost inconclusive Mexican presidential elections (2006) were symptoms of the times and distrust from the voters for their politicians. Although the Electoral Commission and the vote-counters proclaimed Felipe Calderón, the winner by 0.5 percent of the votes, Mexico became politically fragmented and on the brink of a legitimacy crisis. Calderón was inaugurated in an almost secret ceremony. Violence increased in the stalemate for power in an almost failed state. Calderón resorted to the Army and brass-knuckles politics in order to crack down on "trafficking" and social protests. This is a traditional Latin American praxis which had nearly disappeared in Mexico.

The plan Mexico is concocting is to protect Mexican and American interests in the style of the Colombian "narco-terrorist" story. Like in Colombia, it means the presence of private military American contractors.[19] The supply of expensive helicopters and high-tech surveillance equipment were part of the American philanthropy. About 70% of the American cocaine demand is delivered by and through Mexican cartels. Despite the critique of the United Nations and human rights organizations, Calderón's use of the Army in his war against some narco-terrorists was unyielding. Military atrocities and cover-ups against innocent civilians occurred. By 2010, Mexico led the world in journalist casualties. The bystanders only pray that the Dantesque inferno will soon end. The old political Latin American systems are dying and new ones have not yet been born. In some parts of Latin America, we are entering into the age of political inadequacy.

In 1994, the United States, Canada and Mexico created the NAFTA. In the same year, the United States proposed the FTAA, but the latter still remains basically a project of American and Latin American traditional elites. The FTAA wants to open markets for American goods while subsidizing American agriculture and imposing tariffs on Latin American commodities that compete in the United States. The Brazilian President Lula as well as other dissenting voices proclaimed the FTAA as an American annexation plan. However, upon Barack Obama's election as president of the United States, Lula asserted that more positive changes were possible in American–Latin American relations. Furthermore, with the recent accelerated growth of Brazil's economy, its leaders are demanding greater sway in regional and international affairs. By the same token, the FTAA would also limit Asian and European competition in Latin America to the advantage of the United States. Under the American strategy for modernization in the Western Hemisphere, the Mexican elites became the first "upgraded" American trading partners in Latin America.

In the midst of the Mexican neo-liberal reforms and the economic crisis of April 1995, the United States granted Mexico a 53.8 billion-dollar loan. It was the largest loan ever given to any country. The loan was 48 hours away from Mexican insolvency and from having to stop its payments to foreign creditors. The collapse of the Mexican credit system would have also had direct consequences on the American economy. For sure, Mexico is a very important country for the United States and Mexicans as well. However, the real salaries of American workers declined after the first decade of "outsourcing" by the NAFTA.[20] Some Mexicanist experts in the United States assert that the NAFTA is "a virtual laboratory that is defining the process of corporate-centered globalization" in which the elites on both sides of the border are the greatest beneficiaries.[21]

Since Mexico became part of the NAFTA, Mexico has become the second greatest trading partner of both the United States and Canada. About one third of everything produced in Mexico is for export, and 90% of it goes to the United States. Although industrial exports grew by 16% annually from 1995 to 1999, most of the growth was due to the *maquiladora* factories (assembling plants) built near the border for the exclusive purpose of producing labor-intensive components for the United States. The *maquiladora* zones have some of the highest environmental contaminations in the world. The *maquiladora* contribution to internal markets and sustainable development is very minimal. Furthermore, industrial imports and trade deficits increased.[22] Mexico is a major oil supplier to the United States; however, 25% of Mexican gasoline imports come from north of the border.[23] In addition, Mexico imports at least 40% of all its refined oil products.[24] In 1979, Mexico stopped building oil refineries. Though Mexico has less than 1% of the world's proven oil reserves, neo-liberal ideologues and interests continue to advocate for the expansion of production through privatization. Unlike Mexico, Brazil has become virtually self-sufficient in energy because of its recycling of energy technology, ethanol production and the recent discovery of oil.

The NAFTA has resulted in the further internationalization of Mexican capital. By the dawn of the third millennium, Mexico no longer had a nationally owned banking sector. Above all, Citigroup and the European banks own most of the Mexican banking. What happened with the denationalization of Mexican private banking is an example of globalization in the periphery. The sale of native banks means the loss of local control. National resources are being internationalized, and native entrepreneurs are becoming managers and consultants. Strategic alliances of "peripheral" power groups and multinational corporations are underway in the neophyte global enterprises. Service industries are disputing turfs in the international regulations that affect both *North* and *South*. Oil export, *maquiladora* activities and remittances from migrant workers remain as the main legal sources of Mexican foreign earnings.[25]

In the aftermath of the NAFTA, North American capital and agribusiness moved the geographical frontier southward. An influx of subsidized American agricultural products ruined Mexican farming, which used to employ 20% of Mexico's labor force. From being an exporter of potatoes and cotton, Mexico became an importer of those commodities. Moreover, Mexico, which had been self-sufficient in corn and beans, became an importer of the cheaper and genetically produced American corn and beans. By the dawn of the twenty-first century, the United States was supplying about one third of the corn consumption in Mexico. According to Oxfam, American corn-producers that exported to Mexico received from $105 to $145 million annually in government subsidies. Such subsidies were more than the total income of the 250,000 farmers in the corn-producing Chiapas province.[26] Moreover, the same private monopolies that distributed local corn were the importers of American corn.[27] Due to the influx of American corn, about 1.7 million Mexicans lost their jobs.[28] Before the drastic rise of corn prices (*Tortilla Crisis*) due to the American shift to ethanol production, Mexican corn prices had been cut by 70%.[29] Subsidized American agriculture is a problem that Latin American peasants will also have to confront as their governments join the FTAA. Indeed, American agriculture enjoys higher technology and greater state subsidies.

Nevertheless, Mexico has gradually obtained a privileged status within the system of unequal exchanges between the American industrial-complex and underdeveloped Latin America. Despite the asymmetric Mexican-American relations, many Latin American governments and elites have aspired to the American conditions granted to Mexico but have been unsuccessful. Although Mexico has become the eleventh biggest economy of the world, 50% of all Mexicans still live in poverty and more than 500 persons die annually trying to cross the Mexican border to the American "promised land." The NAFTA was advertised by the Mexican ruling elites as a project that would reduce barriers between the peoples on both sides of the Rio Grande. Ironically, it resulted in the construction of ramparts and walls that stop Mexican job-seekers. Historically, the United States has functioned as a safety-valve to Mexican illegal immigrants who send home billions of dollars. Over one million arrests were made while crossing the Mexico-United States border in 2005.

In one of the country's most honest elections (2000), the one-party Mexican system ended when the PRI lost its franchise. When the PRI lost the presidency, the Army also lost its party. New alliances and relations of power are in the making. Indeed, the decline of the almighty PRI marked the end of an era. In retrospect, the Mexican historian Enrique Krauze noted that when the PRI ruled, "the president controlled the legislature, judiciary, natural resources, state-run business, electoral system, monetary policy, and budget and could limit freedom of expression."[30] The conservative and neo-liberal Vicente Fox, of the National Action Party (PAN), took the government but the political establishment, at first, did not allow Fox the power of his predecessors. However, he attempted to continue with the PRI's authoritarian tradition. After Fox took office, he retreated from his promise to support a Truth Commission to investigate the PRI's political assassinations since the 1970s. Power-sharing among elites and anti-elites and the *mordida* became the encouraging enticements in the neo-liberal modernization under *Foxismo*. After a dozen years out of office, the "new" PRI was restored by the vote-counters. Lo and behold, Enrique Peña Nieto faces a deeply wounded nation in search of peace and justice. However, daily violence has not ended.

Mexico has become a Spanish-speaking country where nearly 100 indigenous languages are still spoken. But until the Zapatista revolt, the indigenous ethnicities were seen as "folkloric" curiosities by most Mexicans. The exclusion and discrimination of Amerindians is the untold story of Mexican democracy through information technology. The Zapatista or Maya uprising, which coincided with the NAFTA's official birth, managed to show how humanity's future was linked to an Amerindian struggle for local influence and re-vindication. "Subcomandante Marcos" was the Mestizo ethnification of an Amerindian revolution. Although the right-wing paramilitary group *Peace and Justice* murdered over 200 Maya Amerindians from 1995 to 1998 in Chiapas, the Maya cause survived. The Zapatistas were not obliterated, in great part because their struggle was made public by mostly uncensored Internet technology. They still survive due to these inadvertent and mixed possibilities of globalization. International solidarity and mobilization prevented the Mexican national state from criminalizing the Zapatistas. However, paramilitary operations are still active in Chiapas.

Although the Zapatistas began as guerrillas, their actions defend their community against the lack of political democracy. The Maya Amerindians are not trying to capture the state or impose a "proletarian dictatorship." The peasant struggle, like in other parts of

Latin America, is also an effort to prevent agribusiness from taking over their lands. All the Amerindians of Mexico are generally poor, but there are about 40 million other Mexicans who share such misery. The Zapatista cause enraptured the youngsters from virtually all walks of Mexican society as well as people abroad. *Subcomandante* Marcos claimed that the neo-liberal financial and capital flows were the enemy of the most excluded ethnic groups and the poor. Through the practical pedagogy of the Brazilian Paulo Freire and foreign donations, the Zapatistas are developing an alternative education as well as social services and productive work for their communities. The pedagogy of Freire and the Liberation Theology are promoting education and reeducation. Moreover, the Zapatistas represent a revival of an indigenous movement whose theories of action and mobilization began at home.

Ten thousand years ago, corn was first domesticated in Mexico. The natural genetic diversity of Mexican corn is threatened by artificially produced transgenic varieties. Biological diversity is at stake because transgenic genes are dominant. The agricultural globalization of the North Atlantic economies has prolonged pedigrees of ecological ravage. Mexico is one example of this long history. After a decade of the NAFTA, the Mexican rural masses have been further impoverished. Moreover, there is a very aggressive campaign by the Mexican oligarchy to appropriate state and Amerindian resources beyond Chiapas' borders.[31] The Zapatistas have been marginalized by the traditional Mexican Left and the Mestizo identity. By the same token, *Subcomadante* Marcos has called the leftist movement, led by the Democratic Revolutionary Party (PDR), a bluff and a danger to democracy. But on their twelfth anniversary, the Zapatistas launched a program for a Mexican democratic socialism. A new anti-establishment armed group has emerged and it is based in Oaxaca. The Popular Revolutionary Army (EPR) is connected with urban labor unions, especially the workers of PEMEX. The EPR is sabotaging energy pipelines and it opposes the privatization of the oil industry.

Except for Cuba, until very recently the United States usually got what it wanted in the Latin American "backyard." Despite Republican or Democratic governments in the United States, the modern Cuban-American conflict has not been solved. Individual political actors have been less important in solving structural and historical relationships. President Dwight Eisenhower authorized the CIA to create a Cuban opposition within the island and in the United States on March 17, 1960. Since then, the United States has never tired in undermining the Cuban Revolution. The rhetoric of democracy, freedom and "National Security" camouflaged the American strategic and economic interests. Millions of dollars have been appropriated to create an "internal" Cuban opposition with "international support."

According to the Cuban government, the CIA had made 637 attempts against Fidel's life in 40 years (1999). Moreover, as late as June 28, 2007, Fidel Castro claimed that President George W. Bush had ordered his assassination.[32] Despite the fact that the USSR came to Cuba almost by accident, Cuba irreverently challenges United States authority and ideology. Ironically, by the year 2000, the former Soviet satellites Poland and the Czech Republic, with American sponsorship, persuaded the United Nations into labelling Cuba as a human rights violator. Since the earliest Cold War days, a dispute existed about the two components of the United Nations' definition of human rights. While the West argued for civil and political rights, the Communist bloc defended the socio-economic and cultural aspects. The Cuban state asserts that it respects human rights by providing free education, medical care, housing and food for all. But Cuba still faces a struggle against corporate and global disinformation.

The collaboration of the United States, Poland and the Czech Republic on the condemnation of Cuba is an example of how former communists have joined the Western ideological perspectives on human rights. Furthermore, these two former communist nations have been among the hardest critics of Cuba within the European Union. But on the first secret elections for membership to the Human Rights Commission of the United Nations, the United States was voted out. After a year of American threats to withdraw its financial support from the United Nations, the United States was formally reinstated in the Human Rights Commission. Despite American and European opposition, Cuba was elected by 135 votes of the General Assembly to the neophyte Human Rights Council of the United Nations in 2006. The great difference between the Human Rights Commission and the newly created Human Rights Council was that the latter's members must be the first to be scrutinized. Until the advent of Barack Obama, the United States did not volunteer to be a candidate in the Human Rights Council of the United Nations.

With the collapse of the Soviet economy, Cuba stagnated and nearly imploded in 1994. However, Cuba recuperated and it is beginning to grow despite the economic embargo imposed by the United States.[33] In the labyrinth of solitude caused by the Soviet implosion and the American economic blockade, Cuba has been trying to reinvent itself without giving up Marxist ideals. Despite the overwhelming opposition by the General Assembly of the United Nations, the American blockade continues. Although the Cuban Revolution attempted to avoid the tendency to copy the Soviet model, Fidel Castro emphatically repeated his gratitude for the help of the East European bloc: "I deeply respect that first attempt at building socialism, thanks to which we were able to continue along the path we had chosen."[34] Olof Palme was the first Western head of state to visit Cuba in 1975. Palme noted, "I have met many leaders in communist and socialist countries but never somebody so interested in Swedish industrial democracy and democratic processes as Fidel Castro."[35]

Cuba is making structural changes according to its own needs and priorities. By the year 2012, the state still employed 80% of the work-force (four million employees), while the rest worked in the private sector and cooperatives. Four hundred thousand employees work for the private sector. However, self-employment is very closely regulated. From being a capitalist and mono-cultural export economy, revolutionary Cuba has developed other sectors. But the greatest asset of the island is its "human capital." Ordinary Cubans do not necessarily swallow every description of reality by the government or the enemies of the Revolution. Cubans are among the most educated people of the planet. In addition to sugar and nickel, major sources of income are in the fields of bio-technology, medicine, tourism and services. Over 2,700 medical doctors were serving in the Third World by 2002. Cuba has the highest number of medical doctors per capita in the world. In Cuba, everybody has access to medical care.

Cuba is one of the most advanced nations in bio-medical technology. Unfortunately, because of the American economic blockade, Cuba is not allowed to export and compete freely in the world market. Cuba's merits and weakness in the internal organization of production are not being completely tested by international competition. Cuban accomplishments occurred despite American hostility. According to the Cuban government, the American economic blockade has cost the island $72 billion in 42 years.[36] Official Cuban claims for damages caused by the United States had reached $89 billion in 2007. And the damage claims keep increasing, despite the unreceptive ears of the United States. Despite the restrictions imposed by the United States, the recent discovery of oil in Cuba has brought new possibilities and investments by Canadian, Chinese and other companies. Furthermore, Venezuelan collaboration in the oil industry is increasing. On August 18, 2006, the CIA announced the creation of a new commission to supervise intelligence operations at a strategic level for Cuba and Venezuela.

On May 18, 2001, President George W. Bush officially promised to continue the economic embargo until democracy and freedom were established in the island. Furthermore, his administration announced that Cuba was secretly developing WMD. Before the lack of evidence became proof of the contrary, the Cuban government answered by opening all the suspected sites to international inspectors. For sure, there is a real Cuba as well as the one created by the Western media, one that still is fighting the Cold War. There is an exile government in Miami, which is encouraged by the American neoconservative elites to "liberate" Cuba after Fidel's demise. But perhaps in no other issue is American foreign policy and Latin America more out of tune than in Cuba. The Cuban Revolution was the first to change a structural relationship between the

United States and Latin America.

Cuban history has always been intertwined with that of its Latin sisters, and it precedes pre-Cold War times. Nevertheless, Latin American capitalists keep about 50% of their assets in the United States and outside their own countries.[37] Fidel is both reviled and respected in Latin America. Moreover, the wishful thinking of American policy makers and their favorite Cuban émigrés are ill-prepared for continuity in the island after Fidel. In the imposed solitude, the lonely island searches for the understanding of its friendly neighbors. Unlike in some Latin American countries where 10% of the population controls up to 90% of the national wealth, the state is the biggest economic actor in Cuba. The state still provides education, health-care, work and security. However, a sacralization of a Spartan way of life is promoted by the Cuban state in order to cope with the American blockade. The conspicuous consumption of consumer societies is only a distant fantasy.

Outside Latin America, China and Vietnam have become Cuba's greatest allies. Except for the late Hugo Chávez, most of Cuba's Latin American neighbors had been too intimidated to invest their capital in the island. Although the Cuban and Venezuelan revolutions have different goals and contexts, Chávez loudly declared "Fidel Castro is for me like a father, a revolutionary father and an example of dignity, struggle and resistance against an empire."[38] Upon the death of Chávez, Fidel lamented: "For me, he was like a son." But from the outset, American strategists articulated the possibility that Chávez's Venezuela would try to prevent the Cuban transition to "democracy" after Fidel Castro. Lo and behold, on July 21, 2006, the largest regional Latin American market, *Mercosur* (Argentina, Brazil, Paraguay, Uruguay and Venezuela) also granted Cuba preferential trade tariffs in order to ameliorate the island's isolation. *Mercosur*, like the Association of South East Asian Nations (ASEAN), excludes the United States from their strategic decisions.

Cuba's connections with Venezuela and Asia have opened new markets and possibilities of growth for the island. In 2006, Cuba's GNP expanded by about 12%.[39] With or without Fidel, the Cuban economy will revolve in conjunction with markets. Although Cuba wants to increase production in order to generate further prosperity for the average Cuban, it will not exactly follow the Chinese model because of the ideology and the cadres formed by the Revolution. Moreover, the Brazilian membership in the emerging economies of the BRICS (Brazil, Russia, India, China and South Africa) opens new possibilities for Cuba. The Cuban dilemma is also an issue on how compatible markets and socialism can be as well as who will benefit from the wealth generated by trade. It is not just the opening to market economics that causes conflicts with the United States, but who is to protect the island's national identity and sovereignty.

Cuba is not the country where those who win 51% of the votes dominate the other 49%. Since 1976, Cuba has had parliamentary elections every five years. The deputies of the National Assembly are proposed by their district assemblies and are elected by direct vote. The parliamentary candidates are not required to be members of the Communist Party. Cuba has one of the highest non-obligatory voter participations in the world. Although Fidel Castro acknowledged that a dictatorial system existed in Cuba, he argued that it was not personally his; "it is the dictatorship of the proletariat" and that unlike in the American elections, candidates did not have to be "very rich in the first place." At any rate, money is not a key component of election politics in Cuba. Until his retirement, the National Assembly kept reelecting Deputy Fidel Castro as President of Cuba.

Like in many other parts of the world, Cuban governance is, above all, for the organized-and-engaged. Even though women actively participated in defeating the Batista dictatorship, the Cuban Revolution did not have a special program for the massive mobilization of women until Castro came to power. Cuban women have been mobilized for the goals of the Revolution, but the revolutionary policies "to benefit women have not followed feminist goals."[40] Women won 27.6% of the seats in the parliamentary elections of 1998. Because of their gender activism, the political and social gains of women are on the rise.

The American militant antagonism against the Cuban Revolution continues to facilitate the portrayal of a struggle between David and Goliath on the island and in Latin America. When, on July 31, 2006, Fidel Castro took a leave of absence due to illness, American policy makers expected a political explosion. The bleep rather than the blast is evidence that there is much complacent ignorance among the critics of the Cuban Revolution. Despite Fidel's semi-retirement, the Marxist system prevails on the island. Indeed, the cadres of the "proletariat's dictatorship" are numerous and willing to survive. Likewise, the Bolivian President Evo Morales has openly proclaimed that "the struggle of the Cuban people and Fidel against imperialism has not been in vain."[41] Moreover, a growing number of Cuban-American organizations are advocating for a dialogue with the Cuban government. A poll among Cuban émigrés by Florida International University (2006) revealed that support for a military invasion of the island had decreased from 60% to 33% since 2004.[42] In addition, there is a generation gap among Cuban émigrés. The younger generation of émigrés is more willing to compromise with the Cuban government. Unlike the influential Cuban-American lobby, 65% of Cuban-Americans favor a dialogue with the Cuban government.[43]

In the beginning, the example of the Cuban Revolution brought the belief among many Latin Americans that through guerrilla warfare and popular mobilizations, social change could be carried out. But the traditional ruling elites and reactionary dictators repressed the new activism with vengeance. In 1964, Brazil was the first to be subjected to the technocratic and military administrations, which flourished throughout Latin America for over two decades. Since the 1980s, Latin America began to move away from military coups to elected governments. However, such a transition has not liberated the region from criminal violence, police brutality, unemployment, destitution and political corruption. After the Latin American return to civilian rule and the multi-party systems, 54.7% of the Latin Americans had not noticed existential improvements because of the establishment of democratic elections. Moreover, they were willing to accept dictatorship for the sake of economic betterment.[44]

Dependency pundits have long argued that the neo-liberals from the *North* have preached free trade for Latin America while curtailing competitor textiles, steel, foodstuffs and "non-traditional" products from the *South*.[45] The success and the takeoff in the East Asian economies after the Second World War benefited from the initial receptiveness of the American government and market. Despite the nearly corporatist and dictatorial nature of East Asian economic development, it enjoyed the political and financial goodwill of the United States and the West. Moreover, the United States was willing to reconcile itself with Vietnamese communism than the Cuban brand. The East Asian development model was based on export-led manufacturing with greater rates of return to foreign investors while the state accumulated extensive foreign currency reserves. According to the International Labor Organization (ILO), the largest increase in unemployment worldwide took place in Latin America, while East Asia provided most jobs between 2004 and 2005.

Latin American elites did not succeed in industrializing their economies, even though they were the founders of the first native school of development economics in the Third World. In 1953, the per capita income in Latin America was 260 dollars annually, while for Southeast Asia only 64 dollars per year.[46] The "tiger economies" of East Asian style did not appear in Latin America despite the theoretical sophistication of its intellectuals. The historical experience is that the state participation and subsidies for local industrialization were notoriously wasteful in Latin America. Unlike East Asian governments, Latin America did not invest enough in education and infrastructure. Indeed, underdevelopment is not solely explained by external factors, but dependency and neocolonialism are important causes. In Latin America, 10% of the population still receives at least 40% of the region's income.[47] Ironically, the American majorities, like their Latin American counterparts, have developed the consumer philosophy of living without savings. The Asian culture of savings, prodigious work and entrepreneurship are the internal ingredients that Dependency scholars failed to emphasize in their sweeping perspectives. However, people do die of overwork (*Karoshi*) in Asia and Japan.

Before World War II, the Argentinean agricultural-extractive economy was still bigger than Japan's GNP. After World War II, the United States, while encouraging East Asian corporatist efforts to industrialize, was hostile to the Argentinean aims of similar nature. The Argentinean neo-classical economist Raúl Prebisch (1901-86) had elaborated his theory of the "unequal exchange" and Dependency on the economic-historical relationship between England and Argentina. Although the "unequal exchange" had pundits in Latin America and the Third World, the theory was more specific for the Argentinean case. Prebisch argued that the systemic expansion and underdevelopment are a consequence of capitalist growth on a world scale. Despite American objections, Prebisch and his team were supported by the United Nations on their efforts to industrialize Latin America through import-substitution and state participation. However, neo-liberalism, independent of its own merits, won over Dependency as well as communist solutions.

The Argentinean crisis is a textbook example of the intertwining relationship between the global financial system and the local political economy. *Dependency* has a historical explanation in the Argentinean case. Argentina was the most industrialized Latin American economy with the largest middle class that was de-industrialized and impoverished with neo-liberal economic policies. In the last two decades of the twentieth century, Argentina made the transition from corporatist to neo-liberal capitalism in the periphery of the world system. However, the Argentinean structural changes were presented by the IMF as successful prototypes of neo-liberal reforms. On December 24, 2001, Argentina defaulted on its foreign debt. The Argentine state was unable to service $80 billion worth of government bonds. It was the biggest default in history. The crisis witnessed five presidents in two weeks.

Since the 1930s, Argentina's economic advantage had constantly deteriorated. But in order to solve the stagnation, a statist-capitalist model of economic development (*Justicialismo*) was promoted by General Juan Perón (1895-1974) and his followers since the 1940s. Unlike the promotion of corporatist projects in East Asia during the Cold War, the Argentinean corporatism faced the hostility of American foreign policy and the "native" defenders of *laissez faire*. In 1955, Perón fled for his life and survived for nearly two decades in exile. This charismatic leader was brought back by the ruling elites to solve the socio-political crisis affecting the nation. The right-wing military and their civilian allies defeated leftist Peronists shortly after the death of the *caudillo*. In 1983, the military dictatorship collapsed and the civilians were allowed to manage the government. Six years later, Peronism returned under the leadership of the pro-American civilian Carlos Menem.

In the Argentinean magic realism, the Latin American *Gringos* used to be members of the Third World and the Non-Alignment Movement. President Menem renounced both categories and officially joined the American side. Strictly following the instructions of the IMF, Menem undertook the most aggressive neo-liberal economic policies in Latin America. The Argentine writer Luisa Valenzuela has asserted that during the Menem regime, "our 'carnal relations' with the United States…took the form of spurious privatizations and a fictitious exchange rate."[48] From 1989 to 1999, Argentina received $50 billion in foreign investment. As a consequence of the new "dance of the millions," from 1991 to 1998, the GDP officially rose by 57%. Argentina had a "currency fund" which allowed the printing of money only in proportion to the number of dollars held by the Central Bank. Unwittingly, by establishing monetary parity to an overvalued dollar, Argentinean products were unable to compete in the international markets.

By 1999, Argentina was in deep recession, and the state almost defaulted on the foreign debt. In order to obtain a 25 billion dollar loan from the IMF, President Fernando De la Rúa had to allow the privatization of pension funds and medical care. Despite further cuts on workers' benefits dictated by the IMF, the crisis did not end. It got worse before it became better. De la Rúa reached the presidency with an anti neo-liberal discourse, but six months after his take over, Menem's economic ideologue and finance minister Domingo Cavallo was reinstated. De la Rúa and Cavallo resigned when they failed to receive new loans from the IMF and the United States. Since Menem's presidency, Cavallo had been the "miracle man" who had dismantled a neo-corporatist economy in the capitalist periphery and imposed neo-liberalism. The sale of state monopolies gave way to private monopolists with political connections. Speculative financial operations instead of entrepreneurial investments were the norm.

De la Rúa fled from the presidential palace before the outraged masses had the chance to lynch him. But over $100 billion fled Argentina by electronic means when its economy began to collapse. When restrictions were imposed on the amount of money that could be withdrawn from bank accounts, the state in fact confiscated middle class assets before they left the country. By then, the Argentinean state was paying over one third of its income to service the foreign debt. In 2002, the peso plunged by 80% and the GNP declined by 11% and over 50% of the Argentines were suddenly living under the poverty level. The majority of the neophyte poor came from the middle classes. In the midst of crisis, restrictions on short-term capital flows were enacted by President Néstor Kirchner (2003-07).

In the face of economic and social catastrophe, Argentineans recovered their Latin American identity and Third World solidarity. Kirchner was a leftist Peronist who refused to pay a $2.9 billion loan to the IMF unless it granted new loans to Argentina. Powerful European investors opposed new IMF loans to Argentina unless it recognized their claims. The United States overruled its European allies and the IMF financed Argentinean obligations to the fund for the incoming three years on September 20, 2003. It is germane to note that the majority of creditors to Argentina were Europeans. In that year, Argentina recuperated and grew by 8.4%. But the recuperation was not enough to return to the status quo before the crisis. Furthermore, energy supplies must be secured in order to increase economic development. It will take decades of growth. Even after the Argentinean macro-economy officially recuperated, over 40% of the people were still living under the poverty level. Argentina's capacity to produce food and industrial products are fundamental to its struggle against underdevelopment.

Argentina benefited from high prices for its commodity exports.

But Argentina is also investing in high technology industries with foreign collaboration. Foreign investors who became originally skeptical about Argentinean profitable opportunities are returning despite financial claims against Argentina's default. Moreover, Argentina had demonstrated to its neighbors that it is possible to ignore the IMF. China has also emerged as an alternative financing source. Brazil and Argentina have paid all their debts to the IMF. Like Asian nations, they are creating their "buffer funds" in order to avoid loans from the IMF.[49] The catastrophic failure of neo-liberalism in Argentina became a wake-up call for some of its neighbors. However, as in the first administration of Juan Perón, the landowning magnates and their allies are again opposing subsidies to industrial development and social welfare programs for the urban poor at the expense of agribusiness.

With an initial capital of five billion euros, the *Banco del Sur* (Bank of the South) was inaugurated in Buenos Aires on December 9, 2007. This bank intends to promote economic development, a regional monetary fund, a central bank and a clearing-mechanism for currency exchanges. Furthermore, the Banco del Sur intends to channel South American energy revenues and other investments to finance science, technology and socio-structural development as well as replace the role of the IMF and World Bank in South America. The Banco del Sur also intends to control the energy and natural resources of its member countries. This bank's main office is based in Venezuela. Although Venezuela, Argentina and Brazil provided most of the original capital, all members have equal representation and votes. By the same token, the Banco del Sur intends to attract the Latin American savings, which are traditionally invested in Treasury Certificates of Western nations.[50] If this project succeeds, it would challenge the American financial hegemony over Latin America or renegotiate its position within the global system. Furthermore, the Banco del Sur is emerging in tandem with the Union of South American Nations (*Unasur*). Unasur's goals are the South American integration in social, economic, political and institutional spheres. Unasur is also an institutional challenge to the Organization of American States (OAS).

After Salvador Allende was overthrown in 1973, American-Chilean relations improved, and by the onset of the second millennium, Chile was providing the United States with cheap copper, fruit, salmons and wines. After Mexico and the NAFTA, Chile became the first Latin American country to be granted preferential economic treatment by the United States. Until the Chinese trading success, the United States became Chile's biggest trading partner. Together with Brazil and Mexico, Chile has the second highest GNP per capita in Latin America (2010). Despite the much-avowed Chilean economic miracle, Chile has the second biggest income gap after Brazil in Latin America. But since 1991, Chile has had a tax on the inflow of foreign investments, and the longer the capital investments remain in the country, the lower the taxes become. Although the dictatorial Chilean national state withdrew from production activities, the state still had a central role in the developmental project and the regulation of free trade. Moreover, strategic resources like copper (*Codelco*) remained under state control.[51] At least 10% of the foreign earnings from copper are used for the expansion and modernization of the Chilean armed forces and military industry. The Chilean capitalist upsurge was more similar to the Southeast Asian economic experience than the neo-liberal prototype. Although deficient in energy sources, Chile is rich in natural resources, and it has discouraged speculative international investments in its economy.

In the midst of relative prosperity, a transition has taken place from dictatorial forms of political administration to more institutional and pluralist governments in Chile. This transition has not taken place without profound suffering among the lower classes and dissidents. The defenders of the authoritarian path to capitalism have praised Pinochet and Pinochetism. Despite the undemocratic means, Chile became the Latin American parade example of how internal socio-political adjustments coupled with American goodwill can promote economic expansion. While Latin America drastically stagnated, Chile expanded during the last decades of the twentieth century. Chile has developed entrepreneurial and national elites who invest at home and abroad. They are prospering in alliance with trans-national capital. Chilean private investments abroad are far superior to the foreign debt of the Chilean national state. Although Chile still has an underdeveloped economy, industrialization and modernization have taken place.

Unlike most of Latin America, the Colombian ruling elites keep moving in a right-wing direction. Colombia is one of the most dangerous countries in the world for journalists and teachers. Colombia leads the world in the number of murdered labor leaders. In 2001, eight people were kidnapped and almost 100 were murdered on an average day. Kidnapping became a growing industry which transcended class or ideology. From 1996 to 2006, over 23,000 people were kidnapped by criminals as well as leftist and right-wing terrorists. About a thousand of them died in captivity. During the Cold War, the United States tolerated Latin American politicians, dictators and kleptocrats of every kind as long as they were anti-Communist. After the Cold War, new criteria for favoring Latin American allies were put into motion by the United States in the region.

It is in Colombia that the United States chose to fight the war against Latin American terrorism and drugs. From 1994 to 1998, the United States launched a campaign to remove the Colombian president Ernesto Samper because of his alleged contacts with the drug-mafias. But in Colombia it is difficult to be neutral. The so-called "Plan Colombia" was designed by the United States with the acquiescence of President Andrés Pastrana (1998-2002). Despite all the peace-loving statements, it was a plan for war against the guerrillas. The herbicide glyphosate is being fumigated from airplanes over suspected drug-producing areas. Violence and across-border hot pursuits are spreading along Colombia's perimeter. Colombian refugees are already escaping to Brazil, Ecuador, Peru and Venezuela. The crackdown on "drugs and terrorism" will have very serious consequences on Colombia's neighbors. Colombia became the third recipient in the world of United States military aid, after Israel and Egypt. Colombia is the closest South American ally of the United States. In the synergetic reality, the sale of American helicopters to Colombia came precisely at the moment when the industry was desperately looking for new customers. From 2000 to 2008, American aid amounted to over $6 billion. It keeps increasing.

Colombia produces 80% of the cocaine and 70% of the heroin consumed in the United States. Despite the War on Drugs, drug production has increased in Colombia.[52] Right-wing paramilitary and leftist guerrillas survived because of the drug trade. More than 120,000 people were killed since 1964 to the end of the twentieth century. Over 3,700,000 have fled from their towns and regions. The struggle against Colombian drugs is a redux of the bloody counter-insurgency operations against communism in El Salvador and Central America during the 1980s. Increased privatization and drugs are the additional ingredients in the redux. The Revolution-ary Armed Forces of Colombia (FARC) is the oldest and most powerful Latin American guerrilla movement. During the 1980s, the FARC tried to convert itself into a political party, the Patriotic Union (UP). But right-wing paramilitary forces murdered at least 3,000 members of the UP. Afterwards, the violence and counter vi-olence degenerated into an orgy of brutality and a tit for tat spiral.

Until the military offensive of Plan Colombia, the FARC con-trolled a "demilitarized" area as big as Switzerland.[53] Even before the hard-liner Alvaro Uribe took office as president (2002-10), mil-itary confrontations were very intense outside the demilitarized zone. While the FARC and the Colombian government were talk-ing to each other in one place, they were combating in another. Likewise, the smaller movement of Maoist inspiration, the Army of National Liberation (ELN), also wanted to control a "demilita-rized" zone. Negotiations with the mediation of Cuba, France, Nor-way, Spain and Sweden were taking place before the crusade on terrorism was extended to Colombia. Bush the Younger proclaimed Colombia a strategic partner. But the question is: "strategic" for what, whom or against whom? Uribe emerged at a time when most Colombians were tired of the political violence regardless of who caused it. With American support and military assistance, he brought some stability through high-handed methods ("Democratic Security"). His relative success bestowed him popularity, espe-cially in the rural areas.

After Bush the Younger took office, the Colombian guerrillas were semantically transformed from "belligerent political organizations" and partners for peace into "terrorists." Alvaro Uribe added that the leftist guerrillas had replaced their struggle for social justice with the drug business and criminality. Although the Colombian military avoided the dirty task of suppressing insurgents by delegating orders to paramilitary groups, the Army provided them with logistics and privileges. The conflict goes on and the United States is deeply involved in this containment. In order to bypass congressional restrictions on the use of American troops, the Bush II administration delegated most of its "peace keeping" operations to several international Private Military Companies (PMFs), but the most dominant contractor is the Dyn Corporation from the United States.[54]

The Dyn Corporation is also participating in the fight against the illegal drug traffic throughout Latin America. The Private Military Companies are acquiring a central role in modern counter insurgency operations and war making.[55] By the same token, there is a growing local suspicion about the hidden agendas and mysterious objectives of the military companies. Despite greater security, human rights violations and martial laws continue. However, many Colombians as well as investors supported Uribe's drastic security policies and militarization. Uribe intended a military solution instead of a socio-political one. But this adventure is still without a visible end. Because drug trafficking and guerrilla operations are not the same problem, the defeat of the FARC in itself would not end the dirty cocaine business.

Until the advent of President Uribe, the two-party system had allowed the Colombian elites to survive and flourish in the extensive and diverse geography of valleys, mountains and jungles. The inadequate Colombian national state continues to bleed as it has done for much of its history. This time, the new bloodbath includes powerful foreign actors and interests on the scene. Uribe's approach to peace was to negotiate with the paramilitary groups and confrontation with the leftist guerrillas. And, those who were not with him were against the state. Uribe was a right-wing ruler who attempted to bring "law" and "order" through the massive militarization of "national security." Over 40,000 *paras* were disarmed. The *paras* had protected landowners, drug mafias and helped the Army to fight guerrillas. Many *paras* have become entrepreneurs, right-wing politicians and security experts.

Violence still is an essential part of Colombia's daily democratic life. Moreover, American neoconservative strategists wanted Colombia to become a counterbalancing force to Venezuelan "populism." The American efforts to present Colombia as a democratic success story and prototype of the "war on drugs" to be emulated by Afghanistan are at least premature. As Dan Restrepo has perceptively noted: "the deep connections between Colombia's political and governing class and narco-terrorist paramilitary organizations has began to unravel...it is unclear that U.S. policy in Colombia has been a success."[56] Maybe Colombia and Afghanistan can be compared by American policy-makers, but it could not be for their attributed virtues.

On his Latin American tour (2007), Bush the Younger had to limit his stay in Colombia to only six hours because of security reasons. In the meantime, the Uribe regime accused the political opposition, labor unions, peasant organizations and student movements of apologizers for terrorism. The extra judicial executions and death squads did not stop. From 2003 to 2008, over 936 extrajudicial executions were carried out in Uribe's democracy.[57] Colombia was left with a geography of mass graves. Ironically, Uribe asked Venezuela for help to mediate with the leftist guerrillas in September 2007. However, Uribe, with American acquiescence, recanted from his request in less than three months.[58] Despite his shortcomings, Uribe was loyal to the United States. Not surprisingly, before George W. retired, he granted Uribe the American Medal of Freedom. Apparently, Juan M. Santos, Uribe's successor and scion of the aristocracy, is attempting a negotiated solution. In the meanwhile, Colombia continues to bleed.

Venezuela is the fifth oil producer of the world and paradoxically the United States is its biggest buyer. This trading relationship also explains the difficulties in changing structural conditions despite individual actors. Before the election of President Hugo Chávez (1998), the Venezuelan nomenclature administered an economy, which produces oil. Despite oil and plenty natural resources, about 60% of the Venezuelan population lived in poverty by the end of the twentieth century. The top 20% of the population received more than 50% of the national income. Five percent of the population owned 80% of Venezuelan private land. Venezuela was one of the world's most unequal societies. Furthermore, the Venezuelan economy suffered continuous decline during the last two decades of the twentieth century. Ironically, the rise of Chávez and Uribe was possible by the collapse of the two-party systems, which had allowed the traditional elites to rule Venezuela and Colombia in democracy's name.

From the start, Chávez's "Bolivarian Revolution" advocated for a "Third Way" between unrestricted capitalism and unrealistic socialism. Chávez's openly proclaimed ambition is not to become one more populist ruler in the notorious Latin American tradition. The elites and anti-elites are using their resources in the struggle to steer Venezuela's path. With the rise of *Chavismo*, the traditional elites are being challenged throughout Latin America. One of the darlings of Latin American neo-liberalism and "magic realism" proclaimed that Chávez's constitutional reforms were unnecessary and still had not prohibited "poverty, illness, masturbation and melancholy."[59] However, Venezuela is a divided country, as demonstrated by Chávez's initial failure to amend the constitution that proclaimed Venezuela as a socialist nation.[60] But *Chavismo* has its most numerous clients among the lower classes. After a year of political campaigning and mobilization, the constitution was finally amended through the ballot.

In February 2002, the Venezuelan currency was unpegged from the dollar and allowed to float in the international market. Unlike previous Venezuelan rulers, Chávez refused to let American reconnaissance flights freely enter Venezuela's airspace. Ever since Chávez became president, a power struggle over the control of the oil industry ensued. A pro-American military coup failed to overthrow him on April 11, 2002. According to Chávez, the coup failed when the execution platoon refused to shoot at him. It was a turning point in the radicalization of the Bolivarian socialist revolution. Likewise, the United States is spending millions of dollars through different fronts, institutions and individuals to undermine the Bolivarian Revolution.[61] Except for Haiti, the United States had not supported military coups in Latin America for over a decade.[62]

After Chávez took away the control of the oil industry from multinational corporations and their local allies,[63] he had plenty of money to finance new projects at home and abroad. Chávez also cancelled the contracts of foreign oil corporations, which intended to double Venezuela's oil production. *Chavismo* has its own strategic and political objectives. The Bolivarian Revolution has mobilized the poor and it is attempting a peaceful socio-economic change. Housing projects, running water, electricity, schools, literacy programs and so forth are being promoted among the underprivileged. Due to Chávez's massive literacy campaigns, the United Nations declared Venezuela free of illiteracy in 2005.

The Bolivarian Revolution is launching the biggest land redistribution in Venezuelan history. There is also a political empowerment of "communal councils" at the local level. Bureaucratic corruption is to be confronted by the Bolivarian movement through "a revolution within a revolution." The strategy is to build socialism from the bottom up. Private, collective and social properties are to be protected. The state is to own at least 51% of the strategic industries, such as energy. There is a rollback in neo-liberal economic policies as well as a consolidation of state companies. Co-management and even co-ownership of factories by workers has been introduced. Import-substitution industrialization with state subsidies is being promoted. Rural and urban co-operatives with government support are growing. It is germane to note that per capita income had decreased by 35% from 1970 to 1998.[64] But on the other hand, the number of Venezuelans living in poverty decreased from 44% to 34% during the period 1998-2006, according to government figures.[65] Indeed, the United Nation has confirmed that poverty and unemployment have been reduced in Venezuela.

Chávez's ideological make-up had many sources, among them,

Simón Bolívar, José Martí, José Carlos Mariátegui, the Liberation Theology and the Dependency theoreticians. Chávez founded the Bolivarian Alternative of the Americas (ALBA) as a response to the American-sponsored FTAA. The ALBA trading and development alliance already included Venezuela, Cuba, Nicaragua, Bolivia, Dominica and Honduras by 2009.[66] The ALBA also projects the creation of a united defense council and military force. Furthermore, Chávez promoted the regional integration of the Latin American energy resources. It includes the proposed construction of an 8,000-kilometer long pipeline through Brazil to Argentina. Chávez advocated for Latin American integration in order to interact with the United States and its allies on less unequal terms. Venezuela and Argentina have signed an Energy Security Agreement (2007), and similar projects are in the making with other Latin American nations.

Oil constitutes over 80% of Venezuelan exports. High oil prices are essential to finance the Bolivarian Revolution. Chávez had been an irritation to the American hegemony over Latin America, especially after the failed coup of 2002. He developed an uncanny knack for infuriating American neoconservative pundits. Unlike other Latin American revolutionary movements, the Bolivarian loyalists have the resources to promote goodwill outside Venezuelan borders. Besides ideological differences, the American economy depends on cheap oil. Venezuela is trying to diversify its oil customers and become less dependent on the American oil market. This is a structural condition, which can not be transformed overnight. Because of oil, the United States and Venezuela are still dependent on each other despite the mutual hostile rhetoric and spiting defiance. Both have resources to promote goodwill to their interests and ideologies. But Venezuela is not trying to overthrow the American government.

On May 16, 2004, Chávez officially created the People's Army to supposedly defend Venezuela from paramilitary forces financed by the United States and its local allies. On August 23, 2005, the influential Reverend Pat Robertson, TV evangelist and former United States presidential candidate, openly advocated for the assassination of Chávez. In the meanwhile, *Chavismo* is attempting to make the Bolivarian Revolution a prototype for Latin America and the Third World. Even though Chávez did not invent Venezuelan corruption and actually tried to curtail it, Transparency International (2007) classified Venezuela as one of the world's most corrupt national states. Alas, the Bolivarian Revolution must have enough funds to finance its basic ideals as well as tolerate the corruption levels, which also affect many rich liberal democracies. Corruption, incompetence and inflation could become the biggest internal hazards to the heirs of the Bolivarian Revolution. The "Bolivarian Revolutionaries" would do well to remember that their mentor, Simón Bolívar, proposed a "Moral Power" to keep watch over the ethics of governance.

Even though Venezuela has regular free elections and constant popular referendums, the official articulators of American foreign policy have branded the elected Venezuelan government as a democratic thug government. The George W. Bush administration advocated for a Latin American front against Chávez. American articulators claimed that Chávez was too friendly with Castro and the Colombian guerrillas, and that he did not really support the War on Drugs.[67] Although Chávez had advocated for the declassification of the Colombian guerrillas as "terrorists," he pleaded with them to cease military activities. In Chávez's view, the war on "terrorism" gave the United States the perfect excuse to threaten and keep military bases in Latin America.[68] On May 15, 2006, the United States suspended the sale of weapons to Venezuela because of its lack of collaboration in the war against terrorism. In response, Chávez turned to Russia for military supplies. The Venezuelan leader warned the United States for an Amazonian Vietnam with the Plan Colombia. Venezuela and Colombia share a 2,200 kilometer-long porous border.

Chávez and Fidel Castro were officially proclaimed by the Bush Junior administration as the biggest obstacles to American policy and democratization in Latin America. The essential question is: how many Latin Americans believe such righteous indignations? The oil-rich Venezuela is not isolated by its Latin American neighbors. Even the Colombian government, and close American ally, prefers good relations with Venezuela. Although the Cuban and Venezuelan revolutions are different processes, Chávez transformed his various political supporters into the United Socialist Party of Venezuela. The Latin American governments have been reluctant to join the American project to contain Venezuela. Moreover, in a private conversation between Fidel Castro and Lula, the latter asserted that Brazil planned to collaborate with Chávez.[69] Lula's successors continue to collaborate with *Chavismo*. On October 7, 2012, Chávez was reelected. The former American President James Carter asserted that after having observed 91 elections, he concluded that Venezuela had the best electoral system of the world. The heir to Chávez and *Chavismo*, Nicolás Maduro, pleads for "love, peace and discipline." But it will be difficult to fill the shoes of the charismatic Commandant Chávez.

Because of the growing foreign debt, several Latin American governments were on the brink of defaulting during the 1980s. The Brady bonds were invented by the United States in order to exchange "non-collectable" American debt claims (junk status) against Latin American governments for privatization purchases alongside new investments. The American rescue packages required neo-liberal economic reforms from the recipient states. Most Latin American national states chose to finance their deficits according to the American "recommendations." It resulted in a neo-liberal offensive of global dimensions. But the cherry-picking of valuable state assets by private capital did not solve the North-South structural relationship or the unequal exchange.

Ecuador was the first Latin American nation to default to the Brady bonds (1999). The reaction of the Ecuadorian ruling elite to the economic crisis was to promote further privatizations and make the American dollar the official national currency despite desperate local protests. Military officers, Amerindians and urban masses attempted to capture the government by force in January 2000. Although this revolt against the Ecuadorian neo-liberalism was repressed, two years later, one of the leaders in this movement, Lucio Gutiérrez, was elected president on an anti neo-liberal platform. After taking office, Gutiérrez recanted and dramatically reversed his promises. With his neo-liberal economic policies and despite American support, Gutiérrez lasted only three years before he was deposed by popular uprisings. Ecuador is a deeply divided nation with a very active indigenous political movement. But Ecuador depends on the export of oil and bananas, paid with American dollars.

The Ecuadorian state was spending annually about two billion dollars, or more than one third of its budget, in order to service its foreign debt.[70] Such debt-servicing kept increasing. Ecuador became one of the most expensive Latin American countries, and its exports are being priced out of the international market. In the meanwhile, two thirds of the Ecuadorians live in poverty. The people of Ecuador mitigate their survival on the dollar remittances from Ecuadorian émigrés abroad. But the leader of the "Citizen's Revolution," Rafael Correa, was elected president in 2006. Correa represents the pragmatic new type of Latin American leftist leader who is willing to compromise with market forces and the existing structural realities. He began his political formation in the Liberation Theology movement and was trained as an economist in Ecuador and the United States. The Ecuadorian ruler has asserted: "Foreign investment that generates wealth and jobs and pays taxes will always be welcome."[71] Indeed, Correa's struggle against corporate tax-evaders has brought new fiscal revenues that are helping to finance social services and infrastructure. His governance reduced extreme poverty by 45% (2012). However, Correa is challenging neo-liberal ideologists and interests in a traditional American client-state.

Like Ecuador, Guatemala and El Salvador have dollarized their economies, and most of Central America is moving in that direction. Thus, those nations are also losing control of their monetary policies. While Central America was increasingly moving into the American reinforced hegemony, the former Sandinista president Daniel Ortega was reelected in 2006. Despite open American threats that the return of the Sandinista leader would be negative to Nicaraguan relations with the United States, Ortega was elected.

Ortega returned when the Cold War was over and the communists were no longer the official enemies of the United States in Central America. But after the Cold War, Central America emerged with the most unequal land distribution in the world. Agribusiness and money laundering are on the march in Central America. The structural relations of power were preserved in the most subservient region of the American playground.

When the Sandinistas previously ruled, the Nicaraguan state confronted the "Freedom Fighters" (*Contras*) even though their behavior qualified them as genuine terrorists. By the dawn of the twenty-first century, the United States had found new enemies to contain and they were denominated "terrorists." During the Ronald Reagan years (1981-89), Nicaragua was subjected to intensive military hostility, and the Sandinistas would prefer to avoid a redux. The Central American conflicts during the 1980s and 1990s converted Nicaragua into one of the poorest countries in the world. Ortega had become a pragmatic dealer who was officially religious, and his vice president was a former *Contra*. It is in Central America where the American bare-knuckled diplomacy has its most obvious historical and regional examples. Nicaragua accepts aid from Iran to Venezuela and China while trying to maintain peace with the United States. This is another high-wire act.

By the turn of the twenty-first century, several Latin American governments had been overthrown by social unrest; the Argentinean, Bolivian, Ecuadorian and Paraguayan explosions were caused by the failures of neo-liberal economic policies. All these social upheavals brought drastic political reforms, but perhaps the most profound changes are taking place in the poorest South American country. Bolivia is attempting a transition to a post-neoliberal society. President Evo Morales is an Aymara Indian and a former farmer of coca leaves. His party, MAS (Movement toward Socialism), is attempting to restructure the Bolivian state, promote ethnic democracy and social justice. However, the politically defeated right-wing interests that defend neo-liberalism have constantly boycotted the reforms by the MAS. On November 25, 2007, Morales announced a new *magna carta*. Because of the boycott by the political opposition, the "socialist" constitution was approved by a simple majority. Only 138 of the 255 delegates to the Constitutional Assembly voted. Bolivia has officially become a "plurinational" state.

A socio-political experiment has started in Bolivia. Morales is a new type of national politician and his ethnicity can no longer be avoided by racial politics. Bolivia is primarily an Amerindian country with 36 indigenous cultures. They constitute at least 63% of the Bolivian population. An internal polarization with the mostly European descendants of eastern Bolivia is underway. Their armed bands have intimidated the indigenous population and articulated "the need for ethnic cleansing." The regional oligarchy launched a political mobilization for the legal autonomy and covert separatism of Eastern Bolivia. Santa Cruz, the richest province and the center for agribusiness, leads the separatism. This process is being supported by local and foreign ideologues and interests with neoliberal agendas. The separatism of eastern Bolivia, like that of Zulia province in Venezuela and the Ecuadorian coast is being encouraged by neocolonial interests.

The Bolivian oil and gas are in eastern Bolivia. It includes the region where the Chaco War was fought and lost with Paraguay during the 1930s. Militarization on both sides of the border has been encouraged. Not without reason, the United States has built a military base (Félix Estigarribia) on the Paraguayan side. After Venezuela, Bolivia has the largest gas reserves in South America. Bolivia and Venezuela have also signed a treaty of military collaboration. This agreement is geared to protect the borders of a very poor country, which has historically suffered the plunder of its abundant natural resources. From the outset, Morales has had the hostility of the United States, which considered him too friendly to Hugo Chávez and Fidel Castro. Moreover, the United States has accused Morales of siding with the drug traffickers. Even after Morales became president, the CIA computers had kept him as a possible terrorist and dangerous to air transport.

As soon as Morales became president, he dismissed 28 generals for illegally transferring state secrets and property to the United

285

States. But the pragmatic Morales managed to renegotiate the distribution of Bolivian oil and gas resources with multinational corporations. The reciprocity increased the state revenues from $200 million to $4 billion annually. These re-negotiations did not take place without the threat of force. By the same token, MAS opposes the American efforts to criminalize the cultivation of coca leaves. This plant has been cultivated since Andean antiquity, and it is part of the local diet, medicine and religion. Morales is trying to tell Americans and the world that the coca leaf is not the same as the cocaine sold in the streets of New York. His argument is that if coca leaves are good for Coca-Cola, why are they bad for Bolivia? Although the secret formula of Coca-Cola asserts that the cocaine contents have been eliminated from this refreshing drink, Coca-Cola is still flavored with coca leaves.

The leftist and cross-class political movements, like those of *Chavismo*, Correa and Morales, have been branded as "populist" by local and foreign critics.[72] In the "pigmentocratic" Latin American society, the dark-skinned citizens have been usually kept at the bottom of the social ladder. Chávez, Correa and Morales have their biggest support among the excluded poor. The older generation of populists included Getulio Vargas, Juan Perón, Lázaro Cárdenas and others. This Latin American populism has been defined as a sort of political clientelism, which rewards its supporters. According to this story, Latin American populism supposedly promises what it cannot really deliver and when crisis arrives, the beneficiaries are repressed by all and with all means. Latin American populism and *caudillismo* are historically intertwined. Populists, *caudillos* and charismatic leaders still have support among the Latin American masses because political institutions have not always benefited them.

What are common to the older and newer generation of Latin American "populist" leaders are their social programs for the masses and the efforts to incorporate them in the political process. Populist leaders have patriotic slogans and do not give up their social class. Some would say that they promote revolutions from above, while others sanction: "mere reformism." Although political scientists have noted that "populism" exists in many places of the world, in Latin America is "both more entrenched and more resilient than similar political currents elsewhere."[73] But Joseph Stiglitz has responded to the usage of the "populist" sobriquet in Latin America by noting, "If populism results in the poor getting education, health services for the first time, isn't that what democracy is supposed to produce?"[74] Morales announced that Bolivia had become free from illiteracy on December 20, 2008. The struggle against ignorance is also the struggle for democracy.

The geopolitical survival and identity of Bolivia are at stake. It is a race against time. Morales' arrival to the government was the culmination of recurrent cycles of popular and ethnic mobilizations. But MAS is more popular than an indigenous or ethnic movement. Morales advocates for national unity instead of ethnic identity. In December 2005, Morales was elected with 54% of the popular vote. Moreover, Morales was reelected to a second presidential term with over 64% of the vote; it was the largest margin in Bolivian history. The MAS also has the project to recuperate a portion of the nation's resources from multinational corporations and to distribute land to the landless peasants. A revolutionary transformation of land ownership is promised. Perceptively, the American ethno-historian Catherine Walsh has noted that the contemporary success of the Bolivian and Ecuadorian mass movements owe much to the inability of the Mestizo revolutions to domesticate the spirit of the *Indianidad*.[75] In both Andean nations there is a search to imagine a different future in which the Amerindian cultures would have prominent roles. Morales, like other *caudillos* and charismatic leaders in Latin America who are trying to modernize their societies, also confronts intolerant forces from the Left and the Right. Indeed, this anarchic conundrum is the challenge to the Latin American "open society."

By the turn of the twenty-first century, "New Leftist" movements had emerged throughout Latin America. These socio-political movements also have ethnic characteristics, especially in countries with sizeable indigenous and non-white populations. Such mass movements have a clear tendency to move the Latin

287

American societies to a post neo-liberal model. Some New Leftists have taken political office, and their governments are restructuring their societies as well as making barter agreements, non-dollar transactions with Europe, Asia and other regions. The swift economic growth of Brazil opens new possibilities for regional development and less dependency on the North. However, the geopolitical presence of the biggest economy and the most powerful military power in history will either haunt or open new doors for Latin America.

The United States and Latin America have their interests and structural relations to defend and negotiate. During the Cold War, the North-South conflict was obscured by the East-West rhetoric. But the quest for social justice in Latin America is real, and it is not necessarily anti-American. The challenge for American foreign policy is how to combine its economic and strategic interests with the promotion of durable democratic changes and social justice in Latin America. If the ideals of American democracy and common sense prevail on both sides of the Rio Grande, co-prosperity and reciprocity could be a realistic dream and a promising alternative for the peoples of the Western Hemisphere. For sure, with the Berlin Wall fallen and Wall Street still shaking, it is no time for archaic solutions or arrogance. But Latin America needs more fair trade than foreign aid.

Notes

Introduction

1. Bustelo, Pablo, "La industrialización en América Latina y Asia Oriental," *Comercio Exterior*, Vol. 42, No. 12 (December, 1992), pp. 11-19.
2. Pérez Rincón, Mario, *Comercio Internacional y Medio Ambiente en Colombia* (Barcelona, Spain: Institut De Ciència i Tecnologia Ambientals, 2006), p. 230.
3. Langer, Erick D., "Introduction: Placing Latin America in World History," *The Hispanic American Historical Review*, 84:3 (August, 2004), p. 397.

Chapter I

1. Seed, Patricia, *American Pentimento: The Invention of Indians and the Pursuit of Riches* (Minneapolis: University of Minnesota Press, 2001), pp. 12-28, 151-190.
2. There is a growing literature and debate about the dates, numbers, forms and migration routes to the Americas. See: Klein, Herbert S. & Schiffner, Daniel C., "El origen de los amerindios: Debates actuales," *Revista de Indias*, LXIII, No. 227 (2003), pp. 19-30.
3. Today's commercial cottons originate mostly from cottons cultivated by Amerindians. Burns, Bradford E., *Latin America: A Concise Interpretive History*, Third Edition (Englewood Cliffs, NJ: Printice Hall Inc., 1982), p. 17.
4. Mexicans also had a similar concept in *Cihuacoatl*.
5. Céspedes, Guillermo, *Latin America: The Early Years* (New York: Alfred A. Knopf, 1974), p. 49. There are other calculations of Pre-Columbian demography, bigger and smaller, but they remain theoretical calculations.
6. Precious stones from Brazil have also been found in Peru. See the collection in the Museo de Oro (Lima, Peru). This museum belongs to the Mújica Gallo family.
7. Before the Anglo-Saxon colonization of North America, the great

289

population centers of the Mississippi culture would have been decimated through plagues brought by Spanish explorers. Crosby, Alfred W., *Ecological Imperialism* (Cambridge: Cambridge University Press, 1993), pp. 210-215. See also: Lynda Saffer, *Native Americans Before 1492* (New York: M. E. Sharpe, 1992).

8. Horna, Hernán, "A propósito del descubrimiento asiático de América," *América Indígena* (México, D.F.), LII, 1-2 (January-June, 1992), pp. 275-301.See also: Horna, Hernán, "Asiatic Migrations to the Andean Zone [Chinese]," in *Collected Writings of Asia-Pacific Studies*, Volume 6 (Peking: Peking University Press, 2009), pp. 140-49.

9. There is convincing evidence that human beings were using floating embarkations for colonization and transport about 40,000 years ago as is the case with the colonization of Australia. See: Klein, Herbert S. & Schiffner, Daniel C., "El origen de los amerindios: Debates actuales," *Revista de Indias*, LXIII, No. 227 (2003), p. 29.

10. Peterson, Frederick A., *Ancient Mexico* (New York: Capricorn Books, 1962), p. 40. My colleague Magnus Mörner asserts that the Negroid influences could also be Australoid. I agree with his observation.

11. Campbell, Joseph, *Oriental Mythology: The Masks of God* (New York: Penguin Books, 1991), pp. 398-401.

12. Shao, Paul, *Asiatic Influences in Pre Columbian Art* (Aimes: University of Iowa Press, 1976).

13. Meggers, Betty J., "The Transpacific Origin of Mesoamerican Civilization," *American Anthropologist*, 77: 1 (March, 1975), pp. 1-27. See also: Meggers, Betty J., et al., *Early Formative Period of Coastal Ecuador* (Washington, D.C.: Smithsonian Institute, 1965), p. 158.

14. Horna, Hernán, *La Indianidad* (Princeton, NJ: Markus Wiener Publishers, 2001), p. 21. See also: Horna, Hernán, "A propósito del descubrimiento asiático de América," *América Indígena*, 52: 1-2 (January-June, 1992), pp. 275-301.

15. Adams, Richard E. W. (Editor), *The Origins of Maya Civilization* (Albuquerque: University of New Mexico Press, 1977). See also: Hamond, Norman and Wiley, Gordon P., *Maya Archeology and Ethno-History* (Austin: University of Texas Press, 1979).

16. Lettner, Carlos J., "Las escrituras americanas," *Anuario Indigenista*, Vol. XXXIII (December, 1973), pp. 87-154. See also: Marcus, Joyce, "Zapotec Writing," *Scientific American*, Vol. 242 (February, 1980), pp. 46-60.

17. Knórozov, Y. V.,*Códices jeroglíficos de los Mayas* (Leningrado: Academia de las Ciencias de la URSS, 1975).

18. Coe, Michael D., *Breaking the Maya Code* (London: Thames & Hudson, 1992), p. 32.
19. Arnold, Paul, *El libro maya de los muertos* (México, D.F.: Editorial Diana, 1990), pp. 9-18, 25.
20. Stuart, David, and Houston, Stephen D., "Maya writing," *Scientific American*, Vol. 261 (August, 1989), p. 75.
21. De la Fuente, Beatriz,*Los hombres de Piedra: Escultura Olmeca* (México, D.F.: UNAM, 1977).
22. Adams, *The Origins of Maya Civilization*, pp. 383-423.
23. Entrepreneurial shamans also emerged in the Central American isthmus. See: Helms, Mary W., *Ancient Panama: Chiefs in Search of Power* (Austin: University of Texas Press, 1979).
24. Lothrop, Samuel K., "South America as Seen from Middle America," in *Essays in Pre-Columbian Art and Arqueology*, Edited by Lothrop, Samuel K. et al., (Cambridge, MA: Harvard University Press, 1961), pp. 427-429.
25. *Popol Vuh*, Edited by Recinos, Adrián (México, D.F.: Fondo de Cultura Económica, 1994), p. 105.
26. Scarbough, Vernon L., and Gallopin, Gary G., "A Water Storage in the Maya Lowlands," *Science*, Vol. 251: 4994 (February, 1991), pp. 658-662.
27. Atloloni Lecón, Amalia, "El maya, su esclavitud y su comercio," *Memoria del congreso conmemorativo del X aniversario del Departamento de Etnohistoria*, Cuaderno de trabajo No. 4 (México, D.F.: Instituto nacional de antropología e historia, 1988), pp. 107-120.
28. "Torka utrotade mayafolket," *Illustrated Vetenskap*, 13 (December, 1996), p. 23.
29. Sharer, Robert, "The Maya Collapse Revisited: Internal and External Perspectives," in *Social Process in Maya Prehistory*, Edited by Hamond, Norman (Baltimore: John Hopkins University Press, 1977), pp. 531-552.
30. Georgescu-Rogen, Nicholas, *Energy and Economic Myths: Institutional and Analytical Economic Essays* (New York: Harvard University Press, 1976), p. 6.
31. León-Portilla, Miguel, *De besegrades version* (Stockholm: Panorama, 1971), p. 8.
32. Van Zantwijk, Rudolf, "El origen de la sociedad y el estado azteca así como la historicidad de las fuentes autóctonas, una introducción," *Boletín de estudios latinoamericanos y del Caribe* (Amsterdam), No. 18 (June, 1975), pp. 4-14.
33. Gibson, Charles, *The Aztecs under Spanish Rule* (Stanford: Stanford University Press, 1964), p. 5.

34. Cortés, Hernán, *Cartas de relación de la conquista de México*, Sexta Edición, Colección Austral (Madrid: Espasa-Calpe, 1979), pp. 70-71.
35. López de Gómara, Francisco, *Cortés* (Berkeley: University of California Press, 1966), pp. 345-346, 350-354, 362-364.
36. Gibson, Charles, "The Aztec Aristocracy in Colonial Mexico," *Comparative Studies in Society and History*, Vol. II (1959-1960), pp. 169-170. See also: Rounds, J., "Dynastic Succession and the Centralization in Tenochtitlan," in *The Inca and Aztec States, 1400-1800*, edited by Collier, George A. et al., (New York: Academic Press, 1982), pp. 63-84.
37. Díaz Infante, Fernando, *La educación de los Aztecas* (México, D.F.: Panorama Editorial, S. A., 1988), pp. 36-37.
38. Gibson, Charles, "The Aztec Aristocracy in Colonial Mexico," p. 170. See also: Carrasco, Pedro, "The Economy of the Aztec and Inca States," in *The Inca and Aztec States, 1400-1800*, Edited by Collier, George A. et al. (New York: Academic Press, 1982), pp. 23-39.
39. The best descriptions of courtly life have been written by Bernal Díaz del Castillo, Hernán Cortés and López de Gómara.
40. Sánchez-Albornoz, Nicolás, *The Population of Latin America: A History* (Berkeley: University of California Press, 1974), p. 34.
41. Luxemburgo, Rosa, *Introducción a la economía* (Madrid: Siglo XXI, 1974), pp. 114, 118-122.
42. Burns, E. Bradford, *Latin America: A Concise Interpretive History*, p. 289.
43. Rostworowski, María, *Ensayos de historia andina* (Lima: Instituto de Estudios Peruanos, 1993), p. 39.
44. Bartra, Roger, *El modo de producción asiático* (México, D.F.: Siglo XXI, 1969), pp. 21-231.
45. Gunn, Joel, and Adams, Richard, "Climatic Change, Culture and Civilization in North America," *World Archaeology*, Vol. 13: 1 (June, 1981), p. 93.
46. The late Peruvian ethno-historian Franklin Pease maintained that the break-up of the Inca Empire, *Ayllu* survived during the colonial period. See: Pease, Franklin, *Del Tawantinsuyo a la historia del Perú* (Lima: Instituto de Estudios Peruanos, 1978).
47. Rostworowski, *Ensayos de historia andina*, pp. 105-106, 110.
48. Nordenskiöld, Erland, "The Secrets of the Peruvian Quipus," *Comparative Ethnological Studies* (Gothenburg), Vol. VI, 1-2 (1925).
49. Porras Barrenechea, Raúl, *Fuentes históricas peruanas* (Lima: Mejía Baca, 1945), p. 109.
50. Burns Glynn, William, "La escritura de los Incas," *Boletín de Lima*,

Numbers 12-14 (May-September, 1981), pp. 1-32. See also: Matos Mendieta, Ramiro, "El secreto de la Quilca," *El Comercio* (Lima), November 24, 1985, Dominical, p. 6.

51. Silverman, Gail, *El tejido andino: Un libro de sabiduría* (Lima: Banco Central, 1994), pp. 143, 150, 176.

Chapter II

1. Morison, Samuel Eliot (Editor), *Journals and Other Documents on the Life and Voyages of Christopher Columbus* (New York: The Heritage Press, 1963), pp. 132-133, 215.
2. Morison, *Journals...*, pp. 83, 86.
3. Although Columbus has been accused of exaggerating the quantities of gold in Haiti and the Caribbean, it has been calculated that by 1520, the Caribbean yield had at least doubled the total European production of gold. See: Céspedes, Guillermo, *Latin America: The Early Years* (New York: Alfred A. Knopf, 1974), p. 29.
4. Rouse, Irving, *The Tainos* (New Haven: Yale University Press, 1992).
5. Morison, *Journals...*, pp. 154, 185-186, 271. See also: Friede, "Origenes de la esclavitud indígena en Venezuela," *América Indígena*, XXII, 1 (1962), p. 14.
6. Likewise, when the Portuguese visited Brazil for the first time in 1500, they did not find cannibalism.
7. Clendinnen, Inga, *Ambivalent Conquests: Maya and Spaniard in Yucatán, 1517-1570* (New York: Oxford University Press, 1987), pp. 165, 182.
8. Arens, William, *The Man-Eating Myth* (New York: Oxford University Press, 1979).
9. A French Franciscan André Thevet who lived for several years among the Tupinamba of Brasil in the XVI century, discovered that those Indians also believed in an omnipresent and omnipotent god called Nonan.
10. Burland, C. A., *The Gods of Mexico* (New York: Capricorn Books, 1968).
11. Padden, R. C., *The Hummingbird and the Hawk* (New York: Harper & Row, 1967).
12. Peterson, Fredrick, *Ancient Mexico*, p. 146.
13. Macera, Pablo, *Historia del Perú: La colonia*, 3 Vols., II (Lima: Editorial Bruño, 1985), p. 37.
14. Díaz Del Castillo, Bernal, *The True History of the Conquest of Mexico* (La Jolla, CA: Renaissance Press, 1979), pp. 152-155.
15. Díaz Del Castillo, *The True History of the Conquest of Mexico*, pp.

165-166.
16. Díaz Del Castillo, *The True History of the Conquest of Mexico*, pp. 138.
17. Hassig, Ross, *Mexico and the Spanish Conquest*, (London: Group UK Limited, 1994), pp. 63, 88.
18. Gibson, Charles (Editor), *The Spanish Tradition in America* (New York: Harper & Row, 1968), p. 86.
19. John Murra, *La organización económica del Estado inca* (México, D.F.: Siglo XXI, 1989), pp. 16-17. See also: Rowe, John, "Inca Culture at the Time of the Spanish Conquest," in *Handbook of South American Indians*, II, Edited by Julian Steward (Washington, D.C.: Smithsonian Institute, 1946), pp. 183-330.
20. Wachtel, Nathan, *Los Vencidos* (Madrid: Editorial Alianza, S. A., 1976), pp. 272, 306.
21. Gibson, "The Aztec Aristocracy in Colonial Mexico," *Compartive Studies in Society and History*, II (1959-1960), p. 174.
22. Lynch, John, "The Institutional Fragments of Colonial Spanish America," *Journal of Latin American Studies*, XXIV, Quincentenary Supplement (1992), pp. 78-79. In the eighteenth century, there were 14 Audiencias in Spanish America.
23. Patch, Robert W., "Imperial Politics and Local Economy in Colonial Central America, 1670-1770," *Past &Present*, 143 (May, 1994), p. 77. See also: Patch, *Maya and Spaniard in Yucatán, 1648-1812* (Stanford: Stanford University Press, 1993), pp. 81-90.
24. Ward, Christopher, *Imperial Panama: Commerce and Conflict in Isthmian America, 1550-1800* (Albuquerque: University of New Mexico Press, 1993), pp. 77-78.
25. Real Hacienda (1786), Causas Ordinarias, Legajo 129, Expediente 110, folios 1-8. Archivo Regional La Libertad, Peru.
26. Sección Histórica, Legajo 24, Expediente 365, Año 1633, Archivo Departamental de Cajamarca, Peru.
27. Contreras, Carlos, *Los mineros y el Rey, los Andes del Norte: Hualgayoc 1770-1825*, Serie Estudios Históricos 16 (Lima: Instituto de Estudios Peruanos, 1995), p. 88.
28. Mörner, Magnus, *The Political and Economic Activities of the Jesuits in La Plata Region* (Stockholm: Ibero-amerikanska Biblioteket & Institutet, 1953).
29. Vargas Ugarte, Rubén, *Historia general del Perú*, 6 Vols., II (Lima: Milla Bartres, 1971), p. 206.
30. Burns, E. Bradford, *A History of Brazil* (New York: Columbia University Press, 1980), p. 17.
31. Sweet, David G. and Nash, Gary (Eds.), *Struggle and Survival*

(Berkeley: University of California Press, 1981), p. 18.

32. Poppino, Rollie E., *Brazil: Land and People* (New York: Oxford University Press, 1968), pp. 40-112. See also: Marchant, Alexander, *From Barter to Slavery* (Baltimore: John Hopkins University Press, 1941).

33. Anderson, Robert, "The Quilombos of Palmares," *Journal of Latin American Studies*, XXVIII, 3 (October, 1996), p. 559.

34. Mörner, Magnus, *The Andean Past: Land, Societies and Conflicts* (New York: Columbia University Press, 1985), p. 98.

35. Matos Mar, José, *Yanaconaje y reforma agraria en el Perú* (Lima: Concytec, 1976), pp. 16-36.

36. Schwartz, Stuart B., *Sovereignty and Society in Colonial Brazil* (Berkeley: University of California Press, 1973), pp. 14, 362.

37. Mörner, Magnus, *La corona española y los foráneos en los pueblos de indios de América* (Stockholm: Instituto de Estudios Ibero-Americanos, 1970), pp. 75, 105-106.

38. Mörner, Magnus, *Race Mixture in the History of Latin America* (Boston: Little, Brown and Company, 1967), p. 26. See also: Burns, Kathryn, "Gender and the Politics of Mestizaje," *The Hispanic American Historical Review*, 78: 1 (February, 1998), p. 34.

39. From November 4, 1780 to April 5, 1781.

40. Informe de la captura de Túpac Amaru (1781), folios 179-195, Milicias y Marinas, LXXIX, Sección de la Colonia, Archivo Nacional, Bogotá, Colombia.

41. Bowser, Frederick P., *El esclavo africano en el Perú colonial, 1524-1650* (Mexico, D.F.: Siglo XXI, 1977), p. 402. See also: Informe del transporte de tropas de Panamá al Callao (1784), folios 422-440, Milicias y Marinas, LXXIX; Cartas de Agustín Jauregui al Virrey de Nueva Granada tratando los disturbios internos del Perú (1782), folios 13-15, 17-18, Milicias y Marinas, CXIV, Sección de la Colonia, Archivo Nacional, Bogotá, Colombia.

42. Flores Galindo, Alberto, *Aristocracia y plebe: Lima, 1760-1830* (Lima: Mosca Azul Editores, 1984), pp. 234-235.

43. But the Peruvian exiled Jesuit Juan Pablo Viscardo y Guzmán vainly attempted to obtain British support for Tupac Amaru.

44. Flores Galindo, *Buscando un Inca: Identidad y utopía en los Andes* (La Habana: Casa de las Américas, 1986).

45. Horna, Hernán, *Colombian Archival Sources on Colonial Peru* (Washington, D.C.: Pan American Institute of Geography and History, 1971), pp. 2, 9-29. See also: Marchena Fernández, Juan, *Ejercito y milicias en el mundo colonial Americano* (Madrid: MAPRE, 1992).

46. O'Phelan Godoy, Scarlett, *Rebellions and Revolts in Eighteenth Century Peru and Upper Peru* (Cologne, Germany: Lateinamerikanische Forschungen, 1985), pp. 256-273.

47. Prado, Caio, *The Colonial Background of Modern Brazil* (Berkeley: University of California Press, 1967), pp. 133-134.

48. There is not a record of proceedings about the promotion, but since 1720, the King's representative in Brazil had the title of Viceroy.

49. Stoetzer, Carlos O., *The Scholastic Roots of the Spanish American Revolution* (New York: Fordham University Press, 1979), pp. 60, 79, 92, 249-263.

50. His successor and follower, Jean-Jacques Dessalines, who fought for independence and the abolition of slavery, was killed on October 17, 1806.

51. Fals Borda, Orlando, "La Investigación-Acción en convergencias disciplinarias," *Latin American Studies Association: Forum*, XXXVIII, 4 (Fall, 2007), p. 21.

52. Hobsbawm, Eric J., *The Age of Capital: 1848-1875* (London: George Weidenfeld & Nicolson, 1975), p. 78.

53. Stein, Stanley J. and Stein, Barbara H., *The Colonial Heritage of Latin America* (New York: Oxford University Press, 1970), pp. 45-46.

54. Wolf, Eric R., *Europe and the People without History* (Berkeley: University of California Press, 1997), p. 255.

55. Li, Dun J., *The Ageless Chinese* (New York: Charles Scribner's Sons, 1965), pp. 504-505.

56. Cortés Conde, Roberto and Stein, Stanley J., (Editors), *Latin America: A Guide to Economic History, 1830-1930* (Berkeley: University of California Press, 1977), p. 10.

57. Among the major scholars representing the dependency and system analysis are Raúl Prebisch, Fernando Cardoso, Enzo Faletto, Theotonio Dos Santos, André G. Frank, Celso Furtado, Immanuel Wallerstein, Samir Amin and Emmanuel Arghiri.

58. Amin, *Accumulation on a World Scale* (Sussex: Harvester Press, 1974), p. 40.

59. Braudel, Fernand, *The Structures of Everyday Life: Civilization and Capitalism 15th-18th Century*, 2 Vols., II (New York: Harper & Row, 1982), pp. 267-273.

60. Vilar, Pierre, *A History of Gold and Money 1450-1920* (London: Foundations of History Library, 1976), p. 138.

61. O'Brien, Patrick, "European Economic Development: The Contribution of the Periphery," *The Economic History Review*, XXXV, 1 (February, 1982), pp. 1-18. See also: Wallerstein, Immanuel, "Euro-

pean Economic Development: A Comment on O'Brien," *Economic History Review*, XXVI (1983), pp. 580-585.

62. Braudel, Fernand, *The Structures of Everyday Life: Civilization and Capitalism 15th-18th Century*, 2 Vols., I (New York: Harper & Row, 1979), p. 440.

63. Jenks, Leland Hamilton, *The Migration of British Capital to 1875* (London: Thomas Nelson and Sons Ltd., 1963), p. 193.

Chapter III

1. Rodrigues, José Honório, *Tempo e sociedade* (Petrópolis, Brasil: Editora Vozes, 1986), p. 123.

2. Flores Caballero, Romeo, *Counterrevolution: The Role of the Spaniards in the Independence of Mexico, 1804-38* (Lincoln: University of Nebraska Press, 1974), pp. 8-9, 15-26, 68, 129-136.

3. Halperin-Donghi, Tulio, *The Aftermath of Revolution in Latin America* (New York: Harper & Row, 1973), p. 53.

4. Marichal, Carlos, *Historia de la deuda externa de América Latina* (México, D.F.: Alianza Editorial Mexicana, 1988), pp. 30-31.

5. Jenks, Leland Hamilton, *The Migration of British Capital to 1875* (London: Thomas Nelson and Sons Ltd., 1963), p. 109.

6. Horna, Hernán, *Five Essays on Post Colonial Latin American History* (Uppsala, Sweden: History Institute, 1994), p. 6.

7. Ffrench-Davis, Ricardo, "Latin American Economies, 1950-1990," *The Cambridge History of Latin America*, VI, Part 1, Edited by Bethell, Leslie (Cambridge: Cambridge University Press, 1994), p. 247.

8. Lowenthal, Abraham F., "América Latina ingresa a los 90," *Caretas* (Lima), February 5, 1990, p. 43.

9. *Santa Fe II: Strategy for Latin America in the Nineties* (Washington, D.C.: The Committee of Santa Fe, 1989), pp. 15-16.

10. "Busca la CE a Latinoamérica...," *Excelsior* (México, D.F.), July 8, 1993, p. 2F.

11. Lowenthal, Abraham F., "Latin America: Ready for Partnership?" *Foreign Affairs*, Vol. 72, No. 1 (1993), pp. 74-92. See also: "Euromarché," *L'Echo* (Brussels), June 21, 1993, p. 18.

12. "Region: Energy," *Latin American Weekly Report* (London), July 22, 1993, p. 335.

13. "Entrevista...," *Caretas* (Lima), February 3, 1992, p. 91.

14. Hobsbawm, Eric J., *Industry and Empire: An Economic History of Britain since 1750* (London: George Weidenfeld & Nicolson, 1968), pp. 59-60.

15. Stone, Irving, "Britiska långtidsinvesteringar i Latinamerika 1865-1913," in *Problem i världsekonomins historia*, Edited by Bunte, Rune and Jörberg, Lennart (Lund, Sweden: CWK Gleerup Bokförlag, 1969), p. 297.
16. Lynch, John, *Caudillos in Spanish America, 1800-1850* (Oxford: Claredon Press, 1992).
17. June 26, 1970.
18. Lynch, John, "The Origins of Spanish American Independence," in *The Independence of Latin America*, Edited by Bethell, Leslie (Cambridge: Cambridge University Press, 1989), p. 44.
19. Matthieu, Gilles, *Une ambition sud-américaine: Politique culturelle de la France (1914-1940)* (Paris: L'Harmattan, 1991), pp. 47-48.
20. Ronning, C. Neale (Editor), *Intervention in Latin America* (New York: Alfred A. Knopf, 1970), pp. 25-32.
21. On February 22, 2010, the Community of Latin American and Caribbean States (CELEC) was created in Cancún, Mexico. The CELEC is intended to include all regional organizations and eventually replace the OAS. The United States and Canada are to be excluded.
22. At the II Congress on Latin American Poverty (Quito, November, 1990), it was estimated that there were 270 million (60%) poor in Latin America. See also: "El perfil de la pobreza en América Latina...," *CEPAL*, No. 536 (November, 1992), pp. 1-4.
23. Ermolaev, V. I., "The Emergence of the First Labor Organizations and Marxist Groups in the Countries of Latin America, 1870-1900," in *Soviet Historians on Latin America*, Edited by Bartley, Russell H. (Madison: The University of Wisconsin Press, 1978), pp. 234-55. See also: Tarcus, Horacio, *Marx en la Argentina: Sus primeros lectores obreros, intelectuales y científicos* (Buenos Aires: Siglo XXI, 2007), pp. 12-17, 21-485.
24. "Författare lever farligt,"*Dagens Nyheter* (Stockholm), December 7, 1992, p. A8. Between March and September, 1992, fifty-five writers "disappeared" in the world, and 70% of them in Latin America.

Chapter IV

1. Because several liberal laws originating in the Spanish Constitution of 1812 were incorporated in the Mexican legal system, the North American historian Timothy Anna has argued that there was not a counterrevolution in the independence movement. The Mexican historian Romeo Flores Caballero is of the opposite view. See: Anna, Timothy, "The Independence of Mexico and Central America," in

The Independence of Latin America, Edited by Leslie Bethel (Cambridge: Cambridge University Press, 1989), p. 82; and Flores Caballero, Romeo, *Counterrevolution* (Lincoln: University of Nebraska Press, 1974).

2. Banzant, Jean, "Mexico from Independence to 1867," *The Cambridge History of Latin America*, III, Edited by Bethell, Leslie (Cambridge: Cambridge University Press, 1985), pp. 426-27.

3. Vásquez, Josefina Zoraida, *La Gran Bretaña frente al México amenazado* (México, D. F.: Secretaría de Relaciones Exteriores, 2002).

4. Meyer, Michael C., And Sherman, William L., *The Course of Mexican History* (New York: Oxford University Press, 1983), p. 496.

5. Hart, John Mason, *Empire and Revolution: The Americans in Mexico since the Civil War* (Berkeley: University of California Press, 2002), p. 5.

6. Meyer, Jean, "Mexico: Revolution and Reconstruction in the 1920s," *The Cambridge History of Latin America*, V, Edited by Bethell, Leslie (Cambridge: Cambridge University Press, 1986), p. 167.

7. According to *FORBES*, Carlos Slim became the richest person of the world with $59 billion in 2007.

8. "Rápido crecimiento de los grupos empresariales mexicanos," *Excelsior*, January 6, 1992, p. 8F. See also: "Los 13 grandes multimillonarios," *Proceso* (México, D.F.), July 12, 1993, pp. 6-9.

9. "Mexican Dance: The RR in PRI," *Newsweek*, March 22, 1993, p. 35. See also: "Politics and Finance," *Latin American Weekly Report* (London), July 8, 1993, p. 308.

10. Their political platform was best summarized by Porfirio Muñoz Ledo. See: Muñoz Ledo, Porfirio, *La sociedad frente al poder* (México, D.F.: Editorial Diana, 1993).

11. "Economy," *Mexico & Nafta Report* (London), September 23, 1993, p. 5. It has been estimated that Mexico has a 40% structural unemployment and underemployment, which is mitigated by emigration to the United States. See: *Santa Fe II: A Strategy for Latin America in the Nineties* (Washington, D.C.: The Committee of Santa Fe, 1989), p. 30.

12. "Para su información," *El Financiero* (México, D.F.), July 12, 1993, p. 8.

13. Fauriol, George A., "The Shadow of Latin American Affairs," *Foreign Affairs*, Vol. 69, No. 1 (1990), p. 121.

14. "Cuba: Economy," *Latin American Weekly Report* (London), September 17, 1992, p. 11.

15. Moreno Fraginals, Manuel, "En torno a la identidad cultural en el Caribe insular," *Casa de las Américas*, XX, No. 118 (January-Fe-

bruary, 1980), pp. 42-47.

16. Sepkowski, Tadeusz, *Haiti* (La Habana: Departamento de Historia de América, 1978), p. 54.

17. Bell, Madison Smartt, *Toussaint Louverture: A Biography* (New York: Pantheon, 2007). See also: Davis, David Brion, "He Changed the World," *The New York Review*, May 31, 2007, pp. 54-58.

18. Nicholls, David, *From Dessalines to Duvalier: Race, Colour and National Independence in Haiti* (Cambridge: Cambridge University Press, 1979).

19. Rotberg, Robert I., *Haiti: The Politics of Squalor* (Boston: Houghton Mifflin, 1971), p. 146.

20. Hallward, Peter, "An Interview with Jean-Bertrand Aristide," *London Review of Books*, Vol. 29, No. 4 (February 22, 2007), Internet Edition.

21. Clinton, Bill, "Many Hands Lighten the Load," *Newsweek*, January 25, 2010, p. 30.

22. Munro, Dana G., *Intervention and Dollar Diplomacy in the Caribbean* (Princeton: Princeton University Press, 1964), p. 336.

23. Vega, Bernardo, *Eisenhower y Trujillo* (Santo Domingo: Fundación Cultural Dominicana, 1991).

24. Pratt, Julius W., "The Ideology of American Expansionism," in *Expansion and Imperialism*, Edited by Campbell, A. E., (New York: Harper & Row, 1970), pp. 23-24.

25. Although Batista became the best known victim of such a sobriquet, the American historian Robert F. Smith has noted that it was first applied to the Dominican dictator Rafael L. Trujillo. See: Smith, Robert F., *The United States and Cuba: Business and Democracy, 1917-1960* (New York: Alfred A. Knopf, 1960), p. 184.

26. Pérez, Jr., Louis A., *Cuba and the United States: Ties of Singular Intimacy* (Athens: University of Georgia Press, 1999), p. 174.

27. According to the Cuban government, Batista and his partners escaped with $424 million in state funds. See: *Granma* (Havana), November 9, 2004, Internet Edition.

28. There are several witnesses who claim that Castro proclaimed himself a Communist when he took command of the troops that repelled the Bay of Pigs invasion.

29. Conference by Professor Kiva Majdanik at the Latin American Institute, Stockholm, September 30, 1993.

30. On July 23, 1993, President Bill Clinton decreed limited telephone contacts between the United States and Cuba.

31. The infant mortality rate was 10.7 per 1,000 births (2002) in contrast to 60 per 1,000 births before 1959.

32. "Cuba," *Time*, August 12, 1991, p. 28.
33. Figueras, Miguel, "La producción de bienes de capital en Cuba," *Comercio Exterior*, Vol. 42, No. 12 (December, 1992), pp. 1149-55.
34. In 2009, a 10% commission on the exchange of American dollars was imposed. A convertible local dollar has also been created.
35. Johansson, Kjell A., "Kompisar från Kuba," *Dagens Nyheter* (Stockholm), July 8, 1991, p. B2.
36. July 17, 2010
37. Barredo-Medina, Lázaro, "50 años después," *Granma*, December 30, 2008, Internet Edition.
38. Domínguez, Jorge I., "Revolution and its Aftermath in Cuba," *Latin American Research Review*, Volume 43, No. 2 (2008), p. 227.

Chapter V

1. Woodward, Jr., Ralph Lee, *Rafael Carrera and the Emergence of the Republic of Guatemala, 1821-1871* (Athens: University of Georgia Press, 1993).
2. Cruz, Consuelo, *Political Culture and Institutional Development in Costa Rica and Nicaragua: World-Making in the Tropics* (Cambridge: Cambridge University Press, 2005), p. 181.
3. Reeves, René, *Ladinos with Ladinos, Indians with Indians, and Regional Ethnic Conflict in the Making of Guatemala* (Stanford: Stanford University Press, 2006), p. 6.
4. Stone, Samuel Z., *The Heritage of the Conquistadors: Ruling Classes in Central America from the Conquest to the Sandinistas* (Lincoln: University of Nebraska Press, 1990), pp. 27-28.
5. Gleijeses, Piero, *Shattered Hope: The Guatemalan Revolution and the United States, 1944-1954* (Princeton: Princeton University Press, 1991), pp. 177-182.
6. Handy, Jim, *Revolution in the Countryside: Rural Conflicts and Agrarian Reform in Guatemala, 1944-1954* (Chapel Hill: University of North Carolina Press, 1994), pp. 134-135.
7. Wilkinson, Daniel, *Silence on the Mountain: Stories of Terror, Betrayal, and Forgetting in Guatemala* (Durham: Duke University Press, 2004).
8. Dosal, Paul J., *Power in Transition: The Rise of Guatemala's Industrial Oligarchy, 1871-1994* (Westport, CT: Praeger, 1995), p. 192.
9. "El narcoeslabón centroamericano," *Excelsior* (México, D.F.), June 25, 1993, p. 31.
10. "Abierta lucha por el poder...en Nicaragua," *Excelsior*, February 28, 1991, pp. 1, 5. This amount of money was assigned by the Interna-

tional Court of Justice (Hague) in damages when it declared the
United States guilty of unlawful aggression against Nicaragua.

11. Castañeda, Jorge G., "Lessons for the Left," *Newsweek*, March 12, 1991, p. 4.

12. In 1991, Mrs. Chamorro withdrew the Nicaraguan complain in exchange for the promise of economic aid from the United States.

13. By the end of 1993, the Sandinist army had been reduced from 80,000 to 15,000 but kept General Humberto Ortega as its chief.

14. "Ortega critica a EEUU," *El País* (Madrid), August 1, 1993, p. 7.

15. Lowenthal, Abraham F., "América Latina," *Caretas* (Lima), June 12, 1990, p. 49.

16. In 2008, foreign assistance constituted about 8% of Nicaragua's GNP. However, Nicaragua is not as dependent on foreign aid as most African nations.

17. A United Nations commission led by the former Colombian president Belisario Betancourt concluded that 85% of all human rights violations during the Salvadorian civil war were inflicted by the Army.

18. "U.S., Aware of Killings," *The New York Times*, November 9, 1993, p. A9.

19. *La Jornada* (Mexico, D. F.), January 16, 2007, p. 14.

20. "En crisis…ejército de Honduras," *Excelsior*, July 15, 1993, pp. 2-3.

21. Scott, Peter Dale and Marshal, Jonathan, *Cocaine Politics: Drugs, and the CIA in Central America* (Berkeley: University of California Press, 1992).

22. *Newsweek*, October 27, 2008, p. 72.

Chapter VI

1. *International Herald Tribune*, March 16, 2007, p. 7.

2. Venezuela left the CAN claiming as excuse that Colombia and Ecuador had signed free trade agreements with United States without the approval of the Andean nations.

3. Carrera Damas, Germán, *La crisis de la sociedad colonial* (Caracas: Universidad Central, 1976), p. 80.

4. "Latin America," *Newsweek*, April 17, 1989, p. 42.

5. Bushnell, David, *Colombia* (Berkeley: University of California Press, 1992), pp. 78-81, 107.

6. Green, John W., *Gaitanismo, Left Liberalism and Popular Mobilization in Colombia* (Gainesville: University Press of Florida, 2003), pp. 261-265.

7. Henderson, James D., *Modernization in Colombia* (Gainesville: Uni-

versity Press of Florida, 2001), p. xiv.

8. *International Herald Tribune*, June 11, 2007, p. 14.

9. Pineo, Ronn F., "Reinterpreting Labor Militancy: The Collapse of the Cacao Economy and the General Strike of 1922 in Guayaquil, Ecuador," *The Hispanic American Historical Review*, 68: 4 (November, 1988), p. 711.

10. Rodríguez, Linda, *The Search for Public Policy: Regional Politics and Government Finance in Ecuador, 1830-1940* (Berkeley: University of California Press, 1985), pp. 104, App. B.

11. Marchán Romero, Carlos (Ed.), *Crisis y cambio de la economía en los años veinte* (Quito: Banco Central del Ecuador, 1987).

12. Zook, Jr., David H., *Zarumilla-Marañón: The Ecuador-Peru Dispute* (New York: Bookman Associates, Inc., 1964).

13. Montoya, Rodrigo, *Al borde del naufragio* (Lima: Cuadernos de SUR, 1992), pp. 45, 69-72. See also: Carrasco, Hernán, "Indígenas serranos en Quito y Guayaquil," *América Indígena*, LI, No. 4 (October-December, 1991), pp. 159-83; and Macas, Luis, *El levantamiento Indígena visto por sus protagonistas* (Quito: Abi-Ayala, 1991), pp. 3-23.

14. Jackson, Robert, "The Decline of the Hacienda in Cochabamba, Bolivia," *The Hispanic American Historical Review*, 69: 2 (May, 1989), pp. 259-81.

15. Scott, Rebecca, "Economic Aid and Imperialism in Bolivia," *Monthly Review*, Vol. 24 (May, 1972), p. 54.

16. Klein, Herbert S., *A Concise History of Bolivia* (New York: Cambridge University Press, 2006), p. 222.

17. "Peru," *Latin American Weekly Report* (London), February 25, 1993, p. 89.

18. It has been estimated that from 1840 to 1880, the guano sales amounted to about 150 million British pounds of which 60% went to the state. See: Hunt, Shane, *Growth and Guano in Nineteenth Century Peru*, Report No. 34 (Princeton: Princeton University Press, 1973).

19. The Lima-La Oroya railroad at 4,847 meters above the sea level remained as the highest in the world until the Tibet line was inaugurated in 2006. The latter reached the altitude of 5,072 meters.

20. Matos Mar, José, *Desborde popular y crisis del estado* (Lima: Concytec, 1988), p. 28.

21. Macera, Pablo, "Reflexiones a propósito de la polémica del indigenismo," *Apuntes* (Lima), III, No. 6 (1977), p. 80.

22. Cotler, Julio, *Clases, estado y nación en el Perú* (Lima: Instituto de Estudios Peruanos, 1985), pp. 306-34.

23. Conaghan, Catherine M. and Malloy, James M., *Unsettling State-craft: Democracy and Neoliberalism in the Central Andes* (Pittsburgh: University of Pittsburgh Press, 1994).
24. "Emperor of Peru," *Newsweek*, May 10, 1993, p. 38.
25. Walker, Charles F., "Political Commentary," *LASA: FORUM*, XXXVIII, 1 (Winter, 2007), pp. 28-29.
26. One hundred corporations dominated by foreign capital still produced over 50% of the Peruvian GNP in 2008. See: *La República* (Lima), June 12, 2008, Internet Edition.
27. Burga, Manuel, "El Perú ha perdido el paso [Interview]," *Socialismo y participación* (Lima), No. 91 (October, 2001), p. 101.

Chapter VII

1. "General Confirms...," *Latin American Weekly Report* (London), July 8, 1993, p. 309.
2. "Fyra gatubarn mördas dagligen," *Svenska Dagbladet* (Stockholm), March 1, 1992, p. A4.
3. "Encabeza Brasil la prostitución infantil en AL," *Excelsior* (México, D.F.), June 29, 1993, p. 38A.
4. "Yanqui, Come Here, *"Newsweek*, July 15, 1991, pp. 20-23.
5. Schneider, Cathy, "Chile: The Underside of the Miracle," *NACLA*, XXXVI, 4 February, 1993), pp. 30-31.
6. Dorfman, Ariel, "Pinochet II," *International Herald Tribune*, December 12, 2006, p. 8.
7. Cariola, Carmen and Sunkel, Osvaldo, "Chile," in *Latin America: A Guide to Economic History, 1830-1930*, Edited by Cortés Conde, Roberto and Stein, Stanley J. (Berkeley: University of California Press, 1977), pp. 282-83.
8. Stuven, Ana María, *La seducción de un orden: Las elites y la construcción de Chile en las polémicas del siglo XIX* (Santiago: Universidad Católica de Chile, 2000).
9. Bauer, Arnold J., "Industry and the Missing Bourgeoisie: Consumption and Development in Chile, 1850-1950," *The Hispanic American Historical Review*, 70: 2 (May, 1990), pp. 244-52.
10. Berquist, Charles, *Labor in Latin America* (Stanford: Stanford University Press, 1986), pp. 15, 23.
11. Adelman, Jeremy, "Between Order and Liberty," *Latin American Research Review*, Volume 42, No. 2 (2007), p. 87.
12. Lewis, Colin M., *British Railways in Argentina, 1857-1914* (London: Institute of Latin American Studies, 1983). See also: Wright, Wintrop R., *British-Owned Railways in Argentina* (Austin: Univerity of Texas

Press, 1974).

13. Laclau, Ernesto, "Modos de producción, sistemas económicos y población excedente: Aproximación histórica a los casos argentino y chileno," *Revista latino-americana de sociología*, V (1969), p. 276.

14. Lewis, Arthur W., *The Evolution of the International Economic Order* (Princeton, NJ: Princenton University Press, 1977), pp. 21, 25, 39.

15. Cortés Conde, Roberto, "The growth of the Argentine Economy, c. 1870-1914," *The Cambridge History of Latin America*, V, Edited by Bethell, Leslie (Cambridge: Cambridge University Press, 1986), pp. 355-57.

16. Rock, David, "Argentina a Hundred and Fifty Years of Democratic Praxis," *Latin American Research Review*, Volume 40, No. 2 (2005), p. 227.

17. Haiti and the Dominican Republic, which were under American fiscal supervision, were not allowed to default on their foreign debt.

18. Scobie, James R., *Argentina: A City and a Nation* (New York: Oxford University Press, 1964), p. 227.

19. Rock, David, *Authoritarian Argentina: The Nationalist Movement, Its History and Its Impact* (Berkeley: University of California Press, 1993).

20. Imaz, José Luis de, *Los que mandan* (Those Who Rule), Translated by Carlos A. Astiz (Albany: New York State University Press, 1970), pp. 5-7, 34.

21. MacGann, Thomas F., *Argentina, the United States, and the Inter-American System, 1880-1914* (Cambridge, MA: Harvard University Press, 1957).

22. Dorfman, Adolfo, *Cincuenta años de industrialización en Argentina, 1930-1980* (Buenos Aires: Ediciones Solar, 1983).

23. Lanusse, Alejandro, *Mi testimonio* (Buenos Aires: Laserre Editores, 1977).

24. "Argentina," *Latin American Political Report* (London), February 18, 1977, p. 51.

25. Brysk, Allison, *The Politics of Human Rights in Argentina* (Stanford: Stanford University Press, 1994), p. 58.

26. Lewis, Paul H., *Political Parties and Generations in Paraguay's Liberal Era, 1869-1940* (Chapel Hill: University of North Carolina Press, 1993), p. 29.

27. Warren, Harris G., *Rebirth of the Paraguayan Republic: The First Colorado Era, 1878-1904* (Pittsburgh: University of Pittsburgh Press, 1985).

28. Saeger, James Scholfield, *Francisco Solano López and the Ruination*

of Paraguay: Honor and Egocentrism (Lanham, MD: Rowman & Littlefield, 2007), pp. 193-194.

29. Kleinpenning, Jan M. G., *Rural Paraguay, 1870-1932* (Amsterdam: Center for Latin American Research and Documentation, 1992).

30. Hobsbawm, Eric J., *The Age of Capital: 1848-1875* (London: George Weidenfeld & Nicolson, 1975), p. 78.

31. Finch, Henry, *La economía política del Uruguay contemporáneo, 1870-2000* (Montevideo: Ediciones de la Banda Oriental, 2005), pp. 206-08.

32. Ehrick, Christine, *The Shield of the Weak: Feminism and the State in Uruguay, 1903-1933* (Albuquerque: University of New Mexico Press, 2005).

33. During the 1820s, Lord Cochrane and a number of discharged British officers operated a mercenary naval fleet that fought for pay against the Spanish and Turkish navies in South American and Greek emancipatory wars.

34. In 1836, Garibaldi fled to Rio Grande do Sul for five years. Later, he escaped to Uruguay where he fought on the side of Fructuoso Rivera and the Liberals. In 1848, Rivera and his South American companions fought for the Italian unification. Garibaldi also acquired a Peruvian passport by marrying a Peruvian woman.

35. Viotti da Costa, Emilia, *The Brazilian Empire, Myths and Histories* (Chicago: University of Chicago Press, 1985), p. 212.

36. Graham, Richard, *Patronage and Politics in Nineteenth Century Brazil* (Stanford: Stanford University Press, 1990), pp. 232.

37. Burns, Bradford E., *Nationalism in Brazil: A Historical Survey* (New York: Praeger Publishers, 1968), pp. 74-133.

38. Even the Conservative Janio Quadros had attempted to free Brazilian foreign policy from American control. See: Rodrigues, José Honório, "An Independent Foreign Policy," in *A Century of Brazilian History since 1865*, Edited by Graham, Richard (New York: Alfred A. Knopf, 1969), pp. 214-28.

39. "Opposition in Brazil...," *The New York Times*, February 6, 1975, p. 12c. See also: Drosdoff, Daniel, *Linha dura no Brasil: O Governo Médici, 1969-1974* (São Paulo: Global, 1986).

40. Diniz, Eli, "The Post-1930 Industrial Elite," in *Modern Brazil*, Edited by Conniff, Michael L., and McCann, Frank D. (Lincoln: University of Nebraska Press, 1989), p. 114.

41. Colman Sercovich, Francisco, "The Exchange and Absorption of Technology in Brazilian Industry," in *Authoritarian Capitalism*, Edited by Bruneau, Thomas C., and Faucher, Philippe (Boulder: Westview Press, 1981), pp. 128-29.

42. Becker, Bertha K., and Egler, Claudio A. G., *Brazil: A New Regional Power in the World Economy* (Cambridge: Cambridge University Press, 1992), pp. 163-64.
43. "Region's Military See Threat Ahead," *Latin American Weekly Report* (London), October 28, 1993, p. 493.

Chapter VIII

1. Castro, Fidel, "Una sola China," *Granma* (Havana), April 21, 2006, Internet Edition.
2. *China Daily* (Peking), June 14, 2011, pp. 8, 11.
3. Li, He, "Red Star Over Latin America," *NACLA*, Vol. 40, No. 5 (September-October, 2007), p. 25.
4. In 2011, the American exports in goods and services to Latin America and the Caribbean amounted to $210 billion.
5. *El Comercio* (Lima), December 19, 2005, p. A8.
6. *The Economist*, January 12, 2008, pp. 43-44.
7. Krugman, Paul, "Who Was Milton Friedman?" *The New York Review*, February 15, 2007, p. 30.
8. *Reporte Anual de Economía y Desarrollo 2007-2008* (Lima: Corporación Andina de Fomento [CAF], February 22, 2008). See also: "Pobreza se mantiene en América Latina," *La República*, February 19, 2008, Internet Edition.
9. *The Economist*, May 20-26, 2006, p. 11.
10. *Svenska Dagbladet*, September 13, 2003, p. 11.
11. Petras, James, "Venezuela," *Rebelión* (Havana), January 7, 2008, Internet Edition.
12. *El Universal* (Mexico, D. F.), January 19, 2007, p. B7.
13. Edwards, Sebastian, "Globalization, Growth and Crises: The View from Latin America," *National Bureau of Economic Research*, Working Paper 14034 (May, 2008), p. 2.
14. Vidal Luna, Francisco and Klein, Herbert S., *The World since 1980* (Cambridge: Cambridge University Press, 2006), p. 209.
15. *UNDP Report* (New York: United Nations, 2003).
16. By 2008, Brazilian exports constituted 1.18% of the world's exports and with government subsidies they are to increase to 1.25%.
17. Betto, Frei, "El amigo Lula," *La República* (Lima), November 3, 2002, Internet Edition.
18. *The Economist*, June 23, 2007, pp. 56-57.
19. Castañeda, Jorge, "The Battle to Clean Up Mexico," *Newsweek*, November 5, 2007, p. 39.
20. Stiglitz, Joseph, "Alla tjänar inte på globaliseringen," *Dagens Nyhe-*

ter, May 10, 2004, p. 2.

21. "Study Abroad Program," Mexico Solidarity Network (USA, May 19, 2006).

22. *NAFTA at Seven* (Washington, D.C.: Economic Policy Institute, 2001).

23. *International Herald Tribune*, September 21, 2005, p. 19.

24. *The Economist*, September 15, 2007, p. 61.

25. Alvarez Bejar, Alejandro, "Mexico after the Elections," *Monthly Review*, Vol. 59, No. 3 (July-August, 2007), p. 24.

26. *Dagens Nyheter*, September 5, 2003, pp. 8-9. See also: "U.S. Corn Subsidy Fight," *International Herald Tribune*, August 27, 2003, p. 14.

27. *La Jornada* (Mexico, D. F.), January 16, 2007, p. 21.

28. Mexican imports of American corn increased from 156,000 tons in 1993 to about 10.8 million tons in 2007.

29. *Newsweek*, May 19, 2008, p. 22.

30. Krauze, Enrique, "Bringing Mexico Closer to God," *International Herald Tribune*, June 29, 2006, p. 8.

31. Nahmad, Salomón, "Political Commentary," *Latin American Studies Association: Forum*, XXXVIII, 2 (Spring, 2007), pp. 24-26.

32. Castro, Fidel, "El Buen Dios me protegió de Bush," *Granma*, June 28, 2007, Internet Edition.

33. According to official figures of the Cuban government, the island's GNP grew by an average 4.7% yearly from 1995 to 2000.

34. *Granma*, February 19, 2008, Internet Edition.

35. *Svenska Dagbladet*, February 20, 2008, p. 4.

36. *International Herald Tribune*, September 29, 2003, p. 5.

37. *The Guardian Weekly* (London), December 9-10, 2005, p. 10. According to the United Nations, corporations from Argentina, Brazil, Chile, and Mexico alone had $143 billion in direct investments abroad in 2006. *SvenskaDagbladet*, August 18, 2008, p. 9.

38. *La República* (Lima), November 11, 2007, Internet Edition.

39. According to a report by the Economic Commission for Latin America (ECLA) of the United Nations, 2007.

40. Lavrin, Asunsión, "Women in Twentieth-Century Latin American Society," *The Cambridge History of Latin America*, VI, Edited by Bethell, Leslie (Cambridge: Cambridge University Press, 1994), p. 537.

41. *La Jornada*, January 18, 2007, p. 32.

42. *Financial Times* (London), January 20-21, 2007, pp. 6-7.

43. According to polls (2008) conducted by the sociologist Hugh Gladwin, Florida International University, Miami.

44. *UNDP Report* (Lima: United Nations, April 21, 2004).
45. "Region: Energy," *Latin American Weekly Report* (London), July 22, 1993, p. 335.
46. Gustafsson, Bo, *Från kolonialism till socialism* (Stockholm: Clarté, 1964), p. 13.
47. *Svenska Dagbaldet*, May 28, 2004, p. 20.
48. Valenzuela, Luisa, "Latin America," *International Herald Tribune*, March 20, 2007, p. 6.
49. In 2005, 80% of the IMF's $81 billion loan portfolio was to Latin America. Two years later, it was drastically reduced only to one percent of its $17 billion portfolio.
50. The founding members of the bank are: Argentina, Bolivia, Brazil, Ecuador, Paraguay, Uruguay, and Venezuela.
51. This state company is the biggest producer of copper in the world. It originated with the nationalization of the copper industry by the Allende government in 1971.
52. According to the United Nations, the cultivation areas in Colombia increased by 27% from 2006 to 2007.
53. When, in February 2002, the Colombian army moved into FARC territory, it did not meet any resistance. The guerrilla forces had already moved away.
54. In 2003, the PMF activities represented about $100 billion annually. Among the largest investors in these entrepreneurial ventures were Lockheed-Martin, Northrup Grumman, and Halliburton.
55. The global business of Private Military Companies was estimated in $100 billion in 2007.
56. Restrepo, Dan, "The Wrong Model," *International Herald Tribune*, January 30, 2007, p. 6.
57. Lévano, César, "Uribe: Peón de Bush," *La Primera* (Lima), March 4, 2008, Internet Edition.
58. The official excuse for the cancellation of Chávez's mediation was because Chávez contacted Colombia's Defense Minister without Uribe's permission.
59. Vargas Llosa, Mario, "El suicidio de una nación," *Socialismo y participación* (Lima), No. 86 (December, 1999), p. 162.
60. A national referendum, which would have amended 69 out of 350 articles in the Constitution, was rejected by 51% of the votes on December 21, 2007.
61. Romero, Simón, "US Spending to Finance the Foes of Chávez," *International Herald Tribune*, November 10, 2006, p. 17.
62. In 1991, the United States supported a coup against the democratically elected President Bertrand Aristide. However, three years later

the United States invaded Haiti to restore Aristide. On February 29, 2004, the United States sponsored again a coup against Aristide. The American Deputy Secretary of State for Latin America, Roger Noriega, described the American intervention only as a "non-traditional" type of coup.

63. By 2007, the Venezuelan government had bought a majority ownership in its oil industry. However, the American companies ExxonMobil and Conoco-Phillips refused the compensation. At their request, an international arbitration court froze $12 billion of Venezuelan assets held in the United States, Canada, and England in 2008.

64. Weisbrot, Mark, "Latin America: The End of an Era," *International Journal of Health Services*, Vol. 36, No. 4 (2006), p. 9, Internet Edition.

65. *International Herald Tribune*, December 2-3, 2006, p. 2.

66. After the military coup of June 28, 2009, the new Honduran government withdrew from the ALBA.

67. John Walters, head of the Drug Enforcement Administration (DEA) publicly asserted that Chávez's failure to conduct an effective war against drug traffic made him a supporter of narco-terrorism (January 2008).

68. This appeal was made by Chávez in his weekly TV program on June 8, 2008.

69. Castro, Fidel, "Lula," *Granma*, February 1, 2008, Internet Edition.

70. *The Economist*, November 30, 2002, p. 50.

71. *International Herald Tribune*, November 29, 2006, p. 7.

72. The sobriquet "Populist" was first used by the Russian Social Democrats (Marxists) against the upper class political activists who advocated for radical social change in benefit of the lower classes in the late 19x century.

73. Benton, Lauren, "No Longer Odd Region Out: Repositioning Latin America in World History," *The Hispanic American Historical Review*, 84:3 (August, 2004), p. 426.

74. *International Herald Tribune*, February 14, 2007, p. 12.

75. Walsh, Catherine, *Interculturalidad, estado, sociedad: Luchas (de) coloniales de nuestra época* (Quito: Universidad Andina Simón Bolívar/Abya-Yala, 2009), pp. 65, 95-100.

Bibliography

Archives

Informe de la captura de Túpac Amaru (1781), folios 179-195, Milicias y Marinas, LXXIX, Sección de la Colonia, Archivo Nacional, Bogotá, Colombia.

Informe del transporte de tropas de Panamá al Callao (1784), folios 422-440, Milicias y Marinas, LXXIX; Cartas de Agustín Jauregui al Virrey de Nueva Granada tratando los disturbios internos del Perú (1782), folios 13-15, 17-18, Milicias y Marinas, CXIV, Sección de la Colonia, Archivo Nacional, Bogotá, Colombia.

Real Hacienda (1786), Causas Ordinarias, Legajo 129, Expediente 110, folios 1-8. Archivo Regional La Libertad, Trujillo, Peru.

Sección Histórica, Legajo 24, Expediente 365, Año 1633, Archivo Departamental de Cajamarca, Peru.

Articles, Books, and Printed Documents

Adams, Richard E. W. (Editor), *The Origins of Maya Civilization* (Albuquerque: University of New Mexico Press, 1977).

Adelman, Jeremy, "Between Order and Liberty," *Latin American Research Review*, Volume 42, No. 2 (2007).

Alvarez Bejar, Alejandro, "Mexico after the Elections," *Monthly Review*, Vol. 59, No. 3 (July-August, 2007).

Amin, Samir, *Accumulation on a World Scale* (Sussex: Harvester Press, 1974).

Anderson, Robert, "The Quilombos of Palmares," *Journal of Latin American Studies*, XXVIII, 3 (October, 1996).

Anna, Timothy, "The Independence of Mexico and Central America," in *The Independence of Latin America*, Edited by Leslie Bethel (Cambridge: Cambridge University Press, 1989).

Arens, William, *The Man-Eating Myth* (New York: Oxford University Press, 1979).

Arnold, Paul, *El libro maya de los muertos* (México, D.F.: Editorial Diana, 1990).

Atloloni Lecón, Amalia, "El maya, su esclavitud y su comercio," *Memoria del congreso conmemorativo del X aniversario del Departamento de Etnohistoria*, Cuaderno de trabajo No. 4 (México, D.F.: Instituto nacional de antropología e historia, 1988).

Banzant, Jean, "Mexico from Independence to 1867," *The Cambridge History of Latin America*, III, Edited by Bethell, Leslie (Cambridge: Cambridge University Press, 1985).

Barredo-Medina, Lázaro, "50 años déspues," *Granma*, December 30, 2008, Internet Edition.

Bartra, Roger, *El modo de producción asiático* (México, D.F.: Siglo XXI, 1969).

Bauer, Arnold J., "Industry and the Missing Bourgeoisie: Consumption and Development in Chile, 1850-1950," *The Hispanic American Historical Review*, 70: 2 (May, 1990).

Becker, Bertha K. and Egler, Claudio A. G., *Brazil: A New Regional Power in the World Economy* (Cambridge: Cambridge University Press, 1992).

Bell, Madison Smartt, *Toussaint Louverture: A Biography* (New York: Pantheon, 2007).

Benton, Lauren, "No Longer Odd Region Out: Repositioning Latin America in World History," *The Hispanic American Historical Review*, 84:3 (August, 2004).

Berquist, Charles, *Labor in Latin America* (Stanford: Stanford University Press, 1986).

Betto, Frei, "El amigo Lula," *La República* (Lima), November 3, 2002, Internet Edition.

Bowser, Frederick P., *El esclavo africano en el Perú colonial, 1524-1650* (Mexico, D.F.: Siglo XXI, 1977).

Braudel, Fernand, *The Structures of Everyday Life: Civilization and Capitalism 15th-18th Century*, 2 Vols., I (New York: Harper & Row, 1979).

Braudel, Fernand, *The Structures of Everyday Life: Civilization and Capitalism 15th-18th Century*, 2 Vols., II (New York: Haper & Row, 1982).

Brysk, Allison, *The Politics of Human Rights in Argentina* (Stanford: Stanford University Press, 1994).

Burga, Manuel, "El Perú ha perdido el paso [Interview]," *Socialismo y participación* (Lima), No. 91 (October, 2001).

Burland, C. A., *The Gods of Mexico* (New York: Capricorn Books, 1968).

Burns, E. Bradford, *A History of Brazil* (New York: Columbia University Press, 1980).

Burns, E. Bradford, *Latin America: A Concise Interpretive History*, Third Edition (Englewood Cliffs, NJ: Prentice Hall Inc., 1982).

Burns, E. Bradford, *Nationalism in Brazil: A Historical Survey* (New

York: Praeger Publishers, 1968).

Burns, Kathryn, "Gender and the Politics of Mestizaje," *The Hispanic American Historical Review*, 78: 1 (February, 1998).

Burns Glynn, William, "La escritura de los Incas," *Boletín de Lima*, Numbers 12-14 (May- September, 1981).

Bushnell, David, *Colombia* (Berkeley: University of California Press, 1992).

Bustelo, Pablo, "La industrialización en América Latina y Asia Oriental," *Comercio Exterior*, Vol. 42, No. 12 (December, 1992).

Campbell, Joseph, *Oriental Mythology: The Masks of God* (New York: Penguin Books, 1991).

Cariola, Carmen, and Sunkel, Osvaldo, "Chile," in *Latin America: A Guide to Economic History, 1830-1930*, Edited by Cortés Conde, Roberto, and Stein, Stanley J. (Berkeley: University of California Press, 1977).

Carrasco, Hernán, "Indígenas serranos en Quito y Guayaquil," *América Indígena*, LI, No. 4 (October-December, 1991).

Carrasco, Pedro, "The Economy of the Aztec and Inca States," in *The Inca and Aztec States, 1400-1800*, Edited by Collier, George A. et al., (New York: Academic Press, 1982).

Carrera Damas, Germán, *La crisis de la sociedad colonial* (Caracas: Universidad Central, 1976).

Castañeda, Jorge G., "Lessons for the Left," *Newsweek*, March 12, 1991.

Castañeda, Jorge, "The Battle to Clean Up Mexico," *Newsweek*, November 5, 2007.

Castro, Fidel, "El Buen Dios me protegió de Bush," *Granma*, June 28, 2007, Internet Edition.

Castro, Fidel, "Lula," *Granma*, February 1, 2008, Internet Edition.

Castro, Fidel, "Una sola China," *Granma* (Havana), April 21, 2006, Internet Edition.

Céspedes, Guillermo, *Latin America: The Early Years* (New York: Alfred A. Knopf, 1974).

Clendinnen, Inga, *Ambivalent Conquests: Maya and Spaniard in Yucatán, 1517-1570* (New York: Oxford University Press, 1987).

Clinton, Bill, "Many Hands Lighten the Load," *Newsweek*, January 25, 2010.

Coe, Michael D., *Breaking the Maya Code* (London: Thames & Hudson, 1992).

Colman Sercovich, Francisco, "The Exchange and Absorpion of Technology in Brazilian Industry," in *Authoritarian Capitalism*, Edited by Bruneau, Thomas C., and Faucher, Philippe (Boulder: Westview Press, 1981).

Conaghan, Catherine M. and Malloy, James M., *Unsettling Statecraft: Democracy and Neoliberalism in the Central Andes* (Pittsburgh: University of Pittsburgh Press, 1994).

Contreras, Carlos, *Los mineros y el Rey, los Andes del Norte: Hualgayoc 1770-1825*, Serie Estudios Históricos 16 (Lima: Instituto de Estudios Peruanos, 1995).

Cortés, Hernán, *Cartas de relación de la conquista de México*, Sexta Edición, Colección Austral (Madrid: Espasa-Calpe, 1979).

Cortés Conde, Roberto, and Stein, Stanley J. (Editors), *Latin America: A Guide to Economic History, 1830-1930* (Berkeley: University of California Press, 1977).

Cortés Conde, Roberto, "The growth of the Argentine Economy, c. 1870-1914," *The Cambridge History of Latin America*, V, Edited by Bethell, Leslie (Cambridge: Cambridge University Press, 1986).

Cotler, Julio, *Clases, estado y nación en el Perú* (Lima: Instituto de Estudios Peruanos, 1985).

Crosby, Alfred W., *Ecological Imperialism* (Cambridge: Cambridge University Press, 1993).

Cruz, Consuelo, *Political Culture and Institutional Development in Costa Rica and Nicaragua: World-Making in the Tropics* (Cambridge: Cambridge University Press, 2005).

Davis, David Brion, "He Changed the World," *The New York Review*, May 31, 2007.

De la Fuente, Beatriz, *Los hombres de Piedra: Escultura Olmeca* (México, D.F.: UNAM, 1977).

Díaz Del Castillo, Bernal, *The True History of the Conquest of Mexico* (La Jolla, CA: Renaissance Press, 1979).

Díaz Infante, Fernando, *La educación de los Aztecas* (México, D.F.: Panorama Editorial, S. A., 1988).

Diniz, Eli, "The Post-1930 Industrial Elite," in *Modern Brazil*, Edited by Conniff, Michael L. and McCann, Frank D. (Lincoln: University of Nebraska Press, 1989).

Domínguez, Jorge I., "Revolution and its Aftermath in Cuba," *Latin American Research Review*, Volume 43, No. 2 (2008).

Dorfman, Adolfo, *Cincuenta años de industrialización en Argentina, 1930-1980* (Buenos Aires: Ediciones Solar, 1983).

Dorfman, Ariel, "Pinochet II," *International Herald Tribune*, December 12, 2006.

Dosal, Paul J., *Power in Transition: The Rise of Guatemala's Industrial Oligarchy, 1871- 1994* (Westport, CT: Praeger, 1995).

Drosdoff, Daniel, *Linha dura no Brasil: O Governo Médici, 1969-1974* (São Paulo: Global, 1986).

Edwards, Sebastian, "Globalization, Growth and Crises: The View from Latin America," *National Bureau of Economic Research*, Working Paper 14034 (May, 2008).

Ehrick, Christine, *The Shield of the Weak: Feminism and the State in Uruguay, 1903-1933* (Albuquerque: University of New Mexico Press, 2005).

Ermolaev, V. I., "The Emergence of the First Labor Organizations and Marxist Groups in the Countries of Latin America, 1870-1900," in *Soviet Historians on Latin America*, Edited by Bartley, Russell H. (Madison: The University of Wisconsin Press, 1978).

Fals Borda, Orlando, "La Investigación-Acción en convergencias disciplinarias," *Latin American Studies Association: Forum*, XXXVIII, 4 (Fall, 2007).

Fauriol, George A., "The Shadow of Latin American Affairs," *Foreign Affairs*, Vol. 69, No. 1 (1990).

Ffrench-Davis, Ricardo, "Latin American Economies, 1950-1990," *The Cambridge History of Latin America*, VI, Part 1, Edited by Bethell, Leslie (Cambridge: Cambridge University Press, 1994).

Figueras, Miguel, "La producción de bienes de capital en Cuba," *Comercio Exterior*, Vol. 42, No. 12 (December, 1992).

Finch, Henry, *La economía política del Uruguay contemporáneo, 1870-2000* (Montevideo: Ediciones de la Banda Oriental, 2005).

Flores Caballero, Romeo, *Counterrevolution: The Role of the Spaniards in the Independence of Mexico, 1804-38* (Lincoln: University of Nebraska Press, 1974).

Flores Galindo, Alberto, *Aristocracia y plebe: Lima, 1760-1830* (Lima: Mosca Azul Editores, 1984).

Flores Galindo, Alberto, *Buscando un Inca: Identidad y utopía en los Andes* (La Habana: Casa de las Américas, 1986).

Friede, Juan, "Orígenes de la esclavitud indígena en Venezuela," *América Indígena*, XXII, 1 (1962).

Georgescu-Rogen, Nicholas, *Energy and Economic Myths: Institutional and Analytical Economic Essays* (New York: Harvard University Press, 1976).

Gibson, Charles, "The Aztec Aristocracy in Colonial Mexico," *Compartive Studies in Society and History*, II (1959-1960).

Gibson, Charles, *The Aztecs under Spanish Rule* (Stanford: Stanford University Press, 1964).

Gibson, Charles (Editor), *The Spanish Tradition in America* (New York: Harper & Row, 1968).

Gleijeses, Piero, *Shattered Hope: The Guatemalan Revolution and the United States, 1944- 1954* (Princeton: Princeton University Press,

1991).

Graham, Richard, *Patronage and Politics in Nineteenth Century Brazil* (Stanford: Stanford University Press, 1990).

Green, John W., *Gaitanismo, Left Liberalism and Popular Mobilization in Colombia* (Gainesville: University Press of Florida, 2003).

Gunn, Joel, and Adams, Richard, "Climatic Change, Culture and Civilization in North America," *World Archaeology*, Vol. 13: 1 (June, 1981), p. 93.

Gustafsson, Bo, *Från kolonialism till socialism* (Stockholm: Clarté, 1964).

Hallward, Peter, "An Interview with Jean-Bertrand Aristide," *London Review of Books*, Vol. 29, No. 4 (February 22, 2007), Internet Edition.

Halperin-Donghi, Tulio, *The Aftermath of Revolution in Latin America* (New York: Harper & Row, 1973).

Hamond, Norman, and Wiley, Gordon P., *Maya Archeology and Ethno-History* (Austin: University of Texas Press, 1979).

Handy, Jim, *Revolution in the Countryside: Rural Conflicts and Agrarian Reform in Guatemala, 1944-1954* (Chapel Hill: University of North Carolina Press, 1994).

Hart, John Mason, *Empire and Revolution: The Americans in Mexico since the Civil War* (Berkeley: University of California Press, 2002).

Helms, Mary W., *Ancient Panama: Chiefs in Search of Power* (Austin: University of Texas Press, 1979).

Henderson, James D., *Modernization in Colombia* (Gainesville: University Press of Florida, 2001).

Hobsbawm, Eric J., *Industry and Empire: An Economic History of Britain since 1750* (London: George Weidenfeld & Nicolson, 1968).

Hobsbawm, Eric J., *The Age of Capital: 1848-1875* (London: George Weidenfeld & Nicolson, 1975).

Horna, Hernán, "A propósito del descubrimiento asiático de América," *América Indígena* (México, D.F.), LII, 1-2 (January-June, 1992).

Horna, Hernán, "Asiatic Migrations to the Andean Zone [Chinese]," *Collected Writings of Asia-Pacific Studies*, Volume 6 (Peking: Peking University Press, 2009).

Horna, Hernán, *Colombian Archival Sources on Colonial Peru* (Washington, D.C.: Pan American Institute of Geography and History, 1971).

Horna, Hernán, *Five Essays on Post Colonial Latin American History* (Uppsala, Sweden: History Institute, 1994).

Horna, Hernán, *La Indianidad* (Princeton, NJ: Markus Wiener Publishers, 2001).

Hunt, Shane, *Growth and Guano in Nineteenth Century Peru*, Report No. 34 (Princeton: Princeton University Press, 1973).

Imaz, José Luis de, *Los que mandan* (Those Who Rule), Translated by Carlos A. Astiz (Albany: New York State University Press, 1970).

Jackson, Robert, "The Decline of the Hacienda in Cochabamba, Bolivia," *The Hispanic American Historical Review*, 69: 2 (May, 1989).

Jenks, Leland Hamilton, *The Migration of British Capital to 1875* (London: Thomas Nelson and Sons Ltd., 1963).

Johansson, Kjell A., "Kompisar från Kuba," *Dagens Nyheter* (Stockholm), July 8, 1991.

Klein, Herbert S., *A Concise History of Bolivia* (New York: Cambridge University Press, 2006).

Klein, Herbert S., & Schiffner, Daniel C., "El origen de los amerindios: Debates actuales," *Revista de Indias*, LXIII, No. 227 (2003).

Kleinpenning, Jan M. G., *Rural Paraguay, 1870-1932* (Amsterdam: Center for Latin American Research and Documentation, 1992).

Knórozov, Y. V., *Códices jeroglíficos de los Mayas* (Leningrado: Academia de las Ciencias de la URSS, 1975).

Krauze, Enrique, "Bringing Mexico Closer to God," *International Herald Tribune*, June 29, 2006.

Krugman, Paul, "Who Was Milton Friedman?" *The New York Review*, February 15, 2007.

Laclau, Ernesto, "Modos de producción, sistemas económicos y población excedente: Aproximación histórica a los casos argentino y chileno," *Revista latino- americana de sociología*, V (1969).

Langer, Erick D., "Introduction: Placing Latin America in World History," *The Hispanic American Historical Review*, 84:3 (August, 2004).

Lanusse, Alejandro, *Mi testimonio* (Buenos Aires: Laserre Editores, 1977).

Lavrin, Asunsión, "Women in Twentieth-Century Latin American Society," *The Cambridge History of Latin America*, VI, Edited by Bethell, Leslie (Cambridge: Cambridge University Press, 1994).

Lewis, Arthur W., *The Evolution of the International Economic Order* (Princeton, NJ: Princeton University Press, 1977).

Lewis, Colin M., *British Railways in Argentina, 1857-1914* (London: Institute of Latin American Studies, 1983).

Lewis, Paul H., *Political Parties and Generations in Paraguay's Liberal Era, 1869-1940* (Chapel Hill: University of North Carolina Press, 1993).

León-Portilla, Miguel, *De besegrades version* (Stockholm: Panorama, 1971).

Lettner, Carlos J., "Las escrituras americanas," *Anuario Indigenista*, Vol. XXXIII (December, 1973).

Lévano, César, "Uribe: Peón de Bush," *La Primera* (Lima), March 4,

2008, Internet Edition.

Li, Dun J., *The Ageless Chinese* (New York: Charles Scribner's Sons, 1965).

Li, He, "Red Star Over Latin America," *NACLA*, Vol. 40, No. 5 (September-October, 2007).

Lothrop, Samuel K., "South America as Seen from Middle America," in *Essays in Pre- Columbian Art and Arqueology*, Edited by Lothrop, Samuel K. et al., (Cambridge, MA: Harvard University Press, 1961).

Lowenthal, Abraham F., "América Latina," *Caretas* (Lima), June 12, 1990.

Lowenthal, Abraham F., "Latin America: Ready for Partnership?," *Foreign Affairs*, Vol. 72, No. 1 (1993).

Luxemburgo, Rosa, *Introducción a la economía* (Madrid: Siglo XXI, 1974).

Lynch, John, *Caudillos in Spanish America, 1800-1850* (Oxford: Claredon Press, 1992).

Lynch, John, "The Institutional Fragments of Colonial Spanish America," *Journal of Latin American Studies*, XXIV, Quincentenary Supplement (1992).

Lynch, John, "The Origins of Spanish American Independence," in *The Independence of Latin America*, Edited by Bethell, Leslie (Cambridge: Cambridge University Press, 1989).

Macas, Luis, *El levantamiento Indígena visto por sus protagonistas* (Quito: Abi-Ayala, 1991).

Macera, Pablo, *Historia del Perú: La colonia*, 3 Vols., II (Lima: Editorial Bruño, 1985).

Macera, Pablo, "Reflexiones a propósito de la polémica del indigenismo," *Apuntes* (Lima), III, No. 6 (1977).

MacGann, Thomas F., *Argentina, the United States, and the Inter-American System, 1880- 1914* (Cambridge, MA: Harvard University Press, 1957).

Majdanik, Kiva, "Conference" at the Latin American Institute, Stockholm, September 30, 1993.

Marchán Romero, Carlos (Ed.), *Crisis y cambio de la economía en los años veinte* (Quito: Banco Central del Ecuador, 1987).

Marchant, Alexander, *From Barter to Slavery* (Baltimore: Johns Hopkins University Press, 1941).

Marchena Fernández, Juan, *Ejercito y milicias en el mundo colonial Americano* (Madrid: MAPRE, 1992).

Marcus, Joyce, "Zapotec Writing," *Scientific American*, Vol. 242 (February, 1980).

Marichal, Carlos, *Historia de la deuda externa de América Latina* (México, D.F.: Alianza Editorial Mexicana, 1988).

Matos Mar, José, *Desborde popular y crisis del estado* (Lima: Concytec, 1988).

Matos Mar, José, *Yanaconaje y reforma agraria en el Perú* (Lima: Concytec, 1976).

Matos Mendieta, Ramiro, "El secreto de la Quilca," *El Comercio* (Lima), November 24, 1985, Dominical.

Matthieu, Gilles, *Une ambition sud-américaine: Politique culturelle de la France (1914- 1940)* (Paris: L'Harmattan, 1991).

Meggers, Betty J., "The Transpacific Origin of Mesoamerican Civilization," *American Anthropologist*, 77: 1 (March, 1975).

Meggers, Betty J. et al., *Early Formative Period of Coastal Ecuador* (Washington, D.C.: Smithsonian Institute, 1965).

Meyer, Jean, "Mexico: Revolution and Reconstruction in the 1920s," *The Cambridge History of Latin America*, V, Edited by Bethell, Leslie (Cambridge: Cambridge University Press, 1986).

Meyer, Michael C., And Sherman, William L., *The Course of Mexican History* (New York: Oxford University Press, 1983).

Montoya, Rodrigo, *Al borde del naufragio* (Lima: Cuadernos de SUR, 1992).

Moreno Fraginals, Manuel, "En torno a la identidad cultural en el Caribe insular," *Casa de las Américas*, XX, No. 118 (January-February, 1980).

Morison, Samuel Eliot (Editor), *Journals and Other Documents on the Life and Voyages of Christopher Columbus,* (New York: The Heritage Press, 1963).

Mörner, Magnus, *La corona española y los foráneos en los pueblos de indios de América* (Stockholm: Instituto de Estudios Ibero-Americanos, 1970).

Mörner, Magnus, *Race Mixture in the History of Latin America* (Boston: Little, Brown and Company, 1967).

Mörner, Magnus, *The Political and Economic Activities of the Jesuits in La Plata Region* (Stockholm: Ibero-amerikanska Biblioteket & Institutet, 1953).

Muñoz Ledo, Porfirio, *La sociedad frente al poder* (México, D.F.: Editorial Diana, 1993).

Munro, Dana G., *Intervention and Dollar Diplomacy in the Caribbean* (Princeton University Press, 1964).

NAFTA at Seven (Washington, D.C.: Economic Policy Institute, 2001).

Nahmad, Salomón, "Political Commentary," *Latin American Studies Association: Forum*, XXXVIII, 2 (Spring, 2007).

Nicholls, David, *From Dessalines to Duvalier: Race, Colour and Na-*

tional Independence in Haiti (Cambridge: Cambridge University Press, 1979).

O'Brien, Patrick, "European Economic Development: The Contribution of the Periphery," *The Economic History Review*, XXXV, 1 (February, 1982).

O'Phelan Godoy, Scarlett, *Rebellions and Revolts in Eighteenth Century Peru and Upper Peru* (Cologne, Germany: Lateinamerikanische Forschungen, 1985).

Padden, R. C., *The Hummingbird and the Hawk* (New York: Harper & Row, 1967).

Patch, Robert W., "Imperial Politics and Local Economy in Colonial Central America, 1670- 1770," *Past & Present*, 143 (May, 1994).

Patch, Robert W., *Maya and Spaniard in Yucatán, 1648-1812* (Stanford: Stanford University Press, 1993).

Pease, Franklin, *Del Tawantinsuyo a la historia del Perú* (Lima: Instituto de Estudios Peruanos, 1978).

Pérez Rincón, Mario, *Comercio Internacional y Medio Ambiente en Colombia* (Barcelona, Spain: Institut De Ciència i Tecnologia Ambientals, 2006).

Peterson, Frederick A., *Ancient Mexico* (New York: Capricorn Books, 1962).

Petras, James, "Venezuela," *Rebelión* (Havana), January 7, 2008, Internet Edition.

Pineo, Ronn F., "Reinterpreting Labor Militancy: The Collapse of the Cacao Economy and the General Strike of 1922 in Guayaquil, Ecuador," *The Hispanic American Historical Review*, 68: 4 (November, 1988).

Popol Vuh, Edited by Recinos, Adrián (México, D.F.: Fondo de Cultura Económica, 1994).

Poppino, Rollie E., *Brazil: Land and People* (New York: Oxford University Press, 1968).

Porras Barrenechea, Raúl, *Fuentes históricas peruanas* (Lima: Mejía Baca, 1945).

Prado, Caio, *The Colonial Background of Modern Brazil* (Berkeley: University of California Press, 1967).

Pratt, Julius W., "The Ideology of American Expansionism," in *Expansion and Imperialism*, Edited by Campbell, A. E. (New York: Harper & Row, 1970).

Reeves, René, *Ladinos with Ladinos, Indians with Indians, and Regional Ethnic Conflict in the Making of Guatemala* (Stanford: Stanford University Press, 2006).

Reporte Anual de Economía y Desarrollo 2007-2008 (Lima: Corporación

Andina de Fomento (CAF), February 22, 2008).

Restrepo, Dan, "The Wrong Model," *International Herald Tribune*, January 30, 2007.

Rock, David, "Argentina a Hundred and Fifty Years of Democratic Praxis," *Latin American Research Review*, Volume 40, No. 2 (2005).

Rock, David, *Authoritarian Argentina: The Nationalist Movement, Its History and Its Impact* (Berkeley: University of California Press, 1993).

Rodrigues, José Honório, "An Independent Foreign Policy," in *A Century of Brazilian History since 1865*, Edited by Graham, Richard (New York: Alfred A. Knopf, 1969).

Rodrigues, José Honório, *Tempo e sociedade* (Petrópolis, Brasil: Editora Vozes, 1986).

Rodríguez, Linda, *The Search for Public Policy: Regional Politics and Government Finance in Ecuador, 1830-1940* (Berkeley: University of California Press, 1985).

Romero, Simón, "US Spending to Finance the Foes of Chávez," *International Herald Tribune*, November 10, 2006.

Ronning, C. Neale (Editor), *Intervention in Latin America* (New York: Alfred A. Knopf, 1970).

Rostworowski, María, *Ensayos de historia andina* (Lima: Instituto de Estudios Peruanos, 1993).

Rotberg, Robert I., *Haiti: The Politics of Squalor* (Boston: Houghton Mifflin, 1971).

Rounds, J., "Dynastic Succession and the Centralization in Tenochtitlan," in *The Inca and Aztec States, 1400-1800*, Edited by Collier George A. et al., (New York: Academic Press, 1982).

Rouse, Irving, *The Tainos* (New Haven: Yale University Press, 1992).

Saeger, James Scholfield, *Francisco Solano López and the Ruination of Paraguay: Honor and Egocentrism* (Lanham, MD: Rowman & Littlefield, 2007).

Saffer, Lynda, *Native Americans before 1492* (New York: M. E. Sharpe, 1992).

Sánchez-Albornoz, Nicolás, *The Population of Latin America: A History* (Berkeley: University of California Press, 1974).

Santa Fe II: Strategy for Latin America in the Nineties (Washington, D.C.: The Committee of Santa Fe, 1989).

Scarbough, Vernon L., and Gallopin, Gary G., "A Water Storage in the Maya Lowlands," *Science*, Vol. 251: 4994 (February, 1991).

Schneider, Cathy, "Chile: The Underside of the Miracle," *NACLA*, XXXVI, 4 February, 1993).

Schwartz, Stuart B., *Sovereignty and Society in Colonial Brazil* (Berkeley: University of California Press, 1973).

Scobie, James R., *Argentina: A City and a Nation* (New York: Oxford University Press, 1964).

Scott, Peter Dale, and Marshall, Jonathan, *Cocaine Politics: Drugs, and the CIA in Central America* (Berkeley: University of California Press, 1992).

Scott, Rebecca, "Economic Aid and Imperialism in Bolivia," *Monthly Review*, Vol. 24 (May, 1972).

Seed, Patricia, *American Pentimento: The Invention of Indians and the Pursuit of Riches* (Minneapolis: University of Minnesota Press, 2001).

Sepkowski, Tadeusz, *Haiti* (La Habana: Departamento de Historia de América, 1978).

Shao, Paul, *Asiatic Influences in Pre Columbian Art* (Aimes: University of Iowa Press, 1976).

Sharer, Robert, "The Maya Collapse Revisited: Internal and External Perspectives," in *Social Process in Maya Prehistory*, Edited by Hamond, Norman (Baltimore: John Hopkins University Press, 1977).

Silverman, Gail, *El tejido andino: Un libro de sabiduría* (Lima: Banco Central, 1994).

Smith, Robert F., *The United States and Cuba: Business and Democracy, 1917-1960* (New York: Alfred A. Knopf, 1960).

Stein, Stanley J., and Stein, Barbara H., *The Colonial Heritage of Latin America* (New York: Oxford University Press, 1970).

Stiglitz, Joseph, "Alla tjänar inte på globaliseringen," *Dagens Nyheter*, May 10, 2004.

Stoetzer, Carlos O., *The Scholastic Roots of the Spanish American Revolution* (New York: Fordham University Press, 1979).

Stone, Irving, "Britiska långtidsinvesteringar i Latinamerika 1865-1913," in *Problem i världsekonomins historia*, Edited by Bunte, Rune, and Jörberg, Lennart (Lund, Sweden: CWK Gleerup Bokförlag, 1969).

Stone, Samuel Z., *The Heritage of the Conquistadors: Ruling Classes in Central America from the Conquest to the Sandinistas* (Lincoln: University of Nebraska Press, 1990).

Stuart, David, and Houston, Stephen D., "Maya writing," *Scientific American*, Vol. 261 (August, 1989).

"Study Abroad Program," Mexico Solidarity Network (USA, May 19, 2006).

Stuven, Ana María, *La seducción de un orden: Las elites y la construccion de Chile en las polémicas del siglo XIX* (Santiago: Universidad Católica de Chile, 2000).

Sweet, David G., and Nash, Gary (Editors), *Struggle and Survival* (Berkeley: University of California Press, 1981).

Tarcus, Horacio, *Marx en la Argentina: Sus primeros lectores obreros, intelectuales y científicos* (Buenos Aires: Siglo XXI, 2007).

UNDP Report (New York: United Nations, 2003).

UNDP Report (Lima: United Nations, April 21, 2004).

Valenzuela, Luisa, "Latin America," *International Herald Tribune*, March 20, 2007.

Van Zantwijk, Rudolf, "El origen de la sociedad y el estado azteca así como la historicidad de las fuentes autóctonas, una introducción," *Boletín de estudios latinoamericanos y del Caribe* (Amsterdam), No. 18 (June, 1975).

Vargas Llosa, Mario, "El suicidio de una nación," *Socialismo y participación* (Lima), No. 86 (December, 1999).

Vargas Ugarte, Rubén, *Historia general del Perú*, 6 Vols., II (Lima: Milla Bartres, 1971).

Vásquez, Josefina Zoraida, *La Gran Bretaña frente al México amenazado* (México, D. F.: Secretaría de Relaciones Exteriores, 2002).

Vega, Bernardo, *Eisenhower y Trujillo* (Santo Domingo: Fundación Cultural Dominicana, 1991).

Vidal Luna, Francisco, and Klein, Herbert S., *The World since 1980* (Cambridge: Cambridge University Press, 2006).

Vilar, Pierre, *A History of Gold and Money 1450-1920* (London: Foundations of History Library, 1976).

Viotti da Costa, Emilia, *The Brazilian Empire, Myths and Histories* (Chicago: University of Chicago Press, 1985).

Wachtel, Nathan, *Los Vencidos* (Madrid: Editorial Alianza, S. A., 1976).

Walker, Charles F., "Political Commentary," *LASA: FORUM*, XXXVIII, 1 (Winter, 2007).

Wallerstein, Immanuel, "European Economic Development: A Comment on O'Brien," *Economic History Review*, XXVI (1983).

Walsh, Catherine, *Interculturalidad, estado, sociedad: Luchas (de) coloniales de nuestra época* (Quito: Universidad Andina Simón Bolívar/Abya-Yala, 2009).

Ward, Christopher, *Imperial Panama: Commerce and Conflict in Isthmian America, 1550- 1800* (Albuquerque: University of New Mexico Press, 1993).

Warren, Harris G., *Rebirth of the Paraguayan Republic: The First Colorado Era, 1878-1904* (Pittsburgh: University of Pittsburgh Press, 1985).

Weisbrot, Mark, "Latin America: The End of an Era," *International Journal of Health Services*, Vol. 36, No. 4 (2006), Internet Edition.

Wilkinson, Daniel, *Silence on the Mountain: Stories of Terror, Betrayal, and Forgetting in Guatemala* (Durham: Duke University Press, 2004).

Wolf, Eric R., *Europe and the People without History* (Berkeley: University of California Press, 1997).

Woodward, Jr., Ralph Lee, *Rafael Carrera and the Emergence of the Republic of Guatemala, 1821-1871* (Athens: University of Georgia Press, 1993).

Wright, Winthrop R., *British-Owned Railways in Argentina* (Austin: University of Texas Press, 1974).

Zook, Jr., David H., *Zarumilla-Marañón: The Ecuador-Peru Dispute* (New York: Bookman Associates, Inc., 1964).

Periodicals

1. Articles and Essays

"Abierta lucha por el poder...en Nicaragua," *Excelsior* (México, D.F.), February 28, 1991, pp. 1, 5.

"Argentina," *Latin American Political Report* (London), February 18, 1977, p. 51.

"Busca la CE a Latinoamérica...," *Excelsior*, July 8, 1993, p. 2F.

"Cuba," *Time*, August 12, 1991, p. 28.

"Cuba: Economy," *Latin American Weekly Report* (London), September 17, 1992, p. 11.

"Economy," *Mexico & Nafta Report* (London), September 23, 1993, p. 5.

"El narcoeslabón centroamericano," *Excelsior*, June 25, 1993, p. 31.

"El perfil de la pobreza en América Latina...," *CEPAL*, No. 536 (November, 1992), pp. 1-4.

"Emperor of Peru," *Newsweek*, May 10, 1993, p. 38.

"Encabeza Brasil la prostitución infantil en AL," *Excelsior*, June 29, 1993, p. 38A.

"En crisis...ejército de Honduras," *Excelsior*, July 15, 1993, pp. 2-3.

"Entrevista...," *Caretas* (Lima), February 3, 1992, p. 91.

"Euromarché," *L'Echo* (Brussels), June 21, 1993, p. 18.

"Författare lever farligt," *Dagens Nyheter* (Stockholm), December 7, 1992, p. A8.

"Fyra gatubarn mördas dagligen," *Svenska Dagbladet* (Stockholm), March 1, 1992, p. A4.

"General Confirms...," *Latin American Weekly Report* (London), July 8, 1993, p. 309.

"Latin America," *Newsweek*, April 17, 1989, p. 42.

"Los 13 grandes multimillonarios," *Proceso* (México, D.F.), July 12, 1993, pp. 6-9.

"Mexican Dance: The RR in PRI," *Newsweek*, March 22, 1993, p. 35.

"Opposition in Brazil…," *The New York Times*, February 6, 1975, p. 12c.
"Ortega critica a EEUU," *El País* (Madrid), August 1, 1993, p. 7.
"Para su información," *El Financiero* (México, D.F.), July 12, 1993, p. 8.
"Peru," *Latin American Weekly Report* (London), February 25, 1993, p. 89.
"Pobreza se mantiene en América Latina," *La República*, February 19, 2008, Internet Edition.
"Politics and Finance," *Latin American Weekly Report* (London), July 8, 1993, p. 308.
"Rápido crecimiento de los grupos empresariales mexicanos," *Excelsior*, January 6, 1992, p. 8F.
"Region: Energy," *Latin American Weekly Report* (London), July 22, 1993, p. 335.
"Region's Military See Threat Ahead," *Latin American Weekly Report* (London), October 28, 1993, p. 493.
"Torka utrotade mayafolket," *Illustrated Vetenskap*, 13 (December, 1996), p. 23.
"U.S., Aware of Killings," *The New York Times*, November 9, 1993, p. A9.
"U.S. Corn Subsidy Fight," *International Herald Tribune*, August 27, 2003, p. 14.
"Yanqui, Come Here," *Newsweek*, July 15, 1991, pp. 20-23.

2. Issues

China Daily (Peking), June 14, 2011, pp. 8, 11.
Dagens Nyheter (Stockholm), September 5, 2003, pp. 8-9.
The Economist, November 30, 2002, p. 50.
The Economist, May 20-26, 2006, p. 11.
The Economist, June 23, 2007, pp. 56-57.
The Economist, September 15, 2007, p. 61.
The Economist, January 12, 2008, pp. 43-44.
El Comercio (Lima), December 19, 2005, p. A8.
El Universal (Mexico, D. F.), January 19, 2007, p. B7.
Financial Times (London), January 20-21, 2007, pp. 6-7.
Granma (Havana), November 9, 2004, Internet Edition.
Granma, February 19, 2008, Internet Edition.
The Guardian Weekly (London), December 9-10, 2005, p. 10.
International Herald Tribune, September 29, 2003, p. 5.
International Herald Tribune, September 21, 2005, p. 19.
International Herald Tribune, November 29, 2006, p. 7.

International Herald Tribune, December 2-3, 2006, p. 2.
International Herald Tribune, February 14, 2007, p. 12.
International Herald Tribune, March 16, 2007, p. 7.
International Herald Tribune, June 11, 2007, p. 14.
La Jornada (Mexico, D. F.), January 16, 2007, p. 14.
La Jornada, January 16, 2007, p. 21.
La Jornada, January 18, 2007, p. 32.
La República (Lima), November 11, 2007, Internet Edition.
La República, June 12, 2008, Internet Edition.
Newsweek, May 19, 2008, p. 22.
Newsweek, October 27, 2008, p. 72.
Svenska Dagbladet (Stockholm), September 13, 2003, p. 11.
Svenska Dagbaldet, May 28, 2004, p. 20.
Svenska Dagbladet, February 20, 2008, p. 4.
SvenskaDagbladet, August 18, 2008, p. 9.

Index

CPSIA information can be obtained
at www.ICGtesting.com
Printed in the USA
BVOW08s0840220217
476886BV00001B/74/P